Voices of Islam

VOICES OF ISLAM

Volume 5

VOICES OF CHANGE

Vincent J. Cornell, General Editor

Omid Safi, Volume Editor

PRAEGER PERSPECTIVES

Westport, Connecticut
London

Library of Congress Cataloging-in-Publication Data

Voices of Islam / Vincent J. Cornell, general editor.
  p. cm.
  Includes bibliographical references and index.
  ISBN 0–275–98732–9 (set : alk. paper)—ISBN 0–275–98733–7 (vol 1 : alk. paper)—ISBN 0–275–98734–5 (vol 2 : alk. paper)—ISBN 0–275–98735–3 (vol 3 : alk. paper)—ISBN 0–275–98736–1 (vol 4 : alk. paper)—ISBN 0–275–98737–X (vol 5 : alk. paper) 1. Islam—Appreciation. 2. Islam—Essence, genius, nature. I. Cornell, Vincent J.
  BP163.V65 2007
  297—dc22   2006031060

British Library Cataloguing in Publication Data is available.

Library of Congress Catalog Card Number: 2006031060
ISBN: 0–275–98732–9 (set)
      0–275–98733–7 (vol. 1)
      0–275–98734–5 (vol. 2)
      0–275–98735–3 (vol. 3)
      0–275–98736–1 (vol. 4)
      0–275–98737–X (vol. 5)

First published in 2007

Praeger Publishers, 88 Post Road West, Westport, CT 06881
An imprint of Greenwood Publishing Group, Inc.
www.praeger.com

Printed in the United States of America

The paper used in this book complies with the
Permanent Paper Standard issued by the National
Information Standards Organization (Z39.48–1984).

10 9 8 7 6 5 4 3 2 1

Contents

———————————————————— • ————————————————————

Voices of Islam

———————————— • ————————————

Vincent J. Cornell

It has long been a truism to say that Islam is the most misunderstood religion in the world. However, the situation expressed by this statement is more than a little ironic because Islam is also one of the most studied religions in the world, after Christianity and Judaism. In the quarter of a century since the 1978–1979 Islamic revolution in Iran, hundreds of books on Islam and the Islamic world have appeared in print, including more than a score of introductions to Islam in various European languages. How is one to understand this paradox? Why is it that most Americans and Europeans are still largely uninformed about Islam after so many books about Islam have been published? Even more, how can people still claim to know so little about Islam when Muslims now live in virtually every medium-sized and major community in America and Europe? A visit to a local library or to a national bookstore chain in any American city will reveal numerous titles on Islam and the Muslim world, ranging from journalistic potboilers to academic studies, translations of the Qur'an, and works advocating a variety of points of view from apologetics to predictions of the apocalypse.

The answer to this question is complex, and it would take a book itself to discuss it adequately. More than 28 years have passed since Edward Said wrote his classic study *Orientalism,* and it has been nearly as long since Said critiqued journalistic depictions of Islam in *Covering Islam: How the Media and the Experts Determine How We See the Rest of the World.* When these books first appeared in print, many thought that the ignorance about the Middle East and the Muslim world in the West would finally be dispelled. However, there is little evidence that the public consciousness of Islam and Muslims has been raised to a significant degree in Western countries. Scholars of Islam in American universities still feel the need to humanize Muslims in the eyes of their students. A basic objective of many introductory courses on Islam is to demonstrate that Muslims are rational human beings and that their beliefs are worthy of respect. As Carl W. Ernst observes in the preface to his recent work, *Following Muhammad: Rethinking Islam in the*

Contemporary World, "It still amazes me that intelligent people can believe that all Muslims are violent or that all Muslim women are oppressed, when they would never dream of uttering slurs stereotyping much smaller groups such as Jews or blacks. The strength of these negative images of Muslims is remarkable, even though they are not based on personal experience or actual study, but they receive daily reinforcement from the news media and popular culture."[1]

Such prejudices and misconceptions have only become worse since the terrorist attacks of September 11, 2001, and the war in Iraq. There still remains a need to portray Muslims in all of their human diversity, whether this diversity is based on culture, historical circumstances, economic class, gender, or religious doctrine. Today, Muslims represent nearly one-fourth of the world's population. Although many Americans are aware that Indonesia is the world's largest Muslim country, most are surprised to learn that half of the Muslims in the world live east of Lahore, Pakistan. In this sense, Islam is as much an "Asian" religion as is Hinduism or Buddhism. The new reality of global Islam strongly contradicts the "Middle Eastern" view of Islam held by most Americans. Politically, the United States has been preoccupied with the Middle East for more than half a century. Religiously, however, American Protestantism has been involved in the Middle East for more than 150 years. Thus, it comes as a shock for Americans to learn that only one-fourth of the world's Muslims live in the Middle East and North Africa and that only one-fifth of Muslims are Arabs. Islam is now as much a worldwide religion as Christianity, with somewhere between 4 and 6 million believers in the United States and approximately 10 million believers in Western Europe. Almost 20 million Muslims live within the borders of the Russian Federation, and nearly a million people of Muslim descent live in the Russian city of St. Petersburg, on the Gulf of Finland.

To think of Islam as monolithic under these circumstances is both wrong and dangerous. The idea that all Muslims are fundamentalists or anti-democratic religious zealots can lead to the fear that dangerous aliens are hiding within Western countries, a fifth column of a civilization that is antithetical to freedom and the liberal way of life. This attitude is often expressed in popular opinion in both the United States and Europe. For example, it can be seen in the "Letters" section of the June 7, 2004, edition of *Time* magazine, where a reader writes: "Now it is time for Muslim clerics to denounce the terrorists or admit that Islam is fighting a war with us—a religious war."[2] For the author of this letter, Muslim "clerics" are not to be trusted, not because they find it hard to believe that pious Muslims would commit outrageous acts of terrorism, but because they secretly hate the West and its values. Clearly, for this reader of *Time,* Islam and the West are at war; however the "West" may be defined and wherever "Islam" or Muslims are to be found.

Prejudice against Muslim minorities still exists in many countries. In Russia, Muslim restaurateurs from the Caucasus Mountains must call themselves "Georgian" to stay in business. In China, being Muslim by ethnicity is acceptable, but being a Muslim by conviction might get one convicted for antistate activities. In the Balkans, Muslims in Serbia, Bulgaria, and Macedonia are called "Turks" and right-wing nationalist parties deny them full ethnic legitimacy as citizens of their countries. In India, over a thousand Muslims were killed in communal riots in Gujarat as recently as 2002. As I write these words, Israel and Hizbollah, the Lebanese Shiite political movement and militia, are engaged in a bloody conflict that has left hundreds of dead and injured on both sides. Although the number of people who have been killed in Lebanon, most of whom are Shiite civilians, is far greater than the number of those killed in Israel, television news reports in the United States do not treat Lebanese and Israeli casualties the same way. While the casualties that are caused by Hizbollah rockets in Israel are depicted as personal tragedies, Lebanese casualties are seldom personalized in this way. The truth is, of course, that all casualties of war are personal tragedies, whether the victims are Lebanese civilians, Israeli civilians, or American soldiers killed or maimed by improvised explosive devices in Iraq. In addition, all civilian deaths in war pose a moral problem, whether they are caused as a consequence of aggression or of retaliation. In many ways, depersonalization can have worse effects than actual hatred. An enemy that is hated must at least be confronted; when innocent victims are reduced to pictures without stories, they are all too easily ignored.

The problem of depersonalization has deeper roots than just individual prejudice. Ironically, the global village created by international news organizations such as CNN, BBC, and Fox News may unintentionally contribute to the problem of devaluing Muslim lives. Depictions of victimhood are often studies in incomprehension: victims speak a language the viewer cannot understand, their shock or rage strips them of their rationality, and their standard of living and mode of dress may appear medieval or even primitive when compared with the dominant cultural forms of modernity. In her classic study, *The Origins of Totalitarianism,* Hannah Arendt pointed out that the ideology of human equality, which is fostered with all good intentions by the international news media, paradoxically contributes to the visibility of difference by confusing equality with sameness. In 99 out of 100 cases, says Arendt, equality "will be mistaken for an innate quality of every individual, who is 'normal' if he is like everybody else and 'abnormal' if he happens to be different. This perversion of equality from a political into a social concept is all the more dangerous when a society leaves but little space for special groups and individuals, for then their differences become all the more conspicuous."[3] According to Arendt, the widespread acceptance of the ideal of social equality after the French Revolution was a major reason why genocide, whether of Jews in Europe, Tutsis in Rwanda, or Muslims in the former Yugoslavia, has become a characteristically modern phenomenon.

The idea of equality as sameness was not as firmly established in the United States, claimed Arendt, because the "equal opportunity" ideology of American liberalism values difference—in the form of imagination, entrepreneurship, and personal initiative—as a token of success.[4] This ideology enabled Jews in America to assert their distinctiveness and eventually to prosper in the twentieth century, and it provides an opportunity for Muslim Americans to assert their distinctiveness and to prosper today. So far, the United States has not engaged in systematic persecution of Muslims and has been relatively free of anti-Muslim prejudice. However, fear and distrust of Muslims among the general public is fostered by images of insurgent attacks and suicide bombings in Iraq, of Al Qaeda atrocities around the globe, and of increasing expressions of anti-Americanism in the Arabic and Islamic media. In addition, some pundits on talk radio, certain fundamentalist religious leaders, and some members of the conservative press and academia fan the flames of prejudice by portraying Islam as inherently intolerant and by portraying Muslims as slaves to tradition and authoritarianism rather than as advocates of reason and freedom of expression. Clearly, there is still a need to demonstrate to the American public that Muslims are rational human beings and that Islam is a religion that is worthy of respect.

Changing public opinion about Islam and Muslims in the United States and Europe will not be easy. The culture critic Guillermo Gomez-Peña has written that as a result of the opening of American borders to non-Europeans in the 1960s, the American myth of the cultural melting pot "has been replaced by a model that is more germane to the times, that of the *menudo chowder*. According to this model, most of the ingredients do melt, but some stubborn chunks are condemned merely to float."[5] At the present time, Muslims constitute the most visible "stubborn chunks" in the *menudo chowder* of American and European pluralism. Muslims are often seen as the chunks of the *menudo chowder* that most stubbornly refuse to "melt in." To the non-Muslim majoritarian citizen of Western countries, Muslims seem to be the most "uncivil" members of civil society. They do not dress like the majority, they do not eat like the majority, they do not drink like the majority, they do not let their women work, they reject the music and cultural values of the majority, and sometimes they even try to opt out of majoritarian legal and economic systems. In Europe, Islam has replaced Catholicism as the religion that left-wing pundits most love to hate. Americans, however, have been more ambivalent about Islam and Muslims. On the one hand, there have been sincere attempts to include Muslims as full partners in civil society. On the other hand, the apparent resistance of some Muslims to "fit in" creates a widespread distrust that has had legal ramifications in several notable cases.

A useful way to conceive of the problem that Muslims face as members of civil society—both within Western countries and in the global civil society that is dominated by the West—is to recognize, following Homi K. Bhabha, the social fact of Muslim *unhomeliness.* To be "unhomed," says Bhabha, is not to be homeless, but rather to escape easy assimilation or accommodation.[6] The problem is not that the "unhomed" possesses no physical home but that there is no "place" to locate the unhomed in the majoritarian consciousness. Simply put, one does not know what to make of the unhomed. Bhabha derives this term from Sigmund Freud's concept of *unheimlich,* "the name for everything that ought to have remained secret and hidden but has come to light."[7] Unhomeliness is a way of expressing social discomfort. When one encounters the unhomed, one feels awkward and uncomfortable because the unhomed person appears truly alien. Indeed, if there is any single experience that virtually all Muslims in Western countries share, it is that Islam makes non-Muslims uncomfortable. In the global civil society dominated by the West, Muslims are unhomed wherever they may live, even in their own countries.

This reality of Muslim experience highlights how contemporary advocates of Muslim identity politics have often made matters worse by accentuating symbolic tokens of difference between so-called Islamic and Western norms. The problem for Islam in today's global civil society is not that it is not seen. On the contrary, Islam and Muslims are arguably all too visible because they are seen as fundamentally different from the accepted norm. Like the black man in the colonial West Indies or in Jim Crow America, the Muslim is, to borrow a phrase from Frantz Fanon, "overdetermined from without."[8] Muslims have been overdetermined by the press, overdetermined by Hollywood, overdetermined by politicians, and overdetermined by culture critics. From the president of the United States to the prime minister of the United Kingdom, and in countless editorials in print and television media, leaders of public opinion ask, "What do Muslims want?" Such a question forces the Muslim into a corner in which the only answer is apologetics or defiance. To again paraphrase Fanon, the overdetermined Muslim is constantly made aware of himself or herself not just in the third person but in *triple person.* As a symbol of the unhomely, the Muslim is made to feel personally responsible for a contradictory variety of "Islamic" moral values, "Islamic" cultural expressions, and "Islamic" religious and political doctrines.[9]

In the face of such outside pressures, what the overdetermined Muslim needs most is not to be seen, but to be heard. There is a critical need for Islam to be expressed to the world not as an image, but as a narrative, and for Muslims to bear their own witness to their own experiences. The vast majority of books on Islam written in European languages, even the best ones, have been written by non-Muslims. This is not necessarily a problem, because an objective and open-minded non-Muslim can often describe Islam for a non-

Muslim audience better than a Muslim apologist. The scholars Said and Ernst, mentioned above, are both from Christian backgrounds. The discipline of Religious Studies from which Ernst writes has been careful to maintain a nonjudgmental attitude toward non-Christian religions. As heirs to the political and philosophical values of European liberalism, scholars of Religious Studies are typically dogmatic about only one thing: they must practice *epoché* (a Greek word meaning "holding back" or restraining one's beliefs) when approaching the worldview of another religion. In the words of the late Canadian scholar of religion Wilfred Cantwell Smith, it is not enough to act like "a fly crawling on the outside of a goldfish bowl," magisterially observing another's religious practices while remaining distant from the subject. Instead, one must be more engaged in her inquiry and, through imagination and the use of *epoché,* try to find out what it feels like to be a goldfish.[10]

Through the practice of *epoché,* the field of Religious Studies has by now produced two generations of accomplished scholars of Islam in the United States and Canada. Smith himself was a fair and sympathetic Christian scholar of Islam, and his field has been more influential than any other in promoting the study of Islam in the West. However, even Smith was aware that only a goldfish truly knows what it means to be a goldfish. The most that a sympathetic non-Muslim specialist in Islamic studies can do is *describe* Islam from the perspective of a sensitive outsider. Because non-Muslims do not share a personal commitment to the Islamic faith, they are not in the best position to convey a sense of what it means to *be* a Muslim on the inside—to live a Muslim life, to share Muslim values and concerns, and to experience Islam spiritually. In the final analysis, only Muslims can fully bear witness to their own traditions from within.

The five-volume set of *Voices of Islam* is an attempt to meet this need. By bringing together the voices of nearly 50 prominent Muslims from around the world, it aims to present an accurate, comprehensive, and accessible account of Islamic doctrines, practices, and worldviews for a general reader at the senior high school and university undergraduate level. The subjects of the volumes—*Voices of Tradition; Voices of the Spirit; Voices of Life: Family, Home, and Society; Voices of Art, Beauty, and Science;* and *Voices of Change*— were selected to provide as wide a depiction as possible of Muslim experiences and ways of knowledge. Taken collectively, the chapters in these volumes provide bridges between formal religion and culture, the present and the past, tradition and change, and spiritual and outward action that can be crossed by readers, whether they are Muslims or non-Muslims, many times and in a variety of ways. What this set does *not* do is present a magisterial, authoritative vision of an "objectively real" Islam that is juxtaposed against a supposedly inauthentic diversity of individual voices. As the Egyptian-American legal scholar and culture critic Khaled Abou El Fadl has pointed out, whenever Islam is the subject of discourse, the authoritative quickly elides into the authoritarian, irrespective of whether the voice of authority is

Muslim or non-Muslim.[11] The editors of *Voices of Islam* seek to avoid the authoritarian by allowing every voice expressed in the five-volume set to be authoritative, both in terms of individual experience and in terms of the commonalities that Muslims share among themselves.

THE EDITORS

The general editor for *Voices of Islam* is Vincent J. Cornell, Asa Griggs Candler Professor of Middle East and Islamic Studies at Emory University in Atlanta, Georgia. When he was solicited by Praeger, an imprint of Greenwood Publishing, to formulate this project, he was director of the King Fahd Center for Middle East and Islamic Studies at the University of Arkansas. Dr. Cornell has been a Sunni Muslim for more than 30 years and is a noted scholar of Islamic thought and history. His most important book, *Realm of the Saint: Power and Authority in Moroccan Sufism* (1998), was described by a prepublication reviewer as "the most significant study of the Sufi tradition in Islam to have appeared in the last two decades." Besides publishing works on Sufism, Dr. Cornell has also written articles on Islamic law, Islamic theology, and moral and political philosophy. For the past five years, he has been a participant in the Archbishop of Canterbury's "Building Bridges" dialogue of Christian and Muslim theologians. In cooperation with the Jerusalem-based Elijah Interfaith Institute, he is presently co-convener of a group of Muslim scholars, of whom some are contributors to *Voices of Islam*, which is working toward a new theology of the religious other in Islam. Besides serving as general editor for *Voices of Islam*, Dr. Cornell is also the volume editor for Volume 1, *Voices of Tradition;* Volume 2, *Voices of the Spirit;* and Volume 4, *Voices of Art, Beauty, and Science.*

The associate editors for *Voices of Islam* are Omid Safi and Virginia Gray Henry-Blakemore. Omid Safi is Associate Professor of Religion at the University of North Carolina at Chapel Hill. Dr. Safi, the grandson of a noted Iranian Ayatollah, was born in the United States but raised in Iran and has been recognized as an important Muslim voice for moderation and diversity. He gained widespread praise for his edited first book, *Progressive Muslims: On Justice, Gender, and Pluralism* (2003), and was interviewed on CNN, National Public Radio, and other major media outlets. He recently published an important study of Sufi-state relations in premodern Iran, *The Politics of Knowledge in Premodern Islam* (2006). Dr. Safi is the volume editor for Volume 5, *Voices of Change,* which contains chapters by many of the authors represented in his earlier work, *Progressive Muslims.*

Virginia Gray Henry-Blakemore has been a practicing Sunni Muslim for almost 40 years. She is director of the interfaith publishing houses Fons Vitae and Quinta Essentia and cofounder and trustee of the Islamic Texts Society of Cambridge, England. Some of the most influential families in Saudi

Arabia, Egypt, and Jordan have supported her publishing projects. She is an accomplished lecturer in art history, world religions, and filmmaking and is a founding member of the Thomas Merton Center Foundation. Henry-Blakemore received her BA at Sarah Lawrence College, studied at the American University in Cairo and Al-Azhar University, earned her MA in Education at the University of Michigan, and served as a research fellow at Cambridge University from 1983 to 1990. She is the volume editor for Volume 3, *Voices of Life: Family, Home, and Society.*

THE AUTHORS

As stated earlier, *Voices of Islam* seeks to meet the need for Muslims to bear witness to their own traditions by bringing together a diverse collection of Muslim voices from different regions and from different scholarly and professional backgrounds. The voices that speak to the readers about Islam in this set come from Asia, Africa, Europe, and North America, and include men and women, academics, community and religious leaders, teachers, activists, and business leaders. Some authors were born Muslims and others embraced Islam at various points in their lives. A variety of doctrinal, legal, and cultural positions are also represented, including modernists, traditionalists, legalists, Sunnis, Shiites, Sufis, and "progressive Muslims." The editors of the set took care to represent as many Muslim points of view as possible, including those that they may disagree with. Although each chapter in the set was designed to provide basic information for the general reader on a particular topic, the authors were encouraged to express their individual voices of opinion and experience whenever possible.

In theoretical terms, *Voices of Islam* treads a fine line between what Paul Veyne has called "specificity" and "singularity." As both an introduction to Islam and as an expression of Islamic diversity, this set combines historical and commentarial approaches, as well as poetic and narrative accounts of individual experiences. Because of the wide range of subjects that are covered, individualized accounts (the "singular") make up much of the narrative of *Voices of Islam,* but the intent of the work is not to express individuality per se. Rather, the goal is to help the reader understand the varieties of Islamic experience (the "specific") more deeply by finding within their specificity a certain kind of generality.[12]

For Veyne, "specificity" is another way of expressing typicality or the ideal type, a sociological concept that has been a useful tool for investigating complex systems of social organization, thought, or belief. However, the problem with typification is that it may lead to oversimplification, and oversimplification is the handmaiden of the stereotype. Typification can lead to oversimplification because the concept of typicality belongs to a structure of general knowledge that obscures the view of the singular and the different. Thus, presenting the voices of only preselected "typical Muslims" or "representative Muslims" in a work such as *Voices of Islam* would only aggravate the tendency of many Muslims and non-Muslims to define Islam in a single, essentialized way. When done from without, this can lead to a form of stereotyping that may exacerbate, rather than alleviate, the tendency to see Muslims in ways that they do not see themselves. When done from within, it can lead to a dogmatic fundamentalism (whether liberal or conservative does not matter) that excludes the voices of difference from "real" Islam and fosters a totalitarian approach to religion. Such an emphasis on the legitimacy of representation by Muslims themselves would merely reinforce the ideal of sameness that Arendt decried and enable the overdetermination of the "typical" Muslim from without. For this reason, *Voices of Islam* seeks to strike a balance between specificity and singularity. Not only the chapters in these volumes but also the backgrounds and personal orientations of their authors express Islam as a lived diversity and as a source of multiple wellsprings of knowledge. Through the use of individual voices, this work seeks to save the "singular" from the "typical" by employing the "specific."

Dipesh Chakrabarty, a major figure in the field of Subaltern Studies, notes: "Singularity is a matter of viewing. It comes into being as that which resists our attempt to see something as a particular instance of a general idea or category."[13] For Chakrabarty, the singular is a necessary antidote to the typical because it "defies the generalizing impulse of the sociological imagination."[14] Because the tendency to overdetermine and objectify Islam is central to the continued lack of understanding of Islam by non-Muslims, it is necessary to defy the generalizing impulse by demonstrating that the unity of Islam is not a unity of sameness, but of diversity. Highlighting the singularity of individual Islamic practices and doctrines becomes a means of liberating Islam from the totalizing vision of both religious fundamentalism (Muslim and non-Muslim alike) and secular essentialism. While Islam in theory may be a unity, in both thought and practice this "unity" is in reality a galaxy whose millions of singular stars exist within a universe of multiple perspectives. This is not just a sociological fact, but a theological point as well. For centuries, Muslim theologians have asserted that the Transcendent Unity of God is a mystery that defies the normal rules of logic. To human beings, unity usually implies either singularity or sameness, but with respect to God, Unity is beyond number or comparison.

In historiographical terms, a work that seeks to describe Islam through the voices of individual Muslims is an example of "minority history." However, by allowing the voices of specificity and singularity to enter into a trialogue that includes each other as well as the reader, *Voices of Islam* is also an example of "subaltern history." For Chakrabarty, subaltern narratives "are marginalized not because of any conscious intentions but because they represent moments or points at which the archive that the historian mines develops a degree of intractability with respect to the aims of professional history."[15] Subaltern narratives do not only belong to socially subordinate or minority groups, but they also belong to underrepresented groups in Western scholarship, even if these groups comprise a billion people as Muslims do. Subaltern narratives resist typification because the realities that they represent do not correspond to the stereotypical. As such, they need to be studied on their own terms. The history of Islam in thought and practice is the product of constant dialogues between the present and the past, internal and external discourses, culture and ideology, and tradition and change. To describe Islam as anything less would be to reduce it to a limited set of descriptive and conceptual categories that can only rob Islam of its diversity and its historical and intellectual depth. The best way to retain a sense of this diversity and depth is to allow Muslim voices to relate their own narratives of Islam's past and present.

NOTES

1. Carl W. Ernst, *Following Muhammad: Rethinking Islam in the Contemporary World* (Chapel Hill and London: University of North Carolina Press, 2003), xvii.

2. *Time,* June 7, 2004, 10.

3. Hannah Arendt, *The Origins of Totalitarianism,* rev. ed. (San Diego, New York, and London: Harvest Harcourt, 1976), 54.

4. Ibid., 55.

5. Guillermo Gomez-Peña, "The New World (B)order," *Third Text* 21 (Winter 1992–1993): 74, quoted in Homi K. Bhabha, *The Location of Culture* (London and New York: Routledge Classics, 2004), 313.

6. Bhabha, *The Location of Culture,* 13.

7. Ibid., 14–15.

8. Frantz Fanon, *Black Skin, White Masks* (London, U.K.: Pluto, 1986), 116. The original French term for this condition is *surdéterminé.* See idem, *Peau noire masques blancs* (Paris: Éditions du Seuil, 1952), 128.

9. Ibid., 112.

10. Wilfred Cantwell Smith, *The Meaning and End of Religion* (Minneapolis, Minnesota: The University of Minnesota Press, 1991), 7.

11. Khaled Abou El Fadl, *Speaking in God's Name: Islamic Law, Authority, and Women* (Oxford, U.K.: Oneworld Publications, 2001), 9–85.

12. Paul Veyne, *Writing History: Essay on Epistemology,* trans. Mina Moore-Rinvolucri (Middletown, Connecticut: Wesleyan University Press, 1984), 56.

13. Dipesh Chakrabarty, *Provincializing Europe: Postcolonial Thought and Historical Difference* (Princeton and Oxford: Princeton University Press, 2000), 82.

14. Ibid., 83.

15. Ibid., 101.

INTRODUCTION: ISLAMIC MODERNISM AND THE CHALLENGE OF REFORM

•

Omid Safi

As is the case with a number of other Islamic discourses, it can be hard to locate the precise boundary of Islamic modernism. Few Muslims explicitly self-identify as "Muslim modernists," instead referring to themselves simply as Muslims, Muslims involved in the process of reform and renewal, Muslims committed to democracy, or even Muslims intent on reviving the original spirit of Islam, and so on. In this chapter, Islamic modernism is defined as those discourses of Islamic thought and practice in the last two centuries in which modernity itself is seen as a viable category to be engaged and drawn upon, not merely dismissed or used as a foil to define oneself against. In other words, advocates of Islamic modernism are not simply modern Muslims, but those Muslims who see something (if not all) of modernity as a constitutive element of their worldview and practice.

As is the case with other intellectual and religious traditions, Islamic engagements with modernity have been neither static nor uniform. Traditions ranging from the revivalism of the eighteenth and nineteenth centuries to the rationalizing and Salafi tendencies of the early twentieth century and liberal movements of the twentieth century to the progressive Muslim movement of the twenty-first century can all be discussed under the broad rubric of Islamic modernism. At times, it has been difficult to locate the boundary between Islamic modernists and some nineteenth and early twentieth-century Salafi thinkers. While both advocated fresh interpretations of the Qur'an, the modernists tended to engage modernity explicitly, while many Salafis couched their language in terms of the "righteous forefathers" (*al-salaf al-salih*), the generation of Muslims living with and immediately after the Prophet Muhammad in the seventh century. As the Salafi movement became more intertwined with Wahhabism in the latter half of the twentieth century, the overlap between modernists and Salafis has been greatly reduced.

The discourse of modernity itself has not stayed static, as it has come under severe critique and contestation from feminists, environmentalists, Marxists, subalterns, and others. As the discourse of modernity continues to change, so does the Muslims' engagement with modernity.

There has also been a long-running tendency among Western journalists and even some scholars to look at the more conservative articulations of Islam (such as some traditional religious scholars) and even Muslim extremists as somehow representing "real" Islam. Subsequently, these same sources have not adequately engaged Muslim modernists, who are unfairly dismissed as lacking a constituency or influence. Even more problematic is the view that any explicit reimagination of Islam is no longer proper Islam. Lord Cromer, the British High Commissioner in colonized Egypt, once said: "Islam reformed is Islam no longer." That attitude misses out on the vigorous and dynamic debates that are going on within not only modernist circles but also much wider segments of Muslim societies.

WESTERNIZATION AND ISLAMIC PARADIGMS

Part of the difficulty in establishing the proper boundaries of Islamic modernism has to do with the way that the legacy of Islamic thought in the modern era is conceived. Many Western scholars have seen modernity as the exclusive offspring of the West. As a result, they approach any other civilization that engages modernity through the lens of "westernization." There is no doubt that the encounter with Western institutions and thought has had a profound impact on Islamic modernism both positively (emphasis on human rights, constitutional forms of government, adoption of science, and so on) and negatively (colonialism, support for autocratic regimes). At the same time, many of the issues that Islamic modernism engages in today, such as human rights, democracy, and gender equality, are truly seen as universal struggles. Furthermore, most Muslims who engage in these issues frame their own discourse not as a borrowing or "influence" from Western discourses but rather as a part of indigenous Islamic interpretations. Positioning the Muslims' struggles in these universal arenas as perpetually derivative vis-à-vis Western paradigms robs them of their own legitimacy and dynamism.

The above debate is also related to the question of when one begins the history of Islamic modernism. The older paradigm that viewed Islamic thought as being hopelessly stagnated before being jolted into a renaissance by its interaction with European colonialism is now critiqued by many scholars. Without diminishing the profound experience of responding to the shock, inspiration, and violation of the colonial experience, it is also important to realize that some of Islamic modernism also taps into important reform traditions such as those of Shah Wali Allah of Delhi (d. 1762 CE) and many others that predate the full-blown experience of colonialism.

Many Muslim modernists have readily acknowledged their interactions with Western models, institutions, and figures. At the same time, they have been careful to cast their movement in decidedly Islamic terms. Perhaps the most common strategy for presenting modernism as an indigenously and authentically Islamic movement is through the framework of *ijtihad*. Ijtihad initially had a narrower meaning, referring to the process whereby Muslim jurists would arrive at rulings for unprecedented cases. Modernists have gradually expanded the definition of ijtihad to mean critical, independent reasoning in all domains of thought. In other words, the proper domain of ijtihad was taken to be not just Islamic law, but rather all aspects of thought. In an egalitarian move, modernists often hold that it is not just jurists but all Muslims who have the responsibility to carry on ijtihad. The majority of Islamic modernist writers emphasize the need for ijtihad, often juxtaposing it polemically against *taqlid*. As with ijtihad, modernists often came to reinterpret taqlid. Taqlid had originally meant simply following a school of Islamic law, or a designated authority (*marja'*) in the case of Shi'i Muslims. For modernists, who wished to highlight independent critical reasoning, taqlid came to mean blind imitationism, becoming a symbol of everything they held to be wrong with Islamic thought.

Like many other Muslims, modernists have also cast their own struggles as perpetuating the spirit of the Qur'an and the teachings of the Prophet Muhammad. Modernists often insist that the egalitarian spirit of the Qur'an in areas ranging from women's rights to religious pluralism should take precedence over more conservative later rulings. The distinction between essence and manifestation (universals and particulars, or other similar dichotomies) is a common motif in the history of modern religious thought. Many modernists also argue for a situated and contextualized reading of the Qur'anic revelations.

Modernists find Qur'anic precedence for their own critique of tradition-embedded injustices by pointing to Qur'anic voices (such as Abraham and Muhammad) who challenged their own communities that insisted on continuing "the ways of the forefathers." In appealing to prophetic legitimization, many modernists have recorded the conversation between the Prophet Muhammad and a companion named Mu'adh ibn Jabal (d. 627 CE). Mu'adh stated that if he found no explicit guidance in the Qur'an or the Prophetic Sunna, he would rely upon his own independent reasoning. While the systematic nature of this anecdote may well belie a later juridical desire to legitimize legal methodology, it has served as a powerful tool for modernists to sanctify their own appeal to ijtihad.

Modernists also tapped into other traditions of Islamic legitimacy that predated the encounter with Europe. One of their most powerful means of legitimizing themselves was by adopting the title of "renewer" (*mujaddid*), which recalls a statement attributed to the Prophet Muhammad: "God sends to this nation at the beginning of every century someone who renews its religion."In doing so, modernists lay claim to the mantle of Islamic renewal, following established masters such as Abu Hamid al-Ghazali (d. 1111 CE) whose *Ihya 'ulum al-din* ("Revivification of the Religious Sciences") explicitly evoked the theme of rejuvenation and renewal after death and stagnation.

RELIGIOUS AUTHORITY

The crisis of contemporary Islam is inseparable from the struggle over defining Islam and the concomitant question of who gets to define Islam, using what sources and which methodologies. The question of authority in Islam is today—and always has been—a contested one. It has often been noted that there is no formal church structure in Islam, thus making the basis of religious authority more fluid. However, the lack of a formal structure of authority does not mean that there is *no* religious authority in Islam. Competing groups of Muslims claim authority for themselves by appealing to religious language and symbols. Foremost among them have been the religious scholars (*ulama*) and the mystics (Sufis) of Islam. However, Sufism is a contested category today, and many in the Muslim community who gravitate toward Salafism view Sufis with skepticism. For example, the mainstream Muslim organizations in the United States (ISNA [Islamic Society of North America], ICNA [Islamic Circle of North America], and so on) avoid almost all mention of Sufism (and also Shi'ism). Ismailis, particularly those under the leadership of the Agha Khan, are arguably the most cosmopolitan and modernity-accommodating of Muslims, yet they too are seen by some conservative Sunni Muslims as suspect.

The majority of Muslims turn to the *ulama*, religious scholars, for religious guidance. However, many ulama today are ill equipped to handle the more sophisticated aspects of modernity. Traditional *madrasa* institutions in many Muslim-majority countries no longer offer the highest level of critical thought. Whereas these institutions historically attracted the brightest minds in the community, today they are often a haven for those who have been unable to be admitted to more lucrative medicine, engineering, and computer science programs. By and large, there are very few madrasas for the training of ulama in a curriculum that takes modernity in the sense of engagements with modern philosophy, sciences, politics, and economics seriously. Ironically, while it is modernist Muslims who are often best suited to handle these decidedly modern subjects, many community members view modernist scholars with skepticism because modernists are not usually products of the *madrasa* system. This skepticism of the community members reveals a great deal about the presuppositions of many contemporary Muslims regarding the "purity" of Islamic knowledge, and how it may be "contaminated" by Western training. Ironically, this compartmentalized view of knowledge contradicts both medieval philosophical notions and certain contemporary rigorous interpretations of Islam. As early as the ninth century CE, the philosopher al-Kindi stated: "We should not be ashamed to acknowledge truth and to assimilate it from whatever source it comes to us, even if it is brought to us by former generations and foreign peoples."[1] This epistemological pluralism is also echoed in the works of the Iranian modernist intellectual Abdolkarim Soroush, who states: "I believe that truths everywhere are compatible; no truth clashes with any other truth.... Thus, in my search for the truth, I became oblivious to whether an idea originated in the East, or West, or whether it had ancient or modern origins."[2]

The vision of Islam espoused by many modernists is a more liberal, inclusive, humanistic, and even secular interpretation of Islam that is greatly distrustful of Islamist political discourses. By "secular," what is intended is a model of social relations in which the boundaries between religious discourse and political legitimacy are not collapsed, not one in which one would seek an exile of the religious from all of the public domain. The modernists' suspicion of models of governments that base themselves on Islamic discourses often provides their critics with ammunition to accuse them of laxness of religious practice. Whether it is warranted or not, modernists have often been perceived as being less observant than their conservative coreligionists.

LATE NINETEENTH CENTURY AND TWENTIETH CENTURY

One of the characteristics of the modernist movement in the late nineteenth century and the twentieth century was its transregional, translinguistic, and transnational character. While figures such as Muhammad 'Abduh and Rashid Rida worked in Egypt, others such as Sayyid Ahmad Khan, Muhammad Iqbal, and Fazlur Rahman hailed from South Asia. Figures such as Jamal al-Din "al-Afghani" moved with seeming ease from Iran and Afghanistan to the Ottoman Empire. One could mention other well-known figures such as the Malaysian Chandra Muzaffar, the Indonesians Ahmad Hassan and Nurcholish Madjid, the Algerian/French Mohamed Arkoun, and the American Amina Wadud to give a sense of its global reach.

Still, moving toward and into the twentieth century, a few Islamic modernists stood out above the rest. Almost all later modernists engaged with the ideas of the following figures either explicitly or implicitly.

Jamal al-Din "al-Afghani" (1838–1897): Along with his disciple 'Abduh, Afghani is seen as the most important of the nineteenth-century Muslim modernists. In the Sunni Arab world, he adopted the name Afghani to distance himself from his Iranian Shiite heritage. He was instrumental in arguing for a vision of Islam that adopted modern sciences. He is a good example of the ambiguity many modernists have vis-à-vis realpolitik, at times supporting the British imperial forces, at times opposing them.

Muhammad 'Abduh (1849–1905): Along with Afghani, 'Abduh published the highly influential journal *al-'Urwa al-wuthqa* (The Firm Bond), a title that harkens back to Qur'an 2:256. Initially exiled from Egypt, 'Abduh eventually returned to become Mufti of Egypt. Generally considered the most influential of the nineteenth-century Muslim modernists in terms of his impact on later thinkers, 'Abduh was responsible for many reforms in the educational system.

Rashid Rida (1865–1935): Rida is a link between 'Abduh and twentieth-century modernists. His journal *al-Manar* was one of the most important means for disseminating modernist ideas. He too talked explicitly about the need for renewal (*tajdid*) and renewing (*tajaddud*), connecting these concepts back to the aforementioned hadith that God sends a renewer (*mujaddid*) at the beginning of every century.

Muhammad Iqbal (1877–1938): This South Asian thinker is widely credited for having been the philosophical inspiration behind the creation of the state of Pakistan. One of the few Islamic modernists with a serious interest in poetry and mysticism, he is remembered for having argued for the importance of dynamism in Islamic thought. His widely influential *The Reconstruction of Religious Thought in Islam* simultaneously harkens back to Abu Hamid al-Ghazali's masterpiece *Ihya 'ulum al-din* even as it took its discourse into the twentieth century.

Fazlur Rahman (1919–1988): A British-trained scholar of Islam, Rahman highlighted the importance of educational systems in the reinvigoration of Islam. For the last 20 years of his life he taught at the University of Chicago, beginning a long legacy of exiled Muslim intellectuals who took up teaching posts in Europe and North America. A fierce critic of both fundamentalism and Sufism, Rahman is usually acknowledged as the doyen of Islamic modernism in the latter half of twentieth century. Unlike many modernists, Rahman was profoundly steeped in the tradition of Islamic philosophy, especially that of Mulla Sadra of Shiraz (d. 1632 CE).

PROGRESSIVE ISLAM

One of the most significant developments in modernist Islamic thought in the last generation has been the various understandings of Islam that go under the rubric of "progressive Islam." Fully immersed in postmodern critiques of modernity, progressive Islam both continues and radically departs from the 150-year-old tradition of liberal Islam. Many nineteenth- and early twentieth-century modernists generally displayed an uncritical, almost devotional, identification with modernity, and often (though not always) bypassed discussion of colonialism and imperialism. Progressive understandings of Islam, on the other hand, are almost uniformly critical of colonialism, both in its nineteenth-century manifestation and in its current variety.

Progressive Muslims develop a critical and non-apologetic "multiple critique" with respect to both Islam and modernity. This double engagement with the varieties of Islam and modernity, plus an emphasis on concrete social action and transformation, are the defining characteristics of progressive Islam today.

Unlike their liberal Muslim forefathers (who usually were fore*fathers*), progressive Muslims represent a broad coalition of female and male Muslim activists and intellectuals. One of the distinguishing features of the progressive Muslim movement as the vanguard of Islamic (post)modernism has been the high level of female participation and leadership. This is particularly the case in Western countries where a majority of Muslims who self-identify as progressive are woman. The majority of progressive Muslims also highlight women's rights as part of a broader engagement with human rights.

Progressives measure their success not in developing new theologies, but rather by the amount of ground-level change for good that they can produce in Muslim and non-Muslim societies. As a number of other prominent authors and I have noted in the volume *Progressive Muslims: On Justice, Gender, and Pluralism*, this movement is characterized by a number of themes: striving to realize a just and pluralistic society through critically engaging in Islam, a relentless pursuit of social justice, an emphasis on gender equality as a foundation of human rights, a vision of religious and ethnic pluralism, and a methodology of nonviolent resistance.[3]

Muslim Libera(c)tion

Progressive Muslims perceive themselves as the advocates of human beings all over the world who through no fault of their own live in situations of poverty, pollution, oppression, and marginalization. A prominent concern of progressive Muslims is the suffering and poverty, as well as the full humanity, of these marginalized and oppressed human beings of all backgrounds who are called *mustad'ifun* in the Qur'anic context. The task of progressives in this context is to give voice to the voiceless, power to the powerless, and confront the "powers that be" who disregard the God-given human dignity of the *mustad'ifun* all over this Earth. Muslim progressives draw on the strong tradition of social justice within Islam from sources as diverse as the Qur'an and the Hadith (statements of the Prophet Muhammad) to more recent spokespersons such as Ali Shari'ati. The Qur'an itself specifically links fighting for the cause of God (*Sabil Allah*) to the cause of *mustad'ifun*.

The methodological fluidity of progressive Muslims is apparent in their pluralistic epistemology, which freely and openly draws from sources outside of Islamic tradition, so long as nontraditional sources serve as useful tools in the global pursuit of justice. These external sources include the liberation theologies of Leonardo Boff, Gustavo Gutiérrez, and Rebecca Chopp as well as the secular humanism of Edward Said, Noam Chomsky, and others. Progressive Muslims are likely to combine a Qur'anic call for serving as "witnesses for God in justice" (Qur'an 42:15) with the task of a social critic to "speak truth to the powers."

As is the case with many feminists and African American scholar-activists, progressives do not accept the dichotomy between intellectual pursuits and activism. Whereas many (though not all) of the previous generations of modernist Muslims were defined by a purely academic approach that reflected their elite status, progressive Muslims realize that the social injustices around them are reflected in, connected to, and justified in terms of intellectual discourses. They are, in this respect, fully indebted to the critiques of Edward Said. A progressive commitment implies by necessity the willingness to remain engaged with the issues of social justice as they unfold on the ground level, in the lived realities of Muslim and non-Muslim communities.

Progressive Muslims follow squarely in the footsteps of liberation theologians such as Leonardo Boff, who in his *Introducing Liberation Theology* deemed a purely conceptual criticism of theology devoid of real commitment of the oppressed as "radically irrelevant."[4] He recognized that *liberação* (liberation) links together the concepts of *liber* ("free") and *ação* ("action"): There is no liberation without action. The aforementioned *Progressive Muslims* volume states: "Vision and activism are both necessary. Activism without vision is doomed from the start. Vision without activism quickly becomes irrelevant."

This informed social activism is visible in the many progressive Muslim organizations and movements, including the work of Chandra Muzaffar with the International Movement for a Just World in Malaysia, the efforts of Farid Esack with HIV-positive Muslims in South Africa, and the work of the 2003 Nobel Peace Prize winner Shirin Ebadi with groups such as the Iranian Children's Rights Society. Progressive Muslims are involved in an astonishing array of peace and social justice movements, grassroots organizations, and human rights efforts.

Toward an Islamic Humanism

At the heart of the progressive Muslim interpretation of Islam is a simple yet radical idea: every human life, female and male, Muslim and non-Muslim, rich or poor, "Northern" or "Southern," has exactly the same intrinsic worth. The essential value of human life is God given and is in no way connected to culture, geography, or privilege. A progressive Muslim agenda is concerned with the ramifications of the premise that all members of humanity have the same intrinsic worth because each member of humanity has the breath of God breathed into them: "And I breathed into humanity of my own spirit" (Qur'an 15:29; 38:72). This identification with the full human nature of all human beings amounts to nothing short of an Islamic Humanism. In this global humanistic framework, progressives conceive of a way of being Muslim that engages and affirms the full humanity of all human beings, that actively holds all responsible for a fair and just distribution of God-given natural resources, and that seeks to live in harmony with the natural world.

Engaging Tradition

Progressive Muslims insist on a serious engagement with the full spectrum of Islamic thought and practices. There can be no progressive Muslim movement that does not engage the textual and material sources of the Islamic tradition, even if progressives themselves debate which sources these should be and how they ought to be interpreted. Progressives generally hold that it is imperative to work through inherited traditions of thought and practice: Sunni, Shiite, Sufi, juridical, philosophical, theological, mystical, poetical, "folk Islam," oral traditions—all must be engaged. In particular cases, they might conclude that certain preexisting interpretations fail to offer Muslims sufficient guidance today. However, they can only faithfully claim such a position after—and not before—a serious engagement with tradition.

Social Justice, Gender Equality, and Pluralism

Justice lies at the heart of Islamic social ethics. Time and again the Qur'an talks about providing for the marginalized members of society: the poor, the orphan, the downtrodden, the wayfarer, the hungry, and so on. Progressive Muslims believe that it is imperative to translate the social ideals of the Qur'an and Islamic teachings in a way that those committed to social justice today can relate to and understand. For all Muslims, there is a vibrant memory of the Prophet talking about the true believer as one whose neighbor does not go to bed hungry. Progressives hold that in today's global village, it is time to think of all of humanity as one's neighbor.

Progressive Muslims begin with a simple yet radical stance: the Muslim community as a whole cannot achieve justice unless justice is guaranteed for Muslim women. In short, there can be no progressive interpretation of Islam without gender justice. Gender justice is crucial, indispensable, and essential. In the long run, any progressive Muslim interpretation will be judged by the amount of change in gender equality it is able to produce. Gender equality is a touchstone for the broader concerns for social justice and pluralism. As Ebadi, the 2003 Nobel Peace Prize winner stated, "Women's rights *are* human rights."

Progressive Muslims strive for pluralism both inside and outside of the *Umma*. They seek to open up a wider spectrum of interpretations and practices marked as Muslim, and epistemologically follow a pluralistic approach to the pursuit of knowledge and truth. In their interactions with other religious and ethnic communities, they seek to transcend the arcane notion of "tolerance," and instead strive for profound engagement through both commonalities and differences.

Progressives and Jihad

The pervasive discourse of jihad has become thoroughly associated with Islam, to the point that one may legitimately ask whether the term can be redeemed. Both Muslim extremist groups such as Al Qaeda and Western Islamophobes in fact do use the term to mean a holy war. On the Muslim side, one can point to the public statement of Usama Bin Laden: "In compliance with God's order, we issue the following fatwa to all Muslims: The ruling to kill the Americans and their allies—civilians and military—is an individual duty for every Muslim who can do it in any country...."[5] Scholars of Islamic law have been quick to point out that this alleged "fatwa" violates both the letter and the spirit of Islamic law. At the same time, one has to acknowledge that Bin Laden supports his own recourse to violence through the discourse of jihad. This same sentiment is reflected in the Western Islamophobic side, where many Christian Evangelicals are recasting centuries-old polemics against Islam in a new guise.

Progressive Muslims counter both the Muslim extremists' and the Western Islamophobes' definition of jihad. Instead, they hold firmly to the notion that jihad is key, not in the sense of holy war and violence, but rather in its root meaning of resistance and struggle. In this regard, progressives in the Muslim community emphasize the responsibility to engage the wider social order by confronting injustice and inequality, while always remembering that one must do so in a nonviolent way. In doing so, they are the heirs of Muslim visionaries such as the Sufi Mevlana Jalaluddin Rumi ("Washing away blood with blood is impossible, even absurd!") as well as exemplars of nonviolence such as Mahatma Gandhi, Martin Luther King, Jr., and the Dalai Lama. This new understanding of jihad, which seeks to uphold resistance to well-entrenched systems of inequality and injustice through nonviolent means, is one of the key contributions of progressive Muslims. Building on the comments of religious figures such as the Dalai Lama (in his Nobel acceptance speech), they recognize that even terms like "peace" are insufficient when peace is not connected to justice and the well-being of humanity. The goal is not simply peace in the sense of the absence of war but rather a peace that is rooted in justice.

Also revealing their indebtedness to American voices of social justice, many progressive Muslims are inspired by Dr. Martin Luther King, Jr. For these Muslims, King embodies speaking out for justice from the depths of a religious commitment, from the midst of a faith community to that community and beyond. Thus, he is a great source of inspiration for many progressive Muslims who want to be voices of conscience speaking not in the wilderness but in the very midst of society. Progressives thus seek to be voices for global justice speaking firmly and powerfully to the Powers that Be, while perpetually affirming the dignity of all human beings.

AN ISLAMIC REFORMATION?

Modernist Muslims are often asked whether their project constitutes an "Islamic reformation." They answer the question in both the affirmative and the negative. It is undeniably true that there are serious economic, social, and political issues in the Muslim world that need urgent remedying. Much of the Muslim world is bound to a deeply disturbing economic structure that provides natural resources (oil, and so on) for the global market, while at the same time remaining dependent on Western labor, technological know-how, and staple goods. This economic situation is exacerbated in many parts of the modern Muslim world by atrocious human rights situations, crumbling educational systems, and worn-out economies. Most modernist Muslims would readily support the reform of all such institutions.

However, the term "reformation" carries much baggage. In speaking of the "Islamic reformation," many people have in mind the Protestant Reformation. It is this understanding that leaves many Muslims uneasy. Theirs is not a project of developing a "Protestant" Islam distinct from a "Catholic" Islam. Most insist that they are not looking to create a further split within the Muslim community as much as to heal it and to urge it along. For this reason, iconic figures such as Ebadi eschew the language of "reform" and "reformation" but call instead for a return to a real, just Islam.

A GLOBAL PHENOMENON OR A WESTERN ISLAM?

It would be a clear mistake to reduce the emergence of progressive Islam to a new "American/Western Islam." Progressive Muslims are found everywhere in the global Muslim *Umma*. When it comes to actually implementing a progressive understanding of Islam in Muslim communities, certain communities in Iran, Malaysia, and South Africa lead, but do not follow, the United States. Many American Muslim communities—and much of the leadership represented in groups such as ICNA, ISNA, and the Council on American-Islamic Relations—are far too uncritical of Salafi (if not outright Wahhabi) tendencies that progressives oppose.

Wahhabism is by now a well-known, puritanical reading of Islam that originated in eighteenth-century Arabia. It was not until the discovery of oil in Saudi Arabia that Wahhabism had the financial resources necessary to import its mission all over the world, including to the United States. In spite of their exclusivist ideology, Wahhabis have had a great working relationship first with the British and since the 1930s with the U.S. administration. Lesser known is the Salafi movement, which represents an important school of Islamic revivalism. Salafis espouse a return to the ways of the first few generations of Muslims, the "Righteous Forefathers." Central to their methodology has been a recentering of the Qur'an and the Sunna of the Prophet Muhammad. It would be a mistake to view American Muslim organizations such as ISNA and ICNA as Wahhabi. On the other hand, interpretations of Islam such as Shi'ism and Sufism are usually absent from these organizations, and the representation of important and contested issues such as gender constructions tends to reflect a conservative, Salafi bend as well. It is in opposition to both Wahhabism and Salafism that many Muslim progressives define themselves.

On the other hand, one also has to acknowledge that the European and, more importantly, the North American contexts have provided fertile grounds for the blossoming of progressive Islam. Many participants in this young movement have found a more hospitable and open environment in the North American milieu than in Muslim-majority areas. Even the contested public world of post-9/11 America still offers great possibilities for conducting public conversations about difficult matters of religion and politics. It would be hard to imagine such critical conversations taking place freely and openly in many Muslim countries. Also one has to acknowledge the significance of North American educational institutions, as well as many fruitful cross-pollinations with liberal religious institutions, human rights groups, and so on.

GLOBAL CHALLENGES TO ISLAMIC MODERNISM

In today's political climate, it is a cliché to begin a discourse on Islam and Muslims with talk of "crisis." It is not my intention here to add to an unrelenting assault on Islam and Muslims. Instead, I intend to explore the profound challenges and precious opportunities confronting Muslims who self-identify as progressives or as advocates of Islamic reform.

Muslim modernists face a whole host of challenges. Many modernists have profound internal disagreements on issues ranging from hermeneutical approaches to Qur'an and Hadith, women's rights, and so forth. More problematic is the ongoing question of modernity versus the hegemony of the West. Many modernists have wrestled with the question of how to incorporate political institutions and science from the same Western civilizations that have colonized and exploited much of the third world, including many Muslim-majority countries.

Some initial phases of Islamic modernism became entangled in apologetic presentations of Islam in which Islam was idealized and imagined as a perfect system that had been sullied through the stagnation of later Muslim generations. Such a presupposition does not enable one to deal constructively with problematic questions in the Qur'an or in the lives of the Prophet and the early Companions, even as it dismisses useful resources in later developments.

Other challenges are external. Muslim modernists do not have a natural institutional home, other than in academia and some media outlets. They have continuously struggled to find a home in the *madrasa* system, although in some places they achieved a measure of success because of efforts of Muhammad 'Abduh and others. In other cases, they have been forced to live in exile (Fazlur Rahman, Nasr Abu Zayd, and so on) for having been persecuted in their homeland. Politically they have often come under attack from a number of directions: from state authorities who find the modernists' political critiques disturbing; from secularists who are puzzled by the modernists' continued involvement with Islam; from traditional religious authorities whose own understanding of Islam is undermined by the modernists. Some modernists such as Fazlur Rahman and Iqbal have had the strange distinction of being targets of both persecution and large-scale admiration.

In conclusion, it is clear that Muslims are entering yet another age of critical self-reflection. Given the level of polemics and apologetics, it is extraordinarily difficult to sustain a critical level of subtle discourse. Yet Muslims today are not merely initiating social transformation, they are also reflecting much wider processes at the same time. They are well-situated to provide the most balanced and critical syntheses of Islam and modernity.

Moving more specifically to the North American context, Muslims who seek to engage in the grand project of Islamic reform face a number of challenges. Writing as a self-identifying progressive Muslim, I will here seek to enumerate some of these challenges in order to position progressive reforms as a beacon for—and not against—the community:

(1) Transcending antagonistic attitudes toward mainstream Muslim communities:

There is a substantial difference between being an *alternative* to the mainstream Muslim community (in terms of particular practices such as gender rights, standing up against racism and classism, and so on) and being consistently *antagonistic* to the mainstream Muslim community.

I am very concerned about some statements from some progressive Muslims in North America that repeatedly characterize the mainstream Muslim community as Islamist, Salafi, or Wahhabi. In today's political climate, acting in such a way puts peoples' lives, family, property, freedom, and reputation in danger. All too often those of us in the progressive community have felt that we must be unrelenting in our critiques in order to be effective. Surely, one can be capable of nuance without surrendering the mandate of being radical in the cause of justice and truth.

My own hope is that we in the progressive movement can be a light to the community, a voice of conscience, a mandate of justice, and an example of compassion, so that through the power of our moral calling, we will persuade many in our community to do which is most just, most beautiful, and most compassionate.

(2) Struggling against secular tendencies in the progressive movement:

One of my hopes for the progressive Muslim movement in North America had been that it would create a "big tent" in which Muslims of various persuasions could gather to strive for common projects, some focusing on the interpretation of Islam in the modern world and others working on concrete and grounded social projects. While the openness of this proposition still appeals to me, I have also come to see that in practice it is extremely challenging to create such a "big tent." In particular, one is reminded that just as there are shades and gradations of conservative Muslims, not all Muslims who self-identify as secular are the same. The secular criticism of the Christian Arab writer Edward Said was not the same as the secularism of Karl Marx, or that of contemporary Europe. For Said, part of the process of "secular criticism" was as follows: "In its suspicion of totalizing concepts, in its discontent with reified objects, in its impatience with guilds, special interests, imperialized fiefdoms, and orthodox habits of mind, criticism is most itself, and if the paradox can be tolerated, most unlike itself at the moment it starts turning into organized dogma."[6] It is worth exploring whether the term "Progressive Islam" has become a dogma in itself, and thus ironically unlike itself—as Said suggests. As a loving self-critique, I would suggest that many progressives have become every bit as rigid, authoritarian, and dogmatic as the conservative movements they so readily criticize. This represents a moral and philosophical failure of the highest magnitude.

Among Muslims today, one also finds a variety of secular tendencies. Some Muslims come from a traditional heritage but are essentially agnostic in their outlook (often combined with the most antireligious interpretations of Marxism), whereas others interpret secularism as a call to keep the state powers out of the religious game. I have come to realize that in our desire to establish the widest possible ground for a "big tent" in some progressive Muslim organizations, we have left ourselves open to the problem of not having enough of a common ground. At the risk of overstating the obvious, a progressive Muslim movement has to start with at least a minimum of commitment to a *tawhidic* perspective, the guidance of the Qur'an, and the earnest desire to emulate the Prophetic Sunna. While I will always support those who seek to prevent the state (whether it is the United States, Israel, Iran, India, or any other state) from favoring one religious community over others, I have come to realize that a Marxist interpretation of secularism, with its hostility toward religion as a source of inspiration, presents one of the greatest dangers to the progressive Muslim movement. This danger is all the more pernicious because so many progressives identify with the Marxists' devastating critique of socioeconomic class issues, colonialism, and so on. Yet this ideology actually suffocates the spirit of progressive Islam.

(3) Engagement with the multiple intellectual and spiritual traditions of Islam:

It is not just to outside critics that Muslim progressives have too often seemed "insufficiently Muslim." I think there has been an unfortunate and unnecessary hostility among some of us to take seriously the spiritual and intellectual heritage of Islam, and to draw on the vast resources it offers us for living as meaningful deputies (*khalifa*s, as in Qur'an 2:30) of God in the world today. In the *Progressive Muslims* volume, I stated:

> Progressive Muslims insist on a serious engagement with the full spectrum of Islamic thought and practices. There can be no progressive Muslim movement that does not engage the very "stuff" (textual and material sources) of the Islamic tradition, even if some of us would wish to debate what "stuff" that should be and how it ought to be interpreted....
>
> To state the obvious, a progressive Muslim agenda has to be both progressive and Islamic, in the sense of deriving its inspiration from the heart of the Islamic tradition. It cannot survive as a graft of secular humanism onto the tree of Islam, but must emerge from within that very entity. It can receive and surely has received inspiration from other spiritual and political movements, but it must ultimately grow in the soil of Islam.[7]

My serious concern at this point is that some of the organizations that have adopted the rubric "progressive Muslims" today are dangerously close (if not already there) to falling into the trap of providing an "Islamic veneer" for many positions without seriously taking on the challenge of engaging the traditions of Islam.

(4) Reviving the spiritual core of a reform movement:

One of my great hopes had been that this reform movement would be marked by a genuine spiritual core, something that would combine and yet go beyond the earlier rationalistic twentieth-century movements with Sufi etiquette and postmodern, postcolonial liberation stances. Yet for me the spiritual core has always been and remains at the center. As I see it, there is no way of transforming Muslim society without simultaneously transforming the hearts of human beings.

(5) Recovering courtesy (*adab*) and spiritual manners (*akhlaq*):

It is imperative for the lofty social ideals of progressive Muslims to be reflected in the *adab* and *akhlaq* of our interpersonal relations. I continue to hope that some of the Sufi ethics of dealing with fellow human beings would characterize our dealings with one another, to always recall and remember the reflection of the Divine Presence and the divine qualities in one another.

Some would call this notion romantic or idealistic. Maybe so. I for one continue to hold on firmly to the notion that without romance and idealism we have no hope of being and becoming fully human. Here, as in so many places, Gandhi had a keen observation: "As soon as we lose the moral basis, we cease to be religious. There is no such thing as religion overriding morality."[8]

On far too many occasions, many of us Muslim progressives have lost the moral basis of interpersonal relations. What is particularly disappointing to me is that we have time and again risen to defend those whose points of view and practices have been hard to justify under any existing interpretation of Islam but have been quick to demonize many others who have done no more than simply present what have up until now been traditional and common Muslim attitudes toward issues that are now part of the culture wars.

My hope is that a community marked by true love and devotion for one another would be capable of incredible transformations. That, after all, has been Islam's legacy starting from the time of the prophets, including our own beloved Messenger of God. What a beautiful example this is for each of us to emulate, as we all seek to establish small, humane communities around us. People who are rude and uncivil to one another have no hope of transforming the world, much less themselves.

Love heals. Love transforms. That is why I have felt so strongly that progressive Muslim communities, and indeed all human communities, should be permeated by loving person-to-person relationships.

CONCLUSION

I pray that the above comments, as hard as they have been to write, will inspire some to address the present shortcomings of the progressive Muslim movement. Why bother? Simply because I believe that the ability of Muslims in North America to contribute to the grand project of Islamic reform is at stake.

I recently had a chance to spend a long day in conversation with some Christian activists who had worked with Dr. Martin Luther King, Jr. One of their insightful comments stayed with me: What Martin said was the same as what many Christian preachers had been saying for 100 years. What was new was that people had heard the message so many times that when a charismatic teacher came along, what he said simply resonated with that which they had known to be true in the innermost chambers of their hearts. Our task today is not to simply parody Martin Luther King, Jr., as much as some of us may idealize him. I believe that the best we can do at this moment in history is to work on projects large and small to establish righteous communities and just and compassionate interpretations of Islam. In time, our struggle—indeed, our *jihad* in the sense most relevant for today's condition—will have the benefit of making its truths self-evident in the inner-most chambers of Muslim hearts.

Our struggle is both for ourselves and for our children. We have to be willing to live with the realization that none of us will get to live long enough to actually see the realization of a just world. But in the endeavor to bring that world about, our own lives will have achieved the dignity and meaning to which we are entitled. And we pray that our children may come to live in a world in which their dignity as Muslims, as citizens of this planet, and as human beings is engaged and acknowledged.

THE CHAPTERS IN THIS VOLUME

One of the persistent challenges facing Muslims in the modern era has been in developing a coherent methodology toward tradition. Indeed it would be fair to say that both modernists and their more conservative coreligionists have been guilty of selective and inconsistent appropriations of the existing traditions. Some of these issues are brought up in my discussion above. Umar Faruq Abd-Allah brilliantly examines the ramification this has had for a crucial issue, the boundaries of innovation and heresy in Islam. Mohammed Azadpur explores the most neglected of Islamic sciences in modern times, philosophy. Indeed the whole issue of the extent to which Muslims may (or rather, did indeed) connect themselves to pararevelational wisdom such as that of the Greek masters is a fascinating case for Muslims' ability today to engage the wisdom (and perils) of modernity.

Two of the chapters in this volume, by Jamillah A. Karim and Aminah Beverly McCloud, address the experiences of African American Muslims. For far too long the experiences of "American Muslims" have been read, discussed, and mediated through the lens of first- and second-generation Muslims. This fallacy can be maintained no more. These two chapters remind us that if Muslim brotherhood and sisterhood are to be realized in Muslim America, a new reality must be created. Ziba Mir-Hosseini's chapter is a powerful reminder of how the gender wars are a perennial indication of the struggles that characterize modern Islam. There is indeed no site more contested in the world than the bodies of Muslim women. The chapter by Scott Sirajul Haqq Kugle continues the engagement with gender issues by moving more specifically toward a frank, and no doubt contested, discussion of sexuality. Ebrahim Moosa continues his examination of critical thought in modern Islam by reminding readers that the working out of the challenges facing contemporary Muslims cannot be achieved outside of a thorough and rigorous methodology.

The last two chapters seek to break down the boundaries of the facile dichotomy of "Islam" versus the "West" in different ways. Hugh Talat Halman embarks on a fascinating discussion of the unfolding of spiritual movements in the West that are in many ways as rooted in historical Islamic tradition as they are in the post–World War II West. My culminating chapter seeks to identify the ambitions of some Muslim Neo-conservatives to live in an "us versus them" world, and asks us to strive for a world in which there can be a "rendezvous of victory for all."

NOTES

1. Seyyed Hossein Nasr, *Three Muslim Sages* (Delmar, New York: Caravan Books, 1964), 11.

2. Abdolkarim Soroush, *Reason, Freedom, and Democracy in Islam: Essential Writings of Abdolkarim Soroush,* trans. and ed. Mahmoud Sadri and Ahmad Sadri (New York: Oxford University Press, 2000), 21.

3. Omid Safi, ed., *Progressive Muslims: On Justice, Gender, and Pluralism* (Oxford, U.K.: Oneworld Publications, 2003), 6.

4. See Leonardo Boff, *Introducing Liberation Theology,* trans. Clodovis Boff (Turnbridge Wells, Kent, U.K.: Burns & Oates/Search Press Ltd., 1987).

5. Bin Laden quotation from http://www.fas.org/irp/world/para/docs/980223-fatwa.htm. Arabic original at http://www.library.cornell.edu/colldev/mideast/fatw2.htm.

6. Moustafa Bayoumi and Andrew Rubin, *The Edward Said Reader* (New York: Vintage, 2000), 242. Said further identified "secular criticism" as not a movement opposed to religion, but rather as follows: "It is not practicing criticism either to validate the status quo or to join up with a priestly caste of acolytes and dogmatic metaphysicians. The realities of power and authority—as well as the resistances offered by men, women, and social movements to institutions, authorities, and orthodoxies...," Ibid., 223.

7. Omid Safi, *Progressive Muslims,* 7–8.

8. Mahatma Gandhi, *Quotes of Gandhi,* ed. Shalu Bhalla (New Delhi, India: UBS Publishers, 1995), 25.

1

CREATIVITY, INNOVATION, AND HERESY IN ISLAM

•

Umar F. Abd-Allah

The terminology of Islamic law and theology includes words for innovation, heresy, and related concepts like hypocrisy, masked infidelity, and apostasy. Generally, each term has its own distinct sense, but the term *bid ʿa* (innovation/heresy)—the focal point of this chapter—is the broadest and most problematic. It covers a range of overlapping meanings, allowing for confusion and misuse. The word *bid ʿa* is a familiar part of everyday Muslim discourse, although it is often used with less than optimal understanding. Certain groups are addicted to the term, using it mistakenly and without discretion as a rhetorical sledgehammer to crush ideas and practices they do not like.

When *bid ʿa* is used by itself without qualifying adjectives, it generally has a pejorative sense, although in traditional Islamic usage—especially when qualified—it covered a wide spectrum of connotations, ranging from the highly positive to the utterly reprehensible. A sound feeling for the theological and legal implications of *bid ʿa* and related concepts is as relevant for Muslims today as ever, since it constitutes a defining element in their consciousness and unquestionably affects their behavior. Sherman Jackson emphasizes the need for instilling a critical modicum of Islamic awareness in the Muslim community, which he calls "Islamic literacy."[1] This core understanding must be sufficient to give everyday Muslims basic immunity against the incompetent pseudoscholarly opinions that occasionally bombard them in the name of Islam. As will be shown, Islamic literacy is consistent with the dictates of *ijtihad* (utmost intellectual inquiry), which was not just a scholarly obligation but a requirement of the lay community to pass judgment on the aptitude of scholars.

Bid ʿa connoted both innovation and heresy, and this chapter treats its association with both phenomena. Historically, its association with theological heresy was particularly common. For those familiar with Islamic scholarship, the term *zandaqa* (atheistic heresy) readily comes to mind in the context of the Islamic conception of heresy and is also examined. But, with reference to heresy, *bid'a* was more inclusive, while *zandaqa* tended to be restricted to heresies regarded as so cynical and inherently hostile to religion that, as with apostasy (*irtidad* or *ridda*), jurists censured those who held them.

BASIC TERMS

The concept of *bid'a* was common in pre-Islamic Arab usage. The root from which the word derived is morphologically linked with a distinct but similar radical, *BD'* (the difference being between the final letter *hamza* (') in this root and the final *'ayn* (') in *bid'a*). *BD'* meant "to start or begin something," while the primary meaning of *bid'a* was "to start or begin something novel." Among the various words directly derived from the root of *bid'a* was the noun *Badi'* (Originator), cited in the Qur'an as one of God's attributions: "Originator (*Badi'*) of the heavens and the earth" (Qur'an 2:117; 6:101).[2] Use of *al-Badi'* with reference to God denoted the uniqueness of His creative act and implied that He brought the world into existence without a previously existing prototype.[3] As an adjective, *badi'* was applied to outstanding works of human genius, especially those of great poets and other masters of the spoken and written word.[4]

The term *bid'a* was less nuanced in its pre-Islamic context than in Islamic usage. It was consistently pejorative and was employed to condemn violations of tribal custom. *Bid'a* was applied to actions and ideas that lacked identifiable prototypes in custom and were unauthorized by tribal role models. It constituted a sort of tribal heresy and innovation, deviating from established norms and the ways of great forebears from the past.

The message of the Prophet Muhammad challenged the established order of Arabia and was condemned as *bid'a*. The Prophet countered by making the opposite claim and turned the *bid'a* controversy on its head, undercutting the allegations of his enemies. Islam was neither a heresy nor an innovation, his teaching asserted, but constituted a restoration of the legacy of Abraham, Ishmael, and the earlier Arabian Prophets (Hud and Salih), ancient ancestral traditions that the idolatrous Arab tribes had distorted over time. The ideological battle is mirrored in a Qur'anic verse commanding the Prophet to declare to his opponents: "Say [to them]: I am no novelty [*bid'*] among [God's] Prophet-Messengers" (Qur'an 46:9). *Bid'*, the word used in this verse, is almost identical in meaning and morphology to *bid'a*. While it clearly indicates that the Prophet's message possessed direct continuity with ancient prophecy—a point made explicitly in other texts—it also intimated that the pagan beliefs and customs of Muhammad's contemporaries were *bid'a* because they lacked continuity with antiquity and had veered long ago from the best of ancient Arab ways.[5]

The pre-Islamic concept of *bid'a* belonged to a wider semantic frame that linked it with its opposite, *Sunna* (established tradition). Islam took over the *bid'a–Sunna* paradigm but redefined its content. In pre-Islamic Arabia, *Sunna* constituted the well-known repository of tribal custom and embodied the norms of acceptable thought and practice. Each instance of *bid'a* conjured up the image of a long-established *Sunna* that it threatened. Rooted in tribal practice, the pre-Islamic *bid'a–Sunna* paradigm was doggedly conservative and functioned to insure the status quo.[6]

With the advent of Islam, the term *Sunna* came to be closely connected with the normative teaching and conduct of the Prophet Muhammad. The link between *Sunna* and *bid'a* was maintained, but both concepts were rooted in scriptural authority and complemented by the creative imperative to perform *ijtihad*.[7]

In contrast to *bid'a*, the words *zandaqa* and *zindiq* (heretic/atheist) were foreign loan words and did not occur in Islam's primary sources. They were borrowed from Aramaic or Middle Persian, most likely from the Aramaic *ziddiq* (righteous), a Semitic cognate of the Arabic *siddiq* (eminently truthful). *Ziddiq* was used by Aramaic-speaking Manichaeans[8] for their spiritual elite. In the pre-Islamic period, Oriental Christians applied the word to Manichaeans in general, which accounts for its initial restriction in Islamic parlance to Muslim heretics suspected of harboring Manichaean beliefs.[9]

Zandaqa's foreign origins may account for its comparative lack of semantic breadth in Arabic usage. It was not, as some scholars have mistakenly claimed, the standard Islamic term for sectarian heresy, a role more properly suited for *bid'a*.[10] *Zandaqa* was restricted to particular types of extreme religious infidelity, which were essentially atheistic. Although Muslims first used *zandaqa* for dualistic heresies of a Manichaean variety, the word quickly shifted focus to any cynical or generally mocking frame of mind inimical to religious belief. Consequently, in later juristic and theological usage, *zandaqa* was almost inseparable from hypocrisy (*nifaq*) and apostasy. Because the expression of atheistic beliefs or public mocking of Islam was a capital offense, *zandaqa* was usually concealed or expressed only in private. As such, it took on the sense of "masked infidelity."

By contrast, *bid'a* as a form of heresy rarely referred to people who took their religious convictions lightly or hid them from others. Like "heretics" of other faiths, those of Islam were often zealous and outspoken and undertook missions to win followers. In the standard parlance of jurists and theologians, such highly committed, movement-oriented heretics were not guilty of *zandaqa* but were classified under the label of "people of [various types of] *bid'a* and passionate excesses" (*ahl al-bida' wa al-ahwa'*). *Zandaqa*, on the other hand, seldom constituted identifiable and coherent movements.[11]

Because theological *bid'a* applied only in extreme cases to denial of faith, it was rarely a capital offense, but, since *zandaqa*, if proven, was almost always fatal, it served on occasion as a powerful weapon in the ruler's arsenal to destroy political rivals. When a head of state leveled the charge of *zandaqa* against an opponent, it meant almost certain death. Not surprisingly, the accusation of *zandaqa* in political circles generally had nothing to do with heresy but was so vague and unfounded that it was virtually impossible to determine the exact nature of the victim's alleged offense.[12]

Defining the content of creedal orthodoxy was a primary goal of traditional Islamic theology and reflected a correlated concern with delineating heresy. Theologians often drew sharp lines where the Prophet had not. It was his habit, instead, to suffice with simple declarations of faith, which he was generally willing to accept at face value as illustrated at the death of Abu Talib, his uncle, clan leader, and chief benefactor. Although Abu Talib vigilantly protected his nephew Muhammad from their tribe's hostile and powerful oligarchy, he died without embracing the Prophet's religion. As Abu Talib lay dying, the Prophet stood by his side and implored: "Uncle, [just] say, 'There is no god but God,' a [single] sentence by which I may bear witness on your behalf in God's presence."[13]

A similar doctrinal minimalism is reflected in other frequently attested Hadith (Prophetic Traditions) that report him saying: "Whoever dies knowing that there is no god but God shall enter the Garden."[14] He also taught: "Whoever bears witness that there is no god but God and that Muhammad is God's Messenger, God will forbid the Fire from [touching] him."[15] On one occasion, such divine munificence disconcerted the Companion 'Umar, who challenged another Companion, Abu Hurayra, upon hearing him give the good news of salvation at the Prophet's behest to anyone "who bore witness that there was no god but God, having certainty of it in his heart." 'Umar went to the Prophet immediately and asked: "Messenger of God, did you [truly] send Abu Hurayra...to give good tidings of the Garden to anyone he met who bore witness that there is no god but God, being certain of it in his heart?" The Prophet answered: "Yes." 'Umar replied: "Do not do that. I fear people will place their reliance upon it. Let them keep performing [good] actions." The Prophet replied: "Then let them [keep doing that]."[16]

Conversion to Islam has remained a simple process, requiring little more than the testimony of faith: "There is no god but God, and Muhammad is God's Messenger." But Muslim theologians rarely made it as straightforward to remain orthodox and stay within the fold. Only a few of them were content with the twofold testimony of faith as sufficient proof of accepted belief. Each denomination elaborated its own corollaries of the basic testimony of faith and subsidiary beliefs that they contended the basic testimonies of faith explicitly or implicitly entailed.

BID'A IN ISLAMIC SCRIPTURAL SOURCES

The Qur'an contains one reference to innovation directly derived from the root of *bid'a*. The verse pertains to Jesus and the first Christian believers: "[We] instilled kindliness and mercy in the hearts of those who followed him and monastic practice, which they innovated [*ibtada'uha*]. We did not prescribe it for them but out of the pleasure of God. Yet they failed to observe it as it should have been observed" (Qur'an 57: 27). The passage is especially noteworthy because it refers in an ostensibly favorable light to *bid'a* in a matter of worship, an area where many Islamic scholars deemed innovations most pernicious.

A common reading of the verse, corroborated by its wording, asserts that monasticism was a human innovation, which God did not prescribe for Jesus' followers but which they themselves instituted, seeking God's pleasure. It is not their religious innovation that is reprimanded but their failure to fulfill it. Early Qur'anic exegesis traces this interpretation to a Companion of the Prophet named Abu Umama, who asserted that Jesus' followers "instituted [certain] innovations which God had not prescribed upon them, seeking God's good pleasure through them, but they failed to observe them properly, and God reproached them for their departure from [proper observation]." Consistent with this reading, many classical commentators linked the verse to the Islamic law of ritual vows, which, by their nature, have an improvised quality and generally demand fulfillment once one has chosen to perform them.[17]

Another reading insists that God Himself ordained monasticism; hence, it was not technically a *bid'a*. He intended its practice solely for His pleasure and reproached those monks who fell short of what was required. Others construed the verse as condemning monasticism itself for being a religious *bid'a*, but their reading of the text is the most forced of the three and lacks the textual exactitude required in Islamic jurisprudence to constitute a categorical proof.[18]

References to *bid'a* are common in the Hadith collections of all Islamic sects—Sunni, Shi'i, and Ibadi.[19] One shared hadith on the subject is the well-known admonition of the Prophet: "The worst of things are monstrosities [*muhdathat;* also "innovations"], and every *bid'a* is misguidance."[20] For Sunnis and Shiites alike, this hadith constitutes one of the most categorical condemnations of innovation and was taken at face value by literalists in both communities. But, in both denominations, the dominant opinion held that the Prophet's admonition was not a categorical prohibition of innovative ideas or practices but a warning to stay within sound legal parameters in accepting or rejecting them. New ideas and practices had to be consistent with established precedents and recognized principles.

If it seems far-fetched that the apparently literal condemnation of *bid'a* in this hadith could be honestly construed as anything less than a categorical reprimand against every form of creativity, such a nonliteral approach was not problematic for most classical scholars. Their hermeneutics recognized the polysemic nature of sacred texts, which they interpreted in the light of a number of references like the subtleties of Arabic, historical context, related texts, and relevant Islamic principles. In the case of this hadith, the hermeneutical tradition unhesitatingly limited its meaning to unwarranted *bidʿa*. Thus, despite the hadith's apparent generality, it was understood as implicitly qualified, the typical reasoning for which is illustrated below. As one scholarly commentary states: "[This is a] general statement [understood as having] specific qualifications [*ʿamm makhsus*]."[21]

Another hadith well-attested in Sunni and Shiite collections pertains to the sanctity of the Prophetic city of Medina, which Muhammad proclaimed a religious sanctuary like the ancient Abrahamic city of Mecca: "So whoever introduces [*ahdatha*; also "innovates"] in [Medina] a [monstrous] innovation or gives shelter there to such an innovator, upon him shall be the curse of God, the angels, and mankind. No disbursement shall be accepted from him or any ransom."[22] In a Shiite version, the hadith adds: "'Messenger of God, what is the innovation [intended]?' He replied: 'Whoever [wrongfully] kills a [human] soul without [legal recompense] for [another] soul, maims [a body] without indemnity, innovates a *bidʿa* having no *Sunna*, or [wrongfully] seizes plunder of exceptional value.'" Another Shiite transmission defines the monstrous innovation as murder, and the word *ahdatha* used in this Hadith occurs in a number of Prophetic declarations with specific reference to that crime.[23]

Sunni interpretations of the hadith essentially agreed with the Shiite view. A famous Sunni commentator, Nawawi, parsed the innovation referred to as iniquitous behavior.[24] Ibn Hajar, another renowned Sunni scholar, understood the hadith's broad wording as implicitly delimited by its context in specific reference to the holy city's sanctuary status. Thus, for Sunni and Shiite scholars in general, the illustrations given for the damnable innovations referred to in the hadith clearly involved the gross violation of Medina's sanctuary status, especially by acts of lawless violence.[25]

An intriguing reference to *bidʿa* in Sunni, Shiʿi, and Ibadi Kharijite sources deals with the second caliph ʿUmar's decision to institute supererogatory group prayers during the nights of Ramadan within a decade of the Prophet's death.[26] According to Sunni and Ibadi sources, the Prophet once led his Companions in similar prayers for a few nights of Ramadan shortly before his death but discontinued the practice, expressing concern that, if he continued leading the vigils, God would make them obligatory, which Muhammad feared would impose an excessive burden upon his community.

During his caliphate, ʿUmar observed people praying randomly in the Prophet's mosque during the nights of Ramadan individually and in small groups and took the decision to unite them behind a single prayer leader, instituting the Ramadan vigil as a group prayer. Entering the mosque on a subsequent night and witnessing the congregation praying in unison, he declared: "What an excellent *bidʿa* this is!"[27] Sunni sources emphasize that the Prophet's cousin ʿAli, who later became the fourth caliph and is revered by all Shiʿi schools as their first Imam, endorsed ʿUmar's action and continued his policy. Sunnis report that ʿAli once remarked that

'Umar "illuminated the month of fasting" by instituting the group prayer. Another Sunni version relates that one night in Ramadan during 'Ali's caliphate, he passed by mosques lit up with candles for the people to perform the congregational vigil and said: "May God illuminate 'Umar's grave just as he illuminated for us our mosques."[28]

The Zaydis, generally regarded as the closest of all Shiites to Sunnis, upheld the validity of the Ramadan group prayer, affirming that 'Ali continued the practice during his caliphate.[29] The Imami Shi'i school was generally antagonistic toward 'Umar and viewed the historical record differently, rejecting 'Umar's decision as an unlawful *bid'a*. Like Sunnis, they confirmed that the Prophet led the community in Ramadan night prayers for a short period. Unlike Sunnis, they contended that the Prophet not merely abandoned the prayer but emphatically banned it in groups, concluding with the words: "Every *bid'a* is misguidance, and the path of every misguidance [leads] to the Fire." Imami sources agree that 'Ali allowed the community to continue praying the Ramadan group vigil during his caliphate. Despite the fact that he personally opposed this practice, the pro-'Umar sentiment was too strong, and the people were so attached to this "*sunna* of 'Umar" that it was not politically feasible for 'Ali to ban it.[30]

Like the Qur'anic verse on monasticism, one of the most interesting points about 'Umar's "excellent *bid'a*" is that it falls squarely within the domain of ritual acts of worship and, with the caveat of the Imami perspective, was widely regarded as good. Sunni sources report that Abu Umama—referred to earlier in conjunction with the verse on monasticism—admonished Muslims to be vigilant in observing the group vigil of Ramadan. He linked this practice explicitly to the Qur'anic allusion to monasticism and would say: "You have innovated the [practice of] standing in prayer during Ramadan, although it was not prescribed for you, for only the fasting [of that month] was prescribed. So, now that you have done it, remain constant in keeping up the prayer and never abandon it."[31]

An eminent Sunni scholar, Ibn 'Abd al-Barr, believed that 'Umar called his decision a *bid'a* because the Prophet had not instituted the vigil as a *Sunna* nor had Abu Bakr, the first caliph after him. Nevertheless, 'Umar declared it "an excellent *bid'a*" to indicate its initial legitimacy in the Prophet's eyes and to emphasize to the people that, although it was technically a *bid'a*, they should have no misgivings about it, since the Prophet had only declined to institute it for fear of making it obligatory.[32] The reasoning here is predicated on a standard principle of Islamic jurisprudence that nothing specific to the Prophet's *Sunna* can be given a new legal status—obligatory or otherwise—after his death if he did not indicate that status during his lifetime. Thus, 'Umar's "excellent *bid'a*" put into practice something the Prophet had looked upon favorably, while avoiding the Prophet's fear of its becoming obligatory and burdensome. In the same vein, another famous Sunni jurist, Abu Bakr ibn al-'Arabi, described 'Umar's institution of the prayer as a

Sunna and a *bid'a* at the same time; it was a *Sunna* by virtue of the Prophet's short-term precedent but a *bid'a* because the Prophet declined to institute it. Ibn al-'Arabi concluded: "How excellent was this *bid'a* as a revived *sunna* and fully accomplished act of obedience!"[33]

These and other Islamic sources demonstrate the linguistic range of *bid'a*. In the abstract, however, *bid'a* was generally pejorative, although in certain circumstances, as we have seen, it could be transformed into its opposite. *Sunna,* by contrast, was almost invariably affirmative but had a semantic potential similar to *bid'a* and could take on negative connotations, especially when used for reprehensible types of *bid'a* that became customary. A famous hadith relates: "No human soul shall be killed wrongfully but that Adam's first son shall carry a share of the guilt, for he was the first human to institute the *sunna* of murder."[34] Another Hadith uses *Sunna* in two different ways, first in reference to a good *bid'a* and second with regard to an odious one: "Whoever establishes a good *sunna* [*sunna hasana*] in Islam that is followed in practice afterward, will have recorded to his merit a reward equal to the reward of anyone who practices it, without any of their rewards being at all diminished. Whoever establishes an evil *sunna* [*sunna sayyi'a*] in Islam that is followed in practice afterward, will have recorded against him a burden equal to the burden of anyone who practices it without any of their burdens being at all lessened."[35]

BID'A IN THE LEGAL TRADITION

The *Sunna–bid'a* paradigm was shared by all Islamic denominations. All concurred on the fundamental obligation to follow the Qur'an and *Sunna*. But each sect and every school within a sect espoused different criteria for defining, interpreting, and applying the concepts.

The four principal Sunni schools differed among themselves on how to interpret Qur'anic texts. They concurred on the probity of all the Prophet's Companions as authoritative transmitters of his *Sunna*—a crucial Sunni tenet and major point of difference between them and the Shi'is and Ibadis—but each Sunni school employed markedly different methods in their understanding and utilization of the *Sunna* and, consequently, arrived at diverse conclusions regarding its legal status and content.[36]

The Shi'is, who had distinctive interpretations of the Qur'an, relied no less heavily upon the *Sunna* than the Sunnis. For the Imamis, the *Sunna* went beyond the teachings and normative example of the Prophet to include those of the 12 divinely guided Imams. Despite such differences, Shiite sources contain authoritative texts identical in wording to those of other denominations like: "Follow the reports of God's Messenger, God bless and keep him, and his *Sunna*."[37] The Ibadis ascribed, in principle, to the same obligation to follow the Qur'an and *Sunna* but differed by granting special status in its transmission to the "the just Imams," meaning the first two rightly guided caliphs, Abu Bakr and 'Umar (excluding the caliphs 'Uthman and 'Ali) and to other authoritative figures like the Prophet's wife 'A'isha.[38]

Likewise, regarding *bid'a*, the theologians and jurists of all three Muslim denominations conceived of the term in similar ways. They concurred that the concept of *bid'a* in its negative sense did not connote a blanket condemnation of all innovative ideas and practices simply because they were new, while they rejected all *bid'a* that appeared inconsistent with Prophetic precedent and Islam's underlying principles.[39] The noted jurist and legal theorist Shatibi emphasized that the very notion that Islamic law stood for categorical prohibitions against change was grossly absurd to classical jurists. All scholars, he contended, concurred that it was intellectually repulsive to insist that Muslims could never diverge from the cultural norms of early Islamic Arabia or that any new development in life must be regarded as an unwarranted *bid'a*.[40]

One of the most basic Islamic paradigms is the distinction between matters that are essentially nonritualistic and mundane (*mu'amalat*) and others that are ritualistic and otherworldly in nature (*'ibadat*). The first category refers to matters like war and peace, buying and selling, and marriage and divorce. Such nonritualistic concerns of human societies, although falling under the rubric of divine revelation and relevant to the law, were believed to serve tangible social goals and benefits. Consequently, they had rationales (tangible legal objectives), that lent themselves to rational scrutiny, and were open to legal analysis and amendment. For this reason, many notable scholars held that *bid'a* did not pertain to the domain of nonritualistic matters.[41] By contrast, matters of ritual like belief, prayer, fasting, and pilgrimage were an exclusively divine prerogative related to otherworldly realities like the secrets of salvation and the unseen. They served the purpose of purifying the soul, bringing people close to God, and winning His eternal pleasure. Consequently, they lacked discernable rationales, were inscrutable to reason, and were closed to legal analysis and amendment. For the great majority, ritualistic matters were the primary focus of *bid'a;* for many others, belief and ritual were its sole domain.

Ibn 'Abd al-Barr was among those who held that *bid'a* was strictly ritualistic: "As for making innovations in the practical workings of this world, no constriction and no fault pertains to one who does so."[42] Technological progress, crafts, building projects, urban development, and the like lay, according to this view, totally beyond the purview of *bid'a*. Dissenting scholars who included mundane affairs under the rubric of *bid'a* applied it only to appalling innovations that encroached scandalously upon central precepts of the law like unjust taxation (*maks*), nepotism, administrative corruption, and hanging pictures of judges and rulers in public places, which all scholars, regardless of how they conceived of *bid'a*, agreed were forbidden.[43]

Given the nuances of *bid'a*, classical Islamic jurisprudence evaluated it according to the five ethical categories of the religious law: obligatory, recommended, neutral, disliked, and forbidden. Thus, the gamut ran from obligatory *bid'a* to forbidden. Any *bid'a* that fell into one of the first three categories was regarded as consistent with the precepts and general principles of Islam.[44] Ibn Hajar wrote: "Put precisely, if a *bid'a* comes under the rubric of things regarded as good in the law, it is good. If it comes under the rubric of things ill-regarded in the law, it is ill-regarded. Otherwise, it belongs to the category of neutral things, and [in general] [*bid'a*] may be divided into the five [ethical] divisions."[45] Today, these nuances of *bid'a* have been largely forgotten. For many Muslims, the word is a red flag, invariably designating extreme religious error beyond any possibility of dispassionate discussion. In such cases, it has become a narrowly parochial force of polarization, obsessively opinionated and devoid of critical depth or scholarly protocol.

COUNTERBALANCING *BID'A* WITH *IJTIHAD*

The concept of *bid'a* was classificatory and judgmental. Though it had positive nuances and was not intended to rule out new ideas, it clearly served as a control mechanism and put ideas on trial, exonerating some and disapproving others. Its fundamental conception was conservative and potentially inhibiting. The criteria of *bid'a* imposed a restrictive frame on creative ideas to ensure continuity with tradition and conformity with legal principle. It must be stressed, however, that setting clear parameters does not necessarily encumber creativity and may even facilitate it. Such demarcation of parameters with the purpose of simultaneously facilitating and directing creative thought was clearly central to the original concept of *bid'a*.

The positive potential of *bid'a* as a control mechanism was reinforced by the intellectual process of *ijtihad,* which served as a complement to the notion of *bid'a* but greatly overshadowed it in legal prominence. By nature, *ijtihad* was encouraging, forward looking, and creative. Unlike *bid'a*, *ijtihad* was neither judgmental nor classificatory but constituted a methodological process of judgment. The final results of its diverse procedures of "utmost intellectual inquiry" were ultimately subject to the scrutiny of the *bid'a–Sunna* paradigm and its corollaries, which determined whether the resulting judgments of *ijtihad* were consistent with the Prophetic tradition or not.

Al-Baji, a traditional Sunni jurist, defined *ijtihad* as "expending one's fullest [intellectual] capacity in search for the right ruling."[46] The art of *ijtihad* required "utmost scholarly exertion on the part of the individual jurisconsult with a view to arriving at a personal opinion" regarding a new matter of legal concern.[47] Bernard G. Weiss notes: "The law was not something to be passively received and applied; it was rather something to be actively constructed by human toilers eager to gain the approval of their Lord for their effort."[48]

Ijtihad derives from the same root as *jihad*. Their common radical, *JHD*, denotes expending extreme effort to achieve a difficult but worthy goal or to overcome a great obstacle for the sake of something good. Although *jihad* clearly applies to armed struggle and brings war immediately to mind, the word constitutes a central principle of Islamic ethics. *Jihad* epitomizes faith as active engagement in the world to make it better. Its high point is the inner struggle for discipline and self-knowledge, but it also covers an unlimited array of personal and group efforts as disparate as childbirth, earning a livelihood, getting an education, taking care of family, helping others, and striving for social justice.

Ijtihad shared *jihad*'s ethical force but pertained to the realm of abstractions, ideas, and critical thought in the endeavor to find solutions by expending extreme effort. Fazlur Rahman speaks of *ijtihad* as an intellectual and moral *jihad* but, more concretely, as "the effort to understand the meaning of a relevant text or precedent in the past, containing a rule, and to alter that rule by extending or restricting or otherwise modifying it in such a manner that a new situation can be subsumed under it by a new solution."[49] Weiss contends that *ijtihad*'s primary semantic field originated in ancient Arabia's harsh agrarian culture, so familiar to the Prophet's first followers, most of whom had experienced oasis agriculture at first hand. The word conjured up in their minds "the image of the cultivator toiling daily under the sun, struggling against the adversities of climate, weed, and sometimes intractable soil." He continues: "Given the difficulties encountered in the work of formulating the law, the jurists saw this work as a kind of toil and customarily called it *ijtihad* ('toil,' 'arduous effort,' 'striving')."[50]

To engage in the process of *ijtihad* is an Islamic religious duty of the first magnitude. As George Makdisi notes, it was the imperative to perform *ijtihad* that led to the formation of the classical schools of Islamic law.[51] All Muslim denominations had *ijtihad* traditions, although certain schools within each denomination put greater restrictions upon it than others. As we have seen, all Muslims upheld the validity of the famous hadith: "Every innovation is misguidance." But none understood it as contradicting the necessity of *ijtihad*, however much they differed on details that governed the process.[52]

What made *ijtihad* inherently optimistic was the Prophet's promise that those who practiced it would be rewarded in the next world, even if their answers were wrong. The Prophet stated: "If a judge [*hakim*] does *ijtihad* and gets the right answer, he receives two rewards, and, if he is [honestly] mistaken, he gets one."[53] Similar transmissions asserted that every person performing *ijtihad* was ultimately right—even if technically wrong—which prompted theologians and jurists to debate whether truth was singular or multifaceted in nature and raised the question of there being more than one correct answer for any given question. Some argued that all dissenting legal opinions could be correct in their own right, despite the fact that they were mutually contradictory.[54] Abu Hanifa, eponym of the largest Sunni school of law, said: "Every *mujtahid* (person performing *ijtihad*) is right, although [ultimate] truth in God's presence is [only] one." He explained that a *mujtahid* who fails to discover God's ultimate truth is, nevertheless, deemed right by virtue of the integrity of his personal *ijtihad*.[55] The majority of scholars were content simply to say that every *mujtahid* receives a reward when mistaken, not by virtue of the error but because of obedience to God in fulfilling the command to undergo the labor of *ijtihad*.[56]

Like *bid'a*, a pertinent question regarding *ijtihad* concerned the domains where it was valid and where it was not. Many restricted *ijtihad* to nonritualistic matters, but their opinion was not a matter of consensus. 'Umar's institution of the Ramadan night prayers clearly belonged to the ritualistic domain, as we have seen, and, in Baji's opinion, was a consummate example of *ijtihad*. It must be noted, however, that Baji discerned an important political (nonritualistic) dimension behind 'Umar's decision. The practice of people praying the Ramadan night prayer individually or in small groups had the potential to prove divisive in times of civil discord. A single, unified group of worshippers symbolized and reinforced the community's cohesiveness, but disparate congregations praying at the same time in a common space behind different prayer leaders could—and probably would—be manipulated in times of trouble to underscore factional divisions and accentuate political rivalries.[57]

Ijtihad was a function of the jurisconsult's membership in society.[58] Because the masses were untrained in the religious sciences, classical tradition required them to follow the scholars. Thus, *ijtihad* was not meant to be an ivory-tower pursuit but a living "social partnership" between legal scholars and the society at large, which continually presented them with "real legal problems" and "questions to work with."[59] But even the common people were required to perform their own type of *ijtihad* by striving to discern the competence of individual scholars and selecting the best to follow, a principle emphatically asserted by the majority of the Sunni and Shiite schools.[60]

Ijtihad is a perpetual obligation. A well-known maxim of Islamic law asserts: "There shall be no denunciation of changed legal judgments with changing times, places, and circumstances."[61] Al-Dabbusi, a prominent Sunni jurist, noted that what may be allowable in one time or place may become prohibited in another because of changing circumstances, just as what was prohibited may become allowable by the same criterion. He added that changing times and places are not the only considerations; there are other ones as well, like the social group a person belongs to. What is beneficial for one segment of society may be harmful for another.[62]

The renowned Sunni jurist al-Qarafi asserted that it was a matter of consensus that scholars were wrong to hand down legal judgments without performing *ijtihad* but merely by adhering strictly to ancient texts in their books without regard for cultural realities. The fault of such jurists was inexcusable and constituted disobedience of God. Their blind adherence to their legal compendia was misguidance in the religion of Islam and violated the original objectives behind the rulings of the earlier scholars and great personages of the past whom they claimed to be following.[63] A great jurist of the next generation, Ibn al-Qayyim, commented on al-Qarafi's opinion, saying:

> This is pure understanding of the law. Whoever issues legal rulings to the people merely on the basis of what is transmitted in the compendia despite differences in their customs, usages, times, places, conditions, and the special circumstances of their situations has gone astray and leads others astray. His crime against the religion is greater than the crime of a physician who gives people medical prescriptions without regard to the differences of their climes, norms, the times they live in, and their physical conditions but merely in accordance with what he finds written down in some medical book about people with similar anatomies. Such is an ignorant physician; the other is an ignorant jurisconsult but more detrimental.[64]

Undoubtedly, many traditional jurists not only failed to live up to the standards of Qarafi and Ibn Qayyim but also demonstrated an exasperating lack of creativity and stifled its spirit in others. Their rigidity created the widespread impression among Muslims and Westerners alike (including a surprising number of present-day academics and writers of good standing) that "the door of *ijtihad*" was "closed" as a matter of religious principle. The conspicuous decline of *ijtihad* at certain periods of Islamic history reflected a general social and intellectual malaise but not legal or theological doctrine. In fact, there is little historical evidence that the door of *ijtihad* was ever closed, and, in any case, since Islam has nothing comparable to an ecclesiastical hierarchy, the door of *ijtihad* never had a doorkeeper.[65]

The question of who was qualified to perform *ijtihad* was not set by the Prophet but by traditional scholars. Their stipulations typically required that a *mujtahid* be an upright Muslim of sound mind with full command of the Arabic language and mastery of the core disciplines of Islamic learning, including knowledge of the Qur'an and *Sunna*, consensus, methods of legal reasoning, and the overriding objectives of the law.[66]

It is to the jurists' credit that they did not list gender as pertinent to the requirements for *ijtihad,* and Islamic intellectual history contains several examples of famous women who excelled in the art. Fatima bint Muhammad al-Samarqandi, for example, who lived in twelfth-century CE Syria, ranks as an eminent *mujtahida*. She wrote and taught several works on Hadith and Islamic law, and her husband, Abu Bakr al-Kasani, author of the unique legal compendium *Bada'i al-Sana'i* (Marvels of Things Devised) and one of the most brilliant Sunni jurists, never issued a legal opinion based on his personal *ijtihad* unless his wife, Fatima, reviewed and signed it first.[67]

For more than a millennium, the process of speculative *ijtihad* was virtually the monopoly of traditional scholars, and the requirements they set for it remained largely unchallenged. Their control over *ijtihad* was first systematically called into question during the pivotal eighteenth century—the eve of Muslim modernity—when various Sunni and Shi'i revivalists demanded easier criteria.[68] As a rule, the revisionists of both camps leaned in favor of a textual literalism easy for the common people to grasp but alien to the dominant Sunni and Shi'i traditions. A similar emphasis on literalism reemerged as the major tendency of Muslim Activist (fundamentalist) thought in the twentieth century.

Conceptualization of *ijtihad* underwent even more radical change after the full onslaught of colonial rule and Western modernity in the nineteenth century. New approaches to education and *ijtihad* became primary concerns for the Muslim Modernist movement (1840–1940), which categorically rejected classical criteria for both. As Charles Kurzman observes, the Modernists (who were unfailing supporters of parliamentary democracy) challenged "the authority of the past and the authority of the credential" and, despite a general lack of traditional training, claimed their right to perform *ijtihad*, insisting in some cases that traditional scholastic education had become so sterile and far removed from modern realities that, instead of qualifying scholars for *ijtihad*, it actually disqualified them.[69]

The Muslim Modernist movement suffered greatly with the rise of Western-oriented secular nationalism in the wake of World War II, but the debate over *ijtihad* has continued until the present, especially within the ranks of Activist thinkers, who, like the Modernists before them, generally lack traditional training, claim the prerogative of *ijtihad* for themselves, and reject the authority of classical tradition, often turning it upon its head. The decline of traditional religious authority over the past three centuries not only made radically different criteria for *bid'a* and *ijtihad* possible but has also come to constitute one of the most critical cultural breaks in Islamic history.

As Richard Bulliet notes, the decline of classical authority in modern times was radically precipitated by the ubiquity of a periodical press and modern media coupled with national policies of universal education, which created mass readerships and heightened expectations: "The new technology enabled authors to become authorities simply by offering the reader persuasive prose and challenging ideas." Religious knowledge was removed from the scholastic classroom and pulpit, and various types of new religious authorities emerged who articulated their messages effectively in the language of the people and found large audiences. The classical moorings of *ijtihad* and Islamic thought came undone, and, as a consequence, the Muslim world finds itself today "immersed in a crisis of [religious] authority," the resolution of which is likely to take generations.[70]

The "new authorities" represent a diverse spectrum of intellectuals from liberal Modernists to radical Activists. Numbered among their ranks are the most influential Islamist ideologues of the twentieth century, whose claims to *ijtihad* have driven their agenda of creating a one-dimensional, politicized Islam. Most notable among them are Sayyid Qutb (Egypt, d. 1966), Abu A'la Mawdudi (India/Pakistan, d. 1979), and 'Ali Shari'ati (Iran, d. 1977), and Ayatollah Ruhollah Khomeini (d. 1989). With the exception of Khomeini, all of these "new authorities" lacked classical training and adamantly rejected the relevance of traditional scholarship.[71] In recent years, Usama Bin Laden, an engineer, and his associate Ayman al-Zawahiri, a pediatrician, have emerged as the most notorious "new authorities" and frequently martial the accusation of *bid'a* against their enemies and utilize their personal claim to *ijtihad* to justify "extremist positions."[72]

PRESENT AND FUTURE IMPLICATIONS

An authentic and sophisticated understanding of *bid'a* as a control mechanism and *ijtihad* as an inducement for creativity is vital for Muslims today. Its greatest interpretative resource is the legacy of Islamic thought through the ages. Marshall Hodgson identifies Islam's "great pre-Modern heritage" as, perhaps, the richest source Muslims possess in creating an integral vision of their religion's place in the modern world but notes: "One of the problems of Muslims is that on the level of historical action their ties with relevant traditions are so tenuous."[73]

It is unrealistic, however, and even undesirable to hope for meaningful restitution of the classical tradition and sophisticated application of concepts like *bid'a* and *ijtihad* without the revision and renewal necessary to make the tradition compatible with present-day needs and bring it in harmony with the criteria emphasized above by Qarafi and Ibn Qayyim. Yet without enlightened educational institutions that attract talented students and in the absence of curriculums that impart a mature understanding of modern thought and realities, it is unlikely that a sophisticated understanding of the tradition can ever be fostered, and our multitudes of old books and dusty manuscripts will remain little more than the extraordinary historical fossils of a defunct civilization. Moreover, until classical Islamic learning is made meaningful to contemporary Muslims, it is hard to fault those who question its relevance.

As harmful and heterodox as the "new authorities" sometimes are, they must be judged in the context of our times and not just condemned by citing bits and pieces of scripture or referencing contrary interpretations in the classical tradition. In Islam, like other faith traditions, religious ideas—whether of innovation and heresy, creativity or the lack of it—are never set in stone, nor do they emerge from a vacuum. What people say about the religions they follow reflects the lives they are living, and it is naïve to expect an optimal understanding of any religion in the absence of a tolerable sociopolitical context. Harsh conditions produce callous perceptions, regardless of the people or religion in question. When we attempt to talk about Islam in the modern world, the generally dismal sociopolitical context of its followers is unavoidable. As Gilles Kepel stresses, to ignore that context and focus instead on essentialist pronouncements about Islam or Muslim civilization is "pure Walt Disney."[74]

Classical Islamic thought was the product of a particular sociopolitical milieu. Contrary to the Activist cliché that there is no separation of religion and state in Islam, Muslim religious establishments for more than a millennium were largely free of governmental control and jealously guarded their autonomy. Unlike the Muslim world today, the classical Islamic world was culturally advanced, economically and militarily formidable, and relatively stable politically. Above all, as Rahman stresses, it produced generations of thinkers who were self-assured and psychologically invincible in confronting new challenges.[75] It was conditions such as these that produced urbane scholars who could define and interact with the concepts of *bid'a* and *ijtihad* in an authentic and productive way.

It should be sufficiently clear from what has preceded that *bid'a,* as a control mechanism within the Prophetic law, should constitute a standard of excellence and not be invoked merely to condemn unfamiliar practices, preclude critical thought, or stifle personal expression and community development. Likewise, a sound conception of the process of *ijtihad* should serve as a positive source of inspiration for the entire Muslim community, scholars and non-scholars alike, in the search for meaningful answers to contemporary challenges.

As an American Muslim, I feel it is imperative that our community free itself from erroneous understandings of *bid'a* and develop full competence to perform *ijtihad* independently. Both within the United States and abroad, the growing American Muslim community, which presently constitutes roughly two percent of the nation's population, is one of the most promising and least known Muslim minorities in the world. Like our counterparts in Canada, considerable sectors of the American Muslim community, in contrast to the majority of our coreligionists in the European Union, are highly educated and constitute, per capita, one of the most talented and prosperous Muslim communities in the world. Moreover, American Muslims, at least for the time being, enjoy a relatively favorable sociopolitical context with extensive freedoms and political enfranchisement. Few Muslims in the world today are in a more advantageous position to comprehend the essence of modernity and formulate new directions for *ijtihad* in keeping with the best traditions of Islamic thought and the imperatives of a pluralistic world.

Bulliet suggests that resolution of the present crisis of religious authority in the Muslim world may ultimately fall on the shoulders of the professoriate of Muslim universities, many members of which are already performing *ijtihad* with considerable sophistication. He emphasizes, however, that the professoriate of the Muslim world will only be able to fulfill this task if it extricates itself from governmental control and secures broad freedoms similar to those of tenured professors in the West.[76]

It is worth noting, in conclusion, that Western universities are currently producing highly qualified graduates in Islamic Studies, many of whom are quickly becoming influential intellectuals in the Muslim community and are committed to producing rigorous scholarship as well as fostering Islamic literacy. Perhaps, this new generation of intellectuals will carry the banner of *ijtihad* into the twenty-first century and lay the foundations for a genuinely modern Islamic culture that has intellectual and spiritual depth, is actively committed to humanity and the world, and represents our best hope for quelling the harmful innovations and violent heresies of our time.

NOTES

1. See the American Learning Institute for Muslims (ALIM) homepage. Available at http://www.alimprogram.com/overview/introduction.shtml (accessed May 2006).

2. It is often mistakenly said that, in Islam, God has 99 beautiful names. According to Islamic theology the beautiful names of God are infinite. Those authentically attested in Islamic scripture—the Qur'an and Hadith—are well over 99, the word *al-Badi'*, referenced in the quotation being one of those. The well-known Tradition regarding the 99 names is correctly interpreted, as classical scholars have frequently noted, to mean that God had 99 "special names," listed in some of the pertinent Traditions, such that anyone who memorizes them and preserves their sanctity by behaving in a manner mindful of them in daily life will be rewarded with the Garden.

3. See Ahmad ibn Faris, *Mu'jam Maqayis al-Lugha*, 6 vols. (n.p.: Dar al-Fikr, 1979), 1:209; al-Raghib al-Isfahani, ed., Safwan 'Adnan Dawudi, *Mufradat Alfaz al-Qur'an* (Damascus: Dar al-Qalam, 1992), 111; Abu Ishaq al-Shatibi, *Al-I'tisam*, 2 vols. (al-Khubar, Saudi Arabia: Dar Ibn 'Affan, 1997), 1:49.

4. Al-Isfahani, *Mufradat*, 111; al-Shatibi, *Al-I'tisam*, 1:49.

5. Al-Isfahani, *Mufradat*, 111.

6. G.H.A. Juynboll, "Muslims' Introduction to His *Sahih*, Translated and annotated with an excursus on the chronology of *fitna* and *bid'a*" in *Jerusalem Studies in Arabic and Islam*, no. 5 (1984), 308; Mohammad Hashim Kamali, *Principles of Islamic Jurisprudence* (Cambridge, U.K.: Islamic Texts Society, 1997), 44.

7. Compare Abu 'Umar ibn 'Abd al-Barr, ed. by 'Abd al-Mu'ti Qal'aji, *Al-Istidhkar al-Jami' li-Madhahib Fuqaha' al-Amsar wa 'Ulama' al-Aqtar fi-ma Tadammanahu al-Muwatta' min Ma'ani al-Ra'y wa al-Athar*, 30 vols. (Cairo: Dar al-Wa'y, 1993), 5:152 and Muhammad ibn al-Hasan al-'Amili, *Wasa'il al-Shi'a ila Tahsil Masa'il al-Shari'a*, 20 vols. (Beirut: Dar Ihya' al-Turath al-'Arabi, 1971), 18:97.

8. The Manichaeans arose in the third century of the Christian era, probably out of Judeo-Christian circles in Mesopotamia. Their dualist theology was based on a radical dichotomy between the spirit and the world. The Manichaeans sought

salvation and enlightenment through self-mortification and shunning the pleasures of the world.

9.   A less convincing etymology derives the word from the Middle Persian *Zand Avesta,* in which the term *zand* refers to the translation and commentary of the Zoroastrian Avesta. Accordingly, a *zindiq* meant one who "distorted the exegesis of the Avesta." See "*zandik,*" in *The Encyclopaedia of Islam,* CD-ROM Edition, vols. 1–11 (Leiden: Brill, 2003), cited below as *EI,* 11:510; Sherman A. Jackson, *On the Boundaries of Theological Tolerance in Islam: Abu Hamid al-Ghazali's* Faysal al-Tafriqa bayna al-Islam wa al-Zandaqa (Oxford, U.K.: Oxford University Press, 2002), 56; Maria Isabel Fierro Bello, "Accusations of '*Zandaqa*' in al-Andalus," *Quaderni di studi arabi,* no. 5–6 (1988): 251; Majid Fakhry, *A History of Islamic Philosophy* (New York: Columbia University Press, 1983), 35–36.

10.   See, for example, "*Bid'a,*" in *The Enclyclopedia of Islam,* 1:1197.

11.   See Bello, "Accusations of '*Zandaqa*,'" 251, 257; "*Zindik,*" in *EI,* 11:510.

12.   See Bello, "Accusations of '*Zandaqa*,'" 251, 257.

13.   Abu al-Husayn Muslim ibn al-Hajjaaj, ed. Muhammad Fu'ad 'Abd al-Baqi, *Sahih Muslim,* 4 vols. (Cairo: Matba'at Dar Ihya' al-Kutub al-'Arabiyya, n.d.), 1:54.

14.   Muslim, *Sahih,* 1:55.

15.   Ibid., 1:58.

16.   Ibid., 1:60–61.

17.   See Abu Bakr Ahmad ibn 'Ali al-Razi al-Jassas, ed. 'Abd al-Salam Muhammad 'Ali Shahin, *Ahkam al-Qur'an,* 3 vols. (Beirut: Dar al-Kutub al-'Ilmiyya, 1994), 3:556–557; Abu Bakr Muhammad ibn al-'Arabi, ed. Muhammad 'Abd al-Qadir 'Ata, *Ahkam al-Qur'an,* 4 vols. (Beirut: Dar al-Kutub al-'Ilmiyya, 1996), 4:183; Abu al-'Abbas Ahmad ibn 'Ajiba, ed. Ahmad 'Abd-Allah al-Qurashi Raslan, *Al-Bahr al-Madid fi Tafsir al-Qur'an al-Majid,* 6 vols. (Cairo: Hasan 'Abbas Zaki, 2001), 6:76.

18.   Al-Shatibi, *Al-I'tisam,* 1:371–372.

19.   Sunnis make up the majority of the Muslim community, and, although their schools disagree on many points, all Sunnis share a belief in the probity of the Prophet's Companions, who constitute their chief means of access to foundational Islamic religious knowledge. The Shi'a make up a substantial minority of the Muslim community. Their schools also disagree on many points but share the belief that the Prophet's cousin, 'Ali ibn Abi Talib, was his rightful heir and that the community's spiritual leadership fell by right to various members of the House of the Prophet in subsequent generations, who constitute their principal means of foundational knowledge. The Ibadis make up a small but significant minority in Oman and parts of North Africa and are the only surviving remnant of the ancient Kharijites, although Ibadi doctrines and practices are notably more moderate than those of the early Kharijites.

20.   Muslim, *Sahih,* 2:592; compare al-'Amili, *Wasa'il al-Shi'a,* 11:511–512, 18:40.

21.   Ahmad ibn 'Umar al-Qurtubi, ed. Muhyi al-Din Dib Matu, *Al-Mufhim li-ma Ashkala min Talkhis Kitab Muslim,* 8 vols. (Beirut: Dar Ibn Kathir, 1999), 3:508; Muhammad ibn Khalfa al-Ubbi, *Ikmal Ikmal al-Mu'lim,* 4 vols. (Beirut: Dar al-Kutub al-'Ilmiyya, n.d.), 3:23; Muhammad ibn Muhammad al-Sanusi, *Mukammil 'Ikmal al-Ikmal,* 4 vols. (Beirut: Dar al-Kutub al-'Ilmiyya, n.d.), 3:23.

22. Muhammad ibn Isma'il al-Bukhari, ed. Mustafa al-Bugha, 6 vols. *Sahih al-Bukhari* (Medina: Dar al-Turath, 1987), 2:662, 6:2662; Muslim, *Sahih*, 2: 994–998; al-'Amili, *Wasa'il al-Shi'a*, 19:18.

23. Al-'Amili, *Wasa'il al-Shi'a*, 19:15, 18.

24. Muslim, *Sahih*, 2:994. Although not specifically cited, Nawawi's commentary is given in the margin throughout this edition.

25. See Ahmad ibn Hajar, *Fath al-Bari' bi-Sharh al-Imam Abi 'Abd-Allah Muhammad ibn Isma'il al-Bukharii*, 13 vols. (n. p.: Dar al-Fikr, n.d.), 4:86.

26. For the Ibadis, see Muhammad ibn Ibrahim al-Kindi, ed. 'Abd al-Hafiz Shalabi, *Bayan al-Shar' al-Jami' li-al-Asl wa al-Far'*, 62 vols. in 48 ('Uman: Wizarat al-Turath al-Qawmi, 1982–1993), 15:196–197, 202.

27. Malik ibn Anas, *Al-Muwatta'*, ed. Bashshar 'Awwad Ma'ruf, 2 vols. (Beirut: Dar al-Gharb al-Islami, 1997), 1:169–170; al-Bukhari, *Sahih*, 2:707–708; 'Abd al-Razzaq ibn Hammam, ed. Habib al-Rahman al-A'zami, *Al-Musannaf*, 12 vols. (Beirut: Al-Maktab al-Islami, 1983) 4:258, 264–265; 'Abd-Allah ibn Abi Shayba, ed. Muhammad 'Abd al-Salam Shahin, *Al-Kitab al-Musannaf fi al-Ahadith wa al-Athar*, 9 vols. (Beirut: Dar al-Kutub al-'Ilmiyya, 1995), 2:164; Ibn Hajar, *Fath al-Bari*, 4:250–252.

28. See 'Abd al-Razzaq, *Al-Musannaf*, 4:258; Yusuf ibn 'Abd-Barr, *Al-Tamhid li-ma fi al-Muwatta' min al-Ma'ani wa al-Asanid*, 18 vols. (Cairo: Al-Faruq al-Haditha li-al-Tiba'a, 1999), 4:93–95, 100.

29. Zayd ibn 'Ali ibn al-Husayn, *Musnad al-Imam Zayd* (Beirut: Maktabat al-Hayah, 1966), 158–159.

30. Al-'Amili, *Wasa'il al-Shi'a*, 5:191–193.

31. Ibn al-'Arabi, *Ahkam al-Qur'an*, 4:183; al-Shatibi, *Al-I'tisam*, 1:374.

32. Ibn 'Abd al-Barr, *Al-Tamhid*, 4:93 and *Al-Istidhkar*, 5:136, 147.

33. Abu Bakr ibn al-'Arabi, ed. Muhammad 'Abd-Allah Walad Karim, *Kitab al-Qabas fi Sharh Muwatta' Malik ibn Anas*, 3 vols. (Beirut: Dar al-Gharb al-Islami, 1992), 1:283; compare Ibn Hajar, *Fath al-Bari*, 4:252.

34. Al-Bukhari, *Sahih*, 1:161.

35. Muslim, *Sahih*, 4:2059–2060.

36. They differed, for example, in the use of nontextual sources like the established practice of Medina, recognized as authoritative in the Maliki and Hanbali school, and took different positions on the authority of isolated hadiths, hadiths without complete chains of transmission, and the reports and opinions of the Companions and Successors. See Umar F. Abd-Allah, "Malik's Concept of *'Amal* in the Light of Maliki Legal Theory" (Ph.D. dissertation: University of Chicago, 1978), 1:155–195.

37. See al-'Amili, *Wasa'il al-Shi'a*, 18:22–24.

38. See al-Kindi, *Bayan al-Shar'*, 1:92–93.

39. Al-Isfahani, *Mufradat*, 111.

40. Al-Shatabi, *Al-I'tisam*, 2:568.

41. Al-Shatabi, *Al-I'tisam*, 1:50.

42. Ibn 'Abd al-Barr, *Al-Istidhkar*, 5:153.

43. Al-Shatabi, *Al-I'tisam*, 2:570, 594.

44. Ibn 'Abd al-Barr, *Al-Istidhkar*, 5:152.

45.   Ibn Hajar, *Fath al-Bari*, 4:253.

46.   Sulayman ibn Khalaf al-Baji, ed. Nazih Hammad, *Kitab al-Hudud fi al-Usul* (Beirut: Al-Zu'bi li-al-Tiba'a, 1973), 64.

47.   George Makdisi, *The Rise of Colleges: Institutions of Learning in Islam and the West* (Edinburgh, U.K.: Edinburgh University Press, 1981), 2, 66.

48.   Bernard G. Weiss, *The Spirit of Islamic Law* (Athens, Georgia: University of Georgia Press, 1998), 89.

49.   Fazlur Rahman, *Islam and Modernity: Transformation of an Intellectual Tradition* (Chicago, Illinois: University of Chicago Press, 1982), 7–8.

50.   Weiss, *The Spirit of Islamic Law*, 88–89.

51.   Makdisi, *The Rise of Colleges*, 2, 66.

52.   Discussion of the hadith comes later in the paper. I presume the Ibadis also relate this hadith in their books but did not chance upon attestation of it in the limited number of their works currently available.

53.   'Ali ibn al-Qassar, ed. Muhammad ibn al-Husayn al-Sulaymani, *Al-Muqaddima fi al-Usul* (Beirut: Dar al-Gharb al-Islami, 1996), 114–115; Sulayman ibn Khalaf al-Baji, ed. 'Abd al-Majid al-Turki, *Ihkam al-Fusul Ihkam fi Ahkam al-Usul*, 2 vols. (Beirut: Dar al-Gharb al-Islami, 1995), 2:714–716; 'Ubayd-Allah ibn 'Umar al-Dabbusi, ed. Mahmud Tawfiq al-Rifa'i, *Al-Asrar fi al-Usul wa al-Furu' fi Taqwim Adillat al-Shar'*, 4 vols. (Amman: Wizarat al-Awqaf, 1999), 3:114–116; Ibn Amir al-Hajj, *Al-Taqrir wa al-Tahbir*, 3 vols. (Beirut: Dar al-Kutub al-'Ilmiyya, 1983), 3:306. The Ibadis took essentially the same position. See al-Kindi, *Bayan al-Shar'*, 1:92–93.

54.   See al-Dabbusi, *Al-Asrar*, 3:116; cf. al-Kindi, *Bayan al-Shar'*, 1:92.

55.   Al-Dabbusi, *Al-Asrar*, 3:114.

56.   Al-Kamal ibn al-Hammam, *Al-Tahrir*, 3 vols. (Beirut: Dar al-Kutub al-'Ilmiyya, 1983), 3:306; Ibn Amir al-Hajj, *Al-Taqrir wa al-Tahbir*, 3:306.

57.   Sulayman ibn Khalaf al-Baji, *Kitab al-Muntaqa sharh Muwatta' Imam Dar al-Hijra Sayyidina Malik ibn Anas*, 7 vols. in 4 (Cairo: Matba'at al-Sa'ada, 1984), 1:207–208.

58.   Makdisi, *The Rise of Colleges*, 290.

59.   Weiss, *The Spirit of Islamic Law*, 128.

60.   Al-Baji, *Ihkam al-Fusul*, 2:727; Ibn al-Qassar, *Al-Muqaddima*, 26; Moojan Momen, *An Introduction to Shi'i Islam* (New Haven, Connecticut: Yale University Press, 1985), 204–205.

61.   See Muhammad ibn Abi Bakr ibn Qayyim al-Jawziyya, ed. Muhammad al-Mu'tasim bi-Llah al-Baghdadi, *I'lam al-Muwaqqi'in 'an Rabb al-'Alamin*, 4 vols. (Beirut: Dar al-Kitab al-'Arabi, 1998), 3:5.

62.   Al-Dabbusi, *Al-Asrar*, 3:115–116.

63.   Taken from al-Qarafi's *Furuq* as quoted in the work of my student, friend, and colleague 'Adil 'Abd al-Qadir Quta, *Al-'Urf: Hujjiyyatuhu wa Atharuhu fi Fiqh al-Mu'amalat al-Maliyya 'inda al-Hanabila*, 2 vols. (Mecca: al-Maktaba al-Makkiyya, 1997), 1:64.

64.   Quoted from Ibn Qayyim's *I'lam al-Muwaqqi'in* in 'Adil Quta, *Al-'Urf*, 1:65.

65. Makdisi, *The Rise of Colleges*, 4, 290; Wael B. Hallaq, *A History of Islamic Legal Theories: An Introduction to Sunni Usul al-Fiqh* (Cambridge, U.K.: Cambridge University Press, 1999), 201–202 and 202, 59n; Christopher Melchert, *The Formation of the Sunni Schools of Law, 9th–10th Centuries C.E.* (Leiden: Brill, 1997), 16–17.

66. See Kamali, *Principles of Islamic Jurisprudence*, 374–378.

67. 'Umar Kahhala, *A'lam al-Nisa'*, 5 vols. (Beirut: Mu'assasat al-Risala, 1991), 4:94.

68. See Nehemia Levtzion and John O. Voll, eds., *Eighteenth-Century Renewal and Reform in Islam* (Syracuse: Syracuse University Press, 1987), 3–20; Etan Kohlberg, "Aspects of Akhbari Thought in the Seventeenth and Eighteenth Centuries," in *Eighteenth-Century Renewal*, 133–153; Bernard Haykel, "Reforming Islam by Dissolving the *Madhhabs*: Shawkani and his Zaydi Detractors in Yemen," in Bernard G. Weiss, ed. *Studies in Islamic Legal Theory* (Leiden: Brill, 2002).

69. See Charles Kurzman, ed., *Modernist Islam 1840–1940: A Sourcebook* (Oxford, U.K.: Oxford University Press, 2002), 3–27.

70. Richard W. Bulliet, *The Case for Islamo-Christian Civilization* (New York: Columbia University Press, 2004), 81.

71. See Gilles Kepel, *Jihad: The Trial of Political Islam*, trans. Anthony F. Roberts (Cambridge, Massachusetts: Harvard University Press, 2002), 23–27, 33–35, 39–41.

72. See Bulliet, *The Case for Islamo-Christian Civilization*, 83–86.

73. Marshall Hodgson, *The Venture of Islam*, vol. 3, *The Gunpowder Empires and Modern Times* (Chicago, Illinois: University of Chicago Press, 1974),3:431.

74. See Kepel, *Jihad*, xviii, 24.

75. Rahman, *Islam* (Chicago, Illinois: University of Chicago Press, 1979), 212.

76. Bulliet, *The Case for Islamo-Christian Civilization*, 158–159.

2

Is "Islamic" Philosophy Islamic?

—————————•—————————

Mohammad Azadpur

At the outset, I want to disown two trivializing approaches to the question that guides this chapter. One such approach responds in the affirmative, pointing to the apparent circularity of the question that is posed. The second approach answers in the negative, arguing that Islamic philosophy refers to the species of philosophy (understood as radically other than what constitutes a religious activity) that is cultivated in the Islamic civilizations. Both of these approaches trivialize the relation between philosophy and religion and I mean to underscore that relation. A perhaps more sophisticated take on the question of whether Islamic philosophy is Islamic would be to examine the claims of the various Islamic philosophers in order to determine their conformity to Islamic doctrines. This third approach, however, faces two principal obstacles. On the one hand, it is not easy to come up with a list of beliefs to which a particular philosopher in this tradition has consistently adhered, not to mention one shared by all such philosophers. This is not to say that Islamic philosophers are incoherent; it is rather a declaration that one must exercise caution in ascribing theses to any philosopher. On the other hand, it is even more difficult to subject the beliefs of Islamic philosophers to those constitutive of Islamic faith and measure their allegiance to Islam. To be sure, there are constitutive beliefs such as *tawhid*, the belief in the oneness of God; *nubuwwa*, the belief in the prophecy of Muhammad; and *ma'ad*, the belief in resurrection and the day of judgment. But given the many possibilities of interpretation, the demands of these beliefs are not hard to meet and expanding the set of such beliefs is disputable. To be sure, there have been efforts to assess the Islamic quality of Islamic philosophy by expanding these theses and limiting their interpretations. Abu Hamid al-Ghazali's (d. 1111 CE) polemic against the Islamic Peripatetics is perhaps one such effort and I will return to this later.

My strategy is to answer the question whether Islamic philosophy is Islamic in a metaphilosophical way—that is, I want to begin by asking what philosophy itself is. I do not pretend to be naïve about this question, as I am not interested in proposing an account of philosophy that transcends all cultural and historical constraints; this is not to say that there is no such account. So let me be more precise about my initial step. Islamic philosophers inherited something from the Greeks and they called it *falsafa*, in close adherence to the Greek word *philosophia*. What was that something? I want to argue that the common understanding of what Muslims inherited from the Greeks involves a misunderstanding. Historians of Islamic philosophy consider Greek philosophy to be made up of bodies of rational knowledge formulated by different philosophers or schools of philosophy, but I want to argue with Pierre Hadot that for the Greeks philosophy was primarily the practice of spiritual exercises aimed at the transformation of the self and the acquisition of wisdom. I submit that this is how Islamic philosophers understood what they inherited from the Greeks. If this point is granted, then it is not hard to see that Islamic philosophy is the Islamic practice of philosophical spiritual exercises. Of course, something more needs to be said about this, and I will—by working out aspects of the prophetology that makes the philosophical way of life advanced by Islamic philosophers Islamic.

Hadot, throughout his writings and especially in *Philosophy as a Way of Life,* revives the ancient distinction between philosophical discourse and philosophy itself in order to criticize the condition of modern scholarship on ancient philosophy. He writes: "Historians of philosophy pay little attention to the fact that ancient philosophy was, first and foremost, a way of life. They consider philosophy as, above all, philosophical discourse."[1] By philosophical discourse, Hadot means the production of a "systematic explanation of the whole of reality."[2] In contrast, philosophy, for Hadot's ancient Greek philosopher, is a way of life; it is not in the service of producing a work—a rational account of reality, rather "the goal is to transform ourselves, to become wise."[3] Philosophers, as lovers of wisdom, are in training for wisdom and wisdom is not contained in a philosophical treatise, but it is a condition of the human soul.[4] The significance of the production of systematic philosophical works (for ancient philosophers) was rather in its pedagogical role in the training of the soul. Philosophy yielded systematic texts

> ...in order that it might provide the mind with a small number of principles, tightly linked together, which derived greater persuasive force and mnemonic effectiveness precisely from such systematization. Short sayings summed up, sometimes in striking form, the essential dogmas, so that the student might easily relocate himself within the fundamental disposition in which he was to live.[5]

This, of course, does not exhaust the significance of rationally systematized philosophical treatises. One could think of other functions: for instance, attending to a tightly argued and systematic treatise assists the philosopher in transcending the limits of the empirical self and its preferred modes of reasoning at the service of the appetites, mundane desires, or social conventions.[6]

Hadot's account of ancient philosophy as primarily a way of life or as he says elsewhere, "the practice of spiritual exercises,"[7] accentuates the centrality of ethics in the ancient philosophical enterprise. Famously, ethics concerns the good life, that is, how one ought to live, but most modern moral philosophers construe this concern as directing us to the agent's actions and the articulation of the requirements determining the rightness or the wrongness of those actions. Depending on their preference for intrinsic goodness of acts or human interests and desires, modern philosophers can be divided into deontologists and teleologists, respectively. There are those espousing hybrid theories as well, but what they all share is a focus on actions. Modern philosophy's act-centered ethics is to be contrasted with the agent-centered (Greek) virtue ethics where the focus is on the agent and her character. Virtue ethicists inquire into the cultivation of the character traits that allow the agent to lead the good life.[8] In other words, the moral agent does not resort to an algorithm (deontological, consequential, or a hybrid) to figure out what to do. Her cultivation of relevant character traits enables her to perceive the good in each particular circumstance and to pursue it.

Hadot's reading of the ancients does not simply assert the truism that their version of ethics is a virtue ethics. Rather, he claims justifiably that virtue ethics is the core of their philosophical orientation and that all of ancient philosophical production was at the service of the inner transformation constituting the good life. Even Aristotle, whose account of the highest good as contemplation culminating in thought thinking itself is often invoked to establish the priority of theory over practice, situated theory and its discursive expression in the context of the ethical cultivation of the soul. "It is sometimes claimed that Aristotle was a pure theoretician, but for him, too, philosophy was incapable of being reduced to philosophical discourse, that is, to the production of a body of abstract knowledge. Rather, philosophy for Aristotle was a quality of the mind, the result of an inner transformation."[9] To put it differently, for Aristotle, it is only after acquiring the practical traits of the soul (for example, temperance, courage, and practical wisdom) that one is drawn to and able to cultivate the theoretical intellect. I will get back to this point later.

In this part of the chapter, I want to look at the approaches of some prominent scholars of Islamic philosophy regarding what they take as that which the Muslims inherited from the Greek philosophers. I want to do this through the lens of Hadot's account of ancient philosophy, because it is extremely useful in unveiling the assumptions that obfuscate the genuine sense of philosophy in the Islamic tradition. Richard Walzer, the prominent scholar of the transmission of Greek philosophy into the Islamic world, maintains that Islamic philosophy continued and preserved the Greek philosophical discourse. Walzer's "Islamic philosophers" drew upon the translated Greek philosophical texts and composed works that were a fusion of the views of their Greek predecessors. For him, it seems that genuine philosophy ultimately advances original theses in "rational terms" about relevant topics, and he is adamant that no such original thesis is to be found in the works of Islamic Philosophers. In the case of Abu Nasr al-Farabi (Alfarabi d. 950 CE), for instance, Walzer maintains that the latter's theory of prophecy contains an original synthesis of Greek views on "imitation" and imagination, but he cannot help arguing, "I have not been able to find precise evidence for it in extant Greek tests although it is obviously of Greek origin."[10] Oliver Leaman is correct to diagnose a trace of Orientalism in Walzer's views.[11] Drawing upon Edward Said's influential work, Leaman argues that Walzer's reading is influenced by a colonialist agenda. Orientalists, that is, scholars under the influence of the colonialist program, promote the colonialist agenda by arguing for the superiority of the culture of the colonizer. "Implicit in the Orientalist attitude, therefore, is the belief that the Orient had passed its golden age as the west was being born, and was thus in decline."[12] I find Leaman's diagnosis plausible, but surely, this is not the only Orientalist assumption exhibited in Walzer's approach. Not only are the so-called Orientals currently in decline, but their golden age was not also anything other than an imitation of the Greek original.

It should also be pointed out that philosophical Orientalism is itself premised on the view that philosophy is the production of rational and systematic treatises. Walzer's Greeks take the credit for the conception of philosophy as the production of rational systems and the later Europeans are credited for advancing it. Muslims, in this picture, play the role of transmitters, who lacked the rational prowess and the requisite creativity to build upon it. His philosophical Orientalism in conjunction with his commitment to the account of philosophy as philosophical discourse blinds him to the ways the Muslim philosophers sought to reconcile ancient Greek philosophical practices with their own religious commitments and exercises. As a result, Islamic philosophy is construed as a mere repository of ancient theories in order to preserve them for the later Europeans.[13]

Leaman diagnoses another manifestation of Orientalism in the position advanced by some scholars of Islamic philosophy, principally Leo Strauss, that "Islamic philosophers were not good Muslims, as philosophy and religion could not be reconciled."[14] Strauss, in *Persecution and the Art of Writing,* attributes the "collapse" of philosophy in the Jewish and the Islamic traditions to the conflict between reason and religious practice. He argues that philosophy prospered in the West precisely because Christian theology, the rational defense of Christian dogma, allowed philosophical discourse an important role in the education of clerics.[15] The symptoms of Orientalism are also detectable in this account. It is assumed that there was a collapse of rationalism in the East, since the tenets of philosophy are incompatible with those of Islam and Judaism. Consequently, in this view, Jewish and Islamic traditions of philosophy became disfigured, because philosophers had to conceal Greek philosophical theories in their texts to avoid persecution by the irrational practitioners of faith, who constituted the majority of society. As a result Muslim and Jewish philosophers simply restated what they inherited from the Greeks and their major contribution was developing an art of writing that contained their accounts of Greek philosophy in disguise (so as to avoid persecution).[16]

Strauss' Orientalism, like its counterpart in Walzer, presupposes a notion of philosophy as the production of rational knowledge. The identification of this assumption helps explain more of the details of Strauss's position. Philosophy comes into conflict with religion, in his reading, because it involves rational reflection on the nature of things whereas religion is concerned with practice based on revealed (read impervious to rational scrutiny) doctrines. Perhaps the most striking evidence for his metaphilosophical commitment is his view that philosophy prospered under the protection of Christian theology.[17] According to Hadot, it was precisely under these conditions that philosophy proper was marginalized.

> With the advent of medieval scholasticism, however, we find a clear distinction being drawn between *theologia* and *philosophia*. Theology became conscious of its autonomy *qua* supreme science, while philosophy was emptied of its spiritual exercises which, from now on, were relegated to Christian mysticism and ethics. Reduced to the rank of a "handmaid of theology," philosophy's role was henceforth to furnish theology with conceptual—and hence purely theoretical—material. When, in the modern age, philosophy regained its autonomy, it still retained many features inherited from this medieval conception.[18]

Strauss applauds Christian theology's appropriation of philosophy because he does not see ethics and the practice of spiritual exercises as constitutive of ancient Greek philosophy. For him, philosophy is the manufacturing of rational knowledge and it is under the tutelage of Christian theology that philosophy comes into its own (perhaps for the first time). But even if it does so, unbeknownst to Strauss, it is at the cost changing its essence. It goes without saying that he misses out on the particular character of Islamic philosophy, as a reconciliation of the practice of ancient philosophy and that of Islam.

This approach to Islamic philosophy—relying on the understanding of ancient Greek philosophy as the production of rational discourse, peppered with Orientalism—is not restricted to European and American scholars. The Moroccan Scholar, Muhammad Abed al-Jabri, in *Arab-Islamic Philosophy*, argues that philosophy *qua* production of rational knowledge declined in the Islamic world because of the influence of Persian Gnosticism. For Jabri, Arabic Islam was an ideology "committed to the service of science, progress and a dynamic conception of society."[19] Thus, it embraced Greek rationalism. However, Persian antirationalism (that is, Gnosticism) gave rise to an assault on the Arabic tradition and resulted in its decline.[20] Implicit in Jabri's argument is a call to unfasten the Gnostic, especially the Shiite, element from the Islamic heritage and facilitate a renaissance of Arabism, which is nothing other than Islam at the service of reason and the European idea of progress. For Jabri, the borders of the Orient have shifted further to the East but the same prejudices are present. Jabri's view is especially awkward because it flies in the face of historical evidence. It is well known that the Persian world encouraged the pursuit of philosophy. The flowering of philosophy in the Safavid dynasty and its cultivation in the Shi'a seminaries to this day testify to the problematic nature of Jabri's account of the nature of philosophy and its history in the Islamic world.

Assigning primacy to the production of rational knowledge in defining the Greek philosophical heritage need not always accompany an Orientalist attitude. A good example of a scholar holding such a view is Leaman. As we have seen, Leaman rejects Orientalism but considers Greek philosophy as "the acme of rationality."[21] For him, "The main purpose of philosophy is to understand arguments, and to assess those arguments and construct new arguments around them."[22] He argues not that Muslims were barbarians and against reason (a favorite assumption of his Orientalist counterparts); rather he maintains that Greek philosophy was challenged by a number of other rational modes of discourse. These included Islamic theology, the theory of language, and jurisprudence, and that these modes of rational discourse had already entered the Islamic cultural scene before philosophy came along. Now this view makes some sense of the resistance offered to philosophy by a theologian and jurist like Ghazali, but it is still problematic because it misses out on the significance of philosophy as a way of life and the Islamic appreciation and appropriation of this significance.[23] So, for Leaman, Islamic philosophy is Islamic just as any other production of rational knowledge in an Islamic context is Islamic: "Perhaps the best way of specifying the nature of Islamic philosophy is to say that it is the tradition of philosophy which arose out of Islamic culture, with the latter term understood in its widest sense."[24] To be fair, Leaman admits that Islamic philosophy, when it comes into its own, "involves study of reality which transforms the soul and is never separated from spiritual purity and religious sanctity."[25] Here, Leaman recognizes the significance of Islamic philosophy as the practice of cultivating and transforming the soul, but he does not see its continuity (in this regard) with the Greek past. As a result, he misses out on what is unique in *Islamic* philosophy, what makes Islamic *philosophy* Islamic.

Perhaps one of the most notable proponents of the view that Islamic philosophy involves the practice of transformative spiritual exercises is Seyyed Hossein Nasr. In "the Meaning and Concept of Philosophy in Islam," Nasr claims that "This conception of philosophy as dealing with the discovering of the truth concerning the nature of things and combining mental knowledge with the purification and perfection of one's being has lasted to this day wherever the tradition of Islamic philosophy has continued and is in fact embodied in the very being of the most eminent representatives of the Islamic philosophical tradition to this day."[26] He calls the practice of spiritual exercises "the purification and perfection of one's own being" and insists that it is constitutive of Islamic philosophy. Nasr also recognizes that the Greeks, especially the Platonists and Hermetico-Pythagoreans, under-scored the relation between the theory and the practice of philosophy.[27] But for him, Peripateticism de-emphasizes this relation and one of the virtues of Islamic philosophy proper is the overcoming of the Peripatetic distor-tion.[28] For Nasr, the move away from Peripateticism occurs in the later writ-ings of Abu 'Ali ibn Sina (Avicenna d. 1037 CE), especially in what remains of *al-hikma al-mashriqiyya* (Eastern philosophy), in which Avicenna decries the follies of the Peripatetics and declares his commitment to an approach to phi-losophy that draws from non-Greek sources.[29] Nasr sees in this a revival of perennial wisdom, which involves an alliance between theory and spiritual exercises. He is adamant about the importance of ascetic self-purification and self-discovery for the true notion of philosophy:

> Philosophy [without spiritual exercises] becomes sheer mental acrobatics and reason cut off from both intellect and revelation, nothing but a luciferan instrument leading to dispersion and ultimately dissolution. It must never be forgotten that according to the teachings of *sophia perennis* itself, the discovery of the Truth is essentially the discovery of one's self and ultimately of the Self...and that is the role of philosophy.[30]

Islam, in Nasr's view, is an expression of perennial wisdom as it is essentially an association of theory and practice, truth and spiritual exercises, and *haqiqa* (truth) and *tariqa* (the way). So, according to Nasr, philosophy in the Islamic tradition becomes Islamic when it overcomes the Peripatetic pressures toward pure theory and recognizes the inseparability of truth and spiritual exercises. Nasr then connects Avicenna's Eastern philosophy (*al-hikma al-mashriqiyya*) to the tradition inaugurated by Shihab al-Din al-Suhrawardi's (d. 1191 CE) *hikmat al-ishraq* (Philosophy of Illumination). In the latter, the cooperation between reason and spiritual practice is central and remains so in the later Islamic philosophical tradition mainly because of Suhrawardi's influence.

Although I agree with Nasr that certain Islamic philosophical traditions (including Suhrawardi's Illuminationism) were based on a rejection of aspects of Peripateticism, it is not correct to claim that the Peripatetics divorced theory from practice.[31] It is likely, as I mentioned earlier, that Aristotle's emphasis on thought thinking itself as the highest activity occasions such a reading of his work and that of his successors. A good dose of Aristotelian ethics, however, can help overcome this reading, as it becomes

apparent that for Aristotle—and the successors who took his texts seriously—
the cultivation of the soul and its excellence is presupposed for the life of
contemplation. In other words, it is not clear that Nasr appreciates Aristotle's
virtue ethics and its centrality in the latter's philosophical heritage.[32] Once
we allow Hadot's thesis that all schools of ancient philosophy are focused
on the practice of spiritual exercises and that philosophical discourse is
only ancillary, then Nasr's assumption that Islamic philosophy becomes
Islamic only in establishing a necessary connection between asceticism
and theory becomes suspect. My contention is that we have to be more
precise and identify the particular *way* in which Islamic philosophers
established the assumed connection between theory and spiritual exercises.
In what follows, I argue that this connection is established by Islamic
prophetology, and that the Islamic Peripatetics were the early proponents
of this prophetology.[33]

I submit that it is the prophetology advanced by Muslim philosophers that
makes Islamic philosophy Islamic. By prophetology, I mean the philosophical
inquiry into what constitutes a prophet as the paradigmatic wise person and
man of God. Of course, Islamic prophetology is "philosophical" because it
establishes relevant spiritual exercises for the transformation of the soul of
the philosopher. However, Islamic philosophical prophetology, *pace* Nasr,
is not restricted to the Shi'a (whether Imami or Ismaili), Eastern (Oriental),
Sufi, or the Illuminationist traditions; it is also present in the work of
Alfarabi and the Peripatetic writings of Avicenna. Moreover, this Peripatetic
prophetology is not just a theory. It has an ethical import (drawn from
Aristotle's work) that is essential to my point that Islamic prophetic
philosophy (including the work of Muslim Peripatetics) is an *Islamization*
of philosophy as the practice of spiritual exercises.

In *De Anima*, Aristotle puts forward the notion of a transcendent Active
Intellect. He maintains that "mind, as we have described it, is what it is by
virtue of becoming all things, while there is another which is what it is by
virtue of making all things: this is the sort of positive state like light; for in
a sense light makes potential colours into actual colours."[34] The Active
Intellect or the productive mind (*nous poietikos*) is explained through the
contrast with the mind as passive (*pathetikos*), the conforming mind.[35] One
comes to the vicinity of the Active Intellect when the ordinary intellect—
the conforming mind—is freed of interests and illusions veiling reality;
this freedom comes through the acquisition of virtue through spiritual
exercises.[36] Virtuous people do not impose contingent meanings upon the
objects of cognition but experience them as they are necessarily in themselves. So the conforming intellect in the attempt to approach the Active
Intellect allows the potential intelligibles to become actualized. In a way,
the Active Intellect produces things, as it shines like light on potential intelligibles and illuminates them. This notion of a separate Active Intellect

becomes an important aspect of the psychology of the Peripatetic predecessors of Islamic philosophy.[37]

Islamic Peripatetics supplement the account of the transcendent Active Intellect given by Aristotle and his Hellenic followers by embracing the Platonic view that what makes things intelligible, their forms, have a separate existence. Aristotle rejected Plato's account of the existence of intelligible objects outside of the domain of the sensible objects of human experience, as well as Plato's claim that knowledge is precisely the intellectual perception of transcendent objects. He maintained that forms do not exist independently of sensible objects, but they can be separated from them in thought.[38] Mehdi Ha'eri Yazdi, in his insightful *The Principle of Epistemology in Islamic Philosophy,* claims that Islamic philosophers believe in the harmony between the views of Plato and Aristotle and, as a result, they argue "that the mind is constituted by its nature to function in different ways at the same time; being perceptive of intelligible substances on the one hand, and speculative about sensible objects on the other."[39] In other words, the Active Intellect is, for Islamic Peripatetics, not just a paradigm of clear thinking; it is also the Divine Being that infuses the sensible world with intelligibility; it is the giver of forms (*wahib al-suwar, dator formarum*) in the manner of Plato's Demiurge in the *Timaeus.*[40] Therefore, intimacy with the Active Intellect not only means that one possesses a clear perception of sensible objects, but it also implies that one receives forms directly from the source rather than through the sensible intermediaries.

It is not too far-fetched to relate this synthetic (Aristotelian/Platonic) account of intimacy with the Active Intellect to the Islamic notion of prophetic inspiration. A central feature of the Islamic proclamation of faith is the belief in the prophecy of Muhammad. The Prophet Muhammad is a prophet because he was inspired by the Angel of Revelation, Gabriel, who made him recite the Qur'an in an interval of 23 years. These recitals contain the divine wisdom (*haqiqa*), the divine path (*tariqa*) to reach that wisdom, and the elements of the law (*Shari'a*) for the community of Muslims, literally those who submit to the will of God and His wisdom. Alfarabi's works represent one of the earliest attempts to connect the Islamic notion of prophecy to the Peripatetic account of the perfect man as the intimate of the Active Intellect. In *al-Siyasa al-Madaniyya* (The Political State), Alfarabi identifies the Active Intellect (*al-'aql al-fa'al*) with Islam's Angel of Revelation.[41] Walzer, in his commentary on *al-Madina al-Fadila* (On the Perfect State), writes: "To know the true meaning of the Active Intellect is . . . essential, according to al-Farabi, to an adequate understanding of one of the most fundamental Muslim articles of faith, the transmission of eternal truth to mankind through a man of overwhelming mental power—a philosopher-prophet-lawgiver."[42]

Alfarabi's philosopher is one who has set his soul in order and has subjected his thinking to a rigorous examination of ideas (aided by the light of the Active Intellect). In a treatise titled *The Attainment of Happiness,* Alfarabi distinguishes between true philosophy and its counterfeit. He writes:

> As for mutilated philosophy: the counterfeit philosopher, the vain philosopher, or the false philosopher is the one who sets out to study the theoretical sciences without being prepared for them. For he who sets out to inquire ought to be innately equipped for the theoretical sciences—that is, fulfill the conditions prescribed by Plato in the *Republic:* he should excel in comprehending and conceiving that which is essential…He should by natural disposition disdain the appetites, the dinar, and like. He should be high-minded and avoid what is disgraceful in people. He should be pious, yield easily to goodness and justice, and be stubborn in yielding to evil and injustice. And he should be strongly determined in favor of the right thing.[43]

The cultivation and perfection of character, in a manner continuous with the ancient account of philosophy as the practice of spiritual exercises, constitutes the centerpiece of Alfarabi's notion of true philosophy. For him, the acquisition of justice, the perfection and balance of the soul, paves the way for the intellectual labors of theoretical inquiry. Such a preparation allows the individual to resist extraneous goals and distractions and attend to the problems of thought and action. Theoretical wisdom gets its start from this condition of the soul.

The just person upon engaging in contemplation comes nearer in status to the Active Intellect, the Angel of Revelation. If this nearness is accompanied by a perfected imagination, then the philosopher is also a prophet, a person whose perfected imagination is active and who receives forms from the Active Intellect, the giver of forms, and from the senses. The modification of the imagination by the revelations of the active intellect allows for "prophecy of present and future events and … prophecy of things divine."[44] This divine creativity has been acquired by transcending the limits of the human intellect, which is merely passive in relation to sensory objects. Furthermore, we should not overlook Alfarabi's insistence that the philosopher-prophet is also a lawgiver, a skillful orator, and knows how to guide people toward the achievement of happiness.[45] The Prophet of Islam, in Alfarabi's account, would be one such person, that is, a philosopher–prophet–lawgiver, and the final one.

Avicenna adopts Alfarabi's strategy of identifying the Active Intellect with Gabriel, the Angel of Revelation. However, he modifies some of the details of Alfarabi's account of prophecy. For Avicenna's philosopher, the acquisition of a just and balanced soul must precede theoretical knowledge and the subsequent possibility of conjunction with and enlightenment by the Active Intellect. In the *Metaphysics of the* Healing (*al-Shifa*), Avicenna sets forth the conditions for the cultivation of the Peripatetic ideal of contemplative intimacy with the Active Intellect. He distinguishes between the rational, the irascible, and the appetitive parts of the soul and argues that justice, the balance of the various parts of the soul and the sum of their excellence, is the first step toward the achievement of personal perfection.

> Since the Motivating Powers are three—the appetitive, the irascible, and the practical—the virtues consist of three things: (a) moderation in...the appetites...(b) moderation in all the irascible passions...(c) moderation in practical matters. At the head of these virtues stand temperance, courage, and practical wisdom; their sum is justice, which, however, is extraneous to theoretical virtue. But whoever combines theoretical wisdom with justice, is indeed a happy man.[46]

For Avicenna, the acquisition of justice, the excellence and balance of the soul, paves the way for the intellectual labors of theoretical inquiry. Such a preparation allows the individual to resist extraneous goals and distractions and attend to theoretical problems. Theoretical wisdom should get its start from this condition of the soul and its addition to justice culminates in happiness (sa'ada). However, beyond the happiness in the coupling of justice and theoretical contemplation is that including the quality of prophecy, which is attained through conjunction with the Active Intellect.[47] The benefits of this conjunction include the acquisition of first principles as well as visions brought about in the perfected imagination.

Avicenna also goes on to distinguish between the prophetic insights of the philosophers and those of the prophets. Prophets—God's chosen Messengers—do not require the mediation of practical and theoretical perfection (as necessary in the case of the philosopher). Prophets receive this immediately from the Active Intellect: "That which becomes completely actual does so without mediation or through mediation, and the first is better. This is the one called prophet and in him degrees of excellence in the realm of material forms culminate."[48] The prophet is God's deputy on earth and benefits from unmediated perfection, happiness, and illumination.

Parviz Morewedge, in "The Logic of Emanationism and Sufism in the Philosophy of Ibn Sina (Avicenna)," argues that Avicenna's view of the relation between persons and God differs from that of the connectionists, including Aristotle and Alfarabi. The latter hold that a person can, at best, achieve a connection with God by engaging in the "divine-like" activity of contemplation.[49] Avicenna, however, espouses a different mystical position, according to which the soul, after the death of the body, *unites* with God.[50] Avicenna, as I understand, maintains the Aristotelian connectionist notion in order to account for the insights of philosophers and the revelations of prophets. The union of the person and God, if Morewedge is right, is a postmortem event. It does not conflict with the idea of connection or conjunction (*ittisal*) with the Active Intellect as denoting the experiences of *living* persons. Of course, this is not to deny that the connectionist views (Avicenna's included) do not differ in their details.

Given this peculiarly Islamic philosophy of prophecy, I want to now return to my view of the continuity between Islamic philosophy and Ancient Greek philosophy, seen as the practice of spiritual exercises for the sake of wisdom. The ideal of wisdom, in Islamic Peripateticism, gets articulated as involving some kind of ethical cultivation and growth, culminating in prophetic experiences. Of course, like all good Muslims, Alfarabi and Avicenna do not maintain that they are prophets of the caliber of Prophet Muhammad or that a prophet like Muhammad can emerge in the future. Both Avicenna and Alfarabi, in different ways, distinguish the grandeur of the Muhammadan prophetic experience from what a philosopher might attain. Alfarabi does this by attributing to the prophet a perfected imagination that yields the laws (*Shari'a*) for governing the community, and Avicenna, as we have seen, distinguishes between the qualities of insight bestowed upon the philosopher and the prophet.

It is important to realize that the Islamic Peripatetics, represented by Avicenna and Alfarabi, do not simply strap their philosophical ideal onto the Prophet of Islam. Rather, the Prophet Muhammad's words and deeds play a central role in the cultivation and the articulation of their ideal. This is again in accord with their Peripatetic heritage. According to Aristotle, ethical standards are not abstract moral principles (a view prevalent in modern moral philosophy); rather they are given by moral exemplars, the *spoudaios* or *phronimos,* that is, the practically wise person.[51] One way the *phronimos* educates is by inviting adepts to imitate him, and the prophetologies articulated by Avicenna and Alfarabi are Islamic precisely because they preserve the Islamic accounts of the Prophet Muhammad's practices and sayings, as sources of imitation for the spiritual transformation of Muslims. The Qur'an and the Sunna fit into this philosophical framework and provide the relevant features of the concrete exemplar who guides the Muslim seeker of wisdom. Of course, this requires the cultivation of a relevant hermeneutic for getting at the meaning of the Qur'an and the Sunna, and such a hermeneutic is overseen by an instructor who is immersed in the spiritual practices of the religion and who knows the law. Philosophers in the Sufi and the Shi'a traditions accept the words and the deeds of the Prophet and the authority of the jurists (*fuqaha'*), but they also emphasize the importance of a living exemplar, in the figure of an Imam, the deputies of the Imam, and so on. These exemplars live the Islamic life and are in touch with the truth (*haqiqa*) of the religion. They are not full prophets in the sense of the Prophet Muhammad, but just like the accomplished philosopher in the philosophies of Alfarabi and Avicenna, they are privy to the Muhammadan truth and can be exemplars for the faithful.

The writings of Nasr and Henry Corbin[52] are more than adequate in articulating the scope of philosophical prophetology in the traditions of Islamic philosophy. Here, I do not want to restate what they have established in their works. I want to make a case for the Islamic Peripatetics, a case that must at the outset meet Ghazali's challenge. It is well known that Ghazali accused the Muslim Peripatetics of being heretics on account of their adherence to three specific doctrines. To respond to this challenge, I will draw from the work of the great Andalusian Muslim Peripatetic, Abu al-Walid ibn Rushd (Averroës, d. 1198 CE). In a short work titled *The Decisive Treatise Determining the Connection Between the Law and Wisdom,* Averroës refutes Ghazali's case against the Islamic Peripatetics by rejecting Ghazali's understanding of philosophy as the production of rational knowledge beholden to the beliefs of its Greek founders. Averroës maintains that philosophy as appropriated by Muslims should rather be understood as a legitimate practice within the constraints of Islam.

In *The Incoherence of the Philosophers,* Ghazali maintains that the Islamic Peripatetics held 20 theses that are false, three of which he considered so grave as to constitute heresy (*kufr*). Already in this account we see that Ghazali is approaching his Peripatetic rivals as heretics because of the theses they advance rather than because of their practices. The problematic theses endorsed by Muslim Peripatetics are (1) God does not know particulars, (2) the world is eternal, and (3) bodies are not resurrected. Ghazali refutes each of these theses in a painstakingly rational way, providing evidence from the Qur'an and other relevant sources. I will not relate the details of Ghazali's arguments but rather show how Averroës, in each instance, diminishes the force of the controversy and presents the philosophers as dealing with the Islamic revelation legitimately, albeit differently from Ghazali.

To begin, Averroës argues that philosophers do not claim that God does not know particulars; they rather claim that He does not know them the way humans do. God knows particulars as their Creator whereas humans know them as a privileged creation of God might know them.[53] In regard to the eternity of the world, Averroës shows that the philosophers agree with Ghazali that there is a God, that God created existent things, and that the world (containing the existent things) extends infinitely into the future. What the dispute concerns is merely the past of the world. Philosophers argue that the world is without a beginning in time, whereas Ghazali disagrees. Averroës argues that the scope of this disagreement is insufficient to constitute heresy and he also introduces Qur'anic verses to defend the Peripatetic view.[54] Finally, as to the resurrection of bodies, Averroës argues that Peripatetic philosophers agree with Ghazali that the soul is immortal and that bodies are resurrected on Judgment Day. The dispute rather turns on the issue of whether the bodies that will be resurrected will be the same material bodies that had perished previously. Islamic Peripatetics argue that "existence comes back only to a likeness of what has perished."[55] More precisely, the resurrected body is identical in its attributes to the perished body, but it is not composed of the same material. Again the point is that the difference in the position of the philosophers and that of Ghazali is insignificant and does not constitute grounds for the condemnation of the former as heretics.[56]

Averroës's engagement in the above dialectical joust with Ghazali aims at mitigating the effects of the latter's attack on the philosophers and is not the substance of his critique of Ghazali. This concerns Ghazali's metaphilosophical assumptions. Averroës distinguishes between three forms of reasoning: rhetorical (*al-qiyas al-khitabi*), dialectical (*al-qiyas al-jadali*), and demonstrative (*al-qiyas al-burhani*). Rhetorical reasoning is the mode of discourse suitable to the public preacher and aims at persuasion by appealing to the audience's imagination and passions. Dialectical reasoning is the preferred method of the theologians, those who explore the truth through rational analysis and argumentation. Demonstrative reasoning, however, is the method of the philosopher, and it is interpretation (*ta'wil*) that gets at the origin (*awwal*) of things, in other words their truth. The first two approaches begin with assumptions shared by and *apparent* to the multitude and then proceed to others based either on persuasive or rational norms. Only the demonstrative method goes beyond appearances and gets at the real:

> God has been gracious to His servants for whom there is no path by means of demonstration—either due to their innate dispositions, their habits, or their lack of facilities for education—by coining for them likenesses (*al-amthal*) and similarities of these [hidden things] and calling them to assent by means of those likenesses, since it is possible for assent to those likenesses to come about by means of the indications shared by all—I mean, the dialectical and the rhetorical. This is the reason for the Law (*al-shar'*) being divided into an apparent sense and an inner sense. For the apparent sense is those likenesses coined for those meanings, and the inner sense is those meanings that reveal themselves only to those adept in demonstration.[57]

Demonstration is the method of getting at the reality of things, but God has provided—by means of revelation—likenesses of the real for those disinclined to engage in the demonstrative method. The Law, which includes the Qur'an and the Sunna, contains the images of the real. Theologians and preachers work on these images without seeking the originals. Philosophers, however, pierce the image and unveil the hidden original (*awwal*) through their certain interpretation (*al-ta'wil al-yaqini*). Averroës refers to the demonstrative *ta'wil* as the art of wisdom (*sin'at al-hikma*),[58] a practice that has something to do with aptitude (*al-fitra*), habit (*al-'ada*), and training (*al-ta'allum*). The articulation of *ta'wil* as an art that has to be cultivated in the person points to the practice of spiritual exercises as constituting the core of philosophy, geared toward molding the character and the mind such that one shuns images and falsehoods and becomes intimate with the source of truth, the Active Intellect. It is here that Averroës's principal criticism of Ghazali's attack on the philosophers comes out. Ghazali, according to Averroës, assesses philosophical theses as if they were theological ones (and harshly at that). Rather, philosophical principles, according to Averroës, must be examined for their service to the practice of philosophy and the activity of aiming at the original (*ta'wil*).

Averroës's view also suggests that philosophy as *hikma* is aligned with Islam, but Muslim philosophers have the further advantage of working with the Islamic law and practices, and are therefore capable of a more direct insight into the truth. In the *Incoherence of the Incoherence,* a text devoted to a more detailed refutation of Ghazali's attacks on the philosophers, Averroës writes:

> [Islamic Peripatetic philosophers] are of the opinion that a human being has no life in this abode but by means of practical arts, and no life in this abode or in the final abode but by means of theoretical virtues; that neither one of these two is completed or obtained by him but by means of the practical virtues; and that the practical virtues are not firmly established but through cognizance of God (may He be exalted) and magnifying Him by means of devotions set down in the law for them in each and every religion—such as offerings, prayers, invocations, and similar speeches spoken in praise of God (may He be exalted), the angels, and the prophets.[59]

It is evident then that Averroës follows the earlier Muslim Peripatetics in understanding philosophy as a way of life aiming at the cultivation of virtues. Moreover, this cultivation is in accord with the Islamic revelation as containing the truth and the practices leading to this truth in a way appealing to the imagination and the reason of the multitude. The reliance on Islamic law, practices, and beliefs as supplied by the revelations of the Prophet Muhammad makes Averroës and his Peripatetic predecessors Muslims. This is a point that I have explored above in dealing with earlier Peripatetic prophetology. Perhaps it would be appropriate to end this section with Avicenna's Persian quatrain, which he composed on being accused of heresy:

> It is not so easy and trifling to call me a heretic;
> No faith in religion is firmer than mine.
> I am a unique person in the whole world and if I am a heretic,
> Then there is not a single Muslim anywhere in the world.[60]

My aim in this chapter has been to argue that what makes Islamic philosophy Islamic is the philosophical prophetology advanced by its proponents. The first premise in the argument consists of the claim that philosophy as inherited from the Greeks was a way of life rather than a set of rational theories. This premise was established by reference to the scholarship of Hadot. I also surveyed accounts of ancient philosophy given by some prominent scholars of Islamic philosophy and criticized aspects of these accounts as conflicting with the practical focus of philosophy. The second premise of the argument identifies the elements that constitute the "Islamicity" of Islamic philosophy. I argue that the central element of Islamic philosophy was not, *pace* Nasr, the combination of theory and self-transformative spiritual exercises. This combination, as I showed with regard to the first premise, was already present in ancient philosophy. Nasr's view had as a corollary the privileging of the anti-Peripatetic posture of Avicenna's later work and its relation to the Hermetico-Platonic Illuminationism advanced by Suhrawardi. I maintain that the central element making Islamic philosophy Islamic was the notion of Islamic philosophical prophetology and that versions of this prophetology were embraced by Muslim Peripatetics. In order to emphasize the Islamicity of Islamic Peripateticism, I defend this tradition against the charge of heresy brought to it by Ghazali. I argue with Averroës that Ghazali misinterpreted the activity of philosophy (especially that of the Islamic Peripatetics) and that the charge of heresy is misplaced.

NOTES

1. Pierre Hadot, *Philosophy as a Way of Life* (Oxford, U.K.: Blackwell, 1995), 269.

2. Ibid., 267.

3. Ibid., 268.

4. Ibid., 264.

5. Ibid., 267–68.

6. Refer to my "The Sublime Visions of Philosophy: Fundamental Ontology and the Imaginal World" *Microcosm and Macrocosm,* ed. Anna-Teresa Tymieniecka (Dordrecht, Netherlands: Kluwer, forthcoming).

7. Hadot, *Philosophy as a Way of Life*, 107.

8. I am indebted to Julia Annas's "Ancient Ethics and Modern Morality," in *Philosophical Perspectives* 2 (1992): 119–136, for the distinction between agent-centered and act-centered perspectives.

9. Hadot, *Philosophy as a Way of Life*, 269.

10. Richard Walzer, *Greek into Arabic* (Cambridge, Massachusetts: Harvard University Press, 1962), 213.

11. Oliver Leaman, "Orientalism and Islamic Philosophy," in *Routledge Encyclopedia of Philosophy,* vol. 7 (London, U.K.: Routledge, 1998), 159.

12. Ibid., 158.

13. Another scholar of Islamic philosophy committed to this form of Orientalism is T. J. DeBoer. See his *The History of Philosophy in Islam,* trans. Edward R. Jones (New York: Dover, 1967), 28–30.

14. Leaman, *Routledge Encyclopedia of Philosophy,* 158.

15. Leo Strauss, *Persecution and the Art of Writing* (Chicago, Illinois: University of Chicago Press, 1980), 19.

16.   Oliver Leaman, "Orientalism and Islamic Philosophy," in *History of Islamic Philosophy*, Part II, ed. Seyyed Hossein Nasr and Oliver Leaman (London, U.K.: Routledge, 1996), 1145.

17.   Strauss, *Persecution and the Art of Writing*, 19.

18.   Hadot, *Philosophy as a Way of Life*, 107–108.

19.   Muhammed Abed al-Jabri, *Arab-Islamic Philosophy*, trans. Aziz Abbassi (Austin, Texas: The Center for Middle Eastern Studies, The University of Texas at Austin, 1999), 48.

20.   Ibid., 49.

21.   Oliver Leaman, *An Introduction to Classical Islamic Philosophy* (Cambridge, U.K.: Cambridge University Press, 1985), 16.

22.   Leaman, *Routledge Encyclopedia of Philosophy*, 1145.

23.   This position echoes the approach that some Indian and Pakistani scholars of Islamic philosophy have adopted. They refer to their subject matter as "Muslim philosophy" since they claim it is cultivated by Muslims and is not Islamic; that is, it is not derived from Islamic sources. An example is M.M. Shariff's *A History of Muslim Philosophy* (Wiesbaden: Harrassowitz, 1963–1966).

24.   Oliver Leaman, "Concept of Philosophy in Islam," in *Routledge Encyclopedia of Philosophy*, vol. 5 (London, U.K.: Routledge, 1998), 6.

25.   Ibid., 7.

26.   Seyyed Hossein Nasr, "The Meaning and Concept of Philosophy in Islam," in *History of Islamic Philosophy*, Part I, ed. Seyyed Hossein Nasr and Oliver Leaman (London, U.K.: Routledge, 1996), 24–25.

27.   Ibid., 23.

28.   Ibid.

29.   Ibid., 22. Nasr admits that before Avicenna, the Ismaili philosophers had gone beyond the Peripatetics in combining philosophical theory and the practice of a virtuous life, see ibid., 23.

30.   Quoted by Mehdi Aminrazavi, "The Logic of Orientals: Whose Logic and Which Orient?" in the *Beacon of Knowledge*, ed. Mohammad H. Faghfoory (Louisville, Kentucky: Fons Vitae, 2003), 48.

31.   Dimitri Gutas *Avicenna and the Aristotelian Tradition* (Leiden, Netherlands: E.J. Brill, 1988), 286–296, is perhaps a good antidote to Nasr's postulate of a radical divide between Avicenna the Peripatetic and Avicenna the Oriental.

32.   See for instance his alignment of ethics with the act-centered divine-command principles of the *Shari'a* in "Islamic Philosophy—Reorientation or Re-understanding," in *Islamic Life and Thought* (Albany, New York: State University of New York Press, 1981), 155.

33.   Prophetology assumes a central place in the discussion of Islamic philosophy through the efforts of Henry Corbin [see *History of Islamic Philosophy*, trans. Liadain Sherrard (London, U.K.: Kegan Paul, 1993), 21; see also Nasr's "The Qur'an and Hadith as Source and Inspiration of Islamic Philosophy," in *History of Islamic Philosophy*, Part I, ed. Seyyed Hossein Nasr and Oliver Leaman (London, U.K.: Routledge, 1996), 28 and 38 ftn. 3].

34.   Aristotle, "De Anima," in *The Complete Works of Aristotle*, ed. Jonathan Barnes, trans. W.D. Ross (Princeton, New Jersey: Princeton University Press, 1984), 430a 14–17.

35.   Ibid., 430a 25.

36.   Pierre Hadot, *What is Ancient Philosophy?* trans. Michael Chase (Cambridge, Massachusetts: Harvard University Press, 2002), 79.

37.   Herbert Davidson, *Alfarabi, Avicenna, and Averroës, on Intellect* (Oxford, U.K.: Oxford university Press, 1992), 13–14.

38.   Aristotle, "De Anima," 427–429.

39.   Mehdi Ha'eri Yazdi, *The Principles of Epistemology in Islamic Philosophy* (Albany, New York: SUNY Press, 1992), 9.

40.   Plato, "Timaeus," in *The Collected Dialogues of Plato*, ed. Edith Hamilton and Huntington Cairns (Princeton, New Jersey: Princeton University Press, 1962), 29e–30c.

41.   Abu Nasr al-Farabi, *On the Perfect State*, trans. Richard Walzer (Oxford, U.K.: Oxford University Press, 1985), 406.

42.   Ibid., 406.

43.   Abu Nasr al-Farabi, "The Attainment of Happiness," in *Medieval Political Philosophy: A Sourcebook*, eds. Ralph Lerner and Muhsin Mahdi (Ithaca, New York: Cornell University Press, 1961), 80.

44.   Al-Farabi, *On the Perfect State*, 225.

45.   Ibid., 247.

46.   Avicenna, "*Healing*: Metaphysics X," in *Medieval Political Philosophy: A Sourcebook*, 110.

47.   Ibid.

48.   Avicenna, "On the Proof of Prophecies and the Interpretation of the Prophets' Symbols and Metaphors," in *Medieval Political Philosophy: A Sourcebook*, 115.

49.   Parviz Morewedge, "The Logic of Emanationism and Sufism in the Philosophy of Ibn Sina (Avicenna)," *Journal of the American Oriental Society* 92, no. 1 (1972): 7–8.

50.   Ibid., 8.

51.   Aristotle, "Nicomachean Ethics," in *The Complete Works of Aristotle*, ed. Jonathan Barnes, trans. W.D. Ross (Princeton, New Jersey: Princeton University Press, 1984) 1140a25–28, 1143b21–25.

52.   See especially his *History of Islamic Philosophy*.

53.   Averroës, *Decisive Treatise and Epistle Dedicatory*, trans. and ed. Charles E. Butterworth (Provo, Utah: Brigham Young University Press, 2001), 13.

54.   Ibid., 16.

55.   Ibid., 46.

56.   Ibid., 20–21.

57.   Ibid., 19.

58.   Ibid., 26.

59.   Ibid., 43–44 [The translation is modified at places in keeping with Averroës, *Tahafut al-Tahafut*, trans. and ed. Simon Van Den Bergh (Oxford, U.K.: Oxford University Press, 1954), 539].

60.   S.H. Barani, trans. "Ibn Sina and Alberuni," in *Avicenna Commemoration Volume* (Calcutta, Iran Society, 1956), 8 (with certain modifications by S.H. Nasr; refer to his "The Qur'an and *Hadith* as Source and Inspiration of Islamic Philosophy," 38 ftn. 2). Mehdi Aminrazavi, in "The Logic of Orientals: Whose Logic and Which Orient?" 48–49, argues against the significance of asceticism in Avicenna's personal life. I disagree with his analysis and refer the reader to Dimitri Gutas' discussion of Avicenna's practices in *Avicenna and the Aristotelian Tradition*, 157–194.

3

ISLAM FOR THE PEOPLE: MUSLIM MEN'S VOICES ON RACE AND ETHNICITY IN THE AMERICAN UMMA

Jamillah A. Karim

American Muslims inherit an Islamic cultural legacy colored by a vast array of ethnic groups. In Marshall G.S. Hodgson's study of the Islamic cultural tradition, he writes that Islam "is unique among the religious traditions for the diversity of the peoples that have embraced it."[1] Similarly, Bernard Lewis writes, "Islam for the first time created a truly universal civilization, extending from Southern Europe to Central Africa, from the Atlantic Ocean to India and China." Within "a common religious culture," Islam brought "peoples as diverse as the Chinese, the Indians, the people of the Middle East and North Africa, black Africans, and white Europeans."[2] Umar Faruq Abd-Allah likens the Islamic cultural legacy to "a brilliant peacock's tail of unity in diversity," extending "from the heart of China to the shores of the Atlantic."[3]

As Islam expanded from shore to shore, every ethnic group added another layer to Islam's vast cultural display, each playing its part in the making of a global Muslim community, or *Umma*. Ideally, the Umma represents an international community of Muslims united across race and ethnicity. New to the international Umma, the American Muslim community marks new possibilities within Islam's 1,400-year-old legacy. Already, its most outstanding feature is its striking ethnic spectrum. The American Muslim population reflects a multiethnic mosaic of African American, Anglo, and Latino converts alongside Arab, Asian, African, and European Muslim immigrants. This distinctive display of "unity in diversity" within the American context makes it an *American Umma*. In this chapter, I present voices of Islam in America, the voices of American Muslims as they struggle to create an American Umma, standing as a model of racial harmony, in a racialized society.

SYMBOLS OF UNITY: MALCOLM X AND THE HAJJ

How can we conceive of unity within Islam's vast ethnic diversity? Scholars of Islam point to the Hajj as the most striking model. During the Hajj, Muslims from around the world arrive at a common destination, Mecca, orienting their hearts and prayers to a common house of worship, the Ka'ba, also known as God's house. In a remarkable way, Mecca, a city isolated between two valleys in an otherwise remote desert, is transformed into a microcosm of the world during the Hajj season. "The pilgrimage," Lewis writes, brings about "a great meeting and mixing of peoples from Asia, Europe, and Africa."[4] Similarly, when Hodgson describes Muslims as a group "moved by a sense of universal Muslim solidarity," he refers to "the great common pilgrimage to Mecca where all nations may meet."[5]

The most vivid and compelling accounts of the Hajj, however, come from the voices of Muslims privileged to experience the Hajj firsthand. In the American context, Malcolm X's (d. 1965) famous "Letter from Mecca" stands as the most acclaimed account. "Never have I witnessed such sincere hospitality and the overwhelming spirit of true brotherhood as practiced by people of all colors and races here in this Ancient Holy Land, the home of Abraham, Muhammad and all other prophets of the Holy Scriptures," Malcolm X wrote at the conclusion of his pilgrimage. "There were tens of thousands of pilgrims, from all over the world. They were of all colors, from blue eyed blonds to black skinned Africans. But we were all participating in the same rituals, displaying a spirit of unity and brotherhood that my experiences in America had led me to believe never could exist between the white and non-white."[6]

Many others have written of the Hajj's display of universal brotherhood; however, Malcolm's account is exceptionally priceless because of his legendary role in the struggle against antiblack racism. On the platform of Black Muslim nationalism, Malcolm X tore down white supremacy with his intensely brilliant words and emerged as a hero for African Americans. The Hajj, the quintessential symbol of Malcolm's move from the NOI (Nation of Islam) to Sunni Islam, made him a universal Muslim hero beyond black America. However, his account of the Hajj's racial harmony reverberates so powerfully because of what he stood for in black America: a defiant spokesman against white racism and a sincere fighter for racial justice.

RACE AND AMERICAN ISLAM

The Autobiography of Malcolm X emerges as a common theme in the conversion stories of many American Muslims, Black, Anglo, and Latino. The prominence of Malcolm's Hajj narrative highlights race as a striking feature of American Islam—American Islam understood as one of multiple cultural expressions of Islam. Theorizing this multiplicity, Hodgson argues that cultural traditions and dialogues within specific contexts determine Islam's cultural relevance: only as Islam engaged already existing cultural dialogues could it "become significant for cultural life at large." Islam's cultural relevance, and therefore its cultural expression, was as distinct as the cultures to which Islam spread. In sub-Saharan Africa, for example, Islam came to be associated with literacy. Through the study of the Qur'an and other Islamic literatures, Muslim Africans became the first literate class in an otherwise oral civilization. Even non-Muslims attended the Qur'an schools in West Africa because "they were the only educational structures available."[7] Similarly, in southern Spain, Islam came to be associated with higher learning, cultural prestige, and lyrical eloquence, primarily through the transmission of Arabic texts, "from the poetical to the philosophical."[8] The semantic richness of Arabic allowed Christians to express what they could not express in Latin and inspired Jews to revive their sacred language and express what they had never expressed before in Hebrew. In contrast, as Islam spread in the eastern regions of the Indian subcontinent along the Bay of Bengal, it came to be associated less with intellectual prosperity than with agricultural prosperity, particularly rice cultivation. There, the rural masses came to identify with Islam through the landholders, primarily religious gentry who were authorized by the ruling Muslims. The landholders established mosques at the center of thriving agrarian-based communities, making Islam a familiar part of a "single Bengali folk-culture."[9]

Islam's relevance and social appeal were manifested in distinct ways. In many societies, race and social equality were not central to the cultural dialogue.[10] In the American context, however, race assumed a central place in the cultural dialogue, and, as demonstrated in the converts' common reference to Malcolm X, Islam has significantly addressed this cultural issue. Islam's concern with issues of race represents a critical aspect in conceptualizing a distinctly American Islam. The NOI, in which Malcolm X was a member for 12 years, played an exceptional role in this regard as it projected Islam as a religion that resisted racism. The NOI made its mission to address racial injustice very clear: it taught that Islam was "the Black Man's" *original* religion, and by accepting the religion, blacks were reclaiming their true, dignified identity. With this message, the Nation of Islam unapologetically challenged racist ideologies intent on establishing blacks as an inferior race.

While the Nation's theological position distinguished it from mainstream Islam, it was responsible for introducing Islam to African Americans, and did so "almost single-handedly."[11] The NOI popularized Islam and gave American Muslims substantial cultural capital, primarily in African American communities. American Muslims acquire cultural capital to the extent that they compellingly present Islam as a cultural asset. American Muslim spokespersons increasingly speak to this challenge. Foremost among them is Dr. Umar Faruq Abd-Allah, an Anglo convert admired by his supporters for his credentials both as an American-trained academic and as a scholar of traditional Islamic sciences. In a 2002 lecture in Chicago, Dr. Abd-Allah challenged his majority second-generation American Muslim audience to make themselves "known [in America] and...to make friends [in America]." American Muslims possess an array of "treasures and knowledge" that can together produce "a creative [Muslim] minority," standing for "justice, equality and good." If "we bring together the best of what is here [in American society] and the best of what we [American Muslims] have, we can create something beautiful."[12]

Offering "something beautiful" to American culture, Dr. Abd-Allah speaks about the possibility of American Muslims furthering their cultural capital. "We must make Islam a home and open doors for the black and the white and the Hispanic and the Native American," he states.[13] His focus on native populations, rather than African, Arab, or Asian immigrants, brings home his message of, "What can Islam do for Americans?" Often he refers to the way in which African American Muslims have already laid the foundations in this regard. Another important spokesperson, Dr. Sherman A. (Abd al-Hakim) Jackson, lectures specifically about the cultural contribution of the NOI. An African American convert popular among second-generation American Muslims, also trained in both academia and traditional Muslim discourse, Jackson authored the groundbreaking work *Islam and the Blackamerican*. In it, he refers to how Black Muslims created in their larger black communities awareness of the effects of pork consumption and also inspired "the spread of Arabic names."[14] Both are examples of Islam offering something beneficial to non-Muslim Americans.

THE IMMIGRANT DIFFERENCE

Because ethnic diversity and racial harmony are valued as American ideals, the ability for Muslims to substantially challenge and remove racial inequalities would function as an invaluable source of cultural capital. How can American Muslims capitalize upon the legacies of the Nation and Malcolm X, furthering the link between Islam and black empowerment, on the one hand, and that between Islam and racial harmony, on the other? American Muslim communities would have to demonstrate these ideals in their own communities first. The demographics of the American Umma—its significant African American population (at least one-third) and its ethnic diversity—make these ideals appear reachable.[15] But the reality is that race-class (and also ideological) divides limit racial harmony in the American Umma. Interestingly, in the American Umma, the most pronounced lines run not between black and white but between black and immigrant.

The immigrant difference broadens the problem of race in the American Umma, and in ways that Malcolm X did not fully anticipate when he proclaimed that "Islam is the one religion that will erase the race problem in America." Tellingly if we look back at his "Letter from Mecca," his focus is on black–white relations, and aptly so. When he refers to his *white* "fellow Muslims, whose eyes were the bluest of blue, whose hair was the blondest of blond, and whose skin was the whitest of white," he states that "their belief in one God had removed the 'white' from their minds, the 'white' from their behavior, and the 'white' from their attitude." His thoughts then turn to "what is happening in America between black and white," and he states, "I do believe, from the experience that I have had with them, that the whites of the younger generation, in the colleges and universities, will see the handwriting on the wall and many of them will turn to the spiritual path of truth—the only way left to America to ward off the disaster that racism inevitably must lead to."[16]

Malcolm X could speak confidently about Islam as a model for American whites because he had yet to fully experience the ethnic divides in the American Umma, at least not compellingly enough to acknowledge or speak about them in his autobiography. But these divides did exist as early as the 1930s, indicated by Sunni African American Muslims' reports of negative experiences with their immigrant counterparts.[17] In Malcolm's case, however, his membership in the Nation of Islam restricted his relations with Muslim immigrants and as a result, limited his negative encounters with them. As it relates to future race relations in the American Umma, the issue of timing also explains Malcolm's shortened scope. The year of Malcolm X's death was also the year of the 1965 Immigration Act, which overturned a series of U.S. laws that limited Asian immigration. This act marked the largest influx of Muslim immigrants to the United States, particularly from the Indian subcontinent. Before this time, Muslim immigrants had yet to create the level of visibility that made ethnic divisions as obvious as they are today, particularly through the proliferation of ethnic mosques.[18]

Like Malcolm X, American Muslim leaders today speak about Islam as a model of diversity and racial equality; at the same time, however, they criticize American Muslims for their racism. Imam Zaid Shakir, a popular African American scholar who complements his traditional Islamic pedagogy with his expertise in political science, writes that American Muslims "have a unique opportunity to contribute to" ending racism, but "unfortunately, many Muslims have endorsed this disease through their refusal to acknowledge its existence or through their attitudes and actions toward their coreligionists of darker complexions."[19] Here, Imam Zaid alludes to the black–immigrant divide. The historical black–white color line, which Malcolm X addressed, does matter in the American Umma; however, it functions differently in a context that combines African Americans and immigrants.

The immigrant presence in America draws attention to a continuum of privilege, not exclusively characterized by race—black versus white—but broadened to account for "an unspoken U.S. hierarchical social order"[20] in which whiteness, high income, and quality of education (which includes the ability to speak standard English) work together to locate ethnic groups and subgroups differently along a socioeconomic spectrum. This spectrum illustrates the persistence of the historical color line as it positions rich whites at the top and poor blacks at the bottom. At the same time, it accounts for how other ethnic groups become implicated in "the problem of the color-line"[21] as they attempt to position themselves closer to Anglos along the spectrum of white privilege: "Latinos join Asians and Native Americans as subgroups less privileged than Anglo Americans, though not as underprivileged as African Americans. It is this contest for middle ground that links both Latinos and Asian Americans in an ongoing struggle for recognition."[22]

Among the early Muslim immigrants were some who experienced what it meant to be on the wrong side of the color line, particularly "those whose skin was darker than that of the average American." In the South, they "found that they were treated as 'colored' by local populations and were refused access to public facilities reserved for 'Whites only.' "[23] If we could imagine Jim Crow segregation making Arab and Asian immigrants "bitterly conscious, as [they] never had been before, of [their] brown skin and black hair,"[24] it would come as no surprise that some immigrants would position themselves so as to not be associated with blacks or with their experiences. Vijay Prashad exposes this form of social distancing among South Asian immigrants. "Desis realize they are not 'white,' but there is certainly a strong sense among most desis that they are not 'black.' In a racist society, it is hard to expect people to opt for the most despised category. Desis came to the United States and denied their 'blackness' at least partly out of a desire for class mobility (something, in the main, denied to blacks) and a sense that solidarity with blacks was tantamount to ending one's dreams of being successful (that is, of being 'white')."[25]

This type of social distancing from blacks—especially betrayed by residential patterns in which immigrants choose not to live in black neighborhoods—reflects a common pattern in black–immigrant relations in the larger society. How then would this common trend play out in the American Umma, a community marked as a subset not only of the universal Umma but also of the larger American society? In other words, what does it mean for South Asian and Arab immigrants to find, upon immigrating to the United States, that a substantial part of their new Umma is black? Have shared location in the American Umma created an awareness of the African American experience, support, and solidarity? For the most part, it has not. America's race and class divides extend into the American Umma. Some African American Muslims even contend that the presence of immigrants in the shared Umma presents yet another venue for race discrimination toward African Americans. I present below the voices of Muslim leaders in Chicago as they speak about the way in which race and class inequalities become manifest in the American Umma. I feature Muslim voices as they urge the next generation of American Muslims to build upon an American Muslim legacy marked by resistance to racism, and the restoration of the African American community in particular. I present a spectrum of voices, primarily male voices, as the American Umma struggles to fulfill Malcolm X's vision. I collected these voices in 2002 as part of research on relations between African American and South Asian immigrant Muslims in Chicago. Chicago has substantial representation of both ethnic Muslim groups. The city holds an unrivalled historical relevance as a major site for early developments within American Islam: Chicago was the headquarters of both the Ahmadiyya and the Nation of Islam, groups with both African American and South Asian roots.[26]

ON ACCOMMODATING RACISM— AFRICAN AMERICAN MUSLIM PERSPECTIVES

With an African American population of one million, Chicago remains a very important city for understanding race relations in America. During the Great Migration, Chicago became a major destination for Southern blacks leaving the South to escape the harshness of sharecropping and the horror of lynching. Ever since, Chicago has continued to tell the story of racist residential patterns especially defined by white flight and black ghettos, by quality resources for whites and poverty for blacks: "For every downtown skyscraper that kept jobs and tax dollars in the city, there was a housing project tower that confined poor people in an overcrowded ghetto.... Chicago is one of America's wealthiest cities but, remarkably, nine of the nation's ten poorest census tracts are in Chicago's housing projects."[27] Before they were torn down in 2002, Chicago was the home of the Robert Taylor Homes, a collection of towering high-rise projects built in the 1950s: "Its 4,415 apartments" made "it the largest public housing development in the world." With "fenced-in external galleries," the Robert Taylor Homes were once described as "filing cabinets for the poor."[28]

Abdullah Madyun, an African American Imam in Chicago, was raised in one of Chicago's projects in the late 1960s and 1970s. His parents joined the Nation of Islam when he was a toddler and subsequently followed Imam W.D. Mohammed into mainstream Sunni Islam after abandoning the Nation's black nationalist teachings. (Imam W.D. Mohammed inherited the largest following of African American Muslims when his father, Elijah Muhammad, died in 1975.) Imam Abdullah attended Sister Clara Muhammad School as a boy. He studied in Saudi Arabia in his early twenties, and upon his return, separated himself from the WDM (W.D. Mohammed)[29] community because he disagreed with Imam W.D. Mohammed's religious methodology. Admired in both African American and immigrant communities, Imam Abdullah is known to captivate his audiences with fiery speeches that reveal an eloquent black vernacular, his words flowing with expressions that reflect his experiences growing up in Black Chicago. He also dazzles his audience with his crisp Arabic, easily citing Qur'anic verse and Hadith. I had met Imam Abdullah two years prior to my research when he spoke to a predominantly South Asian and Arab mosque audience. Never before had I heard an Imam criticize immigrant Muslims who try to hide their religious and ethnic identity to pass as white. Bluntly, he addressed real issues of race and class in the American Umma.

Imam Abdullah's critique of Muslim immigrants sounds very much like Prashad's critique of the Desi American community, the bulk of which, the latter states, has "moved away from active political struggles toward an accommodation with this racist polity" in order to "accumulate economic wealth through hard work and guile."[30] Imam Abdullah renders an analysis as thorough as Prashad's but in terms that especially convey the cadence of black urban protest. According to Imam Abdullah, Muslim immigrants are "sinking right away into America's economic, materialistic objective way of life." The American "life" represents a system that has disadvantaged African Americans, largely on account of race. But this same system gives South Asian immigrants abundant opportunities, Imam Abdullah believes, because "it helps America's economy to bring engineers and scientists here. They come from impoverished countries, but once here, we pay them good. They spend their wealth on getting the good life. But African Americans do not have the same opportunities, and, of course, it is designed like that."[31]

While this "design" is terribly transparent to Imam Abdullah, he sees South Asian immigrants as being "clueless" about it: "They are clueless about this whole American life, the traps, the plans, the objectives, the system." Wali Bashir, an African American Muslim activist and friend of Imam Abdullah, shares similar sentiments. "The people buying into the American dream," Wali said, "don't realize that the American nightmare is working right under it. The beauty of America is built on the horror underneath. I don't think a lot of them [immigrants] understand this concept. Most of them don't even know our history."[32] He refers to the over 200 years of labor exploitation, that is, slavery, which made America's advance as a leading industrial nation possible. Whites continue to benefit and blacks continue to lack resources because of the residual capital and liability of slavery.

This reality seems to escape immigrants, as Imam Abdullah states, "Many of the immigrants think that our condition is because we are lazy. They think, 'All you [African Americans] have to do is do like me. I went to school and such and such.' They really can't see. How can you possibly see the mechanism here to oppress one people, and [think that] you are not a part of it, [that] you get everything that you want and these people don't?"[33] He refers to an overarching system of injustice that connects African Americans and immigrants: "Why did you leave your country to come here? Why couldn't you do all these great things that you are doing here there? Why did you break your neck here if it's just that easy?" Pakistani immigrants come here because Pakistan does not have the same resources and opportunities: "You left there to come here because there was a condition there. I can't escape the condition here and go to Pakistan." In other words, the condition of both Pakistan and black America—connected by a lack of resources and of capital—reflects the inequalities and asymmetries of a global world in which white America comes out on top. Most South Asian immigrants escape the poverty of both Pakistan and black America because they represent the elite of their native countries and can come and acquire wealth here because they are affluent, professional, and closer to white. They live well here, and America "keeps perpetuating materialism and capitalism all over the world." Wali supports Imam Abdullah's analysis, "Everything we get here has repercussion somewhere else," in Pakistan and poor communities in Chicago.

Imam Abdullah argues that as affluent South Asian Muslims perpetuate America's economic order, they compromise their faith. "Immigrants have come here and have reaped the benefits to the point that it has killed their Islam. You come here for materialism, but you forget that you are Muslim, and you forget your responsibility to establish Allah's *din*," interpreting *din* [religion] as the means to justice. "The immigrants should be putting forth more of an effort to utilize their resources towards the upliftment of the African American community." The African American community should be a priority because, according to Imam Abdullah, "the most prominent spots to establish Allah's *din* are those places where injustices and poverty exist."

ON ACCOMMODATING RACISM—SOUTH ASIAN MUSLIM PERSPECTIVES

To Imam Abdullah's remarks on the need to address injustices in African American communities, some Muslims would counter that there do exist other ways of standing up for justice. South Asian Muslims remain connected to Muslims abroad who suffer genocide, warfare, poverty, and global racism. This was the sentiment expressed by Dr. Abidullah Ghazi, a middle-aged South Asian immigrant Muslim who directs IQRA International Educational Foundation, an influential Muslim publishing house in Chicago.

In America, "there is a Pakistani association, an Indian Muslim association, a Kashmir association, a Bengali association, and they all have their own issues." Dr. Ghazi made this point, desiring that critical African American Muslims consider how South Asian Muslims already deal with a range of issues within their communities: "We are first generation. We did not know America. We did not come here to live. We came here to earn our degree and go back and live happily in our own country. [But one thing led to another], children were born, we settled down, and now we belong to two

worlds. African Americans don't belong to two worlds." Although recognizing the African American's symbolic connection to Africa, he noted, "They
are not emotionally involved with what is happening there the way we are
when there is nuclear warfare in India and Pakistan, when there is a massacre
in Ahmedabad, Gujarat and 7,000 Muslims are killed, when there are floods
and calamities in Bengal." Even within English-language Pakistani news-
papers like *Pakistani Link,* he said, you will find 95 percent Pakistan news
and maybe five percent American news yet related to Pakistan. "Our frame
of mind is not America. We are not concerned with what's happening with
blacks or whites or the society...as much as we are concerned with what is
happening there, and in one's own specific locale. A Bangladeshi doesn't
know anything about Pakistan although it was once one country."[34]

Dr. Ghazi desires that African American Muslims consider these factors
"before coming to a judgment that" South Asians "don't care about African
Americans." He acknowledged that there are individual South Asians who
are "insensitive," but "the real issue and problem is not between the two
communities at all. Rather the issue is the American issue: African Americans
live in separate neighborhoods; the whites live in separate neighborhoods.
The schools, the standard of life, the security do not compare between the
inner city and the white neighborhoods." Coming to America for a better life
and being interested in the best education for their children, South Asians
choose to live with affluent whites.

Even as South Asian Muslim immigrants live in majority white neighborhoods, some of them recognize the importance of establishing relations with
African Americans. IQRA's main office, for example, sits in an affluent neighborhood on the north side of Chicago. However, the foundation has formed
relations with African American Muslims who live on the South Side of
Chicago through its active recruitment of writers and designers who
represent the diversity of the American Umma. IQRA's commitment to
diversity is especially dear to the executive director, Dr. Tasneema Ghazi,
Dr. Ghazi's wife. She relishes opportunities to speak about *Grandfather's
Orchard,* a children's book written by Dr. Ghazi. Referring to the cover
illustration, she states, "Here you can see the setting is the American South
with an African American family. We are trying to include all Muslims, all
American Muslims who are of every color and every race."[35]

Dr. Talat Sultan, the 2004–2005 president of ICNA (Islamic Circle
of North America) also voiced commitment to good race relations in the
American Umma. I interviewed Dr. Sultan in his office where he serves as
the principal of the Islamic Foundation School, a predominantly South Asian
grade school. Its location in a mosque complex in one of Chicago's north
suburbs demonstrates once again the residential patterns that divide African
American and South Asian immigrant Muslims. He acknowledged these
divides and spoke of South Asians "harboring the same kinds of prejudices,
[though] not to the same level, prevalent in this country."[36] But this

prejudice against African Americans occurs mostly among *secular* South Asian immigrants, Dr. Sultan told me, "whereas the really good Muslims who practice Islam are friendlier with African Americans." The "good" Muslims "make deliberate efforts to have closer relationships with Afro-Americans. I myself taught at an Afro-American college for 14 years in North Carolina, Barba Scotia College in Concord." It was his first job after completing his degree at UCLA (University of California, Los Angeles). "I really became part of the family," he said. He paused for one second and then uttered words that fell short of a complete thought but gave his narrative the perfect frame, "This business of black and white in America at that time." Aware of the color line, Dr. Sultan chose to identify with African Americans. With the "feeling of being a minority in this country," it seems that you would want "to identify yourself with minorities. That is more logical to me than pretending to be a white American. Unfortunately, this is how our secular South Asians are."

DA'WA FOR THE PEOPLE—DEBATING CULTURAL CAPITAL

Dr. Sultan links interethnic solidarity with the sincere practice of Islam. However, many African American Muslims would counter that they have experienced racism at the hands of "good" practicing Muslims, and often in immigrant-majority mosques. Many immigrants have maintained their Muslim identity, but this does not necessarily translate into solidarity with African American Muslims. This was the sentiment of Imam Sultan Salahuddin, the Imam of the Ephraim Bahar Cultural Center, an inner-city mosque in association with Imam W.D. Mohammed. Imam Sultan recognizes the efforts of South Asian immigrants to preserve their Muslim identities and build Islamic institutions. Because of their wealth, they surpass African American Muslims in Islamic institution building. But, Imam Sultan believes, they have created Islamic institutions for their self-preservation, not to advance justice in the larger society.

"Their focus is different than ours," Imam Sultan said of South Asian leaders in Chicago.[37] He sees his community's focus as "bringing all humanity the clarity of religion," whereas he does not see South Asian Muslim leaders in Chicago making it a priority to teach Islam as a means of empowering people. He clarified, "I'm not saying that they are not interested in that, but it seems that a lot of them are just trying to fit in the main America: They are trying to show Americans that I'm like you, not terrorists. We don't have to do that. Our history in this country has qualified us whereas they have to constantly prove themselves." His comments suggest different experiences of oppression among American Muslims: South Asians are profiled and treated as terrorists while African Americans are not. However, African Americans continue to fight race and class injustices in their communities. Their different struggles produce very different types of activist work: "Most of their masjids and homes are in the suburbs, nice and pretty," Imam Sultan said about the neighborhoods of South Asians. "Out there, they don't have to deal with the problems that we have. They don't have to try to save all our people—I don't mean save [literally] because Allah is the only one who makes Muslims— but I mean they don't stay in the community to lend a hand."

The kind of Islamic activism, or cultural capital, to which Imam Sultan refers has roots in the NOI. The strategy of the Nation of Islam, using Islam to improve the general welfare of African American communities at the same time that it gained thousands of converts, best illustrates what I call "*da'wa* for the people," inviting people to Islam by caring for communities. *Da'wa* literally means "invitation," understood as invitation to Islam. The Qur'an urges Muslims to invite others to Islam through beautiful and intelligent dialogue.[38] *Da'wa* represents a shared vision, yet the different contexts in which Muslims carry out this duty, in poor, black neighborhoods or affluent, white suburbs, create boundaries within the Umma.

Geographic location inhibits South Asians from committing to the African American vision of *da'wa* work, making cooperation with South Asian Muslims frustrating for Imam Sultan. A member of the Council of Islamic Organizations of Greater Chicago, which is dominated by South Asians, he recalled his response to an agenda item in one council session to discuss how to better relations with African American Muslims: "The Qur'an has already addressed that, and it really bothers me that they don't know that. It bothers me that they would want us to come way out there to talk about how to help African American Muslims," referring to how the council meetings usually took place in the suburbs, "when our problem is in the inner city, where the majority of Muslims and the people who need help are. The religion of Islam comes to free all humanity, but specifically the oppressed." Hence, Imam Sultan sees *da'wa* as a form of bringing justice, and helping the oppressed change their state. As Ibn Qayyim al-Jawziyya wrote, "God has sent His Messengers and revealed His Books so that people may establish *qist* [justice]."[39] If South Asian Muslims were concerned about justice for the oppressed, Imam Sultan believes, they would already have good relations with African American Muslims by working alongside them in the inner city.

Of all the Imams that I interviewed, Imam Abdullah was the most critical of South Asians for their limited *da'wa* in the inner city. As if to address South Asians, Imam Abdullah asked, "What part have you played in contributing toward this wave of people coming toward Islam?" He noted how all American Muslims like to advertise the fact that "the fastest growing religion in America is Islam," yet it is African Americans who are the ones converting more than any other group. He went further, racializing the issue by framing *da'wa* within black–white residential divides: "If it was a bunch of white folks converting, then we could say, 'Oh, the immigrants are out there living with them. They are giving them *da'wa*.'" Yet "white folks aren't coming into this religion like African Americans," Imam Abdullah stated with invincible conviction. "Are African Americans converting because immigrants have utilized their resources and gone into the inner city building masjids and helping them get jobs and opportunities? No! It's not any of that. It's just straight from Allah, *subhanahu wa ta'ala* [glorified and exalted], guiding the African American to Islam."[40]

Other African American male voices, however, temper Imam Abdullah's criticism as they acknowledge the inner-city *da'wa* work of South Asians. Shakir Lewis, a young Muslim of African American and Anglo background, works at the Reading Room, a *da'wa* center neighboring the Muslim Community Center, which is majority South Asian, on the North Side. Employed by a South Asian immigrant who owns the Reading Room, Shakir recognizes South Asian leaders who specifically encourage work in African American communities. However, he has noticed how South Asians sometimes privilege Anglo converts over African Americans. They believe that "white people will be good for us," meaning that whites will help to enhance the image of Islam in America. But Shakir believes that a *da'wa* movement in white neighborhoods would fail: "I've seen very few white Americans that are receptive to Islam, who don't give you hell for being a Muslim."[41] As for whites who have converted, he insists that they have done very little for establishing Islam in America: "All the real American leaders are either Pakistani or African American, and the greater number are African American: Jamil Al-Amin, Warith Deen Mohammed, Siraj Wahaj, or Malcolm X. Name me any of them who are white."[42] African Americans surpass others, Shakir believes because "they have that fire. They all may not be extremely educated, but their fire usurps the fact that they are not educated." Yet, some South Asians dismiss the value of uneducated African American converts. This disregard becomes especially apparent when South Asians give "less priority" to prison *da'wa* and think that inmates "don't need advanced things about Islam." In the American context, the Islamic concept of *da'wa* takes on meanings of empowerment and restoration for oppressed people. African American Muslims hold this as the highest form of cultural capital and measure how other ethnic Muslims uphold Qur'anic ideals of justice on the basis of the extent to which they pursue *da'wa* "for the people."

INSPIRING CULTURAL CAPITAL IN THE NEXT GENERATION

American Muslim activists hope that *da'wa* "for the people" will increasingly become a shared Islamic ethic among the next generations of American Muslims. One group that has demonstrated a remarkable commitment to developing Muslim youth activism is IMAN (literally translated as "faith"), the Inner City Muslim Action Network. IMAN,[43] established by a group of DePaul University Muslim students in 1995, is known for bringing together Muslims of diverse ethnic backgrounds (African American, Arab, Anglo American, Latino, South Asian, and others) more than any other organization in the Chicago Umma. Aspiring to alleviate poverty and suffering in Chicago's inner city, IMAN offers to the larger non-Muslim community services ranging from after-school tutoring programs, to computer classes, and a free health clinic. Through its vision—"to see the Muslim community in North America work with others to lead the whole of our society beyond innumerable barriers to social justice and human dignity"—IMAN continues the legacy of using Islam to benefit society.

IMAN's executive director is Rami Nashashibi, a Palestinian American in his late twenties. Never before had I met a second-generation immigrant as passionate about African American issues as he. He is equally passionate about exposing race and class prejudice among immigrants. He is greatly admired in the Chicago Umma, especially among young Muslims. His lectures are brilliant and captivating. His persona embodies ethnic movement and dialogue in the Umma and the determination to inspire others to cross borders. Below, I capture his charisma and passion as he delivers a lecture sponsored by the organization "Muslim Youth of Chicago." His audience consists of first- and second-generation immigrant Muslims

Rami talked about IMAN and the organization's work in the inner city, describing substandard housing and educational resources in low-income African American, Latino, and Arab neighborhoods. "Having never had to live in the projects," he referred to his privilege, but he focused more on the blessing to work in an environment with inner-city Muslims who have "suffered the legacy of racism and oppression and have risen to honorable ranks to inspire" more privileged Muslims to use Islam to transform and enhance their lives.[44]

Rami talked about immigrants and their children finding a place in American society, but place in his terms did not mean finding acceptance among the white majority. Rather it meant raising consciousness about poor communities and doing something about it: "We have a place in America, a place not simply black and white, cut and dry, but a place of active work, *da'wa*, getting involved to do something about your environment." He challenged the mostly immigrant Muslim audience to do something about poverty and racism by uniting with Muslims from different race and class backgrounds: "This is your Umma. It is one Umma. Never underestimate a concept that unites beyond ethnicity, class, and race.... It is a lofty ideal but Muslims have championed this concept for 1400 years." American Muslims commonly refer to themselves as an Umma, he noted, but they fail to live up to the concept: "Post 9/11, we have no more time for slogans. We have to be real about this thing."

He confronted his audience about their love for wealth and how it "deludes" and prevents them from helping communities of the poor in America. He reminded them of words of the Prophet Muhammad: "A man came to the Prophet, *sallallahu 'alayhi wa sallam* [may God bless him and grant him peace], and said, 'O Messenger of Allah, show me an act which if I do it, will cause Allah to love me and people to love me.' He, *sallallahu 'alayhi wa sallam,* answered, 'If you distance yourself from the attachment of this world, Allah will love you, and if you prevent yourself from marveling at the possessions of others, you will gain the love of people.'" After suggesting that the pursuit of wealth has cut immigrant Muslims off from the common people, and therefore from "the love of people," he urged his audience to reflect on how the common people have not come to the aid of American Muslims who have suffered discrimination since 9/11. "In the wake of this travesty, we need to reflect on how noble Muslim charities have been shut down with no murmur, no dissent from the people." Muslim charities that aid needy Muslims abroad, particularly refugees of war, were banned by the U.S. government after 9/11, accused of having ties with Al Qaeda. Referring to these Muslim charities, Rami appealed to his audience by addressing issues important to them. Before 9/11, Muslim immigrant dollars heavily supported organizations like Global Relief Foundation, Benevolence International Foundation, and the Holy Land Foundation because they aided poor Muslims "back home." These transnational Umma networks helped to fight injustices against Muslims across the globe.

Rami asked his audience to ask themselves how they expect to gain support from Americans to stop injustices against Muslims around the world when Muslims do nothing for the people here. "We cannot exist in isolation from our communities. When what you do does not affect the daily lives of people, they are not going to weep for you. Why? Because you do not hit them in their hearts." He addressed another central issue for immigrant Muslims: racial profiling post-9/11. He reminded his audience that racial profiling is not new; it represents "a legacy of 300 years for some people," referring to African Americans. Once again, he confronted the self-interests of immigrant Muslims, stating, "and now [all of sudden, because Muslims have become the newest victims of racial profiling,] we are in an uproar." In conclusion, he charged Muslims in America to uphold the values that they claim make Islam the best religion for humanity. "We cannot afford to be a community of hypocrisy. . . . We have to temper self-righteous attitudes and confront racism in our Umma."

AFRICAN AMERICAN MUSLIMS SEEK AUTONOMY IN THE

AMERICAN UMMA

Much of the focus and critique discussed above has been on immigrants and how they contribute to ethnic divides in the American Umma. African American Muslims, however, also perpetuate divides in the American Umma. "We are still kind of wrapped up into our thinking that we don't really need to integrate with immigrant communities," Imam Abdullah said, critiquing his own ethnic group. "We have this ethnic solidarity vibe which is an impediment towards trying to fulfill the objective of Islam, cause this is just one brotherhood."[45] He sees this type of "vibe" especially within communities associated with Imam W.D. Mohammed. African American Muslims not associated with the Imam "are more inclined towards the immigrant communities," whereas WDM Muslims "theoretically say that Muslims are all one," but they do not "push to integrate with the immigrant communities."

The divide between immigrant and WDM Muslims becomes most visible during the annual Labor Day conventions. Every year, the WDM annual Islamic convention runs concurrently with the national convention of ISNA (Islamic Society of North America), an immigrant-majority group. Five times in the last six years, these conferences have occurred in the same city: Chicago. An article in the Associated Press reported on the 2003 conventions: "American blacks and immigrant Muslims are holding separate conventions just three miles apart—underscoring the divide between the two groups that Muslim leaders have been struggling to bridge for years."[46]

"ISNA has tried to have both conventions held under one banner," stated Dr. Ghazi. Mentioning how South Asian Muslims hold Imam W.D. Mohammed and other African American leaders in high regard, he continued, "We prefer that they go and lead us. They *are* our leaders, but there is resistance from the African American community to be a part of the whole."[47] Yet WDM Imams contend that it is Imam W.D. Mohammed who desires a joint convention while South Asian immigrants continue to perpetuate a tone of authority over African Americans. In other words, they have yet to indicate to WDM Imams that they would uphold the mutual respect and shared authority that a joint project would require. "He is waiting on them, I believe," asserted one WDM Imam. "The imam has been ready."[48]

Imam Sultan described immigrant Muslim leaders as generally respecting "our leader," but still underestimating Imam W.D. Mohammed's leadership on how to live Islam in an American context.[49] Imam Sultan questioned how immigrants can "try to be our leaders" when African American Muslims carry a longer cultural legacy in the United States. He argued his point with an analogy: "When I went to Saudi, I didn't try to run nothing over there. What's wrong with them doing the same thing? This is our home."

Ultimately Imam Sultan believes that they can be a mutual resource as both groups negotiate how to live Islam in America. He acknowledges that immigrants have knowledge to offer African American Muslims but wishes that they would offer it with more humility. At the same time, immigrants should more readily ask, "What can I learn from your community?"

But outside the question of whether different ethnic Muslims can show mutual regard, Chicago leaders see the convention divide reflecting natural cultural differences and different interpretations of Islam. "We play music at our conventions and they think of music as *haram*. We have someone playing piano, someone up there singing. Imam Mohammed once said, 'They have their culture and we have ours, but we can unite in prayer together'." Similarly, Dr. Ghazi recognizes "different issues, different problems, different slang and talking" among African American Muslims when he attends the WDM convention. "I don't feel as at home there as when I go to ISNA." Arabs and Bosnians have their own conventions also, and there, he said, "I also feel as an outsider."

Cultural preferences aside, Dr. Ghazi also senses that many African American Muslims believe that they must establish autonomy and independence as part of acquiring self-dignity. "They have lived in America, they have built America, and they have made a tremendous contribution here. They came under slavery, lynching, and discrimination that's still going on. They fought and they won, and we [Muslim immigrants] came when the society is more open. So they don't want to hear us saying, 'Here is a poor person'." I heard African American Muslim voices that reinforced Dr. Ghazi's position, voices that claimed sole accountability for restoring the economy within their communities. They not only recognize the injustice and disadvantage of their location but also the possibility to build strength from within their location. In my interview with Imam Sultan, we talked about Devon Avenue, a South Asian business district in Chicago. Imam Sultan stressed how "we need to do our own work from our own hands," building a comparable African American Muslim business district in Chicago. "You feel more at home with your own. And it's not that we are not one community [meaning one community with non-black Muslims]. It's just that they have worked and they've got their establishment. We need to work to get our establishment."

I heard a range of perspectives about how to achieve economic justice in African American communities. Conversation shifted between philosophies of self-help and the right to economic resources (that is, reparations). The most compelling arguement for self-help I heard was from Dr. Mikal Ramadan, the Imam of the Taqwa Islamic Center, a WDM mosque on Chicago's southwest side. Dr. Ramadan challenged African American Muslims to build, critiquing WDM Muslims for not meeting the challenge of their leaders. "Where's Chicago's strong business thrust that came out of the legacy of the Honorable Elijah Muhammad? Where's Chicago's

continuation of that effort? Where is it for the believers who have pro-
moted Islam in this city for all those years, under the Honorable Elijah
Muhammad and now under the Imam [Imam W. D. Mohammed] in the
past 27 years? What is there in Chicago now to show for all of that?"[50]
African American Muslims in Chicago should have produced more, given
the unique presence of leadership in the city: "We had the Honorable Elijah
Muhammad, we have Jesse Jackson, we have Minister Farrakhan, and we have
Imam Warith Deen Muhammad in this city. We had Malcolm in this city.
The legacy that we have here, I feel a responsibility from that. Shame on us to
have had this, and now to have to say, 'What has been produced from this?'"

Dr. Ramadan does not deny that there has been progress in Chicago's
African American communities. "There's a huge professional, well-off group
[of African Americans] in Chicago," a large percentage of them moving to the
south suburbs. He critiqued the African American middle-class to which he
belongs but not for their choice of residence. "It's natural for people to move.
It's why people move to America, for better opportunities. So I don't fault
them for doing that." Rather the fault comes when they do not go back into
their former communities and "build bridges so that others can do better."
Thus, instead of critiquing professional South Asians, Dr. Ramadan critiques
professional African Americans who have forgotten the struggle of the larger
community. "When you think of the [African American] middle class as a
group, what are they doing? What are their works? What have they
done? What can we point to? What's substantive?" He feels that their work
"is not easily identified." This void, Dr. Ramadan believes, explains Imam
Mohammed's emphasis on collective work. "The Imam has a desire to build
a 'New Africa' community, to have some geography, a place that we can point
to and say, 'That's where they [African American Muslims] are, over there,
and look how well they're doing over there. They're running their own
businesses, their own masjid, their own schools. They're an industrial people.'
That's what the Imam wants."

For Dr. Ramadan, the question remains: how will African American
Muslims arrive at a New Africa? "Are we going to ship in people? Are we
going to bring African American immigrants from out of town to occupy this
place? Who's going to do all these things?" Of course his answer is that
African Americans, Muslims and non-Muslims, must do this, not immigrants. To him, the economic progress of South Asians does not indicate
a responsibility to help build African American communities but rather
a challenge to African Americans to create their own progress. "I say,
'*Alhamdulillah,* go ahead brothers. Do it.' It challenges us. It's like a runner
in a race. You've given us an example and there's no reason why you should
not be able to come to our Devon Street in the South Side. Where are the
African American Muslim streets? So I'm inspired by it and challenged by it.
The key to this is we have not inspired our professional class to do [what
South Asian immigrants have done]."

Dr. Ramadan recognizes the "stronger business and professional class" among South Asian immigrants. They benefit from the "selection process" in immigration policy, and they do not share the "post-traumatic slavery stress" in African American communities. But he refuses to let these disparities become an excuse. "Notwithstanding the challenges, the race is going to go on whether you participate or not. The Imam has said that he wants us to be competitive. We cannot use other folks' feet to stand on, not the White Man's feet, or Pakistanis' or others' to escape doing a job that we as men gotta do for ourselves. This is not [a] racial, radical [position], but [a stance] for individual dignity." When asked if privileged South Asian Muslims have a responsibility to help poor African Americans and others, after a careful, hesitant pause, he responded, "*Zakat*. And if you think any more than that, you become the new beggar."

Even with the Islamic duty to give *Zakat,* he disapproves of the attitude among African American Muslims who feel that others owe them something. "The person who feels, 'They owe us,' is somebody who has lost the race and said, 'I am no longer a competitor. I want you to recognize my disability, and I want you to afford me leeway because I'm deficient.' In a few minutes they will be saying, 'You all over there, y'all owe me. Come back here, you can't leave me'." Dr. Ramadan believes in the open free market. "Just make it fair. Make it close to fair for me, close to fair, and by the help of my God, I'll show you what I can do." With this attitude, Dr. Ramadan believes that African Americans could be the ones providing resources. "Are you asking for charity? Why aren't you giving them charity? Many of them have nothing when they hit these shores, struggling to get a foothold in America. We should be helping them as travelers to the new shores. How does it look? They are hitting the shores, paddling into the mainstream with a fury, and leaving us in the backwater."

As equal competitors, Dr. Ramadan believes that African American and South Asian Muslims can more effectively do cooperative work in the Chicago Umma. He sees African American autonomy as a way of "cooperating but still realizing responsibility." Although Imam Abdullah is more vocal about South Asian responsibility, he also stresses African American responsibility. "African Americans also have to put themselves in a position of independence so that when they come to the table, they come in a position of strength: 'I come with a million, now you come with a million.' If both are on the same level, then you come with dignity."[51]

CLAIMING A COMMON HISTORY

Exposed to the discourses presented above, young American Muslims gradually grow more conscious of ethnic divides in their communities. Challenges remain as they seek to bridge these divides, often because they have yet to develop a substantial context in which to improve intra-Umma relations. One place to start, some suggest, is to claim a common American Muslim history. Conscious of the ways in which our ethnic Muslim histories overlap and sometimes take shape vis-à-vis the other, Muslim youth may develop a greater sense that our future as American Muslims depends on the collective efforts of all ethnic groups in the American Umma to create a fruitful American Muslim experience.

One historical narrative through which African American and South Asian immigrant Muslims can claim a common American Muslim history is the narrative that recounts the beginnings of the Nation of Islam and the legendary Master Farad Muhammad, also known as Fard Muhammad. In July 1930 in Detroit, Master Farad Muhammad began his mission to transform the lives of African Americans. He entered their homes, telling them that he was an Arab from Mecca sent by God to redeem His chosen people.[52] He revealed to his listeners that "African Americans were of the lost, but finally found Nation of Islam, the tribe of Shabazz that had been stolen by the 'Caucasian cave man' or the 'blond blue-eyed devil' and brought as slaves to 'the wilderness of North America.'"[53] Although Master Farad's true identity had been shrouded in mystery, recent historians and experts, including Imam W.D. Mohammed, confirm his South Asian roots.[54]

In 1931, Elijah Poole, a poor migrant from Sandersville, Georgia, attended one of Master Farad's meetings in Detroit. Elijah immediately accepted his teachings and developed a special relationship with Master Farad. After three and a half years of intense instruction and intimacy with Elijah Poole, Master Farad mysteriously departed in 1934. Before his departure, he gave Elijah the name Muhammad.[55] With only a third-grade education, Elijah Muhammad remarkably spread Master Farad's black nationalist teachings to poor blacks in the inner city. It was through this South Asian and African American encounter that America and the world would come to know the most powerful and sustainable black nationalist movement in history, the Nation of Islam.

Growing up as the daughter of former Nation members, I claimed this history. I always enjoyed hearing my parents and community members tell their Nation stories, stories about baking bean pies and whole wheat rolls, about sewing Nation uniforms and bow ties, about selling *Muhammad Speaks* and fish on black street corners, and about hearing the Honorable Elijah Muhammad or Malcolm X speak. What strikes me now is how a South Asian migration narrative, crisscrossing generations of black nationalist aspiration, set in motion some of the most important moments and people in black history. Unexpectedly I discovered American black history reaching back not only to West Africa but also to the Punjab, the birthplace of Master Farad (according to one report),[56] because transmitting the stories of Clara Muhammad,[57] Elijah Muhammad, Malcolm X, and Imam W.D. Mohammed means telling the story of Master Farad.

Unexpectedly, during my research in Chicago, I also discovered South Asian Muslim men sharing in the collective storytelling of NOI history. One of my favorite moments hearing NOI accounts from a South Asian man occurred in an interview with Dr. Ghazi who shared personal stories about his encounter with Elijah Muhammad. To hear stories from a South Asian man that I had imagined only African Americans could tell made me feel as though I had uncovered parts of history that had yet to be told.

It was in 1968 that Dr. Ghazi visited Chicago to attend a Muslim conference. He was determined to see Elijah Muhammad. Dr. Ghazi's friends told him that he was crazy, that he would have to go into a "very dangerous neighborhood." But he told them, "A false prophet doesn't come every day. I just want a glimpse of him." He arrived at Elijah Muhammad's house where he was met by Fruit of Islam body guards. They told him, "The Messenger is speaking to the ladies, come back tomorrow." Dr. Ghazi came back with five other men. All of them were escorted in to sit at the table with Elijah Muhammad. After their meal, Dr. Ghazi asked Elijah Muhammad a series of questions that challenged his teachings. "Islam doesn't distinguish between black and white so how come you say that blacks will receive salvation and whites be condemned?" He recalled Elijah Muhammad's answer: "When God made the dough to make the human being, the devil urinated, and the urine went into part of the dough, so God separated the impure part out to make the white people, and then the black people he made from the pure part.... The nature of the white person is the devil because of those impurities. Any white person who accepts Islam, he acts against his own nature. He can be Muslim, he can be saved, but it's not his nature. The black person, if he is not a Muslim, he's going against his nature. The black person has to be Muslim so I'm bringing the black person back to his true nature."

How often has Dr. Ghazi shared his NOI stories? Did he tell them for the first time because I appeared interested as an African American Muslim researcher? Or had he passed these stories to his daughter as my parents had to me? Whatever the case because of Islam, South Asian migration narratives emerge inextricably linked to African American history, a history that not only African Americans claim and transmit but also South Asians claim. It is a line of transmission threading a narrative through and between ethnic communities.

CONCLUSION

The voices that I have recorded above demonstrate the diversity of the American Umma. Competing with each other at the same time that they complement each other, these voices represent the making of a distinctively American Islam, the pursuit for racial justice reverberating at its core. Committed to the Umma ideal to overcome race and ethnic divides, these voices inherit a time-honored Islamic cultural dialogue at the same that they contribute something new. As Rami articulated most eloquently, "It is a lofty ideal" but one "that Muslims have championed" for over 1,400 years. Their voices do not represent all in the American Umma and certainly not the voices of American Muslim women. Nonetheless, they provide a window onto understanding the role of race and ethnicity in forging a new chapter in Islam's vast cultural history. Challenges remain for the next generation of American Muslims. Yet the greater the challenge, the more celebrated their commitment and creativity in making Islam a benefit for all American people, Muslim and non-Muslims, black, white, and immigrant.

NOTES

1. Marshall G.S. Hodgson, *The Venture of Islam: Conscience and History in a World Civilization*, vol. 1, *The Classical Age of Islam* (Chicago and London: University of Chicago Press, 1974), 75.

2. Bernard Lewis, *Race and Slavery in the Middle East : An Historical Enquiry* (New York: Oxford University Press, 1990), 18.

3. Umar Faruq Abd-Allah, "Islam and the Cultural Imperative," http://www.nawawi.org/downloads/article3.pdf, 2004.

4. Lewis, *Race and Slavery in the Middle East,* 18.

5. Hodgson, *The Venture of Islam,* 78.

6. Malcolm X with the assistance of Alex Haley, *The Autobiography of Malcolm X* (New York: Ballantine Books, 1964), 371.

7. Sylviane A. Diouf, *Servants of Allah : African Muslims Enslaved in the Americas* (New York: New York University Press, 1998), 7.

8. Maria Rosa Menocal, *The Ornament of the World : How Muslims, Jews, and Christians Created a Culture of Tolerance in Medieval Spain* (Boston, Massachusetts: Little, Brown, 2002), 75.

9. Richard Maxwell Eaton, *The Rise of Islam and the Bengal Frontier, 1204–1760,* Comparative Studies on Muslim Societies 17 (Berkeley, California: University of California Press, 1993), 280–281.

10. Richard Eaton states that the emphasis on social equality in Islam is a product of contemporary reform movements. Persian primary sources show that in introducing Islam to Indians, "Muslim intellectuals did not stress the Islamic ideal of social equality as opposed to Hindu caste, but rather Islamic monotheism as opposed to Hindu polytheism." Richard M. Eaton, "Approaches to the Study of Conversion to Islam in India," in *Approaches to Islam in Religious Studies,* ed. R.C. Martin (Tucson, Arizona: The University of Arizona Press, 1985), 110.

11. Claude Andrew Clegg, *An Original Man: The Life and Times of Elijah Muhammad,* 1st ed. (New York: St. Martin's Press, 1997), 282.

12. Author's notes, 13 August 2002.

13. Author's notes, 11 August 2002.

14. Sherman A. Jackson, *Islam and the Blackamerican: Looking toward the Third Resurrection* (New York: Oxford University Press, 2005), 47.

15. A 1999 study put South Asians at 29.3 percent, Arabs at 32.7 percent, and African Americans at 29.9 percent of the U. S. Muslim population. Fareed Nu'man, *The Muslim Population in the United States: A Brief Statement* (Washington, D.C.: American Muslim Council, 1992). A 1992 study put African Americans at 42 percent, Arabs at 12.4 percent, and South Asians at 24.4 percent. Ilyas Ba-Yanus and Moin Siddiqui, *A Report on the Muslim Population in the United States* (New York: Center for American Muslim Research and Information, 1999).

16. Malcolm X, *The Autobiography of Malcolm X*, 371.

17. Dannin describes how corrupt Ahmadiyya leaders exploited their African American followers by raising membership dues so that immigrant leaders could make trips to India and Mecca. Robert Dannin, *Black Pilgrimage to Islam* (Oxford, U.K.; New York: Oxford University Press, 2002), 39. Dannin's is the most thorough work on early African American and immigrant encounters and tensions.

18. The concept of the "ethnic mosque" was theorized in a seminal work in the field of American Muslim studies: Yvonne Yazbeck Haddad and Adair T. Lummis, *Islamic Values in the United States: A Comparative Study* (New York and Oxford: Oxford University Press, 1987).

19. Zaid Shakir, "Islam, the Prophet Muhammad, and Blackness," *Seasons: Semiannual Journal of Zaytuna Institute* 2, no. 2 (2005): 76.

20. Bruce B. Lawrence, *New Faiths, Old Fears: Muslims and Other Asian Immigrants in American Religious Life* (New York: Columbia University Press, 2002), 10.

21. W. E. B. Du Bois, *The Souls of Black Folk,* Bantam classic ed. (New York: Bantam Books, 1989), 1.

22. Lawrence, *New Faiths, Old Fears,* 39.

23. Jane I. Smith, *Islam in America,* Columbia Contemporary American Religion Series (New York: Columbia University Press, 1999), 55.

24. Evelyn Shakir, *Bint Arab: Arab and Arab American Women in the United States* (Westport, Connecticut: Praeger, 1997), 81.

25. Vijay Prashad, *The Karma of Brown Folk* (Minneapolis, Minnesota: University of Minnesota Press, 2000), 94.

26. See Dannin, *Black Pilgrimage to Islam.*

27. Adam Cohen and Elizabeth Taylor, *American Pharaoh: Mayor Richard J. Daley: His Battle for Chicago and the Nation,* 1st ed. (Boston, Massachusetts: Little, Brown, 2000), 11–12.

28. Ibid., 184.

29. I invented the acronym WDM to designate the community and followers of Imam W. D. Mohammed. During the period of my research in Chicago in 2002, his community was named the Muslim American Society (MAS). In the fall of 2002, Imam W. D. Mohammed changed the name from Muslim American Society because an immigrant group also used this name, and he wanted to distinguish his community. He replaced MAS with ASM, the American Society of Muslims. In September 2003, Imam Mohammed resigned from the ASM to commit to other service and business projects and founded TMC, The Mosque Cares, based in Chicago. Because of the constant name changes and the unclear status of the ASM and its relationship

with TMC, I refer to communities and Muslims who affiliate with Imam Mohammed as WDM for consistency. Also, African American Muslims both under and outside of his leadership often refer to his following as Warith Deen Muslims. Previous names include World Community of Islam in the West, the American Muslim Mission, and the Muslim American Society.

30. Prashad, *The Karma of Brown Folk,* 101–102.

31. Abdullah Madyun, interview with author, 29 May 2002, Chicago, Illinois.

32. Wali Bashir (pseudonym), interview with author, 10 July 2002, Chicago, Illinois.

33. Abdullah Madyun, interview with author, 29 May 2002, Chicago, Illinois.

34. Abidullah Ghazi, interview with author, 26 August 2002, Skokie, Illinois.

35. "Abidullah and Tasneema Ghazi," http://www.chicagohistory.org/global/ghazi.html. While this quotation is taken from an online interview with the Ghazis, Dr. Tasneema also talked excitedly about the book in a personal interview with the author.

36. Talat Sultan, interview with author, 9 September 2002, Villa Park, Illinois.

37. Sultan Salahuddin, interview with author, 10 May 2002, Chicago, Illinois.

38. "Invite (all) to the way of your Lord with wisdom and beautiful preaching; and argue with them in ways that are best and most gracious: for your Lord knows best who have strayed from His Path and who receive guidance" (Qur'an 16:125).

39. Farid Esack, *Qur'an, Liberation and Pluralism: An Islamic Perspective of Interreligious Solidarity against Oppression* (Oxford, U.K.; Rockport, Massachusetts: Oneworld, 1997), 103.

40. Madyun, interview with author.

41. Shakir Lewis (pseudonym), interview with author, 11 June 2002, Chicago, Illinois.

42. Shakir ignores Hamza Yusuf, a prominent Anglo American Muslim leader, because he disagrees with Yusuf's ideology.

43. For more on IMAN, especially its formation, see Garbi Schmidt, *Islam in Urban America: Sunni Muslims in Chicago* (Philadelphia, Pennsylvania: Temple University Press, 2004).

44. Author's notes, 6 April 2002.

45. Madyun, interview with author.

46. *The Herald Sun* (Durham, North Carolina), 28 August 2003.

47. Ghazi, interview with author.

48. Author's notes, 17 June 2002.

49. Salahuddin, interview with author.

50. Mikal Ramadan, interview with author, 6 September 2002, Chicago.

51. Abdullah Madyun, interview with author, 29 May 2002, Chicago, Illinois.

52. C. Eric Lincoln, the foremost authority on the Nation of Islam, discusses the import of the timing of W. D. Fard's appearance in the 1930s, the period of both the Great Depression and the Great Migration, as it relates to the Nation of Islam's early success among the underprivileged classes. C. Eric Lincoln, *The Black Muslims in America,* 3rd ed. (Grand Rapids, Michigan: William B. Eerdmans Publishing Company and Trenton: Africa World Press, Inc., 1994), 11–15, 20–21.

53.   Mattias Gardell, *In the Name of Elijah Muhammad: Louis Farrakhan and the Nation of Islam* (Durham, North Carolina: Duke University Press, 1996), 51.

54.   The *Muslim Journal,* the official WDM newspaper, has published articles on both Master Farad (d. 1992) and his wife (d. 2004). Photos of both also confirm their South Asian identity. See *Muslim Journal,* 7 March 2003, and *Muslim Journal,* 19 March 2004. A number of theories have surfaced regarding the identity of Master Farad Muhammad. See Karl Evanzz, *The Messenger: The Rise and Fall of Elijah Muhammad* (New York: Pantheon Books, 1999), 397–417; Gardell, *In the Name of Elijah Muhammad: Louis Farrakhan and the Nation of Islam,* 50–54; Clifton E. Marsh, *From Black Muslims to Muslims: The Transition From Separatism to Islam, 1930–1980* (Metuchen, New Jersey: Scarecrow Press, 1984), 106–107; Richard Brent Turner, *Islam in the African-American Experience* (Bloomington and Indianapolis, Indiana: Indiana University Press, 1997), 163–166. Evanzz gives the most thorough account. The ethnic identity he ascribes to Farad Muhammad conforms with Imam W.D. Mohammed's description of him as South Asian.

55.   For more information on the development of Elijah Muhammad's relationship with W.D. Farad Muhammad, see Hatim Sahib, "The Nation of Islam" (Ph.D. diss., University of Chicago, 1951), 65–98, 118–150, and Clegg, *An Original Man,* 14–40.

56.   *Muslim Journal,* 7 March 2003.

57.   Clara Mohammed was the first to hear Master Farad speak and then she inspired her husband Elijah Muhammad to attend his next meeting. See Rosetta E. Ross, *Witnessing and Testifying: Black Women, Religion, and Civil Rights* (Minneapolis, Minnesota: Fortress Press, 2003), 145.

4

ISLAM IN THE AFRICAN AMERICAN EXPERIENCE

•

Aminah Beverly McCloud

Everywhere in America, especially since September 11, 2001, eyes have been focused on Islam and Muslims in the United States. Those "eyes" have also been trained to see Islam as a religion "over there" and its adherents, immigrants and their children, as its representatives. Political pundits, journalists, members of the press and Congress, teachers, and heads of corporations—almost every courier of information—understand that Islam is a Middle Eastern religion that threatens America and that immigrants have brought a toxin to American shores. African American Muslims are not a part of this conversation. In response to media claims about Islam and Muslims, many immigrant Muslims and their children deny the assertions of violence but embrace the claim of ownership of American Islam. African American Muslims have not been invited to this conversation either. An astute observer might surmise that there are two—an American Islam in process and a Muslim-world Islam in reformation on American soil.

That significant numbers of black Americans could believe in and be fiercely committed to a religious worldview other than the tradition of Christianity that was forced on them is still hard to fathom for many non-Muslims. As a result of this incredulity, everything about Islam in the black community has been reduced to a protest against racism in one form or another. There are even black historians of black American religious history who state in the twenty-first century that they have little if any knowledge of either black Judaism or Islam. This is incredible but true. The black American Muslim experience continues to be one of a quest for ownership of Islam. This process can be seen in many ways and with several ideological stances. However it is understood, it must be made clear that each position/stance furthers the process toward ownership and is honorable and legitimate. This is critical to any understanding of the black Muslim experience. Readers may have noted that I continue to use "black" rather than African American. Here I am not taking a stand in the name game played on Americans of African descent, rather I am making one small attempt to undo the denigration done after a scholar, C. Eric Lincoln, named members of the Nation of Islam by their color rather than their commitment.[1] While Lincoln's naming was innocent, it opened the door for many researchers to assert that the adjective "black" meant that this community was not really Muslim, and thus, every time Islam is mentioned in the community of blacks it is really not Islam but something else such as a protest movement. My choice is to bring voice to these communities of faith and sometimes of protest. However, faith comes first and protest is at best a handmaiden that helps erase the pejorative connotation when it is used.

Thus far, many researchers have overlooked the fact of one process following another in the overarching representation of black people. Until a couple of decades ago, texts on slave religion omitted almost any mention of Islam and African Muslim slaves. One could almost say that many of these texts tended to glorify the transition from an anonymous, quite generic African traditional religion to a blended Christianity. Researchers of Islam in America have cast commitments to Islam in black America as a either "protest" or "failed Christianity" rather than as an alternative religious experience. Black identity formation is still in process in the twenty-first century. The depictions of black faith commitments in the Christian community should not be taken as normative, even though they have dominated for decades. Many minority cultures around the world face physical erasure. African American Muslims face an intellectual erasure of their history and thus the erasure of their contributions to what is quintessentially theirs, an American Islam.

A particular construction of African American Islam is in play today. I cannot put enough emphasis on the fact that this representation is that of an irrational, illogical ascription to an alternative epistemology as a way to protest American racism. This chapter makes no claims to deconstruct previous representations nor will it attempt to offer more than the skeleton of one potentially viable alternative for describing some of the components of this process. Stated another way, what is intended here is to present one potentially plausible description of the ideas of black Muslims in the process of coming to an ownership of Islam.

I want to look at the function of the discourses of the experiences of black Muslims in an environment in which power relations emerged from chattel slavery. In this story discursive practices are interwoven with social practices. We know that knowledge is governed by power relations, whether the context is slavery or religion. Any factual account of the African American Muslim experience must begin with the arrival of African Muslims kidnapped from their countries. While we must begin here, I am most interested in the possible retention of Islam and the possibility of a more direct link to Islam in the twentieth century. Because this is my concern, I am willing to give some credence to evidence provided of such links. I ask the reader to have patience with my position as it is only a suggestion of an alternate narrative.

THE AFRICAN MUSLIM EXPERIENCE OF THE NEW WORLD

Slavery was the common experience of Africans in seventeenth- and eighteenth-century America. It was a journey from a condition of *sui juris* to chattel slavery in a space of warfare and capture, along with a journey of horror aboard slave ships, beginning a life in enduring struggle to retrieve and resurrect a stolen humanity out of loss. Information on African Muslim slaves is provided mainly by three researchers, Allan D. Austin, Sylvaine A. Diouf, and Michael Gomez.[2] All argue several points: (1) the number of Muslims among the African slaves was significant—numbering in the thousands at least, (2) Muslim slaves were adamant about preserving their religion, (3) some aspects of slave life previously identified as emerging solely from African traditional religions mixing with Christianity are in fact heavily influenced by Islam, (4) Islam itself was a major influence in the process of social stratification within the larger African American society, (5) many of the particulars of Islam, including practices and language were lost over time.

Using these points of fact as markers, we can explore the contours of the experiences of African Muslim slaves, which were intimately tied to those of other African slaves on many levels but are also unique in many ways. African slaves knew slavery as a condition that could be manipulated or not, acquiesced to or not, and removed or not. American chattel slavery was a new kind of slavery in which not only were there no negotiations, but also there were religious justifications regarding skin color. American slaves were deliberately deprived of their heritage, their ability to maintain families, and the outward practice of their religion. This erasure of any claim to humanity gave birth to an ongoing restlessness in the black American community well into the twenty-first century. One significant theme of this restlessness is the segregation of Muslims from other parts of the African American community.

Islamic beliefs and practices, while nurturing the soul of the believer, also separate the individual from those who believe differently on some basic levels. But in the black American community this is a persistent tension as black families are multireligious. For example, modesty is a hallmark of Islam, and thus, the American model of providing few clothes for slaves was untenable for Muslim men who had to be covered from navel to knee. Their response was to wear multiple layers of clothing. Muslims also did not eat pork, the staple of the slave diet. This forced some creativity regarding diets that consisted of other meats such as birds and vegetables and strategic fasting. Prayer in Islam does not require much space or ceremony and is a solitary affair further separating Muslims from their companions in servitude. That these slaves were Muslim is a fact affirmed by the presence of Islam in the regions of their origins.[3]

Simultaneous to the period of the transatlantic slave trade (sixteenth- early twentieth centuries) was a period of the spread of Islam in sub-Saharan Africa. Wolof, Mandinka, Sereer, and Fula from Senegambia; Temne, Mende, and Kissi from upper Gambia; and Bights were some of the better-known tribes whose members were kidnapped or sold into slavery. These tribes comprised most of the African Muslim slaves, but not all of them. Many were schooled in Islam and Arabic as shown in Austin's book, which is a collection of Muslim slave autobiographies.[4] These narratives not only demonstrate literacy but also reveal previous intellectual work. Some of these slaves had been Qur'anic teachers and leaders in their communities. Perhaps here we need to make a note of slavery in the Islamic understanding before engaging in a discussion of the presence of Muslims in antebellum America.

Slavery, in all of its varieties, was definitely a known entity before the coming of Islam and most concretely in Qur'anic references to the subject. The Qur'an presumes the existence of slavery and urges manumission and decent treatment. It does not ascribe slavery to the category of God-ascribed inferiority nor does it assign the condition to either the race or the color of a person's skin. Muslim history in various regions bears witness to slavery as a condition that emerges as a result of war, famine, and kidnapping. Yet, slaves could work off their enslavement, have their families buy them out of the situation, or, of course, just remain slaves for generations, as occurred in Mauritania. Slavery in the old world was not designed to strip people of their essence as human beings. This is the understanding of slavery that African Muslim slaves brought with them on the transatlantic passage. Some of the autobiographies that Austin provides attest to this understanding.[5] Additionally, other slaves were aware of the Muslim presence. Gomez asserts: "...many West Africans practicing indigenous religions were nonetheless familiar with and influenced by Islam, having been exposed to Muslim dress, dietary laws, and overall conduct."[6]

Some evidence of Muslims in the slave population is found in runaway slave notices.

> For example, New Orleans' *Moniteur de la Louisiane* called for the return of a runaway from the Hausa nation ("nation Aoussa") in October, 1807. The next month, an auction by Patton and Mossy featured four men and six women "from the Congo, Mandinga, and Hausa nations, in the country eight months, from 11 to 22 years of age."[7]

Interestingly, these researchers (Gomez, Diouf, and Austin) present a challenge to the history that most of us have learned.[8] In many schools, when slavery is taught at all, it is said that slavery totally abolished tribal connections and that slave masters were clever enough to separate tribal members from each other. Gomez asserts that "the Anglophone slavehold-ing society regularly distinguished between the various ethnicities within the African community."[9] These distinctions are seen in runaway notices and further in the retention of original names. Many Muslim slaves apparently managed to keep portions of their names, which though anglicized are recognizable—Bullaly (Bilali), Bocarrey (Bukhari), or Moosa. The evidence produced by these scholars points to an oversight that results in a partial erasure of our knowledge of this population of slaves. Though there is much speculation about possible reasons for the oversight, the end result is confusion about the reemergence of Muslim communities in the twentieth century.

There are also significant data on the active presence of African Muslim slaves through the 1930s from the Works Progress Administration. This group was commissioned to interview ex-slaves and their families. What they discovered was the retention of many of the basics of Islamic practice such as (the possession of) prayer rugs, prayer beads, veiling, head coverings, Qur'ans, knowledge of dietary laws, and ritualized daily prayer. This treasure trove of retentions provides a reasonable backdrop for black Muslim communities in the twentieth century. African Muslim slaves brought Islam to America and though names and rituals were sometimes lost, Islam as a worldview was not. The separation of Muslims from others and their practices is a theme that runs throughout the presence of Islam in America along with Arabic naming and ritual practices.

BLACK AMERICAN ISLAM

The "lost-found nation" of Muslims is in many ways an apt description of much of the experience of black Americans who transition to Islam. In many ways, the experience of black American Muslims in the United States fits this label that Elijah Muhammad assigned to his followers in the Nation of Islam.

Histories of black American Islam usually begin by categorizing black Muslim communities as "failed Christian communities" whose major focus is Black Nationalism or that these communities concocted something called Islam out of disenchantment with Christianity. Either version attempts to erase any legitimate claim to Islam by labeling it "black." Yet despite the lack of historical references until relatively recently, urban rumor has for almost a century carried tales of African Muslim slaves, voluminous slave retentions of Islamic customs, and a much more varied history than that found in African American history texts.[10] Due to omission (and perhaps commission on the part of some) the story of Islam in black America has rarely been presented as standing on its own. Instead, researchers have painted a picture of "racial hatred," seedy characters, and intrigue and have expressed incredulity at claims of authenticity. But this is not the end of the damage. The story of African American Muslims has centered on the story of The Nation of Islam, which has been told as a "failed Christian" story with Black nationalism as its core mission. Scholars have ridiculed the NOI creation story, their desire to separate from whites who kill them, and their demands for freedom and justice.

Other communities of black Muslims (those not in the Nation of Islam) have been relegated to the margins of history or have been ignored, thus affirming a popular though erroneous thesis that all black Americans come to Islam through the Nation of Islam. The majority of black Americans who transition to Islam do so with deliberation and belief in Islam's central tenets and the viability of its disciplines. This brief treatment of black American Islam will offer a different way of understanding the various communities that make a note of a legacy rather than a protest.

By 1700, there were over 50,000 escaped and freed Africans in America.[11] This would lead any investigator to speculate that their progeny multiplied and were able to continue some of their preslavery traditions. Historical records discovered to date do not give a breakdown of country of origin of these free Africans, so we do not know who these men and women were. We do know, however, that not all Africans in America were enslaved. And, while history has focused on eastern seaboard Africans, they lived across the Mississippi in the West too.[12] What we do know from the runaway slave notices is that some slaves were Muslims. We also know that southern states such as South Carolina, Georgia, and Louisiana had the most numerous plantations and ports of entry. We also affirm that two of the most prominent African American communities to affiliate themselves with Islam in the twentieth century were led by men—Noble Drew Ali and Elijah Mohammad—who came from these regions. I would like to suggest a scenario that is woven around the vagaries of life in the early twentieth century for African Americans and the continuing transmission of knowledge about Islam in the first three decades of the twentieth century. Gomez asserts:

> It is therefore with the children and grandchildren of African-born Muslims that the questions concerning the resilience of Islam take on significance. While it cannot be established with certainty that the progeny were Muslim, the Islamic heritage was certainly there, so individuals bore Muslim names and retained a keen memory of the religious practices of their ancestors.[13]

History texts recount President Abraham Lincoln's freeing of the slaves in 1863, but reality teaches us that in some regions, it took quite some time for that information to be passed along. This lack of communication is remembered in Juneteenth celebrations and is noted in several texts.[14] In a brief review of early black legal history we find that under the Republican Party, Congress passed the 14th Amendment (as part of Reconstruction) in 1866 (ratified in 1868), which extended citizenship to blacks and protected their civil rights. In 1870 the states ratified the 15th Amendment, which prohibited the denial of the right to vote on the basis of race. In 1875 Congress passed the Civil Rights Act, which forbade racial discrimination in "inns, public conveyances on land or water, theaters and other places of amusement." Between 1861 and 1865, 20 black men were elected to the U.S. House of Representatives and the U.S. Senate. Southern Democrats, aided by Northern businessmen, ended this period of unusual collaboration with terror. Democrats and groups like the Klu Klux Klan began a reign of terror to keep blacks from the polls and public places and to reinstate a racial divide that lasted for the next 80 years.

This ending of any collaboration between blacks and whites is the beginning of what is known in American history as the "Jim Crow" era, which lasted from 1865 to 1964 with the passage of the nation's second Civil Rights Act. Jim Crow was the system of laws and customs that enforced racial segregation and discrimination throughout the United States. Jim Crow was the name of a character in minstrel shows (in which white performers in blackface used African American stereotypes in their songs and dances); it is not clear how the term came to describe American segregation and discrimination.[15] Nevertheless, this term was widely used and its horrors were widely applied. While this was the social and political arena in which all blacks functioned, there arose the difficulty of what to name the ex-slave population. Rather than just calling them by their names—John or Moosa—whites decided that they must be further distinguished. The first nonderogatory appellation was "African," which was used in the early eighteenth century. This was changed to slave and/or Negro in the 1830s, changed to "colored" after World War II, changed back to "Negro" in the 1950s and early 1960s, changed to "blacks" in late 1960s and early 1970s, changed to "Afro-Americans" in the late 1970s and early 1980s, and finally, though still contentious, changed in the late 1980s to a list of terms— "blacks, blackAmerican or Blackamerican, and African American." Needless to say, naming and identity are still in question as is the relationship of black Americans to Africa.

Gomez postulates that there were several connections between ex-slave communities that continued to practice or at least know something about Islam and leaders of nascent Muslim communities in the twentieth century.[16] This assertion is plausible because there must have been some contact either through cultural lore, and actual meetings of descendents or immigrants. Leaders like Noble Drew Ali and Elijah Muhammad have been continually discredited Islamically in a number of ways, the most consistent of which has been that they had no connection to any Islamic retention. Gomez's *Black Crescent* recounts the stories of the Melungeon and the Ishmaelite communities who lived in overlapping territories and whose self-descriptions linked them to an Islamic past. The Ishmaelite community seems to have had the most direct connection to Islam and certainly, through its members, connects a past Islamic experience to Noble Drew Ali.[17]

I see these broad stances as a tripod of Islamic beginnings in the twentieth century. Other researchers could of course use another rubric but let us explore this paradigm for a moment. This tripod is anchored in an ownership of the Islamic worldview, which can be believed in and practiced with integrity and certainty, and is not dependent on the cultures of other Muslims. By this I mean that there is an inherent legacy, the explanation of a present condition, and a viable way of life in the present and in the future that permit black American Muslims to be independent actors. One leg of the tripod issues from a mixture of available philosophies/worldviews with some form of Islam at the center that black people could know and use to understand their present conditions and give structure to their future. One example (and it is only an example of an approach to embracing Islam) is Noble Drew Ali's Moorish Science Temple founded in either 1912 or 1913 and based on the Holy Qur'an of the Moorish Science Temple, Circle Seven. This thin text is an obvious mixture of materials but also possibly a deliberate one.

The religiously fertile era of American history that Noble Drew Ali lived in is filled with contenders for the souls of black folks. In this scenario, let us speculate that even though there are traces of millenarianism, the beginnings of the Social Gospel Movement, and an ever increasing number of itinerant preachers in this movement, Ali was deliberate in his choice of affiliation with Islam rather than Christianity or some other religion.

Ali's synthesis of various approaches to a God-centered universe along with a guide to ethical living and self-sufficiency is one type of milestone in the development of Islam in black America. This version of Islam chose to root itself in a tragic yet rich cultural legacy. The use of the term ''Moor'' was not as fanciful as many researchers would have us believe. Perhaps its real origin lay in the recountings of Melungeons and Ishmaelites and that some African slaves did indeed come through coastal towns in Morocco. I would question the insistence on ''unknowable origins'' rather than ascribing to an actor the ability to choose. If we are able to see the Moorish Science Temple as playing its role in an ongoing process that places its roots in a slave past, then we can see a different set of correlates in the development of black American Islam.

Ali's formulation of the ethos of his community—love, truth, peace, freedom, and justice—is directly in line with Islamic values. To assist in surviving the psychological ramifications of namelessness, Ali provided a nationality and a way to build a self-sufficient community in Jim Crow America. In this community first names were retained while surnames, most clearly and directly tied to slavery, were changed to Bey or El. Rather than affirming a name based on skin color or the texture of hair, he planted his community's heritage in Morocco—a place that could be identified on a map. The inheritance of the general contours of Islam coming from slave roots resulted in the retention of some basic elements without the particulars. For example, Moors prayed facing east three times daily and in a different posture from other Muslims. In addition, they fasted and congregated on Friday and Sunday. Given the nature of work for black Americans in the first decades of the twentieth century, to take off for a few hours on Friday would have guaranteed dismissal. When the South Asian Ahmadiyyah Muslim Movement brought English translations of the Qur'an to the black community, they studied it, adding its contents to their store of knowledge.

The community of the Moorish Science Temple focused its attention on reclaiming and rebuilding family life on the basis of on an Islamic worldview. They spread up and down the East Coast and into the Midwest attracting, it is reported, some 30,000 members over time.

As one leg of a tripod, this community represents one way of claiming a legacy and also one impulse in black America toward owning Islam. As one modern expression of Islam torn from its roots of learning and community, the Moorish Science Temple represents one picture of a reemergent Islam that had to survive in the midst of terror, chaos, and dehumanization. Black people at the turn of the century were herded into colonies and did not have the freedom of movement that many immigrants had. St. Clair Drake and Horace R. Cayton, in the classic study *Black Metropolis* assert:

> The distinctive thing about the Black Belt is that while other such "colonies" tend to break up with the passage of time, the Negro area becomes increasingly more concentrated.[18]

World War I ushered in a period of austerity and depression. Blacks who had migrated to the Midwest and the Northeast for a "taste of freedom" or at least an absence of reminders of slavery were met with Jim Crow, lynching, and outright hatred. Colony living produced communities of people who relied on each other for survival. Blacks from various regions in the south converged and naturally shared knowledge and experiences.

By the 1920s, Muslims from the Ottoman Empire had emigrated to the United States and white Americans such as Muhammad Alexander Russell Webb had embraced Islam. Muslim immigrants, though not in significant numbers, were in the United States. Among these Muslim immigrants were members of the Ahmadiyyah Movement from India. They were sent as missionaries to America. Though their intended targets for conversion were white Americans, they found their most ardent audience in the black community. This transmission of Islam as a "foreign" worldview forms the second leg of the tripod. This culturally encrusted Islamic worldview cannot be owned; however, it can be rented or leased.

Immigrants and their children own Islam as a worldview that has been in their countries for centuries. Quite naturally, most are only minimally aware of cultural accretions and have little consciousness of the process that gave them ownership of their religion. Also quite natural is their tendency to see a different manifestation of Islam as illegitimate. While looking closely at the process of ownership of Islam in the Muslim world we can easily see that in modern and contemporary times, much of the ownership was formed in colonial and postcolonial contexts, which gave a special hue to the process. Though they are themselves in a reformation period, immigrants bring their various Islams as the only Islam, often divorced from Islam's basic tenets. What this has meant for many black Muslims is that they can never own Islam as they are often castigated about what they do not know. A first-generation immigrant Muslim child can correct a black third-generation Muslim adult on matters of faith and practice.

Islam, as a foreign religion, is by no means unconnected to the first leg of Islam in the black Muslim experience. Struts (binding straps) connect all the legs and permit individuals and sometimes whole communities to move back and forth from one type of Islam to another even though the legs have roots in different histories. For example, some members of the Moorish Science Temple moved to the Ahmadiyyah community and for varying reasons moved again to other communities or back to the Moorish Science Temple. One prominent reason seems to stem from their search for a world-view that they could own.

Islam as a foreign worldview brought culturally constructed Islam to America with its food, dress, behaviors, and names. The Ahmadis introduced an English translation of the Qur'an, books on worship and practice, Hadith literature, books singling out women as an issue, and books on names. In this leg of the tripod, Islam was only tangentially a slave legacy. Rather, Islam in America was portrayed as the direct result of the efforts of immigrant Muslims and their knowledge. Black Muslims influenced by the Ahmadiyyah opened the First Pittsburgh Mosque in the 1920s where there were formal classes in Arabic and classes on how to pray, the requirements of fasting, and so on. Blacks were encouraged to abandon their names for Arabic and/ or Indian names. This leg of the tripod served to separate and isolate black Muslims from both the black community and the Moorish Science Temple, whose efforts at self-sufficiency were rooted in the black community.

However, the Ahmadiyyah Movement opened the world to its black members. Black Muslims ate, prayed, and studied with South Asian Muslims, and sometimes even married them. Many South Asians came to share the horrors of Jim Crow America even though a few claimed Aryan roots as recorded in immigration records. Readers should note that I am not postulating that Muslims in this leg of the tripod did not see Islam as a heritage. What I am saying is that the impetus of this stance is located in a Muslim-world Islam, which has little concern for that legacy.

Whereas the first leg was perhaps self-limiting because of its roots in slavery and new interpretation (to handling new circumstances or new information), the second leg's cultural core demanded constant reinterpretation if only for the reason of immigration to a non-Muslim land. This reinterpretation, however, could only come from the original cultural core—South Asia but not from its *mawali* (clients)—blacks in the United States. Though blacks can admire the cultures of other Muslims, dress like them, and eat what they eat, each culture in the world that has embraced Islam has done so on its own terms. In this leg there is tension between different cultural needs—an almost irreconcilable dissonance. Muslim-world Islam has little, if any, real understanding of the process of transitioning into Islam from another religious background. Immigrants hail from largely homogenous countries and few have members of other faiths in their families. More important, they did not have the basic, though profound, challenges of changing their worldview in a largely Christian land. There is little, if any, compassion for the tensions that arise from this lack of understanding and refusal to recognize cultural needs.

However, in addition to opening minds to the world outside of America, Muslim-world Islam also opened up the world inside the United States. Precisely because this leg of Islam in America is not rooted in a slave legacy, it attracts whites. Thus, it permits on a limited basis, a rare shared experience between black and white Americans in pursuit of a different way of understanding the world. The presence of this leg in the black community influences not just the other two legs but also the black community in general.

Occupying this second leg of Islam in America, as mentioned previously, is psychologically precarious, as a significant part of the new worldview is not easily accessible nor freely given. In the early twentieth century, learning Arabic was difficult, especially for a black community struggling with English literacy. South Asian cultural norms that are presented as Islamic norms are significantly different from black community norms—women serve, men demand; the worldview has a well-defined hierarchy that is as much, if not more, Indian than it is Islamic. Most African American Muslims who have embraced this stance in the process of owning Islam have never achieved mastery of immigrant Islam. Thus, tensions persist and in many ways presage the existence of the third leg of the tripod.

The third leg of the tripod has as its core a notion of black participation in the creation of the world and its subsequent history. Many scholars have attributed this to a fanciful imagination or a piece of mental pathology directly related to slavery. I must admit that it is no more fanciful than the constructed myth of white superiority. Ownership of Islam in this leg usually begins with a creation story of a glorious and just black nation. This nation either created or encountered whites who in time came to enslave them.[19] The ideology of ownership is built around reclaiming those aspects of culture which lead to recreating a nation with Islam as its worldview. Rebuilding the family is also a priority but is not an end unto itself. Families are rebuilt as a necessity of nation building. Rather than the degradation of slavery, the myth of a glorious past is used as a catalyst for a viable present. The Nation of Islam is one model of this type of Islam.

This third leg is as critical to the process of owning Islam as the other two. Here the fight for freedom, justice, and equality is extended to critique the Umma (the world community of believers) and to continue a legacy of self-sufficiency in the attempt to further the process of ownership of Islam. Both Muslims and non-Muslims have refused to recognize this process and have tried unsuccessfully to relegate the cultural focus that sits at the core of this thought to the margins. I find this intriguing since the historical trajectory of this stance mimics so much in Muslim history.

Stories that are positive—filled with heroic deeds, compassionate efforts, gifted people, and loving families—are, as we all know, necessary for the psychological health of any community. Many of these stories are orally transmitted within communities. However, those communities that choose to develop into empires such as Rome and the United States, spread their stories beyond their normal boundaries to those they enslave, thus giving them a suprareality. It seems to me that modern scholarship, known for its lack of an *imaginaire*, has relegated the stories of non-Western peoples to legend—such stories can be entertaining but are definitely without merit. Given this set of circumstances, the stories of subjected/enslaved people are portrayed as fanciful myths whose appearance renders anything and anyone associated with them illegitimate. Stories that challenge power are ridiculed as myth and black Muslims who plant their roots in this leg often have to deal with such ridicule.

I am using this metaphorical tripod as an attempt to provide an alternative entry into the African American Muslim experience. If we now look at the trajectory of this process in the latter half of the twentieth century, we can perhaps note some other, often omitted factors.

Black Muslims from the first and third legs were the first Muslims on record who demanded pork-free diets in government spaces, in this case in the prison system in the 1950s. They also forced the recognition of Arabic and other unusual surnames such as Bey, El, and X in that same system. Black Muslims in the second and third legs brought Islam into the public school system in the early 1960s as they refused coeducational gym classes, refused to pledge allegiance to the flag, and demanded pork-free lunches for their children. These Muslims brought Islam into the professions around the same time that they joined the Civil Rights Movement and assisted in opening the door for the immigration of Muslim immigrants.[20] Muslims in the second leg were offered scholarships to study overseas in Egypt and Saudi Arabia. Muslims in the first and second legs found their greatest challenges in the American black community which was continually under siege.

These challenges and tensions have only increased in the African American Muslim community and in the immigrant community. Rather than under-standing the process any culture embraces when becoming Muslim, many immigrants and most Americans have relegated black Islam to a corner labeled "antiwhite." There is still at this point little ownership of Islam as many in the black community have either spent much of their effort retrieving Islam from its immigrant presentation or have given themselves over wholly to a cultural Islam. However, this is to be expected in a process that has existed in Islamic history in every culture from Morocco to China.[21]

The African American Muslim experience is still very much in process although it is clearly an American religion. Islam will still be present in America, even if every immigrant takes his or her children back to the ancestral home. The events of September 11, 2001, mark another phase of the process just as did the events at the end of 1979 with the Iranian hostage crisis. Neither African American Christians nor Muslims are players on the world stage and, thus, are not consulted by their white brethren about any of the events of the world. This new phase, however, is beginning to mark a pulling away from the second immigrant leg. Muslims are also not joining the ranks of either the first or the third legs and thus probably are a lot closer in the process of gaining ownership of Islam. In this current phase, black Muslims are questioning not only the immigrant claim to superior Islamic knowledge but also the history of contemporary issues in the Muslim world and how that history relates to their own domestic concerns.

Black Muslims have long noted the presence of Arab Muslim liquor stores in their communities selling both liquor and illegal drugs to the community. They have also taken note of the hypocrisy of representation when on television they see immigrant Muslims smiling for the cameras with government representatives and others who they denigrate in Friday sermons. They realize that immigrant Muslims and their children have little investment in urban ghettos to which black Muslims are committed to change. The black Muslim family life is filled with Jews, Christians, Buddhists, atheists, and agnostics from every part of the ideological spectrum. Some have sided with the Palestinian side of the Israeli-Palestinian issue and have struggled simultaneously with the racism of Palestinians toward black people. The limits of the immigrant capacity to embrace the pluralism or interreligious dialogue that black Muslims advocate is another challenge. The struggle for ownership continues.

This ownership will necessarily include white Muslims, Latino Muslims, immigrant Muslims and their children, but the power relationships will change. Muslim-world Islam will be vetoed by all and what will emerge will reflect a fully Western Islamic expression. Those who fear giving up power will be ignored. The various legs of black American Islam and their primary concerns will syncretize into a dynamic expression of Islam that will display marks of the struggle for ownership.

The slave roots of American Islam will be recognized as will stories that relate the tales of conquest, and the extraordinary feats of heroes along with their tragedies. Hopefully, historians will provide more connections that strengthen the heritage of blacks in Islam, which will combine with the presence of Muslims whose heritage comes from the Muslim world. We must all stay tuned for the next phase. The intent of this chapter was simply to present another lens from which to view a varied and rich process in the present.

NOTES

1. See C. Eric Lincoln, *The Black Muslims of America,* 3rd ed. (Wm. B. Eerdmans Publishing Company, 1994).

2. See Michael Gomez, *Exchanging Our Country Marks: The Transformation of African Identities in the Colonial and Antebellum South* (Chapel Hill, North Carolina: University of North Carolina Press, 1998); Sylviane A. Diouf, *Servants of Allah: African Muslims Enslaved in the Americas* (New York: New York University Press, 1998); Allan D. Austin, ed., *African Muslims in Antebellum America: A Sourcebook, Critical Studies on Black Life and Culture,* vol. 5 (New York: Taylor & Francis, 1983).

3. Playwright, Julie Dash portrayed this image well in her movie, "Daughters of the Dusk." Celebrated filmmaker Julie Dash came under the public's eye in 1991 when her feature film "Daughters of the Dust" won for best cinematography at the Sundance Film Festival.

4. Austin, *African Muslims in Antebellum America.*

5. Ibid.

6. Gomez, *Exchanging Our Country Marks,* 68.

7. Ibid.

8. See the film *Amistad* for a visual portrayal of some aspects of the journey and the deliberate efforts made by slaves to not forget who they were.

9. Gomez, *Exchanging Our Country Marks,* 68.

10. See Adib Rashad's *The History of Islam and Black Nationalism in the Americas* (Beltsville, Maryland: Writers', Inc., 1991).

11. See James Oliver and Lois E. Horton, *In Hope of Liberty: Culture, Community, and Protest Among Northern Free Blacks, 1700–1860* (New York: Oxford University Press, 1998); Kimberly S. Hanger, *Bounded Lives, Bounded Places: Free Black Society in Colonial New Orleans, 1769–1803* (Durham, North Carolina, and London: Duke University Press, 1997).

12. For accounts see: *The Treaty of 1866 of the Five Civilized Tribes,* Claudia Saunt's *Black White Indian: Race and The Unmaking of a Family;* Tiya Miles' *The Ties that Bind: The Story of an Afro-Cherokee Family in Slavery and Freedom; Black Seminoles* by Kenneth Wiggins; and *Africans and Seminoles,* by Daniel F. Littlefield.

13. Gomez, *Exchanging Our Country Marks,* 81.

14. Ralph Ellison and Charles Johnson, *Juneteenth: A Novel* (Vintage International, 2000); Angela Leeper, *Juneteenth: A Day to Celebrate Freedom from Slavery* (Enslow Publishers, 2004).

15. Microsoft Encarta Reference Library 2003. © 1993–2002 Microsoft Corporation.

16. Michael Gomez, *Black Cresent: The Experience and Legacy of African Muslims in the Americas* (Cambridge, 2005), 185–214.

17. Ibid.

18. St. Clair Drake and Horace R. Cayton, *Black Metropolis,* vol. 1 (New York: Harcourt, Brace & World, Inc., 1970), 174.

19. See Schuyler's *Black Empire* as one example.

20. This statement does not negate the fact that the United States recruited significant numbers of students and professionals from the Muslim world to fill jobs that Americans were not educated enough to fill in the numbers needed. It adds a perspective.

21. See Dru C. Gladney, *Muslim Chinese: Ethnic Nationalism in the People's Republic* (Cambridge, Massachusetts and London, U.K.: Harvard University Press, 1991); and Jamil M. Abun-Nasr, *A History of the Maghrib in the Islamic Period* (Cambridge, U.K.: Cambridge University Press, 1987).

5

ISLAM AND GENDER JUSTICE

—————————— • ——————————

Ziba Mir-Hosseini

For a century or more, one of the "hottest" areas of debate among Muslims has been the "status of women in Islam."[1] The debate is embedded in the history of polemics between Islam and the West, and the anticolonial and nationalist discourses of the first half of the twentieth century. With the rise of political Islam in the second half of the century, and the Islamist political slogan of "Return to Shari'a," the debate took a new turn and acquired a new dimension. It became part of a larger intellectual and political struggle among Muslims between two understandings of their religion and two ways of reading its sacred texts. One is an absolutist, dogmatic and patriarchal Islam that makes little concession to contemporary realities and the aspirations of Muslims. The other is a democratic, pluralist and rights-based Islam that is making room for these realities and values, including gender equality.

In this chapter I trace the political and textual genealogy of this "rights-based" Islam, and explore its potential for addressing the gender inequalities embedded in prevailing interpretations of the Shari'a. I ask two prime questions: If justice and equality are intrinsic values in Islam, as many contemporary Muslim jurists claim and Muslims believe, why are women treated as second-class citizens in Islamic jurisprudential texts? If equality has become inherent to conceptions of justice in modern times, how can it be reflected in the laws that define the rights of men and women and regulate relations between them in contemporary Muslim societies?

I begin with a note on my own position and conceptual background; then proceed to an examination of notions of gender rights as constructed in classical jurisprudential texts and as debated, deconstructed and reconstructed in the vast twentieth-century literature on "Women in Islam." I end by outlining an emerging gender discourse that is feminist in its aspirations and demands and Islamic in its language and sources of legitimacy.

CONCEPTUAL BACKGROUND

I approach these questions not only as a trained legal anthropologist but also as a believing Muslim woman who needs to make sense of her faith and her religious tradition.[2] I believe in the justice of Islam and place my analysis within the tradition of Islamic legal thought by invoking two crucial distinctions in that tradition. These distinctions are made by all Muslim jurists and have been upheld in all schools of Islamic law, but have been distorted and obscured in modern times, when modern nation-states have created uniform legal systems and selectively reformed and codified elements of Islamic family law, and when a new political Islam has emerged that uses Shari'a as an ideology.

The first distinction is between Shari'a, revealed law, and *fiqh*, the science of Islamic jurisprudence.[3] This distinction underlies the emergence of various schools of Islamic law and within them a multiplicity of positions and opinions. Shari'a, literally "the way," in Muslim belief is the totality of God's will as revealed to the Prophet Muhammad. *Fiqh*, jurisprudence, literally "understanding," is the process of human endeavor to discern and extract legal rules from the sacred sources of Islam: that is, the Qur'an and the Sunna (the practice of the Prophet, as contained in *Hadith*, Traditions). In other words, while the Shari'a is sacred, eternal, and universal, *fiqh* is human and—like any other system of jurisprudence—mundane, temporal and local.

It is essential to stress this distinction and its epistemological and political ramifications. *Fiqh* is often mistakenly equated with Shari'a, not only in popular Muslim discourses but also by specialists and politicians, and often with ideological intent: that is, what Islamists and others commonly assert to be a "Shari'a mandate" (hence divine and infallible), is in fact the result of *fiqh*, juristic speculation and extrapolation (hence human and fallible). *Fiqh* texts, which are patriarchal in both spirit and form, are frequently invoked as a means to silence and frustrate Muslims' search for this-worldly justice—to which legal justice and equality in law are intrinsic. I contend that patriarchal interpretations of the Shari'a can and must be challenged at the level of *fiqh*, which is nothing more than the human understanding of the divine will— what we are able to understand of the Shari'a in this world at the legal level. In short, it is the distinction between Shari'a and *fiqh* that enables me—as a believing Muslim—to argue for gender justice within the framework of my faith.[4] Throughout this chapter, then, the Shari'a (as contained in the Qur'an and the Prophetic Traditions) is understood as a transcendental ideal that embodies the justice of Islam and the spirit of the Qur'anic revelations; while *fiqh* includes not only the vast corpus of jurisprudential texts but also the positive laws and rulings that Muslim jurists claim to be rooted in the sacred texts.

My second distinction, which I also take from the Islamic legal tradition, is that between the two main categories of legal rulings (*ahkam*): between *'ibadat* (ritual/spiritual acts) and *mu'amalat* (social/contractual acts).

Rulings in the first category, *'ibadat,* regulate relations between God and the believer, where jurists contend there is limited scope for rationalization, explanation, and change, since they pertain to the spiritual realm and divine mysteries. This is not the case with *mu'amalat,* which regulate relations among humans and remain open to rational considerations and social forces. Since human affairs are in constant change and evolution, there is always a need for new rulings, based on new interpretations of the sacred texts, in line with the changing realities of time and place. This is the very rationale for *ijtihad* (literally, "self-exertion," "endeavor"), which is the jurist's method of finding solutions to new issues in the light of the guidance of revelation.[5]

Most rulings concerning women and gender relations belong to the realm of *mu'amalat,* which means that Muslim jurists consider them social and contractual matters, and thus open to rational considerations. My objective in this chapter is to show that discriminatory rulings on women are the products of juristic reasoning and sociocultural assumptions about the nature of relations between men and women. In other words, they are "man-made" juristic constructs, which are shaped by, reflect, and change with the reality on the ground.

There are three interconnected elements to my argument. First, assumptions about gender in Islam—as in any other religion—are necessarily social/cultural constructions, thus historically changing and subject to negotiation. The idea of gender equality is among the "newly created issues" (*masa'il mustahdatha*), to use a *fiqh* idiom; that it is to say, it was not an issue that concerned premodern jurists as it was not part of their social experience. Second, Islamic legal traditions do not contain one concept of gender, but rather a variety of inconsistent concepts, each resting on different theological, juristic, social and sexual assumptions and theories. This, in part, reflects a tension in Islam's sacred texts between ethical egalitarianism as an essential part of its message and the patriarchal context in which this message was unfolded and implemented.[6] This tension enables both proponents and opponents of gender equality to claim textual legitimacy for their respective positions and gender ideologies.[7] Third, gender rights as constructed in classical *fiqh*—and reproduced in dominant contemporary discourses—are neither tenable under contemporary conditions nor defensible on Islamic grounds; not only are they contrary to the egalitarian spirit of Islam, but they are also now being used to deny women justice and dignified choices in life.

GENDER IN CLASSICAL *FIQH*

In classical *fiqh* texts, gender inequality is taken for granted, a priori, as a principle. It reflects the world in which their authors lived, a world in which inequality between men and women was the natural order of things, the only way to regulate relations between them. Biology is destiny: a woman is created to bear and rear children; this is her primary role and her most important contribution to society. The notion of "women's rights"—as we mean it today—has no place and little relevance in the world of these texts.

The classical *fiqh* notion of gender is encapsulated in two sets of rulings: those that define marriage and divorce, on the one hand, and women's covering and seclusion, on the other hand. Not only do they contain the core of the patriarchal logic, but they should be seen as two sides of the same coin: they deny women choice or voice, restraining them in the public domain by veiling and seclusion, and subjugating them in private through family law. These rulings legitimated and institutionalized the control and subjugation of women throughout the history of the Muslim world, and continue to do so in modern times. In these matters, the various *fiqh* schools all share the same inner logic and patriarchal conception. If they differ, it is in the manner and extent to which they have translated this conception into legal rules.[8] An examination of these rulings can tell us something of the genesis of gender inequality in the Islamic legal tradition, which, as we shall see, is rooted in the social, cultural, and political conditions within which Islam's sacred texts were understood and turned into law.

Marriage: Union or Dominion?

Marriage, as defined by classical jurists, is a contract of exchange whose prime purpose is to render sexual relations between a man and a woman licit. Patterned after the contract of sale, which served as a model for most contracts in Islamic jurisprudence, it has three essential elements: the offer (*ijab*) by the woman or her guardian (*wali*), the acceptance (*qabul*) by the man, and the payment of dower (*mahr*), a sum of money or any valuable that the husband pays or undertakes to pay to the bride before or after consummation.

The marriage contract is called *'aqd al-nikah* (literally "contract of coitus"). In discussing its legal structure and effects, classical jurists often used the analogy of the contract of sale and alluded to parallels between the status of wives and female slaves, to whose sexual services husbands/owners were entitled, and who were deprived of freedom of movement. Ghazali, the great twelfth-century Muslim theologian, in his monumental work *Revival of the Religious Sciences,* devoted a book to marriage, where he echoed the prevalent view of his time:

> It is enough to say that marriage is a kind of slavery, for a wife is a slave to her husband. She owes her husband absolute obedience in whatever he may demand of her, where she herself is concerned, as long as no sin is involved.[9]

Likewise, Muhaqqiq al-Hilli, the renowned thirteenth-century Shi'a jurist, wrote:

Marriage etymologically is uniting one thing with another thing; it is also said to mean coitus and to mean sexual intercourse…it has been said that it is a contract whose object is that of dominion over the vagina, without the right of its possession. It has also been said that it is a verbal contract that first establishes the right to sexual intercourse, that is to say: it is not like buying a female slave when the man acquires the right of intercourse as a consequence of the possession of the slave.[10]

Khalil ibn Ishaq, the prominent fourteenth-century Maliki jurist, was equally explicit when it came to dower and its function in marriage:

When a woman marries, she sells a part of her person. In the market one buys merchandise, in marriage the husband buys the genital *arvum mulieris*. As in any other bargain and sale, only useful and ritually clean objects may be given in dower.[11]

I am not suggesting that classical jurists conceptualized marriage as either a sale or slavery.[12] Certainly there were significant differences and disagreements about this among the schools, and debates within each school, with legal and practical implications.[13] Even statements such as those quoted above distinguish between the right of access to the woman's sexual and reproductive faculties (which her husband acquires) and the right over her person (which he does not). Rather, what I want to communicate is that the logic of sale underlies the *fiqh*-based conception of marriage and defines the parameters of laws and practices, where a woman's sexuality, if not her person, becomes a commodity, an object of exchange. It is also this logic, as we shall see, that defines the rights and duties of each spouse in marriage and in Ghazali's words makes marriage like slavery for women.

Aware of possible misunderstandings, classical jurists were careful to stress that marriage resembles sale only in form, not in spirit, and drew a clear line between free and slave women in terms of rights and status.[14] They spoke of marriage as a religious duty, lauded its religious merit, and enumerated the ethical injunctions that the contract entailed for the spouses. But these ethical injunctions were eclipsed by those elements in the contract that concerned the exchange and sanctioned men's control over women's sexuality. What jurists defined as the prime "purposes of marriage" separated the legal from the moral in marriage; their consensus held these purposes to be: the gratification of sexual needs, procreation, and the preservation of morality.[15] Whatever served or followed from these purposes became compulsory duties incumbent on each spouse, which the jurists discussed under *ahkam al-zawaj* (laws of matrimony). The rest, though still morally incumbent, remained legally unenforceable and were left to the conscience of individuals.

For each party, the contract entails a set of defined rights and obligations, some with moral sanction and others with legal force. Those with legal force revolve around the twin themes of sexual access and compensation, embodied in the two concepts *tamkin* (access; also *ta'a,* obedience) and *nafaqa* (maintenance). *Tamkin,* defined in terms of sexual submission, is a man's right and thus a woman's duty; whereas *nafaqa,* defined as shelter, food, and clothing, is a woman's right and a man's duty. A woman becomes entitled to *nafaqa* only after consummation of the marriage, and she loses her claim if she is in a state of *nushuz* (disobedience). There is no matrimonial regime: the husband is the sole owner of the matrimonial resources, and the wife remains the possessor of her dower and whatever she brings to or earns during the marriage. She has no legal duty to do housework and is entitled to demand wages if she does. The procreation of children is the only area the spouses share, but even here a wife is not legally required to suckle her child and can demand compensation if she does.

Among the default rights of the husband is his power to control his wife's movements and her "excess piety." She needs his permission to leave the house, to take up employment, or to engage in fasting or forms of worship other than what is obligatory (that is, the fast of Ramadan). Such acts may infringe on the husband's right of "unhampered sexual access."

A man can enter up to four marriages at a time,[16] and can terminate each contract at will: he needs neither grounds for termination nor the consent or presence of his wife. Legally speaking, *talaq,* repudiation of the wife, is a unilateral act (*iqa'*), which acquires legal effect by the declaration of the husband. Likewise, a woman cannot be released without her husband's consent, although she can secure her release through offering him inducements, by means of *khul',* often referred to as "divorce by mutual consent." As defined by classical jurists, *khul'* is a separation claimed by the wife as a result of her extreme "reluctance" (*karahiyya*) toward her husband, and the essential element is the payment of compensation (*'iwad*) to the husband in return for her release. This can be the return of the dower, or any other form of compensation. Unlike *talaq, khul'* is not a unilateral but a bilateral act, as it cannot take legal effect without the consent of the husband. If the wife fails to secure his consent, then her only recourse is the intervention of the court and the judge's power either to compel the husband to pronounce *talaq* or to pronounce it on his behalf.

Veiling or Seclusion?

Unlike rulings on marriage, classical *fiqh* texts contain little on the dress code for women. The prominence of veiling regulations in Islamic discourses is a recent phenomenon, dating to the nineteenth-century Muslim encounter with colonial powers. It was then that we see the emergence of a new genre of literature in which the veil acquires a civilizational dimension and becomes both a marker of Muslim identity and an element of faith.

Classical texts—at least those that set out rulings or what we can call "positive law"—address the issue of dress for both men and women under "covering" (*sitr*), in the Book of Prayer, among the rules for covering the body during prayers, and in the Book of Marriage, among the rules that govern a man's "gaze" at a woman prior to marriage.[17]

The rules are minimal, but clear-cut: during prayer, both men and women must cover their *'awra*, their pudenda; for men, this is the area between the knees and the navel, but for women it means all of the body apart from hands, feet, and face. A man may not look at the uncovered body of an unrelated woman, but a woman may look at an unrelated man. The ban can be removed when a man wants to contract a marriage and needs to inspect the woman he is marrying. The rules concerning covering during prayer are discussed under *'ibadat* (ritual/worship acts), while rules of "looking/gaze" fall under *mu'amalat* (social/contractual acts).

There are also related rules in classical *fiqh* for segregation (banning any kind of interaction between unrelated men and women) and seclusion (restricting women's access to public space). They are based on two juristic constructs: the first is the one that defines all of a woman's body as *'awra*, pudenda, a zone of shame, which must be covered both during prayers (before God) and in public (before men); the second defines women's presence in public as a source of *fitna*, chaos, a threat to the social order.

These are, in a nutshell, the classical *fiqh* rulings on marriage and covering, which many today claim to be immutable and divinely ordained. The model of family and gender relations that they contain has come to be equated with the Shari'a notion of gender and is thereby invoked to legitimate patriarchy on religious grounds.

These rulings have been the subject of intense debate in the literature and among Muslims since the early twentieth century. But before outlining the contours of this debate and the positions taken, there are important questions to be asked: How far does this notion of gender reflect the principle of justice that is inherent in the Shari'a? Why and how does classical *fiqh* define marriage and covering in such a way that they deprive women of free will, confine them to the home and make them subject to male authority? These questions become even more crucial if we accept—as I do—the sincerity of the classical jurists' claim that they derive their ideal model of gender relations from the sacred sources of Islam: the Qur'an and the Sunna.

JURISTIC FOUNDATIONS OF GENDER INEQUALITY

There are two sets of related answers. The first set is ideological and political, and has to do with the strong patriarchal ethos that informed the classical jurists' readings of the sacred texts, and eventually led to the exclusion of women from the production of religious knowledge and their inability to have their voices heard and their interests reflected in law. The second is more epistemological and concerns the ways in which social norms and gender ideologies were sanctified, and then turned into fixed entities in *fiqh*. That is, rather than considering practices relating to the "status of women" or "gender" as social issues, the classical jurists treated them as the subject matter of religious rulings (*mawadi' al-ahkam*). Let me elaborate.

The model of gender constructed by classical *fiqh* is grounded in the patriarchal ideology of pre-Islamic Arabia, which continued into the Islamic era, though in a modified form. There is an extensive debate on this in the literature, which I will not enter here.[18] Suffice it to say that the classical jurists' construction of the marriage contract was based on one type of marriage agreement prevalent in pre-Islamic Arabia. Known as "marriage of dominion," this agreement closely resembled a sale through which a woman became the property of her husband. As John Esposito notes, it "produced a situation in which a woman was subjugated by males, her father, brother or close male relatives when she was virgin and her husband when she became a wife. As a matter of custom, she came to be regarded as little more than a piece of property."[19]

Many passages in the Qur'an condemn women's subjugation, affirm the principle of equality, and aim to reform existing practices in that direction.[20] Yet the classical jurists bypassed the spirit of these Qur'anic verses and reproduced women's subjugation—though in a mitigated form. What they did was to modify the pre-Islamic "marriage of dominion" so as to accommodate the Qur'anic call for reforms to enhance women's rights and protect them in marriage. Women became parties to, not subjects of, the contract and recipients of the dower or marriage gift. Likewise, by modifying the regulations on polygamy and divorce, the jurists curtailed men's scope of dominion over women in the contract, without altering the essence of the contract or freeing women from the authority of men—whether fathers or husbands. Fathers or guardians retained the right to contract the marriages of their daughters or female wards. While some schools gave a woman the option to annul a contract involving her after she reached puberty, in others the guardian was invested with the power of compulsion (*jabr*) that is, he could compel his daughter or ward into a marriage without her consent. This went against the very essence of Qur'anic reforms aimed at abolishing the pre-Islamic practice of coercing women into unwanted marriages.

The same applies to rulings on covering. Compulsory covering and seclusion for women have no basis in the Qur'an, and the *hadith* (Traditions) that some claim to support them have been also forcefully questioned.[21] As recent research has illustrated, the rulings on covering emerged from political and economic developments during the Abbasid period, and were shaped by the presence in public of slave girls and the commodification of their beauty and sexuality. It was then that rulings on covering during prayer, which come under *'ibadat* (ritual acts), were extended to the realm of *mu'amalat* (social acts), but only for free women, to distinguish them from slave women, who were forbidden to cover their hair in public.[22] It was in this context that compulsory covering came about, premised on the imperative of seclusion. The covering or confinement of free women was seen as the best means of protecting them in and from a public space that was deemed contaminated by the presence and sexuality of slave women. Previously, in particular during the era of the Prophet, there was little constraint on women's access to public space and their participation in the political and social affairs of the nascent Muslim community. Women took the oath of allegiance to the Prophet as men did; they fought in wars and prayed alongside men in mosques.

But the further we move from the time of revelation, the more women's voices are marginalized and excluded from political life. By the time the *fiqh* schools emerged, women were already excluded from the production of religious knowledge and their critical faculties were denigrated enough to make their concerns irrelevant to lawmaking processes.[23] Women were among transmitters of prophetic *hadith*, yet, as Sachedina reminds us:

> It is remarkable that even when women transmitters of hadith were admitted in the *'ilm al-rijal* ("Science dealing with the scrutiny of the reports"), and... even when their narratives were recognized as valid documentation for deducing various rulings, they were not participants in the intellectual process that produced the prejudicial rulings encroaching upon the personal status of women. More importantly, the revelatory text, regardless of its being extracted from the Quran or the Sunna, was casuistically extrapolated in order to disprove a woman's intellectual and emotional capacities to formulate independent decisions that would have been sensitive and more accurate in estimating her radically different life experience.[24]

This takes us to the second set of mechanisms by which the egalitarian message of sacred texts was bypassed: the sanctification of patriarchy through *fiqh* rulings that ensured that women remained subordinate to men. In producing these rulings, classical jurists based their theological arguments on a number of philosophical, metaphysical, social and legal assumptions and theories, which in turn shaped their readings of the sacred texts. Salient philosophical/metaphysical assumptions that underline *fiqh* rulings on gender include the following: "women are created of and for men," "God made men superior to women," "women are defective in reason and faith." While these assumptions are not substantiated in the Qur'an—as recent scholarship has shown[25]—they became the main implicit theological assumptions determining how jurists discerned legal rules from the sacred texts.

The moral and social rationale for subjugation is found in the theory of difference in male and female sexuality, which goes as follows: God gave women greater sexual desire than men, but this is mitigated by two innate factors, men's *ghayra* (sexual honour and jealousy) and women's *haya* (modesty and shyness). What jurists concluded from this theory was that women's sexuality, if left uncontrolled by men, runs havoc and is a threat to social order. Feminist scholarship on Islam gives vivid accounts of the working of this theory in medieval legal and erotic texts, and its impact on women's lives in contemporary Muslim societies.[26] Women's *haya* and men's *ghayra,* seen as innate qualities defining femininity and masculinity, in this way became tools for controlling women and the rationale for their exclusion from public life and their subjugation in marriage.[27] The sale contract, as already discussed, provided the juristic basis for women's subjugation in marriage, and the legal construction of women's bodies as *'awra* (pudenda) and of their sexuality as a source of *fitna* (chaos) removed them from public space, and thus from political life in Muslim societies.

I am not suggesting that there was a conspiracy among classical jurists to undermine women, or that they deliberately sought to ignore the voice of revelation. Rather I argue that, in discerning the terms of the Shari'a, and in reading the sacred texts, these jurists were guided by their outlook, the social and political realities of their age, and a set of legal, social, and gender assumptions and theories that reflected the state of knowledge and the normative values and patriarchal institutions of their time. These rulings— which were all the product of either juristic speculations or social norms and practices—came to be treated by successive generations as though they were immutable, as part of the Shari'a. This is what Sachedina calls the crisis of epistemology in the traditional evaluation of the Islamic legal heritage.

> The Muslim jurists, by exercise of their rational faculty to its utmost degree, recorded their reactions to the experiences of the community: *they created, rather than discovered, God's law.* What they created was a literary expression of their aspirations, their consensual interests, and their achievements; what they provided for Islamic society was an ideal, a symbol, a conscience, and a principle of order and identity.[28]

In this way, what were essentially time-bound phenomena were turned into juridical principles of permanent validity, and rulings on "women's status" and gender relations became fixed entities in *fiqh.* This was achieved, first by assimilating social norms into Shari'a ideals, second by classifying rulings pertaining to family and gender relations under the category of *mu'amalat* (social/private contracts, where the rulings are subject to rationalization and change) yet treating them as though they belonged to the category of *'ibadat* (acts of worship where the rulings are immutable and not open to rational discussion). In short, rathar than embodying the principles of justice and equity inherent in Shari'a ideals, the *fiqh* rulings on marriage and covering must be seen as literal expressions of the classical jurists' "ideals" of family and gender relations.

The patriarchal ideology of the time, as reflected in the *fiqh* texts, was so entrenched and so much part of the reality of classical jurists' lives that it left little room for debate and criticism from within. Most women of their time had little difficulty in accepting these rulings, as they reflected the way in which their roles were defined, and more importantly they had no choice but to submit. Women who did not accept such rulings could find some legal leeway, such as the insertion of stipulations in the marriage contract, to enable them to acquire a measure of autonomy in marriage.[29] Women with property and financial means were certainly in a better position—which points to another paradox in the construction of women's rights. While classical jurists recognized women's financial autonomy and right to control property, they denied women the right to control their own bodies or to participate in public life by their rulings on marriage and seclusion.

CONTEMPORARY GENDER DISCOURSES

With the rise of Western hegemony over the Muslim world and the spread of secular systems of education in the nineteenth century, the ideological hold of *fiqh* on social reality began to wane. At the same time, the colonial encounter turned the "status of women in Islam" into a contested issue, a symbolic political battleground between the forces of traditionalism and modernity, a situation that has continued ever since.

New gender discourses emerged and were aired in the vast literature on "women in Islam" that dates from the start of the twentieth century. Produced by religious publishing houses in both Muslim and Western countries, this literature is available (much of it now on the Internet) in a variety of languages, including English. It consists of highly varied texts, ranging from outright polemic to sound scholarship.[30] In terms of their gender perspective, these texts fall into two broad genres. The first, which comprises the majority of available texts and views, I term "Neo-Traditionalist." Its advocates uphold classical *fiqh* rulings and reject legal equality between the sexes as an imported "Western" concept that has no place in an Islamic worldview. Instead they argue for "complementarity of rights," sometimes called "gender equity" or "balance," which as we shall see, is a modified version of the classical *fiqh* gender discourse. The second genre, which I call "Reformist," argues for gender equality on all fronts. It emerged in the last two decades of the twentieth century, is still in the process of formation, and still constitutes only a small part of the literature.

Gender Balance: Inequality Redefined

The roots of the first new discourse can be traced to the nineteenth century and the Muslim world's encounter with Western colonial powers, but its impact is linked with the emergence of modern nation-states in the twentieth century and the creation of modern legal systems inspired by Western models. It was during this period that, in many nation-states, classical *fiqh* rulings on family and gender issues were selectively reformed, codified, and gradually grafted onto a unified legal system.[31] The impetus for reform varied from one country to another. Each Muslim country has followed one of three paths: abandoning Islamic law in all spheres and replacing it with Western-inspired codes (Turkey is the only example); preserving and attempting to apply Islamic law in all spheres of law (the Gulf countries); or retaining and codifying Islamic law with respect to personal status law concerning family and inheritance, while abandoning it in other areas of law (the large majority of Muslim countries).

Those governments that codified family law introduced reforms through procedural rules, which in most cases left the substance of the classical *fiqh* rulings unchanged. Tunisia was the exception, incorporating the principle of gender equity into its 1956 family law.[32]

In the process of adaptation, family law moved from being the concern of private scholars operating within a particular *fiqh* school to the legislative assembly of a particular nation-state. Statute books took the place of *fiqh* manuals and texts in regulating the legal status of women in society. This not only led to the creation of a hybrid family law that is neither *fiqh* nor Western but also a new gender discourse that is neither entirely traditionalist nor modern. Though commonly termed Islamic Modernism, I suggest that "Neo-Traditionalism" is a more apt term for this discourse, as it shares the classical jurists' basic understanding of gender. Where it differs is that, unlike classical jurists, advocates of the new discourse are able to impose their notions through the machinery of a modern nation-state. This has given patriarchal interpretations of the Shari'a a new force and unprecedented powers.[33]

The Neo-Traditionalist gender discourse is found not only in the legal codes of Muslim countries but also in a new type of texts that, unlike classical *fiqh* texts, neither are necessarily produced by jurists nor are strictly legal in their reasoning and arguments, which makes them more accessible to the general public. Largely written by men—at least until recently—the overt aims of these texts are to shed new light on the status of women in Islam and to clarify what they see as "misunderstandings about the law of Islam." The main themes through which the authors of these texts address the issue of gender relations and define a range of positions are women's covering, marriage and divorce laws, and women's right to education and employment. Despite their variety and diverse cultural origins, what these authors have in common is an oppositional stance and a defensive or apologetic tone: oppositional, because their concern is to resist change and suppress voices of dissent from inside, which they see as "invasion of Western and alien values"; apologetic, because by going back to classical *fiqh* and upholding its rulings they inadvertently expose—and have to defend—its inherent and anachronistic gender biases.

Unwilling to accept that the aspiration for gender equality is not just an imported (Western) concept but part of modern realities, these authors often find themselves in a paradoxical position. On the one hand, they adopt an uncritical approach to classical *fiqh* constructions of marriage and gender relations, and on the other hand, they are aware of, and sensitive to, criticisms of patriarchal bias; they begin their texts with abstract and general statements such as "Islam affirms the basic equality of men and women," "Islam grants women all their rights," and "Islam protects and honours women." It is common to find a single text in which the author accepts the principle of gender equality on one issue (usually on women's education and employment, where classical *fiqh* is more or less silent), but rejects it on matters related to covering and family law (where classical *fiqh* is strident).

Neo-Traditionalist texts lack the legal coherence and the sense of real conviction that imbue classical *fiqh* texts. Keen to distance themselves from overtly patriarchal language and concepts, their authors keep silent on the juristic theories and theological and other assumptions that underlie these rulings in classical *fiqh* texts. For instance, they ignore the parallels in the legal structures of the contracts of marriage and sale, and views such as those of Ghazali (quoted earlier), which see marriage as a type of enslavement for women. Such views are so repugnant to modern sensibilities and values, so alien from the experience of marriage among contemporary Muslims, that no defender of *fiqh* rulings can acknowledge them. Yet the patriarchal logic and the notion of sale, implicit in their texts, come to the surface when they resort to legal arguments, as in the following explanation of why women cannot have equal rights to divorce:

> If she were to be given this right, she would grow over-bold and easily violate the men's rights. It is evident that if a person buys something with money, he tries to keep it as long as he can. He parts with it only when he cannot help it. But when a thing is purchased by one individual, and the right to cast it away is given to another, there is little hope that the latter will protect the interest of the buyer, who invested the money. Investing man with the right to divorce amounts to the protection of his legitimate rights. This is also checks the growth of the divorce rate.[34]

A large majority of the Neo-Traditionalist texts place the focus on the ethical and moral rules that marriage entails for each spouse, drawing attention to those Qur'anic verses and *hadith* that affirm the essential equality of the sexes. Yet, they fail to mention that these ethical rules, in effect, carry no legal sanction, nor do they offer any suggestions as to how they can be translated into legal imperatives. Likewise, while rejecting *fiqh* rulings on seclusion, Neo-Traditionalist texts defend the principle of gender segregation and speak of *hijab* (covering) as a religious duty that mandates a woman to cover her hair and body (with the exception of face and hands) when in the presence of unrelated men and in public. A good example is Jamal Badawi's booklet, *Gender Equity in Islam: Basic Principles.* Marriage, Badawi states, "is about peace, love and compassion, not just the satisfaction of men's needs," but then he goes on to reproduce all the *fiqh* rulings on marriage and divorce almost verbatim.[35] In line with other texts in this genre, Badawi is content with simply outlining what he calls "normative teachings of Islam," glosses over male dominance, and imputes the injustices that women suffer in marriage and society to what he calls "diverse cultural practices among Muslims." He seems to be unaware that many of the *fiqh* rulings that he reproduces negate the "basic principles" of "gender equity" that he claims as Islamic in his booklet.

Two texts of this genre that offer a new rationalization and defense of the classical *fiqh* rulings on marriage and covering and contain a theory of gender rights, are Murteza Mutahhari's *System of Women's Rights in Islam* and Maulana Abul A'la Maududi's *Purdah and the Status of Women in Islam.*[36] Both authors were Islamic ideologues, and their writings, rooted in anticolonial and anti-Western discourses, have become seminal texts for Islamist groups and movements. Writing in Urdu in the 1930s, in the context of pre-partition India, Maududi's adamant rejection and condemnation of modernity and liberal values have made him more appealing to radical Islamists. For him, the problem with Muslims is that they have abandoned their own way of life and adopted secular (that is, Western and to some extent Hindu) values that have corrupted them and are destroying their civilization. The solution he offers is an "Islamic state" with the power and inclination to enforce the Islamic way of life, where women's seclusion and control by men are foundational. Mutahhari, writing in Persian in 1960s Iran as part of the religious opposition to the Shah's secularizing policies, is less adamant in his opposition to modernity and less overtly patriarchal: he is more popular with moderate Islamist groups.

These two texts differ in style, language, and sophistication, but they follow the same line of argument, based on the same premises of the "naturalness" of laws in Islam and the "innate difference" between men and women. These two premises become the pillars of a new defense of gender inequality, which goes as follows: though men and women are created equal and are equal in the eyes of God, the roles assigned to them in creation are different, and *fiqh* rules reflect this difference. Differences in rights and duties do not mean inequality or injustice; if correctly understood, they are the very essence of justice. This is so, they argue, because these rulings not only reflect the Shari'a, the divine blueprint for society, but they are also in line with "human nature" (*fitra*) and take into consideration the biological and psychological differences between the sexes.

This new defense has, ironically, further accentuated the internal contradictions and anachronisms in classical *fiqh* rulings. For example, if, as the classical theory of sexuality holds, women's sexual desire is greater than men's, and if laws in Islam work with, not against, the grain of nature, then how can they allow men but not women to contract more than one marriage at a time? Surely God would not give women greater sexual desire, and then allow men to be the polygamists and make covering obligatory for women? The Neo-Traditionalists resolve such contradictions by modifying the classical theory of sexuality, to eliminate its conflict with the newly advocated theory of the naturalness of *fiqh*-based law. Women's sexuality, thus, is now explained as passive and responsive, and men's as active and aggressive—a theory that has indeed little precedent in classical texts.[37]

It is important to note here that, in arguing for such a theory of sexuality, both Maududi and Mutahhari do not quote Islamic texts but Western psychological and sociological studies. Their readings of these—now long outdated—sources are quite selective, and they cite as "scientific evidence" only those that are in line with *fiqh* definitions of marriage. They are also selective in their readings of the sacred texts and in their usage of classical *fiqh* concepts and definitions.

To give a flavor of these arguments, let me quote from Mutahhari's defense of men's unilateral right to terminate the marriage contract. His arguments, in my view, are the most refined among those that give the concept of gender equality no place in Islam. As already mentioned, he argues that "human nature" (*fitra*) is reflected in the naturalness of Shari'a laws. Though his language and his theory of sexuality differ from those of the classical *fiqh* texts, the male-centred view of creation and the notion of marriage as dominance remain the same.

> Nature has devised the ties of husband and wife in such a form that the part of woman is to respond to the love of man. The affection and love of a woman that is genuine and stable can only be that love which is born as a reaction to the affection and admiration of man toward her. So the attachment of the woman to the man is the result of the attachment of the man to the woman and depends upon it. Nature has given the key of love of both sides to the man, the husband. If he loves his wife and is faithful to her, the wife also loves him and remains faithful to him. It is admitted that woman is naturally more faithful than man, and that a woman's unfaithfulness is a reaction to the unfaithfulness of the man.[38]

Having defined women's sexuality as passive and subordinated to that of men, Mutahhari now gives a new rationalization for why *fiqh* gives men the right of divorce.

> Nature has deposited the key of the natural dissolution of marriage in the custody of man. In other words, it is man who by his own apathy and unfaithfulness

toward his wife makes her cold and unfaithful. Conversely, if the indifference begins on the side of the wife, it does not affect the affection of the man, rather, incidentally, it makes the affection more acute.[39]

The logical conclusion to be drawn is that there is no need for any change or reform in the laws of marriage and divorce.

Sometimes these people ask: "Why does divorce take the form of a release, an emancipation? Surely it should have a judicial form." To answer these people it should be said: "Divorce is a release in the same way that marriage is a state of dominance. If you can possibly do so, change the natural law of seeking a mate in its absoluteness with regard to the male and the female, remove the natural state of marriage from the condition of dominance; if you can, make the role of the male and female sexes in all human beings and animals identical in their relations, and change the law of nature. Then you will be able to rid divorce of its aspect of release and emancipation."[40]

Gender Equality: Questioning the Premises of Inequality

With the rise of political Islam in the second part of the twentieth century, and the rallying cry of "Return to the Shari'a" as embodied in *fiqh* rulings, Islamist political movements appropriated these Neo-Traditionalist texts and their gender discourse. Family law reforms introduced earlier in the century by modernist governments in some Muslim countries were dismantled, for instance in Iran, Algeria, and Egypt. In Iran, after the establishment in 1979 of an Islamic state ruled by clerics, women's covering and gender segregation in public space became mandatory. Women from all walks of life came to experience the harsh reality of subjugation to a religious patriarchy fused with the machinery of a modern state.

Paradoxically, the Islamists' slogan of "Return to Shari'a" and their attempt to translate *fiqh* notions of gender into policy became the catalyst for a critique of these notions and a spur to women's increased activism. In Iran and elsewhere, a new phase began in the politics of gender in Islam as growing numbers of women came to question whether there was an inherent or logical link between Islamic ideals and patriarchy. One crucial element of this new phase has been that it places women themselves—rather than the abstract notion of "the status of woman in Islam"—at the heart of the battle between forces of traditionalism and modernism. Using the language of political Islam and advocating a brand of feminism that takes Islam as the source of its legitimacy, women started to challenge the hegemony of patriarchal interpretations of the Shari'a and to question the validity of the views of those who until now have spoken in the name of Islam. Such a challenge was made possible, even inevitable, by the Islamists' ideological construction of Islam, and the very methods and sources that the Neo-Traditionalists used in their defense and rationalization of *fiqh* constructions of gender rights. By relying on arguments and sources outside religion and by imposing their patriarchal vision of the Shari‘a through the machinery of a modern state, the Islamists inadvertently opened the door to a sustained critique of religious patriarchy in ways that were not previously possible.[41]

By the late 1980s, a new way of thinking about gender emerged, a discourse that is "feminist" in its aspiration and demands, yet "Islamic" in its language and sources of legitimacy. Some versions of this new discourse came to be labelled "Islamic Feminism"—a notion that remains contested by both the majority of Islamists and some secular feminists, who see it as antithetical to their respective positions and ideologies, and as a contradiction in terms.[42]

"Islamic Feminism" is part of a new "Reformist" (as I call it) religious thinking that is consolidating a conception of Islam and modernity as compatible, not opposed. Reformist thinkers do not reject an idea simply because it is Western, nor do they see Islam as providing a blueprint, as having an inbuilt program of action for the social, economic, and political problems of the Muslim world. Following and building on the work of earlier reformers such as Mohammad Abduh, Muhammad Iqbal, and Fazlur Rahman, they contend that the human understanding of Islam is flexible, that Islam's tenets can be interpreted to encourage both pluralism and democracy, and that Islam allows change in the face of time, space, and experience.[43] Not only do they pose a serious challenge to legalistic and absolutist conceptions of Islam, but they are also carving a space within which Muslim women can achieve gender equality in law.

Instead of searching for an Islamic genealogy for modern concepts like gender equality, human rights, and democracy (the concern of earlier reformers) the new thinkers place the emphasis on how religion is understood and how religious knowledge is produced. In this respect, the works of the new wave of Muslim thinkers—such as Mohammad Arkoun, Nasr Abu Zayd, and Abdolkarim Soroush—are of immense importance and relevance. In particular, Soroush's interpretative-epistemological theory of the evolution of religious knowledge—known as "The Contraction and Expansion of Shari‘a"—makes possible a reconciliation of faith with rationality and with contemporary notions of justice and women's rights.[44]

In Soroush's words:

Our understanding of revealed texts is contingent upon the knowledge already set around us; that is to say that forces external to Revelation drag our interpretation and understanding of it in various directions.... Believers generally conceive of religion as something holy or sacred, something constant. You cannot talk about change or evolution of religious knowledge. They stick to the idea of fixity. But as I have demonstrated in my work, we have to make a distinction between religion on the one side and religious interpretation on the other. By religion here I mean not faith which is the subjective part of religion but the

objective side which is the revealed text. This is constant, whereas our interpretations of that text are subject to evolution. The idea is not that religious texts can
be changed but rather over time interpretations will change. We are always
immersed in an ocean of interpretations. The text does not speak to you. You
have to make it speak by asking questions of it.[45]

Such an approach to religious texts is opening the way for the radical
rethinking of some *fiqh* rulings to accommodate concepts such as gender
equality and human rights. Though in Iran their views have not yet been
adequately reflected in legislation, reformist clerics have been challenging
old *fiqh* wisdoms and trying to promote gender equality within an Islamic
framework. For instance, since the early 1990s, Mohsen Sa'idzadeh has been
trying to formulate and defend the "gender equality" perspective in *fiqh*,
which he claims to have been supported by a number of eminent jurists in
the past.[46] In 2003, another reformist cleric, Mohsen Kadivar, argued that
over 90 percent of what were considered to be Islamic laws relating to
women needed to be revised and rethought in line with contemporary
notions of justice and gender, as they no longer qualified for the epithets
"Islamic" or "*shar'i.*" According to him, for a ruling or a law to be considered part of the Shari'a it must meet three criteria. The first is the soundness
of its rational basis: it must satisfy the rational demands of the time. Second,
it must be in line with justice of its time. Third, it must be more advanced and
progressive than existing laws in other societies. The laws introduced by the
Prophet met all of these criteria. People accepted them, not because the
Prophet had introduced them, but because they corresponded with their
sense of justice and ideas of rationality as well as being more advanced and
progressive than existing laws.[47]

The new "Reformist" thinking is still evolving and it is too early to outline
the contours of its gender discourse. But it clearly differs from that of the
Neo-Traditionalists in three major ways. First, Reformist discourse does not
see the *fiqh* notion of gender as sacrosanct or its rulings as above critical evaluation. Second, in contrast to Neo-Traditionalist authors such as Maududi
and Mutahhari, who introduce questionable Western sources and "scientific" and naturalist theories to explain and justify the disparity between
men and women's rights in the Shari'a, Reformist thinkers return to Islamic
sources to argue for the necessity of a new reading of these sources in line
with changed conditions and the principles of justice and equality that are
now agreed to be an essential part of Islam's message. Finally, and most
importantly in my view, the Reformists are more or less silent on women's
sexuality, a silence which is important as it not only enables them to promote
an Islamic jurisprudence where women can be treated as social rather than
merely sexual beings but also in time can sever the link (implicit in classical
fiqh rulings) between constructions of gender and theories of sexuality. It is
this link that underlies the inability of Neo-Traditionalist writers to go

beyond old *fiqh* notions of gender rights, despite their success in making equality between sexes in the spiritual realm an undisputed element of contemporary gender discourses.[48]

SOME ANSWERS?

Let me end this chapter by suggesting some answers to my opening questions, which I would now rephrase as: How and why were classical constructions of gender in Islamic law premised on such a strong theory of inequality that they came to by-pass the values and objectives of the Shari'a? Can there be an equal construction of gender rights in Islamic law?

I explored the first question in the context of the classical *fiqh* discourse on gender. The gist of my argument was that the genesis of gender inequality in Islamic law lies in the inner contradictions between the ideals of the Shari'a and the norms of Muslim societies. While Shari'a ideals call for freedom, justice, and equality, their realization was impeded in the formative years of Islamic law by Muslim social norms and structures. Instead, these social norms were assimilated into *fiqh* rulings through a set of theological, legal, and social theories and assumptions that reflected the state of knowledge of the time, or were part of the cultural fabric of society.[49] In this way, Islamic legal tradition became the prisoner of its own theories and assumptions, which in time came to overshadow the "ethical" voice of Islam and its call for justice and reform, thus negating the spirit of the Shari'a.

I raised the second question—the possibility of achieving gender equality within an Islamic framework—through a discussion of two new legal discourses that emerged in the twentieth century. The Neo-Traditionalists succeeded in rounding some of the harsher edges of classical *fiqh* notions of gender, but their defensive and apologetic approach left them in an intellectual cul-de-sac. The Reformists, who emerged in the closing years of the century as part of an internal response to political Islam, display a refreshing pragmatic vigor and a willingness to engage with nonreligious perspectives. They have also sheltered feminist voices and feminist scholarship, which are shifting the old and tired debate on "women's rights in Islam" onto new ground.[50]

These feminist voices in Islam, in my view, are in a unique position to bring about a much needed paradigm shift in Islamic law. They are exposing the inequalities embedded in current interpretations of the Shari'a, not as manifestations of the divine will but as constructions by male jurists. This exposure has important epistemological and political consequences. Taken to its logical conclusion, this argument demonstrates that some rules hitherto claimed as "Islamic" and part of the Shari'a are in fact merely reflections of the views and perceptions of some Muslims, and are rooted in social practices and norms that are neither sacred nor immutable but human and changing.

The political consequence is both to free Muslims from taking defensive positions and to enable them to go beyond old *fiqh* dogmas in search of new questions and new answers.

Both these feminist voices and the reformist Islam of which they are a part are still in a formative phase, and their future prospects are tied to political developments all over the Muslim world—and to global politics. Their hope of redressing the gender inequalities in orthodox interpretations of the Shari'a depends on the balance of power between Neo-Traditionalists and Reformists, and their ability to organize and participate in the political process and to engage with the advocates of each discourse. They have already started to make their impact, as evidenced in the trend of family law reforms in the new millennium, notably the 2004 Moroccan family code that establishes equality in marriage and divorce between spouses within an Islamic framework.[51]

NOTES

1. This chapter draws on and expands the argument of Mir-Hosseini (2003a and 2006). An earlier version was presented in the Ertegun Open Seminar Series at Princeton University in November 2005. I am grateful to Elizabeth Frierson for inviting me to Princeton, and to other participants in the seminar, in particular Christine Stansell for her comments as discussant, and Michael Cook for criticism that helped me to clarify my argument. My warmest gratitude goes to Richard Tapper who read the chapter in its various incarnations and helped in the process of writing.

2. A clear statement of position is important, as the literature on Islam and women is replete with polemic in the guise of scholarship, see Mir-Hosseini (1999: 3–6).

3. Among current scholars of Islamic law, Kamali (1989: 216) and Abou El Fadl (2001: 32–35) use this distinction; An-Na'im (2000: 33–34) does not.

4. For a discussion of conceptions of justice in Islamic texts, see Khadduri (1984). In brief, there are two schools of theological thought. The prevailing *Ash'ari* school holds that our notion of justice is contingent on religious texts: whatever they say is just and not open to question. The *Mu'tazili* school, on the other hand, argues that the value of justice exists independent of religious texts; our sense and definition of justice is shaped by sources outside religion, is innate and has a rational basis. I adhere to the second position as developed by Abdolkarim Soroush, the Iranian reformist philosopher. According to Soroush, we accept religion because it is just, and any religious texts or laws that defy our contemporary sense of justice or its definition should be reinterpreted in the light of an ethical critique of their religious roots. In other words religion and the interpretation of religious texts are not above justice and ethics. In summer 2004, Soroush expounded his argument in a series of four lectures on "Religious Society, Ethical Society," delivered in Amir-Kabir University, Tehran (not yet available in print but available as audio cassettes, Tehran: Sarat).

5. Kamali (1996: 21).

6. Ahmed (1991: 58).

7. It is important to note that, as feminist scholarship on religion teaches us, such a tension is present in other scriptural religions. See Gross (1993) for this tension in Buddhism, Ruether (1983) and Schussler Fiorenza (1984) for Christianity, Herschel (1983) and Plaskow (2005) for Judaism.

8. For differences among the *fiqh* schools, see Ali (2002), Maghniyyah (1997).

9. Ghazali (1998: 89). For another rendering of this passage, see Farah (1984:120).

10. Hilli (1985: 428).

11. Ruxton (1916: 106). Jorjani, another Maliki jurist, defines marriage in the following terms: "a contract through which the husband acquires exclusive rights over the sexual organs of woman" (quoted by Pesle 1936: 20).

12. For similarities in the juristic conceptions of slavery and marriage, see Marmon (1999) and Willis (1985).

13. For these disagreements see Ali (2003: 70–82); for the impact of these disagreements on rulings related to *mahr* and the ways in which classical jurists discussed them, see Ibn Rushd (1996: 31–33).

14. For differentiation by Hanafi jurists between social and commercial exchange, and the valorization of the human body, see Johansen (1995, 1996).

15. For a discussion, see 'Abd Al 'Ati (1997); the last purpose takes the prime place in the writings of radical Islamists such as Maududi (1983, 1998).

16. In Shi'a law a man may contract as many temporary marriages (*mut'a*) as he desires or can afford. For this form of marriage, see Haeri (1989).

17. Many terms commonly used today in different countries for 'the veil', such as *hijab, parda* ('purdah'), *chador, burqa,* are not found in classical *fiqh* texts. For a discussion of *hijab* in *fiqh* texts, see Mutahhari (1992).

18. Some ('Abd Al 'Ati 1997, Esposito 1982) argue that the advent of Islam weakened the patriarchal structures of Arabian society, others (Ahmed 1992, Mernissi 1991) that it reinforced them. The latter also maintain that, before the advent of Islam, society was undergoing a transition from matrilineal to patrilineal descent, that Islam facilitated this by giving patriarchy the seal of approval, and that the Qur'anic injunctions on marriage, divorce, inheritance, and whatever relates to women both reflect and affirm such a transition. Both base their conclusions on the work of William Robertson Smith. For concise accounts of the debate, see Smith (1985), Spellberg (1991).

19. Esposito (1982: 14–15).

20. Of more than 6,000 verses in the Qur'an, only six treat men and women differently; four of these concern marriage and divorce (Qur'an 2: 222, 228 and 4: 3, 34). For a discussion, see Sardar Ali (1998). For egalitarian interpretations of these verses, see Barlas (2002), Guardi (2004), Mubarak (2004), Umar (2004), Wadud (1999, 2004).

21. See Mernissi (1991), El Guindi (1999: 152–7), Abou El Fadl (2001: 209–263), Stowasser (1997).

22. There are two important recent studies of this. Hajjaji-Jarrah (2003) shows the influence of social forces on the way in which the *hijab* verses were understood in the works of two commentators (Tabari and Razi). Clark (2003) shows the lack of concern with women's covering in the Hadith literature, and no explicit reference

to the covering of hair; there are more *hadith* on men's dress and covering their *'awra* than on women's dress.

23.   As Abou-Bakr (2004) shows, women remained active in transmitting religious knowledge, but their activities were limited to the informal arena of homes and mosques and their status as jurists was not officially recognized.

24.   Sachedina (1999b: 149).

25.   See Barlas (2002), Hassan (1987, 1996), Mernissi (1991), Wadud (1999, 2004).

26.   See Mernissi (1985), Mir-Hosseini (2004), Sabbah (1984).

27.   This rationale is found in many contemporary texts on women in Islam; an explicit example is Maududi (1998).

28.   Sachedina (1999a: 29); emphasis added.

29.   Here I am concerned with the theory of Islamic law, not with its practice. It is essential to note that, while at the theoretical level the *fuqaha* claim that Islamic law is immutable, at the level of practice, flexibility and adaptability are two of its salient features, which have enabled it to be meaningful in a variety of cultural and social contexts from the outset. For an insightful discussion of the ways in which women in premodern times related to Islamic law, see Rapoport (2005) and Sonbol (1996, esp. Introduction); for contemporary examples, see Mir-Hosseini (1993), Welchman (1999).

30.   For a discussion of such writings in the Arab world, see Haddad (1998), Stowasser (1993); for Iran, see Mir-Hosseini (1999); for Muslims living in Europe and North America, see Roald (2001); texts in English include Abusulayman (2003), Badawi (1995), Chaudhry (1995), Doi (1989), Khan (1995), Maududi (1983, 1998), Mutahhari (1991, 1992), Rahman (1986), Siddiqi (1952), Al-Sadlaan (1999).

31.   For a concise discussion of the terms of the marriage contract and their adoption by legal codes in Arab countries, see El Alami (1996).

32.   See Nasir (1990:125–142). For reforms and codification of family law in the Muslim world, see Anderson (1976), Mahmood (1972), El Alami and Hinchcliffe (1996).

33.   See Mir-Hosseini (1993: 10–13).

34.   Maududi (1983).

35.   Badawi (1995); a short version of the booklet is posted on several Islamist websites.

36.   Mutahhari (1991), Maududi (1998); both books are available in English and Arabic and have gone through many editions; for a reading of their texts, see Shehadeh (2003).

37.   'Allama Tabataba'i, the renowned Shi'i philosopher, was the first to advance this theory in his monumental Qur'anic commentary known as *Al-Mizan*, written in Arabic between 1954 and 1972; see Mir-Hosseini (2003b).

38.   Ibid., 274.

39.   Ibid., 297.

40.   Ibid., 298.

41.   I elaborate this in Mir-Hosseini (2006).

42.   There is now a growing literature on Islamic feminism; see, for instance, Afshar (1998), Badran (2002), Fernea (1998), Mir-Hosseini (1999, 2006), Mirza (2000, 2006), Paidar (1996), Roald (1998), Shaikh (2003), Yamani (1996).

43.   For the textual genealogy of this thinking, see Kurzman (1998).

44.   Although Soroush himself, in line with many other religious intellectuals in Iran, does not subscribe to the gender equality perspective, his ideas have not only laid the foundation of what later became known in Iran (following President Muhammad Khatami's election in 1997) as the Reform Movement, but enabled religious women like those of *Zanan* magazine to reconcile their faith with their feminism. For Soroush's ideas on gender and my debate with him, see Mir-Hosseini (1999: Chapter 7); for selections of his writings in English, see Soroush (2000).

45.   Soroush (1996).

46.   For his work, see Mir-Hosseini (1999: Chapter 8).

47.   Kadivar (2003).

48.   Mir-Hosseini (2004).

49.   See also Masud (2001).

50.   Many of these scholars still avoid the term 'feminist' and instead call themselves Muslim women scholars or activists (see Webb 2000). A large majority of them have focused their scholarship on Qur'anic interpretation: Barlas (2002), Hassan (1987, 1996, 1999), Jawad (1998), Mernissi (1991), Shaikh (1997), Wadud (1999, 2004). The following deal directly with *fiqh:* Al-Hibri (1997, 2000, 2001), Ali (2002, 2003), Mir-Hosseini (1999, 2003a), Sardar Ali (1998). Abou El Fadl (2001), An-Na'im (2000), Engineer (1992) and Esack (2001) are prominent among male scholars who have written on women's rights.

51.   For the new code see Foblets and Carlier (2005), and for related debates and political context, see Buskens (2003).

SELECTED BIBLIOGRAPHY

'Abd Al 'Ati, Hammudah. *The Family Structure in Islam*. Indianapolis, Indiana: American Trust Publications, 1997.

Abou-Bakr, Omaima. "Teaching the Words of the Prophet: Women Instructors of the Hadith (Fourteenth and Fifteenth Centuries)." *Hawwa: Journal of Women of the Middle East and the Islamic World* 1, no. 3 (2003): 306–328.

Abou El Fadl, Khaled. *Speaking in God's Name: Islamic Law, Authority and Women*. Oxford, U.K.: Oneworld, 2001.

Abusulayman, Abdulhamid A. *Marital Discord: Recapturing the Full Islamic Spirit of Human Dignity*. London/Washington: The International Institute of Islamic Thought, 2003.

Afshar, Haleh. *Islam and Feminisms: An Iranian Case-Study*. London, U.K.: Macmillan, 1998.

Ahmed, Leila. "Early Islam and the Position of Women: The Problem of Interpretation." In *Women in Middle Eastern History,* edited by Nikki Keddie and Beth Baron. New Haven, Connecticut: Yale University Press, 1991.

————. *Women and Gender in Islam: Historical Roots of a Modern Debate.* New Haven, Connecticut: Yale University Press, 1992.

Al-Hibri, Aziza. "A Study of Islamic Herstory: Or How Did We Get Into This Mess." In *Islam and Women,* Special Issue of *Women's Studies International Forum* 5, no. 2 (1982): 207–219.

————. "Islam, Law and Custom: Redefining Muslim Women's Rights." *American University Journal of International Law and Policy* 12 (1997): 1–44.

————. "An Introduction to Muslim Women's Rights." In *Windows of Faith: Muslim Women Scholar-Activists in North America,* edited by Gisela Webb. Syracuse, New York: Syracuse University Press, 2000.

————. "Muslim Women's Rights in the Global Village: Challenges and Opportunities." *Journal of Law and Religion* 15, nos. 1 and 2 (2001): 37–66.

Ali, Kecia. "Money, Sex and Power: The Contractual Nature of Marriage in Islamic Jurisprudence of the Formative Period." (PhD diss., Duke University, 2002).

————. "Progressive Muslims and Islamic Jurisprudence: The Necessity for Critical Engagement with Marriage and Divorce Law." In *Progressive Muslims: On Justice, Gender, and Pluralism,* edited by Omid Safi. Oxford, U.K.: Oneworld, 2003.

Anderson, James Norman. *Law Reforms in the Muslim World.* London, U.K.: Athlone, 1976.

An-Na'im, Abdullahi Ahmed. "Islamic Foundation for Women's Human Rights." In *Islam, Reproductive Health and Women's Rights,* edited by Zainah Anwar and Rashidah Abdullah Kuala Lumpur: Sisters in Islam, 2000.

Badawi, Jamal. *Gender Equity in Islam: Basic Principles.* Indianapolis, Indiana: American Trust Publications, 1995.

Badran, Margot. "Islamic Feminism: What's in a Name?" *Al-Ahram Weekly Online* 69 (17–23 January 2002).

Barlas, Asma. *Believing Women in Islam: Unreading Patriarchal Interpretations of the Qur'an.* Austin, Texas: Texas University Press, 2002.

Buskens, Leon. "Recent Debates on Family Law Reform in Morocco: Islamic Law as Politics in an Emerging Public Sphere." *Islamic Law and Society* 10 no. 1 (2003): 69–131.

Chaudhry, Muhammad Sharif. *The Status of Women in Muslim Society.* Lahore: Al-Matabaat-ul-Arabia, 1995.

Clark, Linda. "Hijab According to Hadith: Text and Interpretation." In *The Muslim Veil in North America: Issues and Debates,* edited by S. Alvi, H. Hoodfar, S. McDonough. Toronto: Women's Press, 2003.

Coulson, Noel, and Doreen Hinchcliffe. "Women and Law Reforms in Contemporary Islam." In *Women in the Muslim World,* edited by Lois Beck and Nikki Keddie. Cambridge, Massachusetts: Harvard University Press, 1978.

Doi, Abdul Rahman. *Women in the Shari'a.* London, U.K.: Ta-Ha, 1989.

El Alami, Dawoud Sudqi. *The Marriage Contract in Islamic Law.* London, U.K.: Graham and Trotman, 1992.

El Alami, Dawoud Sudqi, and Doreen Hinchcliffe. *Islamic Marriage and Divorce Laws of the Arab World.* London, U.K.: Kluwer Law International and Centre of Middle Eastern and Islamic Law, School of Oriental and African Studies, 1996.

El Guindi, Fadwa. *Veil. Modesty, Privacy and Resistance.* Oxford, U.K.: Berg, 1999.

Engineer, Asghar Ali. *The Rights of Women in Islam.* London, U.K.: Hurst, 1992.

Esack, Farid. "Islam and Gender Justice: Beyond Simplistic Apologia." In *What Men Owe to Women.* Albany, New York: SUNY Press, 2001.

Esposito, John. *Women in Muslim Family Law.* Syracuse, New York: Syracuse University Press, 1982.

Farah, Madelain. *Marriage and Sexuality in Islam: A Translation of Al-Ghazali's Book on the Etiquette of Marriage from the* Ihya. Salt Lake City, Utah: University of Utah Press, 1984.

Fernea, Elizabeth Warnock. *In Search of Islamic Feminism: One Woman's Global Journey.* New York: Anchor Doubleday, 1998.

Foblets, Marie-Claire, and Jean-Yves Carlier. *Le Code Marocain de La Famille.* Bruxelles: Bruylant, 2005.

Ghazali, Imam Abu Hamid Al-. *The Proper Conduct of Marriage in Islam (Adab an-Nikah), Book Twelve of Ihya 'Ulum ad-Din (Revival of Religious Sciences).* Translated by Muhtar Holland. Hollywood, Florida: Al-Baz, 1998.

Gibb, Hamilton, and J.H. Kramers. *Shorter Encyclopaedia of Islam.* Leiden: Brill; and London, U.K.: Luzac, 1961.

Gross, Rita. *Buddhism after Patriarchy.* Albany, New York: State University of New York Press, 1993.

Guardi, Jolanda. "Women Reading the Qur'an: Religious Discourse in Islam." *Hawwa: Journal of Women of the Middle East and the Islamic World* 2, no. 3 (2004): 301–315.

Haddad, Yvonne Yazbeck. "Islam and Gender: Dilemmas in the Changing Arab World." In *Islam, Gender and Social Change,* edited by Yvonne Yazbeck Haddad and John Esposito. Oxford, U.K.: Oxford University Press, 1988.

Haeri, Shahla. *Law of Desire: Temporary Marriage in Iran.* London, U.K.: I.B. Tauris, 1989.

Hajjaji-Jarrah, Soraya. "Women in Qur'anic Commentaries." In *The Muslim Veil in North America: Issues and Debates,* edited by S. Alvi, H. Hoodfar, and S. McDonough. Toronto: Women's Press, 2003.

Hassan, Riffat. "Equal Before Allah? Woman-Man Equality in the Islamic Tradition." *Harvard Divinity Bulletin* 7, no. 2 (Jan–May 1987); also in her *Selected Articles* (Women Living Under Muslim Laws), n.d., 26–29.

———. "Feminist Theology: Challenges for Muslim Women." *Critique: Journal for Critical Studies of the Middle East* 9 (1996): 53–65.

———. "Feminism in Islam." In *Feminism and World Religions,* edited by A. Sharma and K. Young Albany, New York: SUNY Press, 1999.

Heschel, Susannah. *On Being a Jewish Feminist.* New York: Schocken Books, 1995.

Hilli, Muhaqqiq. *Sharayi' al-Islam* Vol. II, Persian translation by A.A. Yazdi, compiled by Muhammad Taqi Danish-Pazhuh. Tehran University Press, 1985.

Jawad, Haifaa. *The Rights of Women in Islam: An Authentic Approach.* London, U.K.: MacMillan, 1998.

Johansen, Baber. "Commercial Exchange and Social Order in Hanafite Law." In *Law and the Islamic World: Past and Present,* edited by Christopher Poll and Jakob Skovgaard-Petersen. Copenhagen: Royal Danish Academy of Sciences and Letters, 1995.

———. "Valorization of the Human Body in Muslim Sunni Law." In *Law and Society in Islam,* edited by Devin J. Stewart, Baber Johansen, and Amy Singer. Princeton, New Jersey: Markus Wiener, 1996.

Kadivar, Mohsen. "Hoquq-e Zanan dar Islam-e Mo'aser az Zaviyeh-e Digar (The Rights of Women in Contemporary Islam from a Different Angle)" (lecture given at Mosharekat meeting on 15/6/82), 2003. http://www.kadivar.com/Htm/Farsi/Speeches/Speech820615.htm (

Kamali, Muhammad Hashim. "Sources, Nature and Objectives of Shari'ah." *Islamic Quarterly* 33 (1989): 215–235.

———. *Principles of Islamic Jurisprudence.* Cambridge, U.K.: Islamic Texts Society, 1991.

———. "Methodology in Islamic Jurisprudence." *Arab Law Quarterly* (1996): 3–33.

Khadduri, Majid. *The Islamic Conception of Justice.* Baltimore, Maryland: John Hopkins University Press, 1984.

Khan, Maulana Wahiduddin. *Woman Between Islam and Western Society.* New Delhi, India: The Islamic Centre, 1995.

Kurzman, Charles, ed. *Liberal Islam: A Sourcebook.* Oxford, U.K.: Oxford University Press, 1998.

Maghniyyah, Muhammad Jawad. *Marriage According to Five Schools of Islamic Law,* Vol. V Tehran: Department of Translation and Publication, Islamic Culture and Relations Organization, 1997.

Mahmood, Tahir. *Family Law Reforms in the Muslim World.* Bombay, India: N.M. Tripathi, 1972.

Marmon, Shaun E. "Domestic Slavery in the Mamluk Empire: A Preliminary Sketch." In *Slavery in the Islamic Middle East,* edited by Shaun E. Marmon. Princeton, New Jersey: Department of Near Eastern Studies, 1999.

Masud, Muhammad Khalid. *Muslim Jurists' Quest for the Normative Basis of Shari'a.* Inaugural Lecture, Leiden: International Institute for the Study of Islam in the Modern World, 2001.

Maududi, Maulana Abul A'la. *The Laws of Marriage and Divorce in Islam.* Kuwait: Islamic Book Publishers, 1983.

———. *Purdah and the Status of Women in Islam.* 16th ed. Lahore: Islamic Publication (Pvt) Ltd, 1998.

Mernissi, Fatima. *Beyond the Veil: Male–Female Dynamics in Muslim Society,* rev. ed. London, U.K.: Al Saqi, 1985.

———. *Women and Islam: An Historical and Theological Enquiry.* Translated by Mary Jo Lakeland. Oxford, U.K.: Blackwell, 1991.

Mir-Hosseini, Ziba. *Marriage on Trial: A Study of Islamic Family Law, Iran and Morocco Compared.* London, U.K.: I.B. Tauris, 1993.

———. *Islam and Gender: The Religious Debate in Contemporary Iran.* Princeton, New Jersey: Princeton University Press, 1999.

———2003a. "The Construction of Gender in Islamic Legal Thought and Strategies for Reform." *Hawwa: Journal of Women in the Middle East and the Islamic World* 1, no. 1 (2003a): 1–28.

———. "Women's Rights and Clerical Discourses: The Legacy of Allameh Tabataba'i." In *Intellectual Trends in Twentieth Century Iran*, edited by Negin Nabavi. University Press of Florida, 2003b.

———. "Sexuality, Rights and Islam: Competing Gender Discourses in Post-Revolutionary Iran." In *Women in Iran from 1800 to the Islamic Republic*, edited by Guity Nashat, and Lois Beck. Urbana and Chicago: University of Illinois Press, 2004.

———. "Muslim Women's Quest for Equality: Between Islamic Law and Feminism." *Critical Inquiry* 32, no. 1 (2006).

Mirza, Qudsia. "Islamic Feminism, Possibilities and Limitations." In *Law After Ground Zero*, edited by J. Strawson. London, U.K: Cavendish, 2002.

———, ed. *Islamic Feminism and the Law*. London, U.K.: Cavendish, 2006.

Mutahhari, Murtaza. *The Rights of Women in Islam*. 4th ed. Tehran: World Organization for Islamic Services, 1991.

———. *The Islamic Modest Dress*. 3rd ed., translated from the Persian by Laleh Bakhtiar. Chicago, Illinois: Kazi Publications, 1992.

Mubarak, Hadia. "Breaking the Interpretive Monopoly: Re-examination of Verse 4:34." *Hawwa: Journal of Women of the Middle East and the Islamic World* 2, no. 3 (2004): 290–300.

Nasir, Jamal. *The Islamic Law of Personal Status*. 2nd ed. London, U.K.: Graham and Trotman, 1990.

Paidar, Parvin. "Feminism and Islam in Iran." In *Gendering the Middle East: Emerging Perspectives*, edited by Deniz Kandiyoti, 51–67. London, U.K.: I.B. Tauris.

Pesle, Octave. *Le Mariage chez les Malekites de l'Afrique du Nord*. Rabat: Moncho, 1936.

Plaskow, Judith. *The Coming of Lilith: Essays on Feminism, Judaism, and Sexual Ethics, 1972–2003*. Boston, Massachusetts: Beacon Press, 2005.

Rahman, Afzalur. *Role of Muslim Woman in Society*. London, U.K.: Seerah Foundation, 1986.

Rapoport, Yossef. *Marriage, Money and Divorce in Medieval Islamic Society*. Cambridge, U.K.: Cambridge University Press, 2005.

Roald, Anne Sofia. "Feminist Reinterpretation of Islamic Sources: Muslim Feminist Theology in Light of the Christian Tradition of Feminist Thought." In *Women and Islamization: Contemporary Dimensions of Discourse on Gender Relations*, edited by K. Ask, and M. Tjomsland. Oxford, U.K.: Berg, 1989.

———. *Women in Islam: The Western Experience*. London, U.K.: Routledge, 2001.

Ruether, Rosemary Radford. *Sexism and God-Talk: Toward a Feminist Theology*. Boston, Massachusetts: Beacon Press, 1993.

Ruxton, F.H. *Maliki Law: A Summary from French Translations of Mukhtasar Sidi Khalil*. London, U.K.: Luzac, 1916.

Sabbah, Fatna. *Woman in the Muslim Unconscious*. New York: Pergamon, 1984.

Sachedina, Abdulaziz. "The Ideal and Real in Islamic Law." In *Perspectives on Islamic Law, Justice and Society*, edited by R.S. Khare. New York: Rowman and Littlefield, 1999a.

———. "Woman, Half-the-Man? Crisis in Male Epistemology in Islamic Jurispudence." In *Perspectives on Islamic Law, Justice and Society*, edited by R.S. Khare. New York: Rowman and Littlefield, 1999b.

Sadlaan, Saalih ibn Ghaanim Al-. *The Fiqh of Marriage in the Light of Quran and Sunnah: Covering the Dower, Wedding Night, Wedding Feast and Rights of Husband and Wife.* Translated by Jamaal al-Din M. Zarabozo. Boulder, Colorado: Al-Basheer Co, 1999.

Sardar Ali, Shaheen. "Women's Human Rights in Islam: Towards a Theoretical Framework." *Yearbook of Islamic and Middle Eastern Law* 4 (1997–1998): 117–152.

Schussler Fiorenza, Elizabeth. *Bread Not Stone: The Challenge of Feminist Biblical Interpretation.* Boston, Massachusetts: Beacon Press, 1995.

Shaikh, Sa'diyya. "Exegetical Violence: *Nushuz* in Qur'anic Gender Ideology." *Journal of Islamic Studies* 17(1997): 49–73.

———. "Transforming Feminism: Islam, Women and Gender Justice." In *Progressive Muslims: On Justice, Gender, and Pluralism,* edited by Omid Safi. Oxford, U.K.: Oneworld, 2003.

Shehadeh, Lamia Rustum. *The Idea of Women under Fundamentalist Islam.* Gainesville, Florida: University of Florida Press, 2003.

Siddiqi, Muhammad Mazheruddin. *Women in Islam.* Lahore: Institute of Islamic Culture, 1952.

Smith, Jane. "Women, Religion and Social Change in Early Islam." In *Women, Religion, and Social Change,* edited by Yvonne Yazbeck Haddad, and Ellison Banks Findly. Albany, New York: SUNY Press, 1985.

Spellberg, Denise. "Political Action and Public Example: A'isha and the Battle of the Camel." In *Women in Middle Eastern History: Shifting Boundaries in Sex and Gender,* edited by Beth Baron, and Nikki Keddie. New Haven, Connecticut: Yale University Press, 1991.

Sonbol, Amira El Azhary, ed. *Women, Family and Divorce Laws in Islamic History.* Syracuse, New York: Syracuse University Press, 1996.

Soroush, Abdolkarim. "A Conversation with Abolkarim Sorush." *Q-News International* (British Muslim Weekly) 220–221 (June 1996): 14–27.

———. "The Evolution and Devolution of Religious Knowledge." In *Liberal Islam: A Sourcebook,* edited by Charles Kurzman. Oxford, New York: Oxford University Press, 1998.

———. "Islamic Revival and Reform: Theological Approaches." In *Reason, Freedom, and Democracy in Islam: Essential Writings of 'Abdolkarim Sorush.* Translated and edited with a critical introduction by Mahmoud Sadri and Ahmed Sadri. Oxford, U.K.:Oxford University Press, 2000.

Stowasser, Barbara. "Women's Issues in Modern Islamic Thought." In *Arab Women: Old Boundaries, New Frontiers,* edited by Judith E. Tucker. Bloomington, Indiana: Indiana University Press, 1993.

———. "The Hijab: How a Curtain Became an Institution and a Cultural Symbol." In *Humanism, Culture, and Language in the Near East: Studies in Honor of Georg Krotkoff,* edited by Asma Afsaruddin, and A.H. Mathias Zahnise. Indiana: Eisenbrauns, 1997.

Umar, Nasruddin. "Gender Biases in Qur'anic Exegesis: A Study of Scriptural Interpretation from a Gender Perspective." *Hawwa: Journal of Women of the Middle East and the Islamic World* 2, no. 3 (2004): 337–363.

Wadud, Amina. *Qur'an and Woman: Rereading of the Sacred Text from a Woman's Perspective*. New York: Oxford University Press.

———. "Qur'an, Gender and Interpretive Possibilities." *Hawwa: Journal of Women of the Middle East and the Islamic World* 2, no. 3 (2004): 317–336.

Webb, Gisela, ed. *Windows of Faith: Muslim Women Scholar–Activists in North America*. Syracuse, New York: Syracuse University Press, 2000.

Welchman, Lynn. *Islamic Family Law: Text and Practice in Palestine*. Jerusalem: Women's Centre for Legal Aid and Counselling, 1999.

Willis, John Ralph. "The Ideology of Enslavement in Islam Introduction." In *Slaves and Slavery in Muslim Africa*, Vol. 1, edited by John Ralph Willis. London, U.K.: Frank Cass, 1985.

Yamani, Mai, ed. *Islam and Feminism: Legal and Literary Perspectives*. London, U.K.: Ithaca, 1996.

6

TRANSITIONS IN THE "PROGRESS" OF CIVILIZATION: THEORIZING HISTORY, PRACTICE, AND TRADITION

Ebrahim Moosa

Life changes fast.
Life changes in an instant.
You sit down to dinner and life as you know it ends.
The question of self-pity...
You had to feel the swell change. You had to go with the change. He told me that. No eye is on the sparrow but he did tell me that.

—Joan Didion, *The Year of Magical Thinking*

Clever people are not credited with their follies: what a deprivation of human rights!

—Friedrich Nietzsche, *Beyond Good and Evil*

INTRODUCTION

Those who think that "progressive" Islam is a ready-made ideology or an off-the-shelf creed, movement, or pack of doctrines will be sorely disappointed. It is not even a carefully calibrated theory or interpretation of Muslim law, theology, ethics, and politics. Neither is it a school of thought. Instead, I would argue that progressive Islam is a wish-list, a desire, and, if at all something, then it is literally, accumulated action, as the word "progress" in the phrase "a work-in progress" suggests. At best it is a practice.

Another way of putting it is to say that progressive Islam is a posture: an attitude. What kind of attitude? Here lies the rub. To say *what* that attitude is, to give it content or even to be as bold as to say what it is *not,* is to sound like the high priestess or gatekeeper for "progressive Islam." It is best not to invite such recriminations.

Yet, persons who are tightly or lightly associated with what is broadly identified as "progressive Islam" will propose different practices and accompanying methodologies to verify and justify the content of the ethical propositions, philosophical visions, and contestations of history they hold. All this disagreement and difference is perfectly healthy for creative thinking in Muslim thought, especially ethical thought. What would certainly signal the death-knell for progressive Muslim thought is if there were to emerge a single voice, a unifying institution, a exclusive guild or association of scholars and practitioners who monopolized the epithet "progressive" and dictated its operations, debated its values and determined its content, like an orthodoxy. If so, then the ship of progressive Islam leaves port badly listing.

What goes by the broad rubric of progressive Islam takes many forms. In some places it is the life and death struggles of people who are trying to make sense of the intensities of life whether in repressive patriarchal contexts, in the grips of rampant poverty, famine, and war, or in the midst of disease of pandemic proportions. In more favorable conditions, there too similar challenges await, albeit disguised by affluence and enviable certainty. Relying on their multiple traditions and the resources of transnational civilizations, many Muslims are trying to find meaning for their lives. In ways not yet clearly articulated these individuals and communities are the lifeblood of what I would call progressive Islam. Detailed ethnographies of such communities and the substance of their struggles are documented elsewhere in this volume. In this reflection, I prefer to outline some key concepts and ideas that emerged during my journey and discovery of how to critically engage the Muslim knowledge traditions. As it will forever remain a work-in-progress, I have more questions than answers; some of my observations will come by way of points of clarification and caveats. What might appear to be answers and exhortations, despite their vehemence, I would urge my reader to regard as tentative.

How does one develop a critical approach to tradition? If past experiences became the social laboratory for the making of tradition, why cannot our current experiences as Muslims become the threads to manufacture the garment of tradition? While there is no sensible and intelligent way to know how a revitalized tradition would unfold, the search for emergent knowledge and ethics has to continue energetically. Intellectuals and activists all have a responsibility to recast the knowledge of tradition and thus tradition in light of their contemporary experiences.

WHAT IS IN A NAME?

A great deal is both revealed and repressed in a name. The term "progressive" used to designate a loosely knit group of activists and thinkers advocating a different narrative of Islam compared to the dominant one is to be sure an oppositional term. In fact, for this author, the term "progressive" is itself a source of discomfort for reasons to be explained later, but I continue to employ it with caveats for the lack of a better substitute. As some French philosophers have helpfully suggested, one can use the term under "erasure."

Progressives differ in significant ways from the dominant orthodoxies of Islamic revivalism and traditionalism in their respective methodologies and ideologies. At least, I view myself in a complex relation to the intellectual heritage and multiple cultural formations in which Muslims lived and prospered, flourished and failed, as well as changed and stabilized. One of the major points of departure for progressives is the heightened and surplus freight of ideology evident in the interpretations propounded by representatives of Islamic revivalism, such as the Muslim Brotherhood of Egypt or the Jamat-e Islami of India and Pakistan to the orthodox seminaries of Al-Azhar in Egypt, the Deobandi, Barelwi, and Ahle Hadith schools of India and Pakistan, the schools of Najaf in Iraq, Qum in Iran, and the varieties of puritan (*salafi*) tendencies in the Gulf region and elsewhere, to mention but a prominent few. Each of these groups also have a global presence, as well as representation in Europe and North America where Muslim minorities are on the rise.

To be sure, just as progressives cannot artificially be made to look alike (homogenized), so too it would be wrong to portray contending views to be uniform. However, for the purpose of characterization, but not defamation, I am compelled to resort to a certain strategic essentialism to describe how my views by way of general brushstrokes differ from those of my opponents. A more careful and technically nuanced comparison belongs to another genre of writing and cannot be composed in the brevity of the space and scope allotted here. The assertion that at least some individuals affiliated with the above-mentioned tendencies, vague as it might sound, would endorse certain aspects of progressive methodology and practice while refraining from doing so with respect to other aspects remains true. This observation should put paid to any illusion that progressive viewpoints are solely the preserve of scholars in the North American academy.

Hence, when I allege that some viewpoints held by Muslim groups are ideological, it is animated by some very specific concerns. Perpetuating an inhibiting cultural inheritance suggests a denial of the obvious facts of the world and the absence of common sense. In a nutshell I would say that the major differences between Muslim progressives and their critics would be that the latter are either wedded to dated methodologies or committed to doctrines and interpretations that have lost their rationales and relevance over time. On the other hand, progressives are also painfully aware that to uncritically succumb to every fact and fad also makes little sense, since it results in a Panglossian option of being unwaveringly and unrealistically optimistic about everything in the modern style.

Many find the term "progressive" to be exclusionary. In other words, does it imply that if one does not subscribe to a progressive agenda that one is by default adhering to a retrograde agenda? In my view such an inference is a flawed one. Any definition can be deployed in both an affirmative and a negative manner. To say that one is black, is a statement that primarily affirms one's black identity and does not necessarily imply the negation of white identity. However, what such a claim does propose is to signal a difference in identities. Similarly, to say that one is American or Indian does not mean that one necessarily despises Canadians or Pakistanis. What such a label affirms is a package of loyalties and commitments, which in some rare instances, especially during conflict, might turn out to be badge of hostility and exclusion.

Another shorthand way to describe my intellectual approach would be to designate it as critical traditionalism, for reasons that will hopefully become clear later. But someone could make the point that in the very act of naming, one is implying that others are just the opposite: uncritical traditionalists. In reality one is trying to assert the element that distinguishes one's intellectual agenda from those of others. What is distinctive in my work is to engage with tradition critically: to constantly interrogate tradition and strive to ask productive questions.

AMBIVALENCE OF PROGRESS

If some are drawn to the term "progress" then others are recoiled by its echo. Those who buy into a Hegelian worldview imagine that history is moving toward some clearly defined and concrete end. For believers of this stripe, any change is productive and clearly directed toward a wholesome "progress." Epitomizing this viewpoint is Francis Fukuyama in his controversial book, *The End of History and the Last Man.*[1] For Fukuyama, philosophers of old have held that history has an end, not as events, occurrences, and happenings, but as something more deeply philosophical and profound. In this view "history" means a single, coherent, evolutionary process that takes into account the experiences of all peoples over all times. As an evolutionary process, if not a program, Fukuyama believes that history is neither random nor unintelligible. Societies develop with coherence from tribal ones based on slavery and subsistence agricultures to theocracies, aristocracies to culminate in liberal democracies driven by technology-rich capitalism. All this is the result of "progress" in history.

In Fukuyama's view we have reached such a pinnacle of progress that the principles and institutions underlying liberal democratic societies will no longer be in need of alteration or have to be changed. The evolution of history has determined for us what we should behold as the ideal institutions: not communism but capitalism; not socialism but liberal democracy;

and definitely, no imponderable third way. In his determination to prove the salvific benefits of liberal democratic progress, Fukuyama drifts into the morally unsettling and theologically Christian territory of eschatology that produces utopia and messianism.

However, there is something deeply troubling and unquestioned in such a conception of progress. Progress becomes hubristic when it only emphasizes the mastery of nature but does not recognize the retrogression of society. Such a vision of progress, notes the German thinker Walter Benjamin, displays the technocratic features that was a hallmark of fascism and other kinds of authoritarian societies. Lots of unsavory movements have in the name of progress been treated as historical norms when in fact they were aberrations. Yoked to the tyranny of unchanging principles is a notion of secular progress that is as fundamentalist in its posture as its religiously inspired counterparts.

This view of progress was inspired by certain biblical themes of an apocalyptic end and driven by a mechanistic view to create a New Jerusalem. In numerous apocalyptic writings, Ernest Lee Tuveson comments, history was endowed with a plot and encompassed a narrative of what happened before and what was expected to come. Building on the Hebraic tradition, Christian thinkers and pioneers adapted the moral narratives of the Bible to their own special interpretations of the divine.[2] Later, Protestant attitudes implicitly held that history moves by divinely preordained and revealed stages to the solution of human dilemmas. Gradually this attitude also infected the philosophies of modernity, coming to dominate modern theories of history and science despite a plethora of opposing voices. Notable among these opposing voices were the Romantic thinkers, among them Herder and also T.S. Eliot who did not accept the inevitability of progress as many others conceded. While everyone accepts that the notion of change is the essence of life, the disagreement is about something much more subtle but is pregnant with significant consequences.

What distinguishes a modernist from someone who is less enamored by everything modern is this: the modernist à la Fukuyama believes in the *inevitability* of progress while the opposing view would, sometimes grudgingly, concede to the *possibility* of change or progress. Progress as fortuitous, rather than as inevitable, holds the promise that change might occur in diverse and multiple forms, not the totalitarian narrative of progress driven by scientism and liberal capitalism. The deterministic or apocalyptic theory of progress locks everyone in a Weberian iron cage or in a suffocating straitjacket of a singular modernity. Ignoring this subtlety can produce some of the most irreconcilable dilemmas and offer nonoptions forcing one to choose between science versus religion, rationality versus faith, and progress versus tradition.

Many Muslim thinkers unfortunately have purchased into the inevitability of progress thesis without thinking through its implications. Muhammad Iqbal (d. 1938), the poet and thinker of India, also inadvertently stumbled into some of these thorny patches. He redeemed himself with his poetry that gushed with romanticism and stirrings of the emotive self. For Iqbal's poetry differed greatly with his occasional reflections on scientific modernity that were secreted into his philosophy.

LOCATION OF WORK

In intellectual work, as in real estate, location is everything. In what context or environment one is located will to a large extent identify one's primary audience. The question of audience is a critical element in all interpretive and revisionist projects. Since progressive Islam is not only a theoretical enterprise but is also closely related to practice, location, and audience, these concerns are in many ways decisive. The loose alliance of scholars who today write about progressive Islam in North America hail from different backgrounds and contexts. Some are North American-born or naturalized citizens whose base communities are unmistakably North American. Others, in turn, work in the United States but whose primary social laboratory are communities in Africa, Asia, or the Middle East.

Part of the challenge to grasp the trajectory of progressive Islam is to comprehend the journeys that many individuals associated with this very undefined trend have undertaken through scholarship and activism. In my case, my formative work was done in South Africa and what follows is admittedly a highly truncated slice of a much more complex and detailed narrative. The selective nature of this narrative is to highlight some critical elements of the progressive Muslim struggle in the South African context.

As graduates of the seminaries or *madrasas* of India, Pakistan, and other regions of the Muslim world, several of my contemporaries like myself returned to our native land in the 1980s only to encounter a cauldron of political conflict and social injustice perpetrated by the system of apartheid. Young and inexperienced, we were yet determined to engage in the liberation struggle from an Islamic moral perspective. After all, Islamic discourse was what we knew best and to which our identities were intimately but also complexly related. While several secular organizations were available from which we could participate in the struggle for liberation, many of us also recognized the need to mobilize our communities in the language that they understood best: the language of faith and tradition.

As aspiring scholars and clerics we were convinced that Islam embodied a message of justice, equality, and freedom, a teaching we needed to internalize and practice programmatically. Our primary audience was the minority Muslim community of South Africa whom we had to remind of their moral duty and responsibility to regard legalized racial discrimination as a violation of human dignity and as sinful as if one were complicit in terms of Muslim ethics. While a section of the Muslim community was willing to embrace this message, a larger group was content to go along with the quietist and accomodationist posture that the overwhelming majority of Muslim clerical associations had adopted by tolerating apartheid's horrors.

It was no doubt an uphill battle to persuade many individuals and the leadership in the ulama community that they erroneously deemed certain doctrines to be part of tradition, such as requiring people to obey an oppressive state. Our exigencies required that such doctrines be reviewed. Most Muslim clerics saw it as their primary duty to defend their narrow sectarian and religious interests since they did not feel any obligation to make sacrifices on behalf of a largely non-Muslim and black majority, yoked and dehumanized by decades of legalized segregationist policies and systematic violence. Needless to say, consciously and unconsciously many nonblack communities in South Africa, Muslims included, had also internalized the structural racism of the society which blinded them to the realities of an oppressive state and caused them to ignore the ethical calling of justice demanded by their faith.

For the Muslim progressives this state of affairs required a mini-revolution in traditional juridical ethics (*fiqh*) and theology (*kalam*). The need was to ensure that Muslim ethical deliberations abandoned sectarian interests and developed a humanist and inclusivist vision that embraced all human beings irrespective of color, creed, and race. This meant going against the grain of a very strong exclusivist tradition dating back to the days of Muslim empire.

What made matters a little bit easier was the visibility of the Islamic revolution in Iran in 1979. This revolutionary message empowered disenfranchised people around the world with the promise of emancipation from authoritarian regimes and dictatorships supported by the major powers. Just as the United States was a major backer of the dethroned Pahlavi dictatorship in Iran, it also for a considerable time supported the minority white and apartheid government in Pretoria as a Cold War ally. Furthermore, around the 1980s, Muslim groups in different parts of the majority Muslim areas were also battling authoritarian governments. Solidarity with such liberatory and revolutionary movements, of course, inspired us in South Africa.

But it also dawned upon us that a progressive agenda in South Africa would be radically different from the kinds of developments occurring in Egypt, Iran, Sudan, or Pakistan. In those countries the emphasis was on the application of a full-blooded notion of Shari'a, the content of which produced bloody consequences and shocking miscarriages of justice. In South Africa our search was for a Shari'a that took into account our realities that were at once very different from those of Muslims in majority contexts.

Often we found voices located on the margins of the Muslim intellectual traditions: particularly attractive were those messages, ideas, and concepts that had resonance with our experiences. For instance, the mainstream and canonized tradition forbade alliances with non-Muslims and harbored suspicions about our associations with Jews and Christians, given a long and unsavory history of political hostilities with these communities over centuries dating back to nascent Islam in Arabia and the Crusades. Over time these attitudes crystallized into a virtual separatist Muslim theology that at least in theory kept associations with Jews and Christians to a minimum save for some notable exceptions in Muslim Spain. In addition, narrow juridical interpretations devalued the role of women in public life and politics.

Large chunks of this inherited tradition were unhelpful to our context, leaving activists agonizing over the psychological barriers such teachings produced. Many clerics and opponents of the progressive Muslim political cause repeated the authoritative readings that they had dredged from texts in order to discredit our meager new readings. Since only scant and selected authorities—past and present—in the tradition offered any kind of help to our context, our liberation theology and juridical ethics had to rely on new readings of the Qur'an and selections from the prophetic tradition. In his noted text *Qur'an, Liberation and Pluralism,* Farid Esack carefully documents the outlines of our ethical struggles and demonstrates how we retrieved the messages of liberation and pluralism from the narratives of the Qur'an. In the frighteningly repressive political climate and life and death struggles that characterized South Africa, it was comforting to read that God was on the side of the oppressed and righteous who were patiently and justly steadfast in God's cause.[3]

During the 1980s we hardly had the luxury to think through the complicated issues of Muslim ethics in a systematic and theoretically rigorous manner. The Muslim equivalents to theorists such as Marx, Engels, and Lenin were the writings of Qutb, Mawdudi, and Khomeini: the latter were rhetorically persuasive but intellectually limiting, if not at times castrating.

Given the exigencies of the struggle we were instantly required to produce reliable ethical positions on a host of issues. In hindsight, our writings were humane in their vision, but thin in intellectual depth; strong on polemics but weak on politics. Critical re-readings of the tradition in a systematic manner that would enable us to theorize our lived experiences in the tradition were a luxury and in short supply at the time.

What awaits those engaged in progressive Muslim discourses in the heat of crisis is to partake in critical reflection on those experiences. Many lessons are to be learned and an equal number had to be unlearned. High priority should be given to theorizing these experiences and practices. This is a task that a range of Muslim progressives needs to accomplish with the hope that our efforts from the geographical margins, as well as the edges of intellectual power vis-à-vis the prevailing orthodoxies, could foster new debates and diversify the tradition.

PROGRESSIVE TRADITION?

Progress is Janus-faced: it has opposing sides to it. Progress also signifies a particular relation to history; that history has an end (*telos*) and a predetermined goal. In a more benign way progress could mean advances in knowledge and the acquisition of some abilities and the loss of others, without making this contingent on the philosophy of history. In his *Theses on the Philosophy of History,* Benjamin meditates on the painting of the Swiss painter, Paul Klee (d. 1940), called the *Angelus Novus.* The image of the angel is for Benjamin the beguiling image of the angel of history. Here Benjamin's caution and deep ambivalence toward historicism surfaces strongly, for in his view the adherents of historicism, like Fukuyama, tend to empathize with the victors in history.

What intrigues Benjamin in the Klee painting is *how* the angel flies: his wings are spread but his face is turned towards the past. The wings of the angel cannot close because they are kept open by a violent storm from Paradise that propels him into the future. With a strong dose of irony, Benjamin comments: "This storm is what we call progress."[4]

At the very time when the helpless angel of history is pushed into the future by the storm of progress from Paradise, he heroically and against the odds resists the storm by turning his face towards the past. The turning back is suggestive of history and tradition, both of which Benjamin believes will restrain a hubristic and a runaway idea of progress.

In order to avoid the negative sense of the word "progress," says Benjamin, one needs to resist some senses of the word.[5] To understand "progress" as involving the transformation of the entirety of humankind is a hubristic posture, to say the least. Yes, indeed, one can acknowledge human advances in ability and knowledge. But to view progress as meaning the infinite perfectibility of humankind in competition with nature sits oddly with the notions of humility and balance advocated in Muslim ethical discourse. Of course, the struggle to reach moral and spiritual perfection is at the very core of Muslim ethical teaching but is very different to a historicist notion of perfection.

For some progressives knowledge of the tradition is important. I do not advocate that one should view knowledge of the tradition as sacred and unchanging; rather, it is subject to interrogation, correction, and advancement. For the upshot of all knowledge is not that it should be adored and worshipped but that it must be put to use and result in ethical practice. Therefore, the major question, if not the most challenging one that arises is whether a practice has to perpetually resemble its origin. The answer to this rhetorical question is not easily soluble: the answer is negotiated in the tradition, the state of *what* one is, and more importantly, *how* one exists.

One thing is for sure: tradition is definitely not a collection of texts. That would be only one source of knowledge of the tradition. Tradition is a state

of mind and a set of embodied practices. As practice, tradition undoubtedly
has authority and operates by certain rules of the game. Tradition, to use
the felicitous words of Pierre Bourdieu, is what the body learned or what
was "learned by body"; it is not something one acquires like knowledge,
but *what* one is.[6] Put differently, one could say that tradition is the self-
intelligibility of the past in the present; a continuously evolving and mutating
intelligibility or state of being. One could also say that tradition has everything to do with one's subjectivity.

The critical element, in order to be a person of tradition, is to have a
historical sense "not only of the pastness of the past," as T.S. Eliot noted,
"but of its presence."[7] The notion of tradition implies more than an awareness of the temporal and the timeless. To be a person of tradition one must
conceive of the temporal and timeless together; one must acutely become
aware of one's place in time and of one's own contemporaneity. Instead of
living in the present, a writer or thinker who engages with tradition lives in
the "present moment of the past" and shows an awareness, in Eliot's words,
"not of what is dead, but of what is already living." Since tradition in Islam is
so much about practices, it is then those practices that are learned by the
body. Tradition, like the body, does not memorize the past but "enacts the
past, bringing it back to life."[8]

Tradition is unlike palingenesis where certain organisms only reproduce
their ancestral characters without modification. Rather tradition works more
like kenogenesis: it describes how in biology an organism derives features
from the immediate environment in order to modify the hereditary development of a germ or organism.

If tradition has fallen into disrepute, it is because some who claim to be
traditionalist practitioners think of tradition, not as dynamic practices, but
rather confuse the knowledge of the tradition with tradition itself. From such
a perspective, tradition is reduced to a set of memories. Under trying and
negative circumstances, these memories give rise to self-pitying nostalgia.
Since some representatives of contemporary Muslim orthodoxy happily confuse knowledge with tradition, they err in imagining tradition to be immune
to environmental influences. Hence, seminal figures and agents in the history
of tradition are turned into unique and idealized personalities in an almost
mythical past. In this scheme, history is elevated to mythology and the human
beings who authored tradition are turned into hagiographical figures, beyond
the scrutiny of historical evidence. It is this excessive reverence for the past, in
my view, that in fact paralyzes dogmatic traditionalists. Paradoxically, what
happens within the ostensible centers of traditionalism is that time is flattened
and homogenized. Unfortunately, time looses its density and complex nature
and is reduced to a secular version with a superficial overlay of piety.

One of the hallmarks of the ideology of progress, one that violently
militates against notions of tradition, is that it considers and imagines time
as being homogenous and empty. Subtly, such a notion of time eradicates

difference: differences between people and in human experiences. In turn, it inspires the fantasy of a utopian historical process driving all nations toward the secular and hurtling toward an undifferentiated modernity. What differentiates the modern style—for that is what modernity really is, a style rather than a rupture—as opposed to its predecessors is the fundamental shift in the notion of time, which is antithetical to persons of tradition.

In the imagination of modernity, Reinhart Koselleck tells us, "Time is no longer simply the medium in which all histories take place, it gains a historical quality. Consequently, history no longer occurs in, but through time. Time becomes a dynamic and historical force in its own right."[9] By dynamic he means that time is credited with creative force, not with will and desire. And, in order to continuously create and re-create this dynamism, time must become singular and homogenous. In other words, time is no longer the vehicle in which history occurred, but rather time has become the driver who is on autopilot. All the passengers in the vehicle are completely at the driver's mercy. The passengers have no will to decide which cars, makes, or models they will drive since the driver cannot take instructions for he is a factory-made automaton! Where conceptions of time were once shaped by the specificities of distinct environments, rhythms, and rituals, now these are eroded.

On this front Muslim progressives must be extremely cautious. If there is a wish to engage knowledge of tradition, one should resist the desire to reduce traditions to "things," or a "single" interpretation, and deem tradition as only "one" practice. While certain forms of dogmatic traditionalism often portray themselves as the singular and authentic voices of Islam, a more careful investigation of Muslim knowledge traditions would often show that the very issues in question have been debated, contested, and disagreed upon and hence, less authoritarian. However, when tradition itself is imagined as a kind of prefabricated design of being then it is a sure sign of traditionalists gone berserk, obsessed with power but paradoxically also dressed in the imperial garb of the modern. This is what I would call designer traditionalism.

Progressives should heed the caution of Michel Serres and his student Bruno Latour and not fall prey to something we all fall prey to from time to time: the issue of period-dating. Seventeenth century intellectual thought (a product of critique-thinking) artificially separated the modern from the premodern.[10] Early science and capitalism, Latour points out, needed to engage in a reductionist philosophy in order to constitute reality into a nature-culture division with the view to accelerate technological-scientific advances. Making such arbitrary divisions in a "work of purification" was now indefensible. It arbitrarily splits objects from subjects and separates nature/earth from human/science. Ironically, this valuable insight itself assaults the term "progress," for progress facilitates the false separation since it assumes that its opposite is static. (I have already explained that I use the term under protest.)

A great responsibility rests on the shoulders of progressives to revive tradition in all its vibrancy, intelligibility, and diversity. One might have to avoid the error made by some Christian and Jewish thinkers and schools of thought who uncritically bought into the inevitability thesis of progress.

Here I wish to offer the view that one should begin to aspire to the *possibility* of progress by engaging the knowledge of tradition without marginalizing it or neglecting its wisdom. Indeed, most people who think of themselves as traditionalists might be surprised to learn that every enactment of tradition also involves a critique. A progressive intellectual posture involves a critical interrogation of the conveyerbelt of tradition, namely texts, practices, and histories, by posing a series of questions to the inherited knowledges of the tradition. In other words, a critical Muslim or a progressive Muslim is also engaged in critical traditionalism. Critique of tradition is not to debunk tradition, but it is rather an introspection of what one is: a continuous questioning of one's being. Recall that I earlier said that tradition is all about what one is: it is more than identity, more than texts and practices, more than history. It is all that, plus more: the additional element remains undefined, but it involves all those things that make one feel that you belong.

TRANSITIONS, NOT CONCLUSIONS: KNOWLEDGES IN THE *DIHLIZ* (INTERSTICE)

Throughout this chapter I have not discussed the specifics as to what the content of anything conceivably called progressive Islam should look like. That was intentional. Rather, I reflected on my experiences in encountering the knowledge of tradition and tried to provide some "after the fact" theoretical reflections and self-critique. There is a reason why I am reluctant to be prescriptive about content. If the progressive movement is going to be prescriptive, then it is going to end up in a one-size fits all version of progressive Islam with predictable disasters in tow. Once one advocates a specific content for progressive Islam, then it becomes an institution with ideological interests that will cauterize its dynamism. And, from a practical point of view if progressives are going to take upon themselves the institutional representation, they take on a burden greater than they can bear. One can hardly forecast all scenarios and contexts in one country or region, let alone do advocacy for a global audience. Rather, I view the momentum toward progressive Islam to be a catalyst for other existing tendencies in Islam, not as a replacement. In fact, progressives must engage and challenge the existing practices and interpretations as members of those communities and not as a separate church or tendency whose credentials are questioned because of a certain aloofness from the larger communities. This is the hard and more challenging part of being an advocate of progressive Islam since it is easy to preach and work with like-minded people. The challenge is to engage people with whom one disagrees. Second, I fear that once progressive practices of Islam are institutionalized and imposed from the top, it will have a number of deleterious effects. Like the well-intentioned labors of Muslim modernists a century ago, progressive Muslims run the risk of becoming servants of power. The state-driven modernizing of Islam has turned Muslim modernists into partners and servants of the most brutal authoritarian regimes from Egypt to Pakistan, and from Tunisia to Indonesia. Muslim progressives might have to consider the value of entering the democratic base of their societies rather than placating elites. Needless to say, this is much easier said than done and a great deal more thought has to be invested to configure the most effective strategies. Third, Muslim progressives must avoid running the risk of appearing to confect some version of a civilizing mission for Muslims. Showing vigilance for the designs of power to co-opt progressives for Neo-conservative, imperialist, or nationalist projects, be they Islamic or non-Islamic is a first step. Continuous self-critique and debate will help us avoid repeating the missteps that our well-meaning predecessors committed.

Critical or progressive approaches to the practice of Islam, especially questions directed at the knowledge traditions together with their relevant answers, are determined by specific contexts. In fact, the context is an undeniable part of the question of practice; it imprints itself on the tradition. To provide prescriptive answers from outside that specific context would be a colonizing posture to be avoided at all costs. Yet, it is an altogether different matter if people in one context wish to learn from the experiences of another context in order not to reinvent the wheel in analogous issues. In such a case, when people do accept the insights derived from another experience, then they do so voluntarily without dictation from outside and they own the idea and practice as their own.

By allowing the interpretation and practice of Islam to be context-driven one also ensures a robust diversity and pluralism. But more importantly, it takes the experiences of each context seriously. While the idea and practice of Islam were inspired by nonhistorical impulses of prophecy and revelation, everything after that initial moment occurs in the full light of history. For this reason it is imperative that Islamic norms be informed by peoples' historical experiences. Thus, if interfaith dialogue and solidarity, and gender justice were burning issues in the South Africa of the 1980s, to cite one example, then it does not mean that these would be the same priorities in the twenty-first century. Hypothetically, Muslims in Egypt may well deem political pluralism and justice to be their urgent priorities, while in America women's access to mosques and the right to religious leadership might be regarded as urgent.

Often practices and experiences are not driven by clear-cut theories and policies that are applied in sanitized environments. To the contrary, practices are produced in much messier contexts and contingent circumstances. In recounting the experiences of Muslim progressives in South Africa,

I observed that theoretical reflection was a luxury and more often than not, practical necessity, common sense, and ethical vision coupled with a certain pragmatism informed our practices in that specific theater of struggle. Theory usually occurs after practice, just like the disciplines of legal theory (*usul al-fiqh*) and the theory of theology (*usul al-din* or *'ilm al-kalam*) emerged as theoretical reflections after the practice of law, ethics and speculative theology had been in vogue for some time.

Theory is necessary for several reasons. One of the more obvious needs for theory is to provide some intellectual coherence and social intelligibility to existing practices. Theory has the ability to finesse and sharpen the rationales underlying practices and also to refine practices. And, theory makes complicated ideas and experiences accessible and digestible for pedagogical ends. Universality of ideas and practices combined with the brevity of abstraction facilitates easy transmission from one context to another. Evidently, the plurality of theories inherited from the past and those manufactured in the present constitute tangible evidence of the different Muslim experiences that need to be sustained at all costs if one wishes to avoid totalitarian outcomes in religious thought.

A plurality of experiences is borne due to differences in knowledge. The fallibility of human knowledge is made manifest in the inescapable diversity and hybridity of knowledge. Fallibility is an imperfection but a necessary one that makes the search for knowledge imperative. No wonder that some of the best exemplars of the Islamic tradition starting from the Prophet, the Companions to later figures like Abu Hamid al-Ghazali (d. 1111 CE), Abu al-Walid Ibn Rushd (d. 1198 CE), Muhyi al-Din Ibn Arabi (d. 1240 CE) made a virtue of intellectual promiscuity. Ghazali demonstrated this diversity in his monumental writings, pressing the value of in-between space (*dihliz*) of daily living and reflection.[11] The spatial metaphor of a threshold or portal, a *dihliz*—an intermediate portal separating the Persian home from its exterior—is also a productive dialogical space. From Ghazali and countless others we learn how intellectual productivity was enhanced at the interstices of cultures. Ghazali imagined and theorized all thought and practice to be a continuous dialogical movement between the inner and the outer; the esoteric and the exoteric; body and spirit in a productive fashion. He did not configure the dialogic in a simplistic binary relation but imagined these to be the polarities of a force field.

Suspended within this force field was the subject diligently tending to the needs of both matter and spirit. Underlying all our critical activity is a complex hybridity and fuzziness, despite our every pretension to smooth it out. And while over the longer duration we can sometimes observe dramatic shifts in knowledge, on most occasions we pass through transitions, creases, and folds in knowledge and time.

The perpetual quest is to seek emergent knowledge arising out of our struggles and transitions for alternative futures. We do know one thing taught by experience: that the dominant paradigms need to be continuously contested with alternative ways of knowing, different types of knowledge and models for society building. The future, as Boaventura de Sousa Santos pointed out, has become a personal question for us, a question of life and death.[12] In order to pursue such futures we also need to resort to the past not as a ready-made solution, but as a creative problem susceptible to opening up new possibilities. "Certainly we need history," Nietzsche wrote. "But our need for history is quite different from that of the spoiled idler in the garden of knowledge," he continued, adding: "...[W]e require history for life and action, not for the smug avoiding of life and action, or even to whitewash a selfish life and cowardly, bad acts."[13]

Both Ghazali and Ibn Arabi, just like Nietzsche later, were compelled to reread the past as a prophecy that would change the present. Unfortunately, too many thinkers have understood the progress of civilization in stoutly economistic terms linking the division of labor to the development of society. It may well be part of the truth, but certainly not the whole of the truth. But it is the prophetic activity dedicated to life that we seek in its intensities. A life premised on balance and distribution is necessary in order to avoid the nihilistic end that beckons without it. The progress we make in giving shape to that prophetic spirit—a life of practice and will to power—opens up the *possibilities* of new histories, not their inevitability and least of all the end of history, which is in reality a disguised theology of eschatology unique to a certain Christian worldview, but not necessarily shared by all. It is precisely because of the possibility of history and the will to power that Fukuyama's end of history prophecy, now running aground in the ruins of Mesopotamia and the Hindu Kush mountains as well as in the ashes of the World Trade Center in New York, proves that he was so grotesquely wrong. The neoconservatives and liberal capitalists who are riding the crest of history for now are confident about the inevitability of progress. But will their terminus also signal the crash of civilization? For those who view history as a continuous struggle, a gift carrying the possibilities of progress, the cultivation of civilization remains inviting and utterly tempting.[14]

NOTES

1. Francis Fukuyama, *The End of History and the Last Man* (London, U.K.: Hamish Hamilton, 1992).

2. Ernest Lee Tuveson, *Millennium and Utopia: A Study in the Background of the Idea of Progress* (Berkeley & Los Angeles: University of California Press, 1949), 5.

3. Farid Esack, *Qur'an, Liberation and Pluralism: Towards an Islamic Perspective of Inter-Religious Solidarity against Oppression* (Oxford, U.K.: Oneworld Publications, 1997).

4. Walter Benjamin, "Theses on the Philosophy of History," in *Illuminations: Essays and Reflections,* ed. Hannah Arendt (New York: Schocken Books, 1986), 257–258.

5. Ibid., 260–261.

6. Pierre Bourdieu, *The Logic of Practice,* trans. Richard Nice (Stanford, California: Stanford University Press, 1990), 73.

7. T.S. Eliot, "Tradition and the Individual Talent," in *Selected Prose of T.S. Eliot,* ed. Frank Kermode (London, U.K.: Faber & Faber, 1975), 38.

8. Bourdieu, *Logic of Practice.*

9. Reinhart Koselleck, *Futures Past: On the Semantics of Historical Time,* trans. Keith Tribe (Cambridge, Massachusetts and London, U.K.: The MIT Press, 1985), 246.

10. Donald Wesling, "Michael Serres, Bruno Latour, and the Edges of Historical Periods," *CLIO: Journal of Literature, History and the Philosophy of History* 26, no. 2 (1997): 200.

11. Ebrahim Moosa, *Ghazali and the Poetics of Imagination* (Chapel Hill, North Carolina: University of North Carolina Press, 2005).

12. Boaventura de Sousa Santos, *Toward a New Common Sense: Law, Science and Politics in the Paradigmatic Transition* (New York and London, U.K.: Routledge, 1995).

13. Friedrich Nietzsche, *On the Advantage and Disadvantage of History for Life,* trans. Peter Preuss (Indianapolis, Indiana: Hackett Publishing Company, 1980), 7.

14. Ahmet Karamustafa, "Islam: A Civilizational Project in Progress," in *Progressive Muslims: On Justice, Gender and Pluralism,* ed. Omid Safi (Oxford, U.K.: Oneworld, 2003).

7

SEXUAL DIVERSITY IN ISLAM

•

Scott Sirajul Haqq Kugle

In the name of God, the compassionate One, the One who cares. Praise be to the singular One by whose will diversity was created and to whose unique Oneness all bewildering multiplicity points in signs, for that One promises, "We will show them [human beings] our signs, upon the horizons and within themselves" (Qur'an 41:53).

I became a Muslim in response to the moral challenge of the Qur'an. Over years of study and reflection, I was drawn to its vision of human responsibility in the cosmos whose diversity and multiplicity testifies to the unity of the One who creates and sustains. The ethical challenge to form a just community that respects and encourages diversity is a key component of its message. One of the most pressing ethical challenges for adherents of all religions in contemporary times is how to respond to diversity in sexuality and gender identity, that is how they respond to lesbian, gay, and transgendered members of their religion. Muslims are not exempt from this challenge, though many flee it. However, when Muslims face the issues squarely, they find that the Qur'an offers many resources to creatively, compassionately and caringly address sexuality and gender diversity.

Diversity in the world is a fact. Pluralism is a political response to that fact, asserting that the moral order should promote respect and dignity for all, despite diversity, difference and division. We often associate pluralism with "secularism," but it is not in principle antagonistic to religion, for Muslims in Indonesia and India have developed a definition of secularism as pluralistic religious devotion. From an Islamic orientation, one can advocate "tawhidic pluralism," a religious response to diversity that embraces pluralism as a positive moral state, acknowledging that a single God purposefully creates and nurtures a cosmos and humanity characterized by deep diversity. My approach in this chapter is that promoting dignifying respect, mutual responsibility, and reciprocal care for all despite their diversity is the way to witness the oneness of God (*tawhid*).

ISLAM AND MUSLIMS

Who am I to write this essay? To better help my readers understand what I write, it is important to specify from what position I speak. I am an American Muslim who grew up in a largely Christian environment but has lived and worked many years in Islamic environments (from Muslim majority contexts like Morocco and Pakistan to Muslim minority contexts like Canada and India). I am a scholar of Islamic religion and culture, with a Ph.D. in Religious Studies, basic training in Islamic disciplines of knowledge (*usul al-din* including the Qur'an, Hadith, and *fiqh*), and the ability to read and translate Islamic texts in Arabic, Persian and Urdu. I belong to the often-oppressed and silenced minority of homosexuals who, along with transgendered people, exist in all cultures though in different roles. I myself identify as a gay man who was "out" before I became a Muslim and am still a gay man after having become a Muslim—some things do not change. In my experience, being gay is a deeply embedded element of one's personality. I find strength in knowing that I am not alone; as more people who are raised as Muslims find the courage to accept their homosexuality and build support and advocacy groups, they are joined by increasing numbers of homosexual women and men who have converted to the faith.[1]

How I can be both a Muslim and a gay, people often ask—this is both a naïve question and a profound one. Speaking frankly, sexual orientation was simply not an issue in my conversion, which was inspired by the Qur'anic vision of the universal message of all religions. But I tell those who ask that it all depends on what kind of Islam one adopts, for it is no longer a simple matter to be a Muslim, if it ever was. What kind of Muslim am I? The violent and crisis-ridden times we are living in demand that we give a complex answer to that question. I am a non-sectarian Sunni with a progressive approach to religion. I value the Shari'a for how its ritual worship offers a means to live an ethically engaged life based upon intellectual principles guided toward humane goals. I approach law (*fiqh*) as a follower of Abu Hanifa (d. 767 CE) and I am a reformist within the Hanafi legal method (*madhhab*) that values rational assessment of traditional sources like hadith reports as essential to the growth and internal renewal of Shari'a. I approach theology (*kalam*) as an admirer of Maturidi (d. 944 CE), who forged a middle way between extreme rationalists (like the Mu'tazila) and dogmatic literalists (like the Hashawis of the past and the Hanbalis and Salafis of the present), for Maturidi never abandoned dialectic between reason and revelation to achieve human justice, as the Sunnis mainly did. I uphold the rational observation of philosophy/science as a student of Ibn Rushd (d. 1198 CE), who affirmed that the natural world is in harmony with revelation and that revelation should be interpreted in ways guided by reason and scientific discovery, not just tradition. I approach ethics (*akhlaq*) as an adherent of Nizam al-Din Awliya (d. 1325 CE), a Sufi exemplar who taught a delicate balance of love and justice, in which the sincerest way to worship the One who creates all is to care for the vulnerable with selfless humility.

This is who I am, as shaped by my teachers, religious exemplars, and spiritual ancestors in Islam. Because I was not born into a Muslim family, I have had greater need to find ancestors and specify who they are and why I follow them. If any Muslim tries, she or he can clarify ancestors who have shaped her or his personality, religious sensibility, and practical method of Islam. I think this is an ethical necessity, to clearly state who we follow and why, so as not to abdicate responsibility and blindly imitate our parents, friends, or local leaders (*taqlid*). Both reason and sincerity urge us to critically examine our beliefs so that we will not repeat what the Qur'an condemns: "Surely we found our parents of that persuasion, and only by their footsteps do we guide ourselves!" (Qur'an 43:23).

Most people cling to presumptions when it comes to issues of sexuality and gender, and feel that they already know "what Islam says" without reflecting on whether they based their opinion on patriarchal culture or knowledge of religion. Maturidi eloquently specifies how we know about religion: "The principle of what we know as religion—for it is necessary that people have a religion upon which they come together and a principle to which they take recourse—has two dimensions, namely transmitted tradition (*sam*) and discerning reason (*aql*)."[2] We come to know the reality of anything, including religion, through three means: what we sense directly (*ayan*), what we learn from others (*akhbar*), and what we deduce by reasoned research (*nazar*). We know of religion mainly through learning from others, for we know the Qur'an by continuous and multiple transmission to us (*tawatur*), vouchsafed by the Prophet Muhammad's honesty about what he sensed directly; similarly we know of the Prophet's behavior through hadith reports transmitted by people who witnessed his words and actions, some of which may have reliable transmission but many of which do not. However, we can never reduce religion down to transmitted tradition, as comforting as that would be to many who seek security in the world from the world. In accepting tradition and especially acting upon it, we need to rely on reason. As Maturidi teaches us, "The human being is specially endowed with the moral responsibility to manage the affairs of the created world, to meet people's needs through labor, to seek the most beneficial circumstances for their powers of reason and choose what is best for them and while protecting them from what is contrary to this—there is no way to achieve this except by using discernment through reasoned researched into the nature of things.... For reason gives us evidence of the reality of things and leads us to grasp their meaning in the same way we rely upon sight to recognize color, hearing to understand sound, and each sense to perceive the reality we experience. We rely on reason for understanding just like we rely on our senses for perception, and there is no power but with God."[3]

Many values we Muslims commonly attribute to Islam do not come from the most highly revered sources of the religion (foremost the Qur'an) but rather from patriarchal culture. Patriarchy is the ideology instituting dominance of elder straight males over all others, specifically women of all ages, younger men, and minority males who do not accept patriarchal roles that reinforce masculine power. As observed by Islamic feminists, patriarchy existed before the advent of the Qur'an and the Prophet Muhammad's example, which deeply challenged it. In later generations after the Prophet's death, Muslims built the Shari'a in ways that inscribed patriarchal values deep into Islamic culture, compromising the Qur'an's ethical voice. Because of this, Muslims for many centuries did not seriously consider either the issue of women's equality with men, did not allow dignified roles for homosexual persons or countenance transgendered persons in Muslim communities. Rapid changes in society under the impact of modernity, along with advances in scientific knowledge in the fields of psychology, sociology, and genetic biology, make reassessing the classical Shari'a a vital necessity. In addition, the voices of previously marginalized minorities, like women, lesbian, gay, and transgendered Muslims, insist on justice after such a long imposed silence. Previously marginalized groups offer important ethical insights into non-patriarchal interpretations of Islamic scripture, insights not available to those who have not suffered similar experiences of existential exclusion.

The goal of this chapter is to show that homosexual and transgendered Muslims exist, that they speak in a voice which offers a constructive and reformist critique of classical Islamic thought, and that Islamic theology has previously untapped resources to comprehend them and give them a dignified role in contemporary Islamic communities.[4] As Maturidi reminds us above, our sincere practice of Islam depends upon constant application of "discernment through reasoned research into the nature of things." Such research may change our view of religion depending on new developments in politics, social organization, and scientific understanding. All these things impact our view of sexuality and homosexuality, and demand that we apply reason to scripture and traditional custom.

DIVERSITY AND SEXUALITY

The Qur'an assesses diversity as a positive reality in the created nature of things. Diversity and multiplicity in the cosmos, in humanity, and between social groups is an integral part of God's creative will. It is an indispensable challenge to moral systems. Islamic feminists have explored the Qur'anic description of gender, such as "O people, stay aware of your Lord who created you all from a single self and created from it its mate and spread from those two many men and women" (Qur'an 4:1). The creation of women was not a mistake, a lessening of the moral standard, or a faulty copying of the perfect male, all of which were suggested by later patriarchal interpretations of Islam encoded in the Shari'a.[5] Diversity in gender is intimately related to diversity in human communities between tribes, sects, nations, and civilizations: "O people, We created you all from a male and female and made you into different communities and different tribes, so that you should come to know one another, acknowledging that the most noble among you is the one most aware of Allah" (Qur'an 49:13). There is a moral purpose behind the single God's creation of conflicting human types: it challenges us to restrain our egoistic aggrandizement, practice ethical compassion toward others, protect the vulnerable in their socially-defined difference, and through this stay conscious of God's presence. "If God had willed, God would have made you one single community, but rather God brings whomever God wills within divine compassion—yet the unjust oppressors have no guardian and no helper" (Qur'an 42:8).

Our human diversity that is so often a cause for exclusion and violence, is actually God's way of challenging us to rise up to the demands of justice beyond the limitation of our individual egoism and communal chauvinism. Deep diversity confronts us with a bewildering pattern of differentiation. Yet difference too often leads us to exclude others in hopes of building a firm community or with ambition to create a hierarchy of power to assert some moral order. However, the Qur'an warns us against going to extremes to exclude others, reminding us that not a single life is dispensable: "Whoever kills an innocent life, it is as if he had killed all of humanity. And whoever gives life to one, it is as if he had revived all of humanity. We have sent them our prophets with clear teaching, but subsequently many of them have gone willfully astray" (Qur'an 5:32). All people, despite their apparent and real differences, are part of a greater whole; safeguarding the dignity of each is essential to achieving one's own dignity and upholding the rights of each is integral to securing justice for oneself.

The diversity of human communities comes not just from appearance, which our society's racial ideology commonly associates with skin color (for Muslim societies are not immune from racism or the institution of slavery), but also from the subtler hues of language and shades of belief. The Qur'an says, "One of God's signs is the creation of the heavens and the earth and the diversity of your tongues and your colors, in which there are signs for those who know" (Qur'an 30:22). The Qur'anic term for "color," in the richness of Arabic metaphors, could refer not just to visible hues, but also to other different sensations like the "taste" of different dishes of food or aromas.[6] Our diversity as human beings goes much deeper than the color of the skin or surface appearance but rather extends into the inner core of our personalities where language, concepts, beliefs and experiences lie. With such a radically positive assessment of human diversity on the epistemological and ethical levels, one can justifiably wonder whether the Qur'an addresses diversity in sexuality as well.

What do we mean by sexuality? Deep in the core of the human personality lies our sense of sexuality, which is far more subtle and pervasive than just sexual acts. By sexuality, we mean a kind of self-awareness that is not just an urge (like lust) but also a passion that grants us emotional fulfillment, sparks in us expansive joy and urges us toward existential coming-to-completeness through encountering another person in a way that unites body, soul, and spirit. Sexual acts bring us as close as possible to "tasting" another person, not just in bodily sensations but also in terms of comprehending the other person's sense of self. Just like tasting food, one comes to sense another's presence by taking her or him into one's own body, dissolving the barrier between self and other through harmonious movement, intense intimacy, and ecstatic rapture. This is why sexual acts are so powerful, and why sexuality is such an intimate part of each individual's personality and an integral component in each person's appreciation of beauty or apprehension of emotional intensity.

Sexuality is made up of many components, making its manifestation in any individual unique. These components include strength of sex drive, frequency of sexual contact, a continuum of style from aggressively passionate to delicately tender, and variation in intensity of response. Of course, an integral component of sexuality is sexual orientation, that is whether one is attracted to a partner of the same gender or the opposite gender (or perhaps to both and possibly to neither). Is this concept found in scripture or in Islam? What we term "sexuality" was discussed by classical Islamic theologians and jurists in ways detailed later in this chapter; however, they did not reflect systematically on what we call "sexual orientation." Before we turn to their opinions, upon which the classical Islamic tradition is based, we need to develop a sufficiently subtle model, based on the Qur'an, for understanding personality and how sexual orientation is related to it.

NATURE AND PERSONALITY

Sexual orientation is one of the "color" differences that make people distinct from each other. Yet those who oppose homosexuality call it "un-natural" or against human nature. In contrast, homosexuals attest that it is an expression of their innate personality and sense of self that is so deep as to be beyond the rational capacity to alter. This attestation is supported by clinical research of professional psychiatric associations, which have removed homosexuality from the category of "personality disorder" and disavowed techniques previously claimed to be able to "correct" sexual orientation. Clearly, the argument is over what constitutes human nature. From an Islamic perspective, we can ask how does God create human beings? What roles do sexuality and orientation play in the personality? Do human beings "choose" their sexual orientation? Is it alterable by choice or habit?

Are we morally accountable for sexual orientation if is part of the subrational elements of personality? The questions raised are profound and the answers are not obvious.

Modern psychiatry increasingly holds sexual orientation to be an inherent part of an individual's personality, elements of which may be genetic, influenced by hormonal balances in the womb, and shaped by early childhood experiences, the cumulative effects of which unfold during adolescence and early adulthood. Most psychiatrists in the West (and increasingly among professionals in Muslim communities) hold that the attitude toward one's sexual orientation is largely cultural and that behavior based upon one's sexual orientation is subject to rational control and clinical modification, but the underlying sexual orientation is not. In premodern times, philosophers also observed that sexual orientation was largely determined outside the choice of the individual; lacking knowledge of genes, hormones, and psychiatric research, they usually speculated that determination was by astrological influences.[7] The personal accounts of lesbian and gay Muslims testify to the early and deep feeling of being different, followed by long and difficult struggles to understand that this difference was due to homosexual orientation and to find ways of explaining this to family and friends while striving for emotional satisfaction within the limits of one's sexual possibilities. In contrast, Muslim communities are undecided as to whether to accept modern psychiatric research. One gay Muslim who grew up in Syria, Muhammad Omar Nahas, visited several psychiatrists to seek a "cure" for his homosexuality, and found some of them advocating therapy to change his sexual orientation while others held that only behavior could be changed not one's internal disposition.[8]

As professionals in Muslim communities slowly adopt clinical approaches based on research and modern medicine, they will advocate a nonjudgmental approach. At the same time, Neo-Traditionalist Muslims caricature homosexuality as a crime, a disease, or an addiction and have a wide audience. Many Muslims are willing to accept modern medical knowledge and techniques in an *ad hoc* manner, to solve particular problems, but shy away from developing a coherent theory of the human personality, based either upon medical practices and scientific discoveries or upon their own religious scripture. However, Muslim theologians, especially the Sufis among them, developed a theory of personality that most contemporary Muslims who oppose homosexuality ignore. We must continue to build upon their insights, to integrate into them new complexities revealed by contemporary psychiatry, so that our notions of morality are firmly grounded in the reality of human personality.

Personality is made up of many levels, and in my understanding of the Qur'an I find reference to at least four: outer appearance, inward disposition, genetic pattern, and inner conscience. The outer form in which we appear is *sura,* as the Qur'an says, "O human being, what has deceived you from your

Generous Lord who created you well-shaped and balanced you and set you into whatever form [*sura*] God desired" (Qur'an 82:6–8). Many other verses describe the stages in which God creates each person's form or *sura*, in the mother's womb as a physical growth and later after breathing into it of the spirit, as a new being with consciousness, and continuing to develop and grow through birth, infancy, childhood, and adolescence. *Sura* unfolds into fullness as we reach adulthood and act autonomously as moral agents and are held accountable for our actions. However, our personality consists of far more than our outward appearance and rational actions.

From experiences in infancy and childhood, each person develops an inward disposition, a set of traits, potentials, or characteristics that are more or less innate, which the Qur'an calls *shakila*. This disposition determines how we react to experiences, as profoundly as shaping our potential to have faith. "We reveal of the Qur'an that which is healing and compassion for the believers yet which gives the oppressors nothing but loss. When we bless people they turn away and act proudly, but when harm brushes them, they despair. So say, 'All act according to their own disposition [*shakila*], yet your Lord knows best who is on the most guided path'" (Qur'an 17:82–83). Disposition is made up of factors beyond our conscious decision and often beyond our awareness: childhood experiences, infant memories, emotional, and intellectual capabilities. In short, it is our psyche through which the ego manifests itself.

Through contemporary science, we are discovering that genetic patterns in our biological material not only determine our outward form but also greatly affects psychic disposition. Genetic inheritance is a third level of our personality. The Qur'an refers to this material substrate of organic life by pronouncing "We created the human being from a quintessence of clay" (Qur'an 23:12). In Arabic, this is called *tabi'a* (one's "physical stamp" that determines one's temperamental nature), a term adopted not from the Qur'an but from Greek science. From this genetic stamp embedded deep in our organic tissue, the Qur'an depicts the development from zygote to fetus to infant, referring to this intimate relationship between genetic material, biological organism, and moral agency: "Then we made the human being a spermazoid firmly embedded, then we created from the spermazoid a clot of mucus and created from the mucus a lump of flesh, then created from the flesh bones, then clothed the bones with muscle, then we transformed it into another creation—so blessed be God, the best of creators!" (Qur'an 13:14). As a Muslim, I uphold that the choices we make based upon genetic potential and constrained within environmental limitations generate our moral worth. I certainly do not argue that genetics determines everything about us in a way that excuses moral failings, any more than I would agree with a deterministic theology that imagines that God wills the corrupt and unjust oppressors into hell by *fiat* (a position toward which much of classical Islamic theology veers dangerously close). However, moral worth must not be prejudged, and each person must be given a reasonable chance to assess her or his potential for growth and ground for sincerity, based upon a realistic, reasonable and compassionate assessment of one's own position and personality: "God does not make persons responsible for what is beyond their capacity" (Qur'an 2:233; 6:152; 7:42; 23:62). For everyone has the capacity to apprehend God, as the Qur'an optimistically affirms.

This is the fourth layer of personality, one's inner conscience nestled subtly within one's outer appearance and accessible only through one's inward disposition. This is the part of our personality in which our true humanity lies. It is our original nature or *fitra*, the deep core of our being that touches on the spirit and stays aware of the presence of God. Our outer form may grow and decay while our inward disposition may become refined or lapse into rawness, but our inner conscience remains fresh if our awareness is not distracted from it. "Set your face to the moral challenge [*din*] in a pure way, according to the original nature of God upon which [God] based humanity, for there is no changing the creation of God" (Qur'an 30:30). We were created to be aware of God's presence (through all of God's qualities, majestic, and awe-inspiring qualities as well as beautiful and love-invoking qualities), and nobody is excluded from this original nature that is never lost. This *fitra* provides us with our conscience; it is the seat of intention and sincerity by which actions will be judged for their moral worth, as the Prophet is reported to have taught: "Surely actions are by intentions and each will get that for which they intend."[9]

Sexual acts, too, should be judged by the intention with which they are performed, an intention formed within the heart of sincerity and fully colored by the filter of inward disposition before being expressed through the physicality of apparent action. Sexual orientation is latent within each individual, emerging in complex interactions between the genetic *tabi'a* and early childhood *shakila*. Current research is pushing slowly but steadily toward the conclusion that sexual orientation is largely inherent, psychiatrists investigating early childhood experience and biochemists discovering hormonal influence during fetal development and genetic inheritance even before birth. The truth probably lies between the two, but in any case sexual orientation is firmly in place before rational thought or adolescent maturity. Judging sexual acts without a theory of sexuality will lead to injustice and will betray the most fundamental Islamic teaching that actions are assessed by the intention behind them.

SEXUAL DESIRE IN THE QUR'AN

Classical Islamic theologians and jurists interpreted the Qur'an without a theory of sexual orientation. Although the Prophet's life provided a model of sexuality and positive morality, they mainly discussed sexuality in negative terms, as the power of lust (*quwwa shahwaniyya*). For example, Fakhr al-Din Razi (d. 1209 CE) claims that the power of lust leads to unrestrained and immoral acts, including sex but not unique to it.[10] The key term in their discussion is *shahwa*, meaning lust or sensual desire. However, the Qur'an uses this term in nuanced ways, sometimes positively and sometimes negatively, to mean desire as appetite, the pleasurable delight of consuming. The Qur'an uses *shahwa* as a verb in conjunction with food as well as sex, pleasures as that promised to souls in heaven, the absence of which torments souls in hell.[11] On a more worldly level, the Qur'an warns of *shahwa* as desire for all domestic delights that give the soul satisfaction and the body ease, which if unbridled can become lustful: "Made beautiful to people is the love of desires, for women and children and treasures hoarded of gold and silver and well-bred horses and livestock and crops—that is a transient worldly life given them by their lord, but with God is the best return" (Qur'an 3:14). Clearly, *shahwa* as lust is harmful, for it distracts one from God's presence, incites greed, and leads to committing immoral deeds. "Desires" appear in the plural, to show the variety of directions in which lust can move: toward food, sex, pride in family (the mention of children), wealth (gold and silver, livestock and crops), status and power (horses).

These objects of desire are not bad nor is the pleasurable enjoyment of them, so they are not prohibited in themselves. Rather, the psychic state of the desire, *shahwa*, makes such enjoyment lustful. Bodily pleasures can be saturated with egoistic pleasures, and the Qur'an juxtaposes the term *shahwa* with another *bagha*, meaning ardent desire or covetousness.[12] *Bagha* is less about bodily pleasure or concupiscence and more about getting egoistic satisfaction, getting one's way.[13] Yet the Qur'an asserts that seeking and desiring is not bad in itself but depends upon its intent and sincerity. If one seeks and desires while acknowledging the bounty of God (*fadl*) and giving thanks for getting one's way (*shukr*) without damaging others (*darar*) or transgressing their rights (*huquq*), then braving the dangerous waves of desire may not be reprehensible: "It is God who made subservient the sea, that you may eat from it fresh flesh and extract from it ornaments to wear, thus you see the ships cleaving through it, that you might seek your desires from God's bounty and that you may give thanks" (Qur'an 16:14). What God demands from believers is mindfulness, sincerity, and thanks for every benefit, whether it is corporeal delight or egoistic desire.[14] Sex is included with food, wealth, and power as among our desires, which might be good or bad depending on the intent, intensity, and ethical comportment of the desiring, more than on the specific object or experience desired. The Qur'an warns everyone about sexual lust, regardless of sexual orientation or marital status. Even heterosexual sex with one's legal spouse can be lustful, as implied by the above-quoted verse, if it leads to greed, selfishness, or abuse.

Does the Qur'an contain indications about sexual orientation? Its language specifically addresses heterosexual persons. This is no surprise, since they constitute the vast majority in any society, including the Prophet Muhammad's immediate environment in Arabia. In one sense, heterosexual relationships are most important for society at large, especially a small one under threat, as was the early Muslim community, since procreation, child-rearing, and family lineage are consequences of heterosexual relationships. For this reason, the Qur'an directly addressed adultery along with legitimacy and inheritance. In contrast, the Qur'an does not clearly and unambiguously address homosexuals in the Muslim community, as there is no term in the Qur'an for "homosexual." This is true despite the fact that many classical Muslim jurists identify the Qur'anic narrative of Lot's struggle with his tribe (*qawm Lut*) as addressing homosexual sex. The Prophet Lot's tribe means the people of Sodom and Gomorrah, as described in the Torah. All Muslim interpreters condemn how the men of Lot's tribe rejected Lot's authority over them by trying to deprive him of the right to extend hospitality and protection to strangers, to the extent of demanding to use the male strangers in a coercive same-sex act. However, some classical interpreters who were jurists "read into" the scriptural text the conclusion that Lot was sent primarily to forbid anal sex between men, which was the principle act of Lot's tribe which constituted their infidelity; there is no opportunity here to give details of their interpretive logic, which I have written about elsewhere.[15] The classical interpreters always discussed sex acts (with almost exclusive attention to anal sex between man and man, sometimes extended to anal sex between man and woman). However, they never discussed sexual orientation as an integral aspect of personality.

If they had, they would not have read the narrative of Lot and his tribe as addressing homosexual acts in general, but rather as addressing male rape of men in particular. Their acts would appear analogous to soldiers using rape as a weapon, as happened in the Balkan wars against men and also women, or analogous to interrogators using sexual acts as tools of domination, as happened in Abu Ghraib, Guantanamo Bay, and elsewhere. Read with a psychological theory of sexual orientation, it appears that the men of Lot's tribe were actually heterosexual men attempting to aggressively assert their power over other vulnerable men. These "men" were the angels who appeared in their city as strangers and wayfarers, to whom Lot offered hospitality and protection in an assertion of his Prophetic authority. The mob attempted to rape the men motivated by rejecting the Prophetic authority of Lot and asserting their own egoistic status and power rather than by sexual desire and bodily pleasure.

Following this line of interpretation actually makes more sense of the many verses that comprise the story of Lot than does the classical interpretation. The verses should be read in context, as inter-referential, in order to interpret the meaning of any particular word or phrase. "And Lot when he said to his people, 'Do you commit the indecency that nobody in the wide world has done before? You do men in lust (*shahwa*) besides women, indeed you are a people who transgress!' His people answered him with nothing but, 'Drive them out of your town, for they are people who make themselves to be purer!' So we delivered him and his followers, except for his wife—she was one of the goners" (Qur'an 7:80–83. The other versus that tell Lot's story are Qur'an 6:86; 11:77–81; 15:61–72; 21:71–75, 26:161–174; 27:54–57; 37:133–134). If the indecency were sex acts by men with men, then why was Lot's wife also destroyed by God's punishment? Clearly, she was involved in "the indecency," the network of idolatry and exploitation that characterized the city's population, including its women and children who were not involved in the sex acts. The fact that the attacking men had wives and children warns us that their crime, as they *do men in lust besides women,* was not homosexuality or even sex acts *per se,* but rather infidelity and rejection of their Prophet. This is what they have in common with the other destroyed peoples, who are always mentioned before and after them: the people of Noah, Salih, Hud, and Shu'ayb who found innovative ways to drive their Prophets from their midst and undermine their authority. In fact, the chronologically earliest revelation that mentions Lot simply tells us that "the people of Lot treated the warning as a lie...they accosted his guests but we blinded them" (Qur'an 54:33–37), with no mention of sex acts.

In another verse, Lot challenges his attackers: "Do you do males from the wide world and leave what mates God has created for you? Indeed you are people exceeding in aggression!" (Qur'an 26:165–166). Here Lot specifies that these men already have mates (*azwaj*), wives whom God has created for them, and yet they aggressively exceed the bounds of propriety by demanding Lot's guests in disregard for the rights that their spouses have other them. The issue here is the men's disregarding their spouses to attack strangers. But could not one argue that the gender of their victims is actually the problem, while the men's leaving their spouses is just a necessary condition? Another verse addresses the question of gender directly, as Lot confronts his assailants: "His tribe came to him rushing at him and before this they had been practicing bad deeds. Lot said, 'O my people, these are my daughters—they are purer for you so be mindful of God and do not humiliate me over my guests!" (Qur'an 11:78). Some readers might rush to judge that Lot is saying women are purer for the men who are rushing at him, meaning that women are more suitable for sex and are legal as spouses for men. However, to read this verse as an assertion that heterosexual desire is normative takes it totally out of context.

Would anyone believe that a Prophet would offer his daughters to assailants intent on rape, as if their raping women would make the act legitimate and "pure"? Rather, Lot makes a sarcastic comparison to show his assailants how wrong it is to rape guests over whom he has extended protective hospitality. Both he and his tribe know that it is far from pure to take his daughters, whose dignity he protects; Lot argues that assaulting his guests is even worse in his sight than fornicating with his daughters! Far from giving them license to rape his women, he is expressing to them, with sarcasm born of despair, that vulnerable strangers are as valuable to him as his own children. On the surface, he may appear to talk about the correct gender for men's sexual orientation, while in reality he argues that both men and women deserve protection from rape and humiliation, as a consequence of the ethic of care which fuels his Prophetic mission. The comparison by gender is only to drive home to his audience that strangers of either gender deserve the same protection one gives to daughters. This ethical message comes through clearly in another verse's narration of these events: "Lot said, 'Surely these are my guests, so do not dishonor me—stay mindful of God and do not humiliate me.' They said, 'Have we not forbidden you [granting others protection] from the wide world?' Lot said, 'These are my daughters, if you are intent on doing it'" (Qur'an 15:68–71).

In conclusion, one can argue that the story of Lot is not about homosexuality at all. Rather, Lot criticizes the practice of sex-as-weapon—using sex acts in coercion, as with rape. This is a critique of male sexuality driven by aggression and the urge to subjugate others under their power by force, not male homosexuality in particular. It is incidental to the story that Lot's guests, who are the targets, are men. We can imagine the same story with guests who are women, if the Islamic imagination would allow angels to appear as women. Jurists who have interpreted the story to be about homosexual acts have missed the point. This confirms a persistent pattern in Islamic law, that verses in the Qur'an which critique and limit patriarchy are systematically ignored or distorted to allow men's exertion of power: they allowed polygamy when the Qur'an warns against it, legalized concubines when the Qur'an urges believers to free slaves, and enforced seclusion upon women alone when the Qur'an enjoins both men and women with upholding modesty and fidelity.

Of course, homosexuality does not just involve men whom we call "gay" but also women whom we call "lesbian." Lesbian women face a dual challenge, first as women in Muslim communities and second as women who are sexually attracted to other women. For many lesbian Muslims, the first challenge is the most difficult, since before one can even discuss sexual orientation, one must address whether women are treated as rational and fully human beings, as legally autonomous agents, as morally equal to men, and as subjects with sexual drives that deserve satisfaction beyond their role in procreation. Muslim jurists and interpreters in the classical period produced some amazingly female-affirmative decisions. They acknowledged that women enjoy sex and are entitled to satisfaction from their partner, affirming the existence and potency of female orgasm and ejaculate. They emphasized equal participation of male and female liquids in conception, imagining the donors of egg and sperm to be equal and autonomous agents who come together to draw up a contract of mutual obligation, in radical contrast to earlier Hellenic, Jewish, and Christian theories of sex and fertility in which

only the man and his sperm were active agents.[16] Most jurists not only
asserted the legality of nonreproductive sexual intercourse but also affirmed
its positive role in cultivating pleasure and generating tenderness between
partners—they even lauded foreplay, caressing and sexual activity for pleasure
(not restricted to procreative intent) as following the *Sunna* of the Prophet
Muhammad).

Despite this elite discourse that gives a positive role to women's sexuality
and sexual pleasure, actual practice did not often live up to its ideals. Local
communities and individual families often stressed the "uncleanliness" of
women's sexual organs due to the issue of menstruation and often spun this
into a theory of women's inherent moral brokenness. Though Muslims
generally accept that women feel and desire sexual satisfaction, patriarchal
men often exaggerated this into an uncontrollable force that overwhelms
women and corrupts their rational faculties, justifying male control over their
movement and social interactions. Too often, discussion of female sexuality
was reduced to urging women to satisfy the male prerogative of penetration
and preventing any social, spiritual, or intellectual activity of women that
might threaten this prerogative. In general, Muslim jurists did not even
address sexual acts between two women, because they defined sexual intercourse as penile penetration. They hardly addressed the obvious question of
whether penetration, whether with a male penis or anything else, is the
epitome and extent of female sexual satisfaction.

The story of Lot does not address sexual acts between women in any way.
There are no other verses in the Qur'an clearly addressing lesbians or same-
sex acts between women, though some interpreters have searched for one
in Qur'an 4:15: "As for those of your women who perpetrate immorality
(*al-fahisha*), have four from among yourselves bear witness against them.
If they do witness, then confine them [the women] to their rooms until death
causes them to perish or until God makes for them a way [of release]."
A tenth-century Mu'tazili interpreter, Isfahani, seems to be the first to argue
that this verse concerns "immorality" identified as same-sex acts between
women (*sihaq*), a suggestion repeated by later interpreters like Zamakhshari
and Baydawi in medieval times and Rashid Rida in modern times.[17] This
was apparently due to the insistence on four eye witnesses, which is the same
requirement for punishing heterosexual acts of fornication; however, the
punishment required here is not similar at all to that for fornication (lashing)
or adultery (stoning). Why should the immorality discussed in the verse be
assumed to be sexual, especially when the grammatical plural "your women"
clearly refers to a group of three or more? The immorality it refers to is
ambiguous, as the term *fahisha* could refer to a wide range of immoral deeds
that are not sexual at all.[18] In fact, the context of these verses (the many
preceding it and following it) is about the inheritance of wealth and its just
distribution, not about sex or sexual orientation. Fraud in division of inheritance wealth, which could be perpetrated by a group of women, is probably

what the Qur'an warns against and punishes. The assertion that this verse
condemns lesbianism and specifies punishment for homosexual acts is quite
flimsy. Because of this, some Shiite scholars assert that "the Companions of
Rass," mentioned obliquely twice in the Qur'an, were a people destroyed
because of widespread lesbianism, though there is not a word in the Qur'an
to substantiate such a position.[19]

Conventional interpretations often bypass ethical teachings on distributing
wealth to prevent hoarding, misallocation of funds, and exploitation of the
vulnerable by creating sexual diversions. Although Qur'anic verse 4:3 does
say to men, "marry those of the women that appear good for you—two,
three or four," it says this in the context of protecting orphans and warning
the men who act as their guardians not to consume unjustly the wealth
entrusted to them as the orphans' inheritance. The whole verse reads, "Give
to the orphans their wealth without exchanging what is good for what is
spoiled. Do not consume their wealth as part of your own wealth, for that is a
profound outrage. If you fear that you cannot deal justly with the orphans,
then marry those of the women that are good for you—two, three or four.
But if you fear that you cannot act justly, then just one..." The ethical
context is clearly one of treating orphans justly and managing their wealth
without fraud, and the license to marry the women among them (as a way
of insuring them logistical and financial support) is given as a last resort if
one cannot live up to the expectation of financial care. It was not meant to
be taken out of context to justify plural marriages as a social norm for the
wealthy elite, though the male jurists did just this. Similarly, the verses
allegedly forbidding lesbian sex actually address financial honesty and fraud,
which male jurists and interpreters either misrecognized or obscured.

SHARI'A BEYOND THE QUR'AN

Instances like this abound in classical interpretations of the Qur'an and
persist in conventional modern interpretations based upon the classical heritage, due to patriarchal assumptions that are "read into the text" at the most
basic level. Such assumptions are largely unconscious, being part of the cultural worldview of the male interpreters, a worldview consistent with pre-
Islamic practices and shared by other religious traditions in the Middle East.
Islamic liberation theology (by women, homosexuals and other marginalized
groups) seeks to critically specify these instances of patriarchal presumption.
They endeavor to interpret the Qur'an in such a way as to free its ethical
message from the limitations of former interpretation and implementation
in the Shari'a.

Muslim jurists built Islamic law, taking it upon themselves to judge acts
without investigating the intentions behind them. They formulated norms
and punishments to regulate sexual behavior with exclusive focus upon

physical acts and anatomical organs. In general, they forbade homosexual acts between men, just as they forbade heterosexual penetrative sex with a partner without the legal relationship of a contract of marriage, ownership through slavery, or oral contract of temporary union (*mut'a* as allowed by Shiite jurists though rejected by Sunnis). When it comes to homosexual acts, the laws in the Islamic jurisprudential tradition are not actually based upon the Qur'an, as will be discussed below. Far from explicitly forbidding homosexuality, the Qur'an arguably contains inferences to the existence of homosexual persons in the Muslim community. Explicating these hints requires interpretation, but so does ignoring them! Both hints occur in the Qur'anic discussion of gender segregation. Both are exceptions to a general rule that men and women should not freely mix if they are not related by blood, marriage, or a contract that can regulate their affairs.

The Qur'an gives a long and detailed list of the kinds of men with whom women can behave more freely: after listing relatives, it says "their womenfolk, their slaves, or their followers among the men who have no wiles with women or children who do not recognize the sexual nakedness of women" (Qur'an 24:31). The "followers among the men who have no wiles with women," preceded by "womenfolk" and followed by "children who do not recognize the sexual nakedness of women" suggests that these men (like heterosexual women or preadolescent children) have no sexual desire for women and are therefore exempt from the general rule of separation. Classical interpreters thought this verse applied to elderly men or impotent men, whom they assumed were exempt by fiat or age or anatomy. However, with the emergence of a modern social category of "gay men," we should extend the interpretation to include them. If we do, we conclude that the Qur'an mentions gay men in an indirect but potent way, recognizing the unique characteristic that sets them apart from other adult men—their not sexually desiring women and therefore not being a threatening presence in their intimate company—with no condemnation.

In a similar way, there is a verse that hints at the existence of lesbian women in the Muslim community. The Qur'an addresses men on issues of gender separation and the preservation of domestic privacy for women: "Yet if your children have reached sexual maturity, then require them to ask permission before entering, like those mentioned before, for in this way God clarifies for you God's signs, and God is a knowing One, One most wise. Of the women, those not reproducing who do not wish for intercourse, it is no harm for them to lay aside their clothing as long as they do not overtly display their beauty [in the company of men]" (Qur'an 24:60). The key term is "those not reproducing" (*al-qawa'id*). It describes fertility, meaning withdrawn from reproductive activity, like a field left to rest and not sown with seed or a date palm not pollinated. The Qur'an clarifies this term, saying that such women do not wish for sexual intercourse, which is the same word in Arabic for marriage (*nikah*). Classical interpreters described such women as elderly, beyond the capacity to become pregnant. However, we know from sexological research that postmenopausal women are still sexually active and often desire intercourse. Therefore, the verse seems to invite a deeper interpretation. The reason such women are not reproducing is because they do not desire sexual intercourse with men, due to their sexual orientation rather than merely their supposed lack of fertility or libido.

Such a sexuality-sensitive interpretation accords with both reason and the literal meaning of the scriptural text, and therefore according to classical principles of Qur'anic interpretation or *tafsir*.[20] It deserves recognition as one of several possible meanings, all equally valid. From this perspective, the Qur'anic verses conventionally held to condemn homosexual acts do not actually address homosexuality, and other verses conventionally held to address the nonsexual elderly actually refer to the presence of homosexual members of the Islamic community in a non-condemning way. Without a concept of homosexuality, a psychological theory of sexual orientation, one misses these inferences. They have gone unnoticed by classical Muslim interpreters and are deliberately ignored by modern interpreters who are Neo-Traditionalists and assert unsophisticated notions of "human nature."

Such a theory of homosexuality is available to us today, in ways that were not articulated in the past, either in the West or in Islamic societies. We need to examine the origin of the term homosexuality itself. It was coined first by doctors to diagnose an "illness" in the late nineteenth century and was quickly used by homosexual advocates to argue for decriminalization of particular sex acts and social justice for marginalized minorities. The invention of the term "homosexuality" occurred amid changes in social organization and economic life associated with capitalism and industrialization, which expanded the potential for individualism, buttressed by a liberal ideal of human rights. It is nestled within a series of revolutions: a bourgeois revolution against aristocracy in the late eighteenth century, a workers' revolt against unfettered oligarchy in the mid-nineteenth century, women's opposition to male superiority in the early twentieth century, a nonwhite uprising against colonial domination in the 1940s, and a youth rebellion against patriotic norms in the 1960s. These overlapping revolutions allowed homosexuals to assert their humanity and rights, first in the early twentieth century in Europe (until snuffed out by fascism) and later in America from 1969. The invention of the term homosexuality helped shift the terms of discussion from the Church's rhetoric of "sodomy" and the police's rhetoric of "buggery" to the psychologist's rhetoric of "sexual orientation."[21]

With cycles of success and failure, legal recognition and protection of homosexuals has taken root in certain areas (especially Scandinavia and the Netherlands, followed by other nations in Continental Europe, Britain, and Canada). Other areas where Catholicism or Evangelical Protestantism remains a force in political life, like the United States and southern Europe, have lagged a bit behind. Similarly, Muslim majority nations in which secularism is strong (either in the form of anticlericism like in Turkey, or in the form of pluralistic government above multiple religious communities as in Lebanon, India, and Indonesia) are moving slowly toward decriminalizing homosexual acts and allowing homosexual people to build civic organizations for legal protection and human rights. All these cases, Euro-American or Islamic, have two factors in common: economic and social development that foster individual autonomy, and political and cultural development that keep religion separate from government.

These replicate the changes in the social order in Western Europe and North America which were necessary preconditions for the emergence of a concept of homosexuality: economic prosperity, urbanization, and the emergence of the nuclear family so that individuals could assert a greater degree of individuality. They also include political liberalization, so that citizens are granted rights as autonomous agents outside of their family, communal, or religious institution. These social changes are reinforced by greater depth of technical expertise in medical and psychological research that offer a more "secular" definition of human nature outside the purview of traditional authorities, whether these are tribal leaders, patriarchal households, or religious scholars.

This history explains how the term homosexuality first came into use to describe an emerging modern concept that was not available to classical Muslim interpreters. However, it would be wrong to assume that homosexuals did not exist before there was a clinical name for them. Homosexuals have always existed as a minority within every cultural group, even if an abstract term like "homosexuality" was not there to label them. There may have been different social constructions as roles for homosexual people (priest, artist, seer, joker, heretic, criminal to name just a few examples), and such social constructions change over time and vary between communities, yet the essential psychological element, difference based on sexual orientation and expression, was present in every place beneath the variety of names and concepts. It is essential to bear in mind that what modern researchers mean by "homosexuality" is not at all what classical Muslim scholars meant by "sodomy" (*liwata*). *Liwata* denoted anal penetration as an act and said nothing about the intention, the sexual orientation, or the inner disposition of the person performing the act.

Do contemporary Muslim scholars recognize this difference? How do they react to these social changes and their scientific challenges to religious orthodoxy? We can observe a "Neo-Traditionalist" reaction that is very powerful today, that combines traditional Shari'a rhetoric with more modern secular denunciations without really accepting contemporary scientific research. One such scholar from the Deoband Academy, Maulana Zahir al-Din, wrote a book against homosexuality which he titled *Suicide,* claiming it to be "the first scholarly book on un-natural sexual desire, meaning the act of Lot's people, and the hatefulness and corruption of its proponents, researched in

the light of the Qur'an and Prophetic example and history and medicine."
The title literally means "killing one's future progeny" and reflects the
modern patriarchal analysis that homosexuality is predominantly the lack of
heterosexual procreation and amounts to killing one's family line, and is
therefore "against the civilizational way of life" promoted by Islam. However, Zahir al-Din freely mixes sacred and secular arguments, as when he
writes that "It is not permitted in any revealed religion, that is not in Islam
and not in any other religion, that a person can fulfill sexual desires with a
person of his own sex, meaning a man with another man or a woman with
another woman.... It is the strangest, most bizarre and most anxiety-
provoking thing in this world for a man to choose to fulfill his sexual desire
with another man, and we should understand the extremes of this as a kind
of insanity. This is because it is an act against human nature (*khilaf-i fitrat
fi'l*) that is not just about sexual appetite but also about satanic delusion."[22]
Such Neo-Traditionalist scholars reify Shari'a norms and adopt *ad hoc*
notions of "nature" from the nineteenth century that support patriarchal
presumptions, while ignoring the contemporary social and scientific research
that places them in question.[23]

Such reactions are insufficient and disappointing. Scientific advances challenge Muslims to rethink their tradition and open up new ways of asserting
the relevance of the Qur'an to contemporary realities. To address these
opportunities, religious scholars (*ulama*) would have to be open to sharing
authority with "secular" scholars and scientists. If they were confident and
flexible with an inner strength, they could do this; but alas, they are stiff
and fragile with a sense of embattled defensiveness that closes their minds
and rusts their hearts. This attitude does not live up to the Islamic tradition
of the past, which never accepted a cleavage between scientific discovery
and scriptural revelation, as both were rooted in the sincere application of
God's gift of reason. Contemporary Neo-Traditionalists are more concerned
to "defend the Shari'a" than to sincerely confront the challenge of the
Qur'an, and this is the cause of their rigidity. To be very honest, I find this
posture one of idolatry, for they have raised the Shari'a, a product of human
hands and minds, to the level of the Qur'an which is God's speech to humankind. The question for critical believers is whether the rulings enshrined in
the Shari'a represent accurate conclusions from the Qur'an and justice-
embodying extensions of the Prophet's example, or rather represent the
all-too-human prejudices of patriarchal jurists in generations after the
Prophet passed away.

The Shari'a punishments for homosexual acts, both between men and
between women, are well known and much debated. However, it is seldom
acknowledged that the Shari'a punishments are not derived from the Qur'an,
no matter what interpretation one accepts of Lot and his tribe. Even before
hadith reports attributed to the Prophet were collated and collected into
books, the punishment for men having sex with other men had already been

decided, not by the Prophet himself but by some of his followers. The issue of deciding which hadith reports are accurate and authentic is very difficult, and then deciding whether they have legal force is quite complex; reviewing these reports for authenticity is the key to reforming the Shari'a from within. Despite the fact that this was an invaluable activity by Islamic scholars in the past and is essential to the livelihood of the Shari'a as a system, it is now considered taboo, and anyone who brings up the subject can expect swift denunciation by guardians of the status quo.

There are many hadith in circulation about punishing men for homosexual acts and several about punishing women, and a few about cursing those who transgress gender norms. As a case study, let us focus here on the punishment for a man's having sex with another man, as this is the obsession of jurists and set the denunciatory tone for the modern treatment of gays, lesbians, and transgendered persons. Whether hadith reports on this subject are authentic or not needs to be determined by focused research using traditional *isnad* criticism and *matn* criticism. *Isnad* is the chain of authorities who narrated the report, while *matn* is textual content of the report itself. Hadith science, in theory, allowed reports to be rejected if their content contradicted reason, medical reality or scientific observation.[24] Sadly, most Neo-Traditionalists are loath to actually use these traditional tools, as the results of sincere research will most likely go against their vested interests.

Whether judged authentic or not, it is clear that these reports do not represent the Prophet Muhammad's actual decision of a concrete case (in contrast to the hadith reports about heterosexual adultery cases). They reinforce decisions that were made by the early Islamic community, based upon their own presumptions. The earliest known case occurred during the vice-regency of Abu Bakr al-Siddiq, after the Prophet's death. Khalid ibn Walid wrote him a letter asking for a decision on what to do with a man found having sex with another man as if he were having sex with a woman. Abu Bakr summoned important Companions of the Prophet to make a decision. Among them was 'Ali ibn Abi Talib, who is reported to have said, "This is a sin which no community was known to have done except one community and God did to them what you well know, so I think we should burn him with fire." Based on this opinion, Abu Bakr ordered that the man be burned.[25]

Close attention to this narrative (*khabar*) reveals many key points. First, the vice-regent called for counsel because there was no precedent in the Prophet Muhammad's own actions. Second, the council included some of the Prophet's closest followers who would have related the Prophet's own words on this subject, if any had been known. Third, none of the Companions related a teaching of the Prophet on this issue, throwing into grave doubt whether any of the hadith reports later attributed to the Prophet are authentically from him. Fourth, 'Ali made a decision based upon his own reasoning, to burn the man alive in imitation of how God punished the people of Sodom and Gomorrah by raining down upon them burning stones. Fifth, this decision was based on informal comparison, not on formal judicial reasoning which is the basis for Islamic law. Sixth, we have no other example of such a comparison used to justify punishments for other acts (for instance, God destroyed Noah's people for idolatry in the great flood but Islamic law does not punish idolaters with drowning, and God destroyed Salih's people for killing His sacred camel in a volcanic eruption but Islamic law does not punish wrongful slaughter of animals with asphyxiation). Seventh, such informal comparison is not allowed to justify legal decisions in the Shari'a. These points highlight the fact that 'Ali and the early Companions were doing what they thought was right but were not acting according to direct guidance from the Prophet or upon an explicit command of the Qur'an. No matter how much we respect these early leaders of the Muslim community, we must admit that they acted upon their opinion and cultural presumptions—therefore their actions are open to review and reassessment.

After reviewing this report (*khabar*), we can better understand why hadith reports were later circulated that justified capital punishment in the name of the Prophet rather than 'Ali and companions. This report offers a rather flimsy justification for taking the life of a believer, even if it is accepted that he sinned in his act. Some people in Medina continued to burn men found having sex with other men, but others found it to be out-of-line with the emerging practice of Islamic law, which tried to decide if homosexual acts were the same as heterosexual acts without a contract (*zina*). If so, the punishment would be lashing, rather than burning. The naïve reader might ask what is the difference if the result is death? The difference is tremendous. The punishment for heterosexual intercourse without a contract between the partners (*zina*) is clearly stipulated in the Qur'an and was carried out by the Prophet. If the punishment for homosexual sex were, by formal analogy, declared to be like adultery, then the punishment could be argued to be based on the Qur'an, extending the punishment for one crime to that of an analogous crime. Also at issue is whether homosexual intercourse is a crime against God (*hadd*) as is heterosexual adultery (*zina*).[26] There are some reports that 'Ali himself ordered men who had sex with men to be stoned; either he changed his mind to seal the analogy with *zina* as adultery or he was reported to have done so to support the jurists who argued by this analogy.

The opinion of the early jurist, Imam Malik ibn Anas (d. 795 CE), shows a transitional state which favors stoning but not through analogy with *zina*. His book, *al-Muwatta,* one of the earliest collections of hadith reports, does not substantiate his ruling on male homosexual intercourse with a hadith report because, one suspects, there were none in circulation at that time. Rather he supported the stoning rule solely on the fact that the people of Medina did this: "He is to be stoned whether he is married or unmarried."[27] This second phrase, "married or unmarried," reveals that Malik's ruling is still based on a unique punishment and not on an analogy with *zina,* for

which punishment is stoning if one is already married but is a lesser lashing if
unmarried. It was not until the time of Shafi'i (d. 820 CE) that jurists' decisions had to be based upon the Prophet's Sunna as defined solely by hadith
reports, rather than by community practice as in the opinion of Malik or by
reliance on reasoned deduction as in the opinions of Abu Hanifa
(d. 767 CE). From this time, hadith reports had a great significance whereas
before they were often held in suspicion. Subsequently, many hadith reports
that circulated orally were written down for use in the law, and reports that
may have originated with Companions and Followers were claimed to
actually be from the Prophet. With this change in legal thinking, there developed intense pressure to give even weak reports adequate chains of transmission, and to justify prior decisions that may have come from followers of the
Prophet as having come directly from him. Accordingly, we find Shafi'i and
Hanbali jurists with hadith reports, allegedly from the Prophet's lips, which
earlier jurists and even Abu Bakr give no evidence of having known. Not
surprisingly, these alleged reports substantiate the ruling that homosexual
intercourse is analogous to heterosexual intercourse outside of a contractual
relationship (*zina*). In his collection of hadith reports, the *Musnad*, Ahmad
ibn Hanbal (d. 855 CE) includes reports specifying death by stoning, with
some variation in the wording, reports that stricter hadith scholars, like
Bukhari (d. 870 CE) and Muslim (d. 875 CE), did not include in theirs. The
flood-gates were thus opened for all sorts of reports alleged to be from the
Prophet; some are quite far-fetched and medieval scholars have thrown them
out as falsifications, like the reports that say homosexual men will be raised on
Judgment Day as pigs and apes, or that when a man mounts another man the
earth beseeches God to allow it to convulse and swallow them up to conceal
their act, or that no young man is more shameless than one who allows himself to be entered from behind.[28] Despite being debunked by medieval scholars, Neo-Traditionalists still use these alleged hadith reports against anyone
who dares to discuss homosexuality.

My own research has been accused of being "glib" and "unscholarly"
for raising the issue of the authenticity of these reports.[29] In reality, for
Neo-Traditionalists the pertinent issue is not which reports are authentic
and which are not, but whose voice is authoritative in having the right to
speak about them. It is my suggestion (and it remains a hypothesis until more
research is done on Hadith by all voices in the current debate) that such
reports do not represent authentic teachings of the Prophet. Rather, they
represent homophobic prejudice common to patriarchal cultures, whether
Arab, Hellenic, Jewish, or Byzantine. Like misogynist values, they were
inscribed in the Shari'a from an early time, even though they were not part
of the Prophet Muhammad's example.[30] Cultural prejudices could have been
reinforced by a concept of sacred history adopted from Jewish culture,
notions of imperial law adopted from Byzantine sources, and medical theories adopted from Greek sources, all of which saw women in general and

homosexual men, as incomplete beings compared to the ideal of the patriarchal empowered man. It would be a fascinating but very long journey to trace in detail all of these cultural streams that flowed into the sea of Islamic society during the formative period of its law, theology, and cultural worldview. My contention is that much of Islamic theology and law is based upon a view of human nature that is cultural and not scriptural, and is therefore contingent and not eternal; as our understanding of what human nature is grows and develops, Islamic theology and law deserves to be held up to scrutiny in the light of justice, social benefit, and reasoned observation, since the Qur'an addresses itself to the human being and not to the Arab male, or to the medieval Persian sultan, or to the Pakistani grandmother. In fact, it is not just a right but also a duty for sincere Muslims to scrutinize their inherited traditions in order to live up to the Qur'anic challenge. Inevitably, believers will disagree over the method and intensity of this scrutiny, but as long as this disagreement is tempered by mutual respect, it is part of the magnificent diversity of Islam and in accord with the Prophet's teaching that "difference of opinion in my community is a mercy."

PAIRS AND PARTNERS

There were disagreements between different schools of law (*madhhab*) over whether homosexual penetrative sex was equivalent to heterosexual adultery (*zina*), for which the punishment was lashing (for an unmarried participant) or stoning to death (for a participant married already to someone else). For instance, Hanafi jurists argued that homosexual sex was not the same as *zina,* since the Qur'an specifies that *zina* is sex between a man and a woman; instead they argued that punishment for homosexual penetration was not stipulated by the Qur'an and was up to the discretion of judges (*ta'zir*) and could change depending on social conventions. Behind these disagreements were differences in philosophy: were only penetrative behaviors considered "sex acts"? Were homosexual acts a sin against God or merely against human convention? Were they forbidden because of the same-sex nature of the couple or because the couple did not have a contract to legalize their union?

This is no place to enter these fascinating and complex legal discussions, which I have written about earlier. Let me make just a few observations. Although classical Islamic law generally forbids same-sex acts, there was not juridical consensus (*ijma'*) as to why, under what conditions and with what punishment. We can safely assert that the subject should still be discussed and, in the light of new evidence and under unprecedented social conditions, be open to revision through *ijtihad*. Classical Islamic law forbids same-sex actions but did not address same-sex relationships, allowing us to ask whether, if there could be legal contracts of marriage or civic union between same-sex partners, the sex acts would still be illegal or immoral.[31] Jurists ruled on same-sex acts on the basis of hadith reports not the Qur'an, for verses about the Prophet Lot, even if they are interpreted as being about homosexuality, do not have legal specificity as required to formulate rulings in the Shari'a. These hadith reports are of questionable authenticity, as some have broken chains of transmission and most of them have single-transmission chains that, in Islamic legal theory, can lead to speculative opinion but not to obligating certainty. Hanafi jurists, for instance, refused to rely on single-transmission hadith reports, especially if the decision could lead to corporal punishment as it could in the issue of penetrative homo-sexual sex acts. Though Hanafis held that same-sex intercourse is immoral, they asserted that it was not a *hadd* crime, insisting that there should be no capital punishment but rather that government authorities could punish it as they see fit.[32] Implicit in their position is that the government's assessment could change as social conditions change, making their position a promising place to begin reform.

I am afraid that contemporary jurists do not have the confidence to open these crucial questions for reassessment, but perhaps they will surprise us! Their voices are often superceded and drowned out by dema-gogues and ideologues, who shout representations of the Shari'a without being educated about the complexities of jurisprudence. Examples of this rhetoric are legion in pamphlets and Internet *fatwas*, like some of those on "IslamOnline."

The Qur'an talks about sexual pairing and partnerships in ways that are much deeper than Islamic law and theology, and this should be the starting place for a reconsideration of sexuality and homosexuality among Muslims. "Glory be to the One who creates the mates, all of them, in what grows upon the earth and from themselves and from what you do not even know!" (Qur'an 36:35–36). The Qur'an invokes pairs and partners in ways too com-plex to be reduced to a heterosexual pair of man and woman (or even a hetero-plurality of man and women). Certainly, Adam and Eve are termed "a pair" who mate at God's direction to provide each other with rest and tranquility. In the Qur'an, all life is created in pairs, "male and female," to insure reproduction and growth, among animals and fruits and plants. However, the Qur'an does not limit the mysterious principle of growth to gendered pairs but extends it to all pairs. To say "God created Adam and Eve, not Adam and Steve" would be a gross reduction of the Qur'an's teaching about mating in pairs!

In recognition of this, classical interpreters of the Qur'an have considered the soul in intimate harmony with the body it animates to be "a pair of mates." Sufi thinkers have reflected very deeply about the nature of the soul and how God interacts with the human being, and Ibn 'Arabi (d. 1240 CE), for example, has explained how the "mating" of masculine and feminine forces in the cosmos and in the human personality drives the perpetual creation and re-creation of the world. His exposition reinforces the ideal that God creates humanity and the universe out of love, and shows how our own innate sexuality leads us through erotic experiences that can be refined into spiritual reflection, even if it does reify conventional notions of male and female.[33] We can follow Ibn 'Arabi's spiritual guidance to explain how all the levels of the human personality described above (*fitra, tabi'a, shakila,* and *sura*) are formed by a union of forces that come together as mates. By picturing these in Figure 7.1, we can understand how sexuality is woven deeply into our nature, regulating the union of self-and-other which shapes us at each level. Figure 7.1 may be abstract, but it tries to picture the complexity of our human nature and how its levels are interwoven by sexuality. I developed this figure in light of the Qur'an and commentaries upon it in Islamic ethics developed by Sufis, and integrated into it insights by Western psychologists.[34]

One should read Figure 7.1 from top to bottom to understand the different dimensions of the human personality. Each dimension appears as two halves of a sphere, representing self and other which come together into a whole. The intimate interaction between self and other at each level is conditioned by the sphere above. For clarity, each sphere is represented as distinct, emerging one from another in a series: starting with the human spirit's confrontation with God as the "primal other" at the level of *fitra*, extending from that into the soul's integration with the body as the "material other" at the level of *tabi'a*, progressing to the psyche's experience of family and environment as the "social other" at the level of *shakila*, and leading to the more everyday dimension of the ego's negotiation with particular relationships, like with a sexual partner or spouse as the "community other" at the level of *sura* at the bottom of Figure 7.1.

While this depiction suggests a hierarchy, in reality all dimensions are in constant interaction. The top-to-bottom depiction of different levels suggests growth. *Fitra* arises from our engagement with God at a time extending from before creation (the day of the primordial covenant) until beyond eternity (the day of reckoning and its consequences), as stated in Qur'an 7:172. *Tabi'a* takes form from our soul's integration with the material body, beginning with conception and progressing through animation, birth and rearing. *Shakila* develops from our experience with our environment, physical, linguistic, social, and emotional, especially in childhood but continuing throughout maturation, as our inward disposition takes shape from biological, material and genetic forces, influenced by our parents' and their social world. *Sura* is the outward appearance of these invisible forces and developmental processes, and we come into its fullness through adolescence and young adulthood; then we reach sexual maturity, assert some measure of independence from parental control, and develop a personal sense of

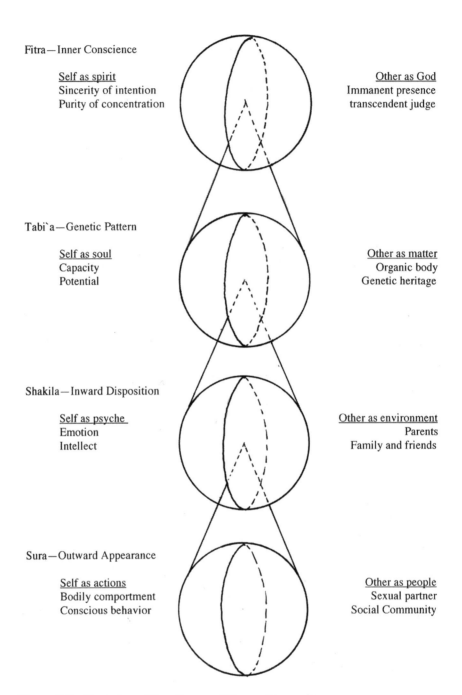

Fitra—Inner Conscience

Self as spirit
Sincerity of intention
Purity of concentration

Other as God
Immanent presence
transcendent judge

Tabi`a—Genetic Pattern

Self as soul
Capacity
Potential

Other as matter
Organic body
Genetic heritage

Shakila—Inward Disposition

Self as psyche
Emotion
Intellect

Other as environment
Parents
Family and friends

Sura—Outward Appearance

Self as actions
Bodily comportment
Conscious behavior

Other as people
Sexual partner
Social Community

Figure 7.1   Depiction of Four Layers of Human Personality

responsibility for our actions. This is why Islamic law considers youngsters legally responsible for their acts only after puberty.

SEXUAL ETHICS

Sura describes our outward manifestation, not just in looks but also in deeds. Through our outward manifestation, we interact with others in rituals of worship, contracts of business, social engagements of all kinds, and sexual intercourse with a partner. All these acts are outwardly manifested deeds but are deeply rooted in the multiple layers of our personalities, involving what is observable (like the deed itself), what is sbtle (like the emotion and intention that motivates any deed), what is microscopic (like the genetic pattern that allows us to act) and what is invisible to observation (like the sincerity behind the deed and its spiritual worth). Our outward manifestation, in *sura* and in acts, is not separable from other layers of our personality. Any religious discourse that judges matters of sex and sexuality without considering these complexities commits injustice (*zulm*) in the name of moral order.

Many of my fellow Muslims will take alarmed exception to the statement above. They might see it as leading to an erasure of moral guidance right in the heart of the family, where norms of gender and limits on sexual expression are learned and enforced. However, I do not make the statement in order for it to be taken to an extreme of moral nihilism. Rather, it should be seen as a moderate plea for cautious moral relativism, rational scrutiny, and ethical self-restraint. It should be placed in the context of developing a "progressive Islam" that embraces contemporary scientific and sociological facts, while questioning the self-righteousness of much of what passes for Islamic "orthodoxy" today. I am not calling for moral absolutes to be abandoned, but for their definition to be adjusted to the lived realities of diverse and pluralistic communities and for their application in discrete cases to be tempered by ethical sensitivity. A call for this change is well within the boundaries of the Islamic tradition, as upheld by the best of Islamic law.

One can see this quality at work in the treatment of theft. Although the Qur'an is very clear that the punishment for theft is severing the hand of the thief, Muslim jurists consistently applied rational scrutiny, sociological context, and ethical restraint in passing judgments about theft, in direct proportion to the severity of punishment. This means that "theft" is defined by the situation of the act, rather than by moralistic indignation or populist legislation about what constitutes theft.[35] For instance, a thief who steals because her family is impoverished would not be punished as severely as if she had stolen out of greed. Judges were more interested in promoting social welfare and preserving human reason than in reifying moral absolutism.

It is this ethical spirit that used to animate Islamic law that we Muslims seem to have lost in contemporary times. Assessing the ambiguity of individual cases and granting leeway to diverse situations was not seen as an affront to the Shari'a, but was its very purpose as an ethical framework rather than a code of rules.[36] Jurists never "defended the Shari'a" by meting out violence upon individuals, especially those who were vulnerable or whose social standing was ambiguous. How different this classical spirit of Islamic law is from its contemporary analogues! The revolutionary regime in Iran, the cultic Salafis of the Taliban, and the Wahhabi monarchy in Arabia pride themselves in meting out capital punishment for homosexuals, as if the blood of scapegoats washed away their many highly immoral policies. The vulnerability of homosexuals to the political expediency of immoral regimes is evident even in states where Islamic law is not applied as national law, as in recent persecutions of gay men in Egypt as the government of Hosni Mubarak tries to deflect attention away from corruption and economic reforms that hurt the poor while trying to defuse fundamentalists' critiques of their legitimacy. Accusations of homosexuality are also common ways for the powerful to eliminate political opposition, as with the Malaysian politician, Anwar Ibrahim. Such examples of power abuse should spark the ire of moderately conscientious and progressively engaged Muslims. It should fuel their resolve to reform how homosexuals are treated within Muslim communities, both at home and in the wider *Umma*. A moratorium on capital punishment within the Shari'a, as advocated by Tariq Ramadan, is a good first step; it must be reinforced by an ethical consensus that Muslims will not kill or injure other Muslims, whether due to sectarian politics, dogmatic chauvinism (*takfir*), or moral policing.[37] This must, of course, be coupled with a renewal of an ethic of care that upholds the dignity of each human being and protects the rights of each, whether Muslim or not, whether male or not, whether straight or not, whether married or not.

So far I have argued that sexuality should not be used to victimize Muslims, whether it is women accused of adultery or lesbians and gays accused of immorality. Such ethical abuses of sexuality should be seen in continuity with rape, sex used as torture or punishment, sexual abuse within the family, or sexual coercion within marriage. Muslim communities need to break the silence of shame around these abuses, for silence only allows the victims' wounds to fester and the perpetrator's injustice to continue. Reexamining attitudes toward sexuality is also acutely necessary for Muslim minority communities living in Western democratic states, where they are legally and moral bound as citizens to uphold the constitution, which often grants rights and protection to women, lesbians and gays, and transgendered persons in ways not found in traditional Shari'a. For Muslim minorities in these conditions there are two choices: either the Shari'a needs deep reform to bring its practices into congruence with constitutional democracy or consensus must develop that the Shari'a is applicable only to explicitly ritual matters (*'ibadat*), leaving civic matters (*mu'amalat*) to be governed by the laws and mores of the nation in which they live. If minority Muslims in

Western states cannot reconcile their sense of religious conscience with their civic obligations under a constitution, they are morally bound to emigrate to a place where they feel a Muslim majority is upholding the Shari'a in the way they think necessary.

What about sexual ethics in a more positive sense? Can Muslim communities accommodate lesbian and gay members who are also Muslims? Can the Shari'a be adapted to a more pluralistic ethic that celebrates sexuality and embraces sexual diversity? If so, what would "Islamic" gay and lesbian life be like? These are not utopian questions but are rather intensely practical, and are actually being worked out, slowly and tentatively, by gay and lesbian Muslim support groups. Fortunately, the Qur'an offers amazing resources for this project, if Muslims gather the courage to engage in *ijtihad*. The Qur'an challenges each person to find a suitable mate or partner. The term for partner, *zawj*, is ambiguously gendered: it is a masculine noun grammatically even when describing female persons. Homosexual pairs could also, within this wide and varied framework, be considered mates as the Qur'anic language is suitably abstract. "One of God's signs is that [God] created for you mates from amongst yourselves that you might find repose in them, and generated between you love and compassion, for surely in this are clear signs for those who ponder!" (Qur'an 30:21). We must keep in mind that this level of abstraction traces the general and universal pattern, while the story of Adam and Eve as the primordial mates is a specific instance of it: "It is God who created you all from a single self and made of it a mate, that one might take repose in the other" (Qur'an 7:189). In this specific case as in many other places, the Qur'an talks of male and female being a pair, but not in a prescriptive way, for the Qur'an also talks of night and day being a pair, or light and dark, or the soul and body. God creates for each person a mate or mates "of it" or of the same pattern and suitable for the two to join together, in love and compassion, to reach a greater emotional and ethical completion. The purpose is for each of us to overcome our self-centered pride and through loving one another to realize that God created us all, all of humanity, *from a single self.*

Sexual intercourse and intimacy is part of this ethical training and spiritual refinement. Islam is challenging in that it does not condemn sexual pleasure in favor of ascetic renunciation and does not limit sexuality to procreation.[38] In this way, Islam is unique among world religions, though Muslim communities have not always lived up to this challenge! However, the Qur'an is clear that sexual pleasure and satisfaction, while good in themselves, should be pursued within ethical limits. Partners should establish between themselves a contract or agreement, through which they acknowledge their legal, financial, and ethical obligations to each other: obligations which include comfort and care, keeping of secrets, upholding the other's public dignity, and safeguarding the other's health, both physical and psychological. Interactions with others outside the purview of a contract should be conducted within accepted norms of modesty: without invasive staring, manipulative strategies, or abusive cunning. The Qur'an enjoins both men and women to wear modest clothing (though what constitutes modesty is left to social norms), speak respectfully, and lower the gaze. In general, the Qur'an announces the principle of avoiding objectifying others in a sexual way to uphold our common humanity. It permits pleasure bounded by care. It enjoins reciprocity, both of rights and pleasures, within a relationship.

This basis of sexual ethics applies to men as well as to women. In a pluralistic Islamic community, it would apply to homosexual couples as well as to heterosexual ones. The purposes of "finding one's mate" are the same for hetero- and homosexual couples, so the ethical guidelines for establishing relationships should also be the same. Fortunately for Muslims, the marriage contract is not a sacrament as in Christianity but a contract; in form and substance is it quite close to a secular "civil union" that is increasingly being adopted by Western democracies. Heterosexual Muslims living as citizens of Western countries register their marriages as civil unions, even if they have a religious ceremony to mark the occasion. Legally, this is no different than homosexual unions under those governments that allow same-sex marriage or civic union, such as Canada, Britain, many European states, and South Africa. In these places, homosexual Muslims can now form legal unions between same-sex partners, which have equal legal status to their heterosexual neighbors. Would Muslim citizens of such nations recognize the legality and validity of same-sex marriage contracts, even if they found them morally questionable or even repugnant? Increasingly, Muslims living in the West will be have to confront this reality, and in places like the Netherlands the answer Muslims give may determine whether they are seen to be citizens who accept the laws and values upon which the nation rests or outsiders who are a threat. Sadly, on-line *fatwas* document how Neo-Traditionalists fail to live up to this challenge.[39]

JUSTICE AND BEAUTY

Why is it important to grant homosexuals the same right to marry and establish ethical contracts between partners? It is not a matter of pleading for "special rights." It is not merely demanding equal rights, to have the same possibilities and responsibilities as heterosexual couples. It is a matter of justice, of clearing a way for homosexual Muslims to partake, with honesty and dignity, in the Prophet Muhammad's paradigm so that they can cultivate an ethical life along with their heterosexual sisters and brothers in finding a sincere way to return to God. This is because the four levels of personality development outlined above are not just descriptive but rather establish a framework for each person's spiritual development, for one cannot return to God except through one's own distinctive personality. Sufi psychologists have distilled from the Qur'an four distinct phases of the soul's struggle toward God, and each corresponds to a level of the personality. If the levels of personality mark a descent deep into the world of materiality, embodiment, particularity, and contingency, then the four phases of the soul's return to God mark an ascent (*mi'raj*) through sincere awareness toward greater spiritual refinement and universal love.

The soul while struggling in outward behavior, the level of *sura,* can be called *the soul that commands toward evil.* At this stage, the soul strives to understand right and wrong, beneficial and harmful, conditioned by its particular place and personality resources (Qur'an 12:53). After maturing through that struggle, the soul is refined a little and can identify with greater clarity the sources of its selfish urges and repressed pain; it can struggle with the subtler forces of egoism and family trauma at the level of *shakila,* and can be called *the soul full of blame.* At first, the soul criticizes others for its pain while later, as insight grows, it blames itself (Qur'an 75:2). Resigning itself from blame and gaining greater self-knowledge through exploration, prayer, and meditation, the soul engages its primal limitations at the level of *tabi'a,* confronting its material limitation, its penchant to decay, and its body's ultimate mortality; the soul that comes to peace with this reality can be called *the tranquil soul,* for it is at ease in humble harmony with its limitations (Qur'an 89:27). Finally, through tranquility and inner peace, the soul can gain sustained contact with its original nature at the level of *fitra,* to worship with utter sincerity and act in the world with pure spirituality, acknowledging God directly as its only Lord; such a soul can be called the soul *well-pleased and well-pleasing,* the state of the souls called into paradise (Qur'an 89:28). In Islam, none of these stages of spiritual development are obstructed by sexuality or sexual relationships, although if they are not in balanced harmony, sex and family life can certainly distract one from spiritual aspiration and hard work (Figure 7.2).

Developing a well-tempered personality in the downward arc toward diversification and individualization is a necessary condition before one can aspire to complete the cycle, pursing the upward arc toward spiritual realization. This is because sincerity is the only fuel for the journey, as a great Sufi jurist expressed, saying "Whoever journeys to God through his own nature, his arrival to God is closer to him than his own nature, and whoever journeys to God through abandoning his own nature, his arrival to God is dependent on his distance from his own nature; attaining distance from one's own nature is difficult indeed."[40] In other words, those who know themselves know their Lord. Clearly, if people are in denial of their true natures or are denied the dignity of expressing their true nature, internal and external pressures obstruct them from aspiring to return to God with sincerity. This is true whether people's personalities are under pressure by racism, by sexism, by poverty, or by homophobia. It is a matter of justice to clear away such obstacles,

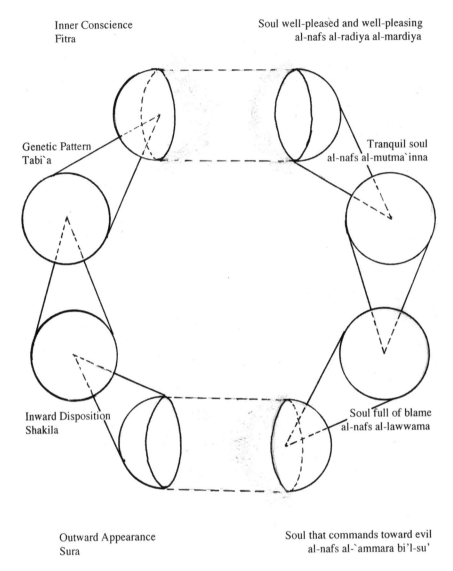

Figure 7.2 Depiction of States of the Soul in Relation to the Layers of Personality

whether they are caused by internalized fear, social stigma, or a moral system based on patriarchal prejudices. It is necessary for homosexual Muslims
to achieve a minimum of justice in their families, communities, and religion
before they can help themselves and their heterosexual neighbors to do
what is beautiful, to achieve ethical refinement—"God enjoins acting justly
and doing what is beautiful."[41]

At the end of the day, many Muslims will respond that it is too much for lesbian, gay, and transgendered Muslims to ask for Islam to change to accommodate them. However, this is not really what they are asking for. In reality, they assert that Islam must change to grow, to continue growing as it had in the past, confident that in facing new challenges with a keen sense of justice Muslims will renew the roots of their faith. Lesbian, gay, and transgendered Muslims assert that they may be agents in this slow but necessary change, along with women, youth, and other disempowered groups. But that is only because of God's granting them a pivotal place in the diversity of humanity—at the edge, a place of both danger and insight. In reality, they ask only to be treated as fully human, while those who believe insist on being recognized if not embraced as equals in faith. For they know that in the end, they are responsible before God through God's Prophet, rather than to any other authority; and God will ask whom they have injured in being homosexual or transgendered and who has committed injustice against them. They can answer with words the Prophet conveyed, "If I err, I err only against my own soul, and if I follow a right direction, it is because of what my lord reveals to me, for God is surely One who hears, an intimate One" (Qur'an 34:50).

NOTES

1. Scott Kugle, "Living Islam the Lesbian, Gay and Transgendered Way: a View of the Queer Jihad from Cape Town, South Africa," *ISIM Review* 16 (Summer 2005). I give many thanks to colleagues and friends in the Al-Fatiha Foundation, Salam Queer Community, The Inner Circle and other support groups for sharing their experiences and interpretations with me. All of them are reflected in this essay, with special thanks to Khalida, Daayiee Abdallah and Muhsin for offering constructive advice.

2. Abu Mansur al-Maturidi, *Kitab al-Tawhid,* 2nd ed. (Beirut [Lebanon]: Dar el-Machreq Editeurs Sarl, 1982), 3.

3. Maturidi, *Kitab al-Tawhid,* 10.

4. Though homosexuals and transgendered persons share many challenges, there are also important differences between them. In this chapter, I focus on homosexuality rather than transgender experiences, solely because of the limited space and not to imply any hierarchy of importance. I hope to give transgender experiences detailed attention in later writings.

5. Asma Barlas, *Believing Women in Islam: Un-reading Patriarchal Interpretations of the Qur'an* (Austin, Texas: University of Texas Press, 2002).

6. The Qur'an uses "colors" to speak of the varieties of plants which grow in the earth (16:13), of food crops (39:21), of fruits and soils (35:27), diverse hues and tastes of medicinal honey (16:69), as well the diverse natures of humankind, beasts of burden and animals of the fields (35:28).

7. Bernadette Brooten, *Love Between Women: Early Christian Responses to Female Homoeroticism* (Chicago, Illinois: University of Chicago Press, 1996), 115–142

documents astrological theories of pre-determined sexual orientation common in Greek, Roman and Early Christian contexts.

8. Muhammad Omar Nahas, *al-Junusiyya: nahw namudhaj li-tafsir al-junusiyya* (Roermond, The Netherlands: Bureau Arabica, 1997). My own documentation of lesbian and gay Muslim's life stories can be found in Kugle, "Living Islam the Lesbian, Gay and Transgendered Way: a view of the Queer Jihad from Cape Town, South Africa," *ISIM Review* (August 2005).

9. Bukhari, *Sahih*, bk. 1, chap. 1, report 1.

10. Fakhr al-Din Razi, *Mafatih al-Ghayb* (Cairo, 1346–1354 A.H.), 2:383.

11. For the use of "desire" in descriptions of heaven, see Qur'an 21:2, 41:31, 43:71, 16:57, 56:21 and 77:42. For the use of "desire" the fulfillment of which is absent in hell, see Qur'an 34:54.

12. See Qur'an 19:59, for example, where sensual desire and egoistic desire are juxtaposed to describe why people have perverted the prophets' teachings that have come before Islam.

13. Egoistic desire is clearly more dangerous than simply desiring bodily pleasure, for the legal terms for prostitution and violent rebellion are derived from the same linguistic root as *bagha*.

14. See Kugle, trans. *The Book of Illumination* (Louisville, Kentucky: Fons Vitae, 2005), 161–177.

15. See Scott Sirajul Haqq Kugle, "Sexuality, Diversity and Ethics," in *Progressive Muslims: on Gender, Justice and Pluralism*, ed. Omid Safi (Oxford: Oneworld Press, 2003) where I discuss in detail the interpretive assumptions of Tabari and Qurtubi. Others were more broad-minded to include same-sex acts as only one type of a range of actions that constituted their infidelity, from murder and robbery to public nudity, gambling and idolatrous worship (as mentioned in Surat al-'Ankabut 29-26-35).

16. Basim Musallam, *Sex and Society in Islam: Birth Control Before the Nineteenth Century* (Cambridge, U.K.: Cambridge University Press, 1983).

17. G..HA. Joynboll, "Sihak" in *Encyclopedia of Islam* 2nd ed., vol. 9, 565–566.

18. Amreen Jamel, "The Story of Lut and the Qur'an's Perception of the Morality of Same-Sex Sexuality," *Journal of Homosexuality* 41/1 (2001): 1–88.

19. The Companions of Rass are mentioned only in Qur'an 25:38 and 50:12; the cause of their destruction is never specified.

20. Farid Esack, *The Qur'an: a Short Introduction* (Oxford, U.K.: Oneworld, 2002) provides an excellent overview of the tools for and varieties of tafsir.

21. Historians who assert the "social construction" of homosexuality sometimes claim that homosexuals did not exist before the term was invented to name them; same-sex acts may always have existed between man and man or between woman and woman, they contend, but homosexuality as a concept did not. I would not go to this extreme, and instead follow a more moderate course between constructivism and essentialism, as charted by John, Boswell, "Concepts, Experience and Sexuality" in *Forms of Desire*, ed. E. Stein (New York: Routledge, 1992).

22. Zahir al-Din Miftahi, *Nasl-Kushi: ghayr-fitri jinsi maylan ya'ni 'amal qawm lut aur us ke dawa'i ki qabahat o mafasid pur pehli muhaqqiqana kitab* (Deoband, India: Salim Company, 1982), 20–21.

23. Bruce Bagemihl, *Biological Exuberance: Animal Homosexuality and Natural Diversity* (New York: St. Martin's Press, 1999); Joseph Alper, ed., *The Double-Edged Helix: Social Implications of Genetics in A Diverse Society* (Baltimore, Maryland: Johns Hopkins University Press, 2002), chaps 9–10.

24. There have been many proponents of Hadith scrutiny, from Syed Ahmed Khan in the mid-nineteenth century through the contemporary Muhammad al-Ghazali, in his *The Sunna of the Prophet: Between the Legists and the Traditionists* of 1989. For an excellent and even-handed summary of this debate, see Daniel Brown, *Rethinking Tradition in Modern Islamic Thought* (Cambridge, U.K.: Cambridge University Press, 1996), 81–112.

25. Shihab al-Din al-Nuwayri, *Nihayat al-Arab fi Funun al-Adab* (Cairo: Dar al-Kutub al-Misriyya, 1964), 206.

26. Arno Schmitt, "Liwat im Fiqh: Männliche Homosexualität?" *Journal of Arabic and Islamic Studies* 4 (2001–2002): 49–110 is the most complete study of the legal sources for rulings on male homosexual acts.

27. Malik ibn Anas, *al-Muwatta* (Lichtenstein: Thesaurus Islamicus Foundation, 2000), Kitab al-Hudud 41, 41. chap. 1, report 11. "Malik told me [Yahya ibn Yahya al-Laythi] that he had asked Ibn Shihab [al-Zuhri] about those who commit the act of the people of Lot; Ibn Shihab said, 'He is to be stoned, whether he is married or unmarried.'"

28. Muhammad ibn Tahir Patani, *Tadhkirat al-Mawdu'at* (Bombay: Maktaba al-Qayyima, 1343 A.H.), 107.

29. Noor al-Deen Atabek, "The Modernist Approach to Hadith Studies" (2004), posted at IslamOnline www.islamonline.net/english/Contemporary/2004/09/Article03.shtml.

30. Fatima Mernissi, *The Veil and the Male Elite:A Feminist Interpretation of Women's Rights in Islam* (Reading, Massachusetts: Addison-Wesley Publishing, 1991) presents this argument about misogynistic teaching alleged to be Prophetic Hadith.

31. This question will be addressed below in the section on "pairs and partners."

32. Hanafi jurists defended their caution against capital punishment by citing another hadith, "The blood of a Muslim is not liable to be shed, except in these three cases: fornication (*zina*) after marriage, infidelity after adopting Islam, and murdering an innocent person." See Abu Bakr Ahmad al-Jassas, *Ahkam al-Qur'an* (Beirut: Dar al-Kitab al-'Arabi, 1978), 2:363.

33. Sachiko Murata, *The Tao of Islam: A Sourcebook on Gender Relationships in Islamic Thought* (Albany, New York: SUNY Press, 1992). The discussion will be refined and sharpened by the able analysis of Sa'diya Sheikh, *Spiritual Cartographies of Gender: Ibn Arabi and Sufi Discourses of Gender, Sexuality and Marriage* (Chapel Hill, North Carolina: University of North Carolina, forthcoming).

34. Freud was the pioneer who rejected the conventional notion that sexuality is a "problem" to be solved by morality and convention and argued instead that sexuality was an inherent force in each person from infancy, a force that threatens social order but also can spur individuals to greater personal development and insight. Freud saw homosexuality as a pathological condition (rather than as a crime or sin), but psychologists who came after him have seen homosexuality as a deviation from the norm that

is not pathological, degenerative or liable to reduce the value of an individual within society. Jung reinterpreted Freud's ideas with greater attention to religion and spiritual archetypes, toward the goal of balance within the individual rather than conformity to social norms. Finally, Lacan refined psychoanalysis further, arguing that sexuality is not a primordial force in the personality as Freud theorized, but is rather one manifestation of the primal confrontation between self and other which shapes the ego at multiple levels, which brings psychoanalysis into even closer dialogue with Sufi metaphysics, as illustrated in Katherine Pratt Ewing, *Arguing Sainthood: Modernity, Psychoanalysis and Islam* (Durham, North Carolina: Duke University Press, 1997).

35.   Judges apply rational criteria to measure the situation: adult responsibility of the thief (*baligh* and *'aqil*), intent (*niya*), minimum value of the stolen object (*nihab*), type of good stolen (*mal*), relation of the thief to the victim, and the location of the stolen object (*hirz*), as described by David Forte, "Islamic Law and the Crime of Theft," *Cleveland State Law Review* (vol. 34–35), 54.

36.   The best exposition of the purposes of the *Shari'a* (*maqasid*) which limit dogmatic literalism by rational understanding of social welfare is by the Maliki jurist Shatibi. His ideals are much needed today, and one work attempts to reintroduce them into contemporary discussions: Muhammad Khalid Masud, *Islamic Legal Philosophy: a Study of Abu Ishaq al-Shatibi's Life and Thought* (Islamabad: Islamic Research Institute, 1977).

37.   Article available at www.tariqramadan.com/article.php3?id_article=0264& lang=en

38.   Abdelwahab Bouhdiba, *Sexuality in Islam* (London, U.K.: Routledge and Kegan Paul, 1985).

39.   For instance, on 17 May, 2004, www.islamonline.net posted a *fatwa* to the query "My brother, who is not Muslim, is homosexual. Now it is legal in Ontario for same sex couples to get married. I am worried that he may wish to do this. I get along very well with my brother. In fact, when I became a Muslim he was the only one in my whole family who supported me and helped me. We are very close. If he decides to have a marriage ceremony, would I be committing a sin if I attended?" The response by a mufti in Toronto, calls homosexuality *fahsha'*, an atrocious and obscene act, and states that "Islam teaches that believers should neither do obscene acts, nor in any way indulge in their propagation," quoting Qur'an 24:19: "Those who love to see obscenity published broadcast among the Believers will have a grievous penalty in this life and in the hereafter." The ruling offered is that "You are not allowed in Islam to attend a so-called marriage ceremony between homosexuals. By 'marrying' so, those people are waging an open war against Allah Almighty. Remember, homosexuality is the most heinous sin because of which Allah destroyed an entire nation. So, never mind your good relationship with your brother. You should never attend such a ceremony." There are several difficulties with this response. The verse quoted discusses the "obscenity" of false accusation of adultery (specifically about accusation against 'A'isha), not about any sex act or about homosexuality. The response also ignores the reality of law in Ontario, in which these "so-called marriages" are actual marriages. The ethics of commanding a brother to refuse to attend his brother's wedding is, of course, questionable.

40.   Ahmad Zarruq, *Sharh Asma' Allah al-Husna* (mss. Rabat: al-Khizana al-'Amma), 249 paraphrases a teaching of Shaykh Abu al-Hasan al-Shadhili (d. 1258 CE).

41.   Qur'an 16:90. "God enjoins acting justly and doing what is beautiful, providing for those near you in need and God forbids indecency, evil and rebellion, admonishing you so that you might be mindful." It is very significant that the formative principles of "acting justly and doing what is beautiful" come before specific ritual demands (providing for those in need through *Zakat*) and before legal or moral restraints (forbidding indecency, evil and rebellion).

8

SUFISM IN THE WEST: ISLAM IN AN INTERSPIRITUAL AGE

Hugh Talat Halman

He who knows himself knows his Lord.

—Hadith attributed to the Prophet Muhammad[1]

There are as many ways to reach God as there are created souls.

—Hadith attributed to the Prophet Muhammad[2]

Lo, for to myself I am unknown, now in God's Name what must I do?
I adore not the Cross, nor the Crescent, I am not a Giaour or a Jew.

—Jalaluddin Rumi[3]

INTRODUCTION

Some might interpret these lines from the Prophet Muhammad and Jalaluddin Rumi as describing a "spirituality" beyond the conventional boundaries of religious affiliation. This kind of worldview has often been associated with a "New Age Movement," or what some observers have now begun to call the "Interspiritual Age"[4] and a "second Axial age."[5] Under whatever name, participants, advocates, and enthusiasts of this view envision personal, social, and ecological transformation rooted in universal peace and unity among religious traditions. This chapter explores how Islam might be related to this "Interspirituality" and if so, how. Is there a bridge between the Religion of the Final Prophet and the Age of Aquarius?

To explore this question, this chapter describes four universalist Sufi teachers and their movements: (1) Hazrat Inayat Khan, (2) Samuel Lewis, (3) Meher Baba, and (4) Bawa Muhaiyaddeen. These teachers and their lineages had a major presence as New Religious Movements before and during the 1960s and 1970s when the New Age Movement emerged. Each teacher had an Islamic background and taught at least some elements of Islam. Hazrat Inayat Khan (1882–1927) came to the United States from India in 1910 and became the first Sufi teacher in The United States and Europe. His son and successor Pir Vilayat Khan (1916–2004) presented Sufism with inspiration and vigor for 40 years during the New Age Movement's development. Samuel Lewis, a disciple of Hazrat Inayat Khan and "teacher to the hippies," introduced the popular "Sufi Dancing" in San Francisco in the late 1960s. Avatar Meher Baba (1894–1969) began coming to Europe and America in 1931, attracted "Baba lovers," established centers worldwide, and chartered a Sufi organization. Bawa Muhaiyaddeen (1884–1986) came from Sri Lanka to Philadelphia in 1971 and developed the Bawa Muhaiyaddeen Fellowship. He also encouraged Coleman Barks to translate the poetry of Mevlana Jalaluddin Rumi (1207–1273 CE) a process that resulted in Rumi becoming popularly described as "America's best-selling poet." All of these teachers have been recorded in film and audio formats.

In the 1970s New Age participants—both practitioners and consumers—pursued psychotherapies, social movements, and cosmologies connected by an alternative "holistic" framework.[6] This movement was summarized in Marilyn Ferguson's *The Aquarian Conspiracy* as a "Paradigm Shift," or a transformation of "worldview" and "practices." Ferguson's holistic paradigm emphasized humankind's shared interconnectedness and the individual and collective power to create change.

> The social activism of the 1960s and the "consciousness revolution" of the early 1970s seemed to be moving toward a historic synthesis: social transformation resulting from personal transformation—change from the inside out.[7]

This description suggests that the movement emerged with the baby-boomer and post baby-boomer generations. Once the 1965 Immigration Act lifted quotas for Asians, numerous spiritual teachers came to the United States, especially from India and Japan. Additionally global mass media, the civil rights movement, the counter culture, the Peace Movement, feminism, world music, and Internet technology all further contributed to developing conditions setting the stage for the Interspiritual Age.

Sociologist Steve Bruce[8] presents a four-part model to describe the New Age Movement:

New Science/New Paradigm. People who identify themselves, or are labeled as proponents of a New Age culture typically borrow, embrace, and apply new philosophies of science as a teaching about spirituality. They apply holistic methods based on the interconnection of matter and energy, especially in pursuit of healing—personal, social, and planetary.

New Ecology. The New Age vision sees the earth as a holistic organism and its proponents are devoted to developing new ways to take care of the earth and ways of living in communities which nurture that goal, especially through "intentional communities" such as Findhorn in Scotland and Auroville in south India. This perspective is at the root of such early New Age classics as Schumacher's *Small is Beautiful* and James Lovelock's *Gaia.*

New Psychology. The New Age Movement embraces psychological models such as Transpersonal and Depth Psychology that envision mental health as reaching beyond normal functioning to release a human being's fullest potential.

New Spirituality. Some examples we would list include:

- Yoga (Swami Satcidananda, Swami Muktananda)
- Organic Gardening and Whole Foods
- Environmentalism and Ecology (Stewart Brand, James Lovelock)
- Green Peace
- Transpersonal Psychology (Baba Ram Das, Ken Wilbur)
- Mother Goddess Worship (Starhawk)
- Quantum Physics and the New Physics (David Bohm, Fritjof Capra)
- Alternative and Complementary Medicine (Deepak Chopra, Larry Dossey)
- Creation Spirituality (Matthew Fox)
- Quantum Healing (Deepak Chopra)
- Interspirituality (Wayne Teasdale)
- Integral Philosophy (Ken Wilbur)
- Biology (Rupert Sheldrake)
- Pagan Spirituality (Starhawk)

Brother Wayne Teasdale identified this new paradigm as the "Interspiritual Age," which he described as a "dawn of a new consciousness" marked by seven shifts in our understanding: (1) ecological awareness; (2) sensing the rights of other species; (3) recognizing our interdependence; (4) abandoning "militant nationalism" and embracing "essential interdependence"; (5) experiencing community between and among religions; (6) opening to the inner treasures of the world's religions through their individual members; and (7) opening to the cosmos and the "larger community of the universe."[9] One important difference in Teasdales' concept of an Interspritual Age relates to the question of relativism. Teasdale, who practiced both Christian and Buddhist monasticism, ultimately advocated standing in one tradition as one's root. His own teacher the Benedictine monk Bede Griffiths (d. 1993) who was one of the twentieth century's most outstanding practitioners of the dialogue between Christian and Hindu ideas and experience remained a Christian even though he had also taken Hindu renunciant (*sannyasi*) vows. Many who have belonged to the "New Age Movement" have rejected such exclusive identification as a limitation on spiritual unfolding.

Karen Armstrong calls our period a "second Axial Age," tracing its roots to the sixteenth and seventeenth centuries when colonialism and later, globalization triggered significant social, political, economic and intellectual revolutions. In response to these revolutions, as Armstrong describes it, people have begun seeking "new ways of being religious" by "building on the insights of the past." Armstrong notes the similarity of these approaches to the first Axial Age (800–500 BCE) when many of the world's religions came into being. She points to a similar combination of "...a recoil from violence with looking into the heart"[10] joined with the search for "an absolute reality in the depths of [one's own] being."[11] Unlike Teasdale, Armstrong (a former nun) no longer belongs to a formal religion.

SYNCRETISM IN ISLAM; SYNCRETISM IN THE INTERSPIRITUAL AGE

The Interspiritual Age is partly characterized by trends toward synthesis and syncretism. Have Muslims engaged in similar tendencies? Throughout Islamic history we find Muslims who have creatively combined religious ideas and practices. Especially in Africa, Iran, Turkey, Central Asia, India, China, and Indonesia, we find that this syncretism contributed to the spread of Islam, For example in Indonesia, some of the nine saints (*Wali Songo*) who spread Islam in Java adapted the Javanese Hindu versions of the heroic Hindu epics, the *Mahabharata* and the *Ramayana* to teach and spread Islam. What differentiates Islamic syncretism from New Age syncretism is that many in the New Age Movement have not considered one religion to be the final and supreme revelation and overarching metanarrative.

THE FOUR DIMENSIONS OF ISLAM

Many Muslims describe Islam in two aspects and four dimensions. Because the four teachers discussed here use these models, they are essential for our comparison. Here we will look at some examples from Indonesia and Turkey. Muslims speak of two parts of Islam: the outer or exoteric (*zahir*) and the inner or esoteric (*batin*) (Qur'an 57:2). From this pair the four dimensions unfold. Anthropologist Clifford Geertz[12] reports how an Indonesian Muslim explained them: (1)*Shari'a*, involves "the carrying out of the usual duties of Islam." *Shari'a* describes normative doctrines, rituals, and mainstream community organization(s); (2) *Tariqa*, includes "the special mystical techniques." *Tariqa* ("the path") encompasses the fellowship, spiritual practices, and relationship to spiritual teachers and guides, that is, Sufism; (3) *Haqiqa* means truth, reality, and realization of mystical union; (4) *Ma'rifat* translates as *gnosis*, meaning inner discernment.It is these three dimensions beyond *Shari'a* which provide a useful way to compare Islam with the New Age Movement.

In Turkey, John Birge received this explanation following the analogy of sugar:

> One can go to the dictionary and find out what sugar is and how it is used. That is the *Shari'a* Gateway to knowledge. One feels the inadequacy of that when one is introduced directly to the practical seeing and handling of sugar. That represents the *Tariqa* Gateway to knowledge. To actually taste sugar and have it enter into oneself is to go one step deeper into an appreciation of its nature, and that is what is meant by *ma'rifat* If one could go still further and become one with sugar so that he could say, "I am sugar," that and that alone would be to know what sugar is, and that is what is involved in the *Haqiqa* Gateway. (Birge, p. 102)

This *haqiqa* experience of mystical union, also called in classical Sufism *wahdat al-wujud* (the unity of existence) and *wahdat al-shuhud* (the experience of oneness), provides an important correlation between Islamic and Interspiritual thinking. This perspective is an example of what Teasdale in his sixth point calls "one of the inner treasures of the worlds' religions."[13]

Now we turn to assess four significant Sufi teachers who led movements in Europe and America and evaluate how they may have helped contribute to the Interspiritual Age.

Pir-O Murshid Hazrat Inayat Khan (1882–1927)

One of the most significant presences in American Sufism has been Pir-O Murshid Hazrat Inayat Khan. Inayat Khan was a harbinger of the attitudes, styles, and approaches of the Interspiritual Age whose influence extended to contact with thousands of people in at least eight countries in Europe and America, including composer Claude Debussy, the pianist Scriabin, psychologist Roberto Assagioli, and automaker Henry Ford. Inayat Khan was a master musician who had also trained in Sufism, Hinduism, and Zoroastrianism. Fluent in English and highly charismatic, he has the distinction of being one of the earliest Islamic teachers in the United States (1910) as well as being the first teacher of Sufism in Europe and America. In 16 years of public teaching, he initiated 200–300 people including four women whom he appointed as *murshidas* (spiritual guides). As he introduced a Universal Sufism in the context of what he called "spiritual liberty," thousands of people encountered basic elements of Islamic teaching, culture, and spirituality.

His collected works, *The Sufi Message of Spiritual Liberty* comprise 14 volumes. To date his teachings have been published under at least 40 titles. Currently the first four volumes of an ongoing reediting of his *Collected Works* have been published. His work has continued as a major presence in American Sufism and in the New Age Movement through his major successors, his son Pir Vilayat Inayat Khan (1916–2004) and Murshid Samuel Ahmad Murad "Sufi Sam" Chishti Lewis (1896–1971) as well as others we will mention.

Born in Baroda, India, his grandfather founded a music academy and his father was also a master musician and singer. In addition to attending a Hindu school, Inayat Khan witnessed and met musicians and other family friends and associates from diverse religious backgrounds. After close training with his grandfather, Inayat Khan toured India as a young boy and was honored by the Nizam of Hyderabad. Under the auspices of his virtuoso family of musicians Inayat Khan became a master of the *vina*, India's oldest musical instrument.

His parents brought him to yogis, saints, and sages of Hindu, Muslim, and Parsi (Indian Zoroastrian) backgrounds. In Nepal he met an old Sufi master whose glance charged him with exaltation. After working as a music professor, Inayat Khan then traveled throughout India alone and saw in a dream a beautiful face, a vision he took as a sign to search for a spiritual guide (*murshid*). In Hyderabad, in 1903, he saw the man whose face he had seen in the dream: Sayyid Mohammed Abu Hashim Madani. Until his death in 1907 Madani served as both Inayat Khan's initiatic and academic teacher in Sufism and issued Inayat Khan the following commission: "Go, my child, into the world, harmonize the East and the West with the harmony of thy music; spread the wisdom of Sufism, for thou art gifted by Allah, the most Merciful and Compassionate." Later that year Inayat Khan met with the prominent Brahman guru Manik Prabhu who deepened his understanding of the link between Sufism's doctrine of oneness of being (*wahdat al-wujud*) and Vedanta's non-duality (*advaita*). Inayat Khan's particular lineage the Chishtiyya provided him with an example of initiating non-Muslims into Sufism.[14]

At a musical presentation at the Hindu Temple in San Francisco in 1911, Inayat Khan met Ada Martin, whom he initiated with the name Rabia and whom he ultimately designated as his immediate successor. In 1915, after traveling in America, Russia, and England, Inayat Khan established the headquarters of the International Sufi Order in London. At this time, he composed an as-yet unpublished spiritual biography of the Prophet Muhammad. Within a few years though, some of the Muslim members of the Sufi Order asked Inayat Khan to require the non-Muslims to convert to Islam. Instead Inayat Khan upheld the right and value of each person to seek truth under the Murshid's guidance without being required to label themselves, and without the requirement to accept, reject, or adopt a particular faith or creed.[15]

Indeed Inayat Khan's sense of the "Message" and his "mission" involved restraint with regard to religious doctrine. His first book, aptly titled, *A Sufi Message of Spiritual Liberty,* opens: "Beloved ones of Allah, you may belong to any race, caste, creed, or nation, still you are all impartially loved of Allah."[16] And Inayat Khan inventively expressed the integral relationship between Sufism and Islam: "The idea that Sufism sprang from Islam or from any other religion, is not necessarily true; yet it might be rightly called the spirit of Islam, as well as the pure essence of all religions and philosophies."[17]

Inayat Khan's description of the Prophet Muhammad's mission illustrates how he envisioned Islam beyond dogma:

> At last he began to hear a word of inner guidance, "Cry out the sacred name of thy Lord"; and as he began to follow this advice, he found the echo of the word which his heart repeated in the whole of nature.... When once he was in tune with the Infinite, realizing his soul to be one, within and without the call came, "Thou art the man; go forward into the world and carry out our Command; glorify the Name of God; unite those who are separated; waken those who are asleep, and harmonize one with the other, for in this lies the happiness of man."[18]

Inayat Khan emphasized that Islam was a revelation based on the theophany of nature. While most Muslims share this perspective, Inayat Khan's special emphasis on nature as scripture heralds values that will emerge in the New Age Movement :

> Islamic worship shows an improvement upon the older forms of worship in human evolution, for Islam prefers nature to art and sees in nature the immanence of God.... It is said, "Cry aloud the name of thy Lord, the most beneficent, who hath by his nature's skilful pen taught man what he knew not," which means: who has written this world like a manuscript with the pen of nature. If one desires to read the Holy Book, one should read it in nature.[19]

These references to the "tongue of nature" and the "pen of nature" reach succinct expression in Inayat Khan's third of "Ten Sufi Thoughts": "There is one Holy Book, the sacred manuscript of nature, the only scripture which can enlighten the reader."

In his first book, *A Sufi Message of Spiritual Liberty,* Inayat Khan described the ultimacy of the Prophet Muhammad's mission and of Islam:

> ...[T]he work was thus continued by all the prophets until Mohammed, the *Khatim al-Mursalin,* the last messenger of divine wisdom and the seal of the prophets, came on his mission, and in his turn gave the final statement of

divine wisdom, "None exists but Allah".... There was no necessity left for any more prophets after this divine message, which created the spirit of democracy in religion by recognizing God in every being. By this message man received the knowledge that he may attain the highest perfection under the guidance of a perfect *murshid* or spiritual teacher.[20]

Inayat Khan's position on the Prophet Muhammad differentiates him from New Age thinkers who more readily rank Christ or Buddha as exemplars of New Age values. Although Inayat Khan did not require his initiates to become Muslim, but instead stressed the primacy of mystical realization lying outside conventional doctrinal and institutional boundaries, he still affirmed the supremacy of Muhammad's mission and revelation as final and as an integrating context for all forms of religious and spiritual expression. Lewis later recounted: "In his first sessions on Sufism, Pir-O-Murshid placed Muhammad as the Perfect Man of All Times."[21]

Inayat Khan describes the four stages of Sufism *Shari'a* (Law), *tariqa* (Way), *haqiqa* (Truth), and *ma'rifat* (Knowledge) in a way that prefigures Interspiritual Age ideals of flexibility:

Although the religious authorities of Islam have limited this law to restrictions, yet in a thousand places in the Qur'an and Hadith one can trace how the law of Shariat is meant to be subject to change, in order to suit the time and place.[22]

After explaining *tariqa* as understanding the cause behind *Shari'a*, he describes *haqiqa* and *ma'rifat* as:

...knowing the truth of our being and the inner laws of nature. This knowledge widens man's heart...he has realized the one Being.... This is the grade in which religion ends and Sufism begins. *Marefat* means the actual realization of God, the one Being where there is no doubt any more.[23]

Sufism, he concludes, arises from attaining all four levels, which are the "inner teachings of the knowledge of God" into which the Prophet Muhammad initiated Ali and Abu Bakr.[24] Inayat Khan did not train his children to perform the *Salat* prayer and did not continue to practice *Salat* after he came to the West. He did, however, instruct his *murida* (disciple) Rabia Martin to learn and practice *Salat,* but not in order to become a Muslim.[25] In India Inayat Khan had practiced *Salat* and other Islamic observances, but ceased after coming to America and Europe.

Instead of *Salat,* Inayat Khan instituted a new prayer regimen. The core prayer known as the Invocation reads:

Toward the One, the Perfection of Love, Harmony, and Beauty,
the Only Being United with All the Illuminated Souls
who form the Embodiment of the Master, the Spirit of Guidance.

Inayat Khan understood all the Prophets and Masters as part of one being. In this he had behind him the Sufi tradition of the *Nur Muhammad*,[26] the idea that all the Prophets emanated from one primordial "Light of Muhammad." In Inayat Khan's text of the afternoon prayer, devotees address the "Master, Messiah, and Savior of all Humanity":

> Allow us to recognize Thee in all Thy holy names and forms:
> as Rama, as Krishna, as Shiva, as Buddha,
> Let us know Thee as Abraham, as Solomon, as Zarathustra,
> as Moses, as Jesus, as Muhammad, and in many other names
> and forms known and unknown to the world...
> O Messenger! Christ! Nabi the Rasul of God.[27]

The Sufi Order's five "concentrations" established by Inayat Khan embody Interspiritual Age ideals and practices: the Universal Worship, the Esoteric School, the Healing Order, Ziraat (Gardening), and the Kinship Concentration.

Originally intended as the Sufi Order's public face, Universal Worship expresses the New Age ideal of honoring all religions. Its worship service features candles for each of the major traditions and one for all traditions unnamed or unknown "who have held aloft the light of truth." Also named the Church of All and All Churches, its ministers (*Cherags*, "lamps") perform marriages and other sacraments. When Inayat Khan offered Universal Worship in New York on May 7, 1921, 50 people attended. In 1926, 500 people attended.

The Esoteric School encompasses the framework of a relationship between *murids* (disciples) and *murshids* (guides) who have been empowered by the Pir. The current Pir is Hazrat Inayat Khan's grandson, Pir Zia Inayat Khan (b. 1971) who continues to develop the curriculum of his father and grandfather. *Murshids* concentrate on guiding *murids* in their practices and aim to avoid the guru-like intercession of advising *murids'* on all areas of their lives. By doing these practices, *murids* are meant to develop their "inner guidance." The Esoteric School also offers retreats ranging between one and forty days.

The Healing Order, begun in 1925, offers a group healing service that attends to healing at a distance through attunement, prayer, breath, and concentration. Since 1979, the Sufi Healing Order has organized 26 national conferences on science and spirituality. Led until recently by Himayati Inayati (John Johnson) the Healing Order also features a more comprehensive healing modality called the Raphaelite Work (named after the angel of healing). As in many New Age healing movements, "healing" is distinguished from "curing" by focusing primarily on the transformation of consciousness, the healing of the heart and soul, or the improvement of quality of life of the person healed.

The Ziraat Concentration uses farming as a metaphor and a spiritual practice for transformation, restoring harmony between the inner and outer: "We respond to the call to become mature gardeners of both our inner being and of our planet." Ziraat cultivates the sacredness of life through meditation, horticulture, and environmentalism. Pir Vilayat linked Ziraat's agricultural mystery rite to deep ecology.[28]

The Kinship Concentration (originally called Brotherhood) is rooted in the universal morality of caring for one another. This service includes work in schools, food banks, counseling, birthing and health clinics, prison book funds, to say nothing of the Hope Project in Delhi. The Hope Project "provides food, education, medical and social services for the destitute shanty dwellers surrounding the tomb of Hazrat Inayat Khan in Delhi."[29]

In 1912 Inayat Khan married an American, Ora Ray Baker (renamed Amina Begum), with whom he sired four children. His eldest son Pir Vilayat was born in London in 1916. Archival film shows Hazrat Inayat Khan in the year before his death passing on succession to Vilayat, who was then ten years old. In World War II, Pir Vilayat served as a minesweeper and later as a journalist in North Africa, and his reporting aroused international acclamation.[30] Vilayat also studied with the Islamic Philosopher Henry Corbin at the Sorbonne where he received his Ph.D. After the war, he traveled throughout India and other countries seeking out "dervishes, Hindu yogis, and *rishis* as well as Buddhist and Christian monks."[31] Since a number of his father's relatives and others had also laid claim to succession,[32] in 1957, Pir Vilayat revived the Sufi Order his father had chartered in London in 1915 and named it the Sufi Order in the West (later, Sufi Order International). Pir Vilayat was not at odds with the other successors but was committed to fulfilling his father's commission.[33] Toward that end he had received authorization to teach from Pir Fakhruddin, the son of Abu Hashim Madani, his father's Chishti *pir*. In the 1970s he established a Sufi Community, the Abode of the Message in New Lebanon, New York, and later the Omega Institute in Rhinebeck, New York, a commercial New Age Workshop facility.

Author of seven books and many articles, Pir Vilayat was admired by his followers as a meditation master, and as an inspired teacher who lucidly invigorated and updated diverse spiritual teachings into an integral framework. He was fond of interpreting the Qur'anic phrase "…light upon light…" as describing "the light of intelligence strikes and your whole aura bursts into brightness more intensely than ever before."[34] In teaching the practice of *dhikr* repeating *la ilaha illa Allah,* Pir Vilayat combines spiritual and scientific references as he describes "…building a temple of light out of the fabric of our aura and a temple of magnetism out of electromagnetic fields, with our heart as the altar in this temple."[35] Concerning the Prophet Muhammad, Pir Vilayat explains that "[Muhammad] gave the final statement of Divine Wisdom: 'None exists but Allah.'"[36] Describing the "spirituality of the future," Pir Vilayat sets forth three points similar to the character of the

Interspiritual Age: (1) it will be a spirituality free of dogma and "replacing theoretical belief with direct mystical experience; (2) "...a recognition of the need for seekers to trust their conscience and assume responsibility... rather than relying on role models to dictate prescriptive 'do's and don't's'"; and (3) an new image of the Divine: "...the Universe is a Global Being of which the cosmos is a body whose intelligence flashes through our thoughts and emotions...."[37]

Pir Vilayat's son and successor Pir Zia Inayat Khan (1971–) who received investiture in 2001 also traveled widely to study with Sufi masters. He holds a B.A. from the School of Oriental and African Studies of the University of London and an M.A. from Duke University. When Pir Vilayat brought Pir Zia[38] to study Buddhism under the auspices of the Dalai Lama, Kalu Rinpoche, a highly respected Kagyu master, bestowed on Pir Zia the designation of *tulku*—a reborn Tibetan teacher. Pir Zia decided that since he did not remember his previous life as a *tulku* and that it made no sense to him, he would rather not accept the honor. In this decision he also consulted with the Dalai Lama.[39] Since assuming the mantle of succession, Pir Zia has encouraged traditional Muslim practice in the Sufi Order. This is reflected in inviting Imam Bilal Hyde to offer seminars in Islam at the Abode of the Message and on the Anjumani Listserve. Pir Zia also brings a renewed appreciation of the Indian Chishti Sufi lineage from which the Inayati–Chishti lineage stems. Members visit the tombs of both Hazrat Inayat Khan in Delhi and Moinuddin Chishti in Ajmer. A recent initiative by Pir Zia is the Suluk Academy of Sufi Studies. Its brochure states:

> The Suluk Academy offers a course of focused spiritual study to cultivate meditative techniques and perspectives grounded in the traditional yoga of Sufism (*suluk*) which support the natural unfoldment of the soul in life.[40]

In 2006, the Academy will offer a course on "Green Hermeticism." Its three teachers bring eclectic backgrounds in alchemy, Kabbalah, herbal medicine, Celtic Christianity, and Sufism—both mainstream and antinomian. In addition to theoretical study, participants will practice *spagyrics* (plant alchemy), investigating how this knowledge can address ecological problems. [41]

Inayat Khan, as a virtuoso musician, was very much a forerunner of the New Age Movement which appreciates music as a spiritual and healing resource. But Inayat Khan sacrificed his own musical career to teach and did not incorporate music directly into his teaching. That musical impulse would revive through Samuel Lewis.

Samuel Ahmad Murad Chisti (Samuel L. Lewis) (1896–1971)

Lewis is probably the most actively eclectic spiritual explorer in this chapter. After majoring in Agriculture at Columbia University, he began in

1919 to live in an intentional community of Sufis in Fairfax, California that practiced the teachings of Inayat Khan.

Initiated in 1923 by Inayat Khan, Lewis was both overwhelmed by a blinding light and comforted by a kind presence. In comparison to Rinzai Zen masters Sogaku Shaku, Shaku Soyen, and Nyogen Senzaki with whom he had studied, he felt that Inayat Khan was the "first person to deeply touch and awaken his heart." (Lewis often wrote in the third person.) During a retreat in Fairfax in 1925, Lewis received three visitations from the immortal Prophet Khidr[42] who conferred the gifts of poetry and music. These visits were followed by the appearances of Shiva, Buddha, Zoroaster, Moses, Jesus, Muhammad, and finally Elijah who bestowed "the Robe."[43] In 1926, after six interviews with Lewis, Inayat Khan conferred upon him the title "Protector of the Message."

While continuing his Zen training, in 1938 Lewis met Ramana Maharshi's disciple Paul Brunton with whom he achieved immediate *samadhi* (divine union). After Rabia Martin turned over authority for the Sufi Order to Meher Baba (see a discussion of this below), Lewis, who disagreed with this decision, maintained his contact with Inayat Khan on the inner planes. In 1946 the Prophets Muhammad and Jesus appeared to Lewis:

> Around 1946, the writer entered into *fana-fi-rassul* [absorption into the Prophet Muhammad]. Although this came from Mohammed, the Khatimal Mursaleen [Seal of the Chain-of-Prophets], it was followed almost immediately by a similar experience with Jesus (Isa).[44]

After this visit with Brunton, Lewis received the name Ahmad Murad. In 1947, he experienced an inner visit from Inayat Khan who assigned him to the direct guidance of Jesus and Muhammad.

In the 1950s and 1960s Lewis worked on salt-water conversion projects. Then after reading Rachel Carson's *Silent Spring*, he worked on nonpoisonous pesticides at City College of San Francisco. In addition he proposed a comprehensive agricultural program inspired by Islamic symbolism in which North African soil would be rejuvenated through planting dates, figs, olives, and grapes. He traveled widely, especially to Egypt, India, and Japan and studied with Sufi, Hindu, and Buddhist masters.

In 1956 in Japan Lewis said the relationship between Amida Buddha and Shakyamuni Buddha, "is exactly the same as that between Allah and Muhammad."[45] Lewis later declared: "Both Sufism and Mahayana Buddhism teach the transcendentalism intuition (*kashf* or *prajna* and no-nonsense)."[46] His ecumenism and intention to harmonize religion and science exemplify ideals of the New Age Movement and the Interspiritual Age.

Lewis trained further with Zen and Sufi masters before returning to America in 1962. Pir Maulana Abdul Ghafor, a Chishti shaykh, initiated Lewis and appointed him to serve as a spiritual inspiration like Shams-i

Tabrizi to Inayat Khan's disciples. Lewis maintained that his authority as a
Sufi teacher derived from his training with numerous Sufis, especially five:
Inayat Khan, Abdul Ghafor, Barakat Ali, Pir Dewal Shereef (President of
the Board of Directors of Islamabad University), and Sidi Abusalam
al-Alawi.[47] Murshid Sam wrote, "I never used this term 'Sufi' [as a
self-referential title] until it was publicly announced by Pir Sufi Barakat Ali
of the Chishti Order in 1961 at Salarwala, West Pakistan."[48] From this point
Lewis would be known as Murshid S.A.M. (Samuel Ahmad Murshid).

In April 1967, while hospitalized for ptomaine poisoning, "...the voice
of Allah appeared to Lewis and said, 'I make you spiritual teacher to the
hippies.'"[49] These words came to life in 'Sufi Dancing." Lewis made a direct
and lasting Sufi contribution to the New Age Movement through these
"Dervish Dances" (now, the "Dances of Universal Peace"):

> Well, the voice of Allah came to me and presented more visions of Dervish
> Dances. These dances are based only slightly on the methods of the Mevlevi
> School. They have in them elements of the Rufai and Bedawi [Sufi] Schools.
> And along with them the operative aspects of *kashf* [insight].... [A]nd from that
> moment a new type of *Qawwal* [sacred song] was born.[50]

Lewis claimed a divine and Islamic inspiration for the dances and described
some of the chanting as *qawwal*, a South Asian devotional genre. As he continued to "receive" these dances he consulted with Ruth St. Denis "my fairy
godmother, so to speak."[51] Again we see a truly New Age eclecticism.
The dances integrated singing and dancing from all the sacred traditions
of the world. Some of the earliest included *Bismillah; As-Salaam Aleikum;
Ya Hayy, Ya Haqq; Ya Muhammad Abdullah;* together with Hindu and
Christian dances. This syncretistic and inclusive framework certainly belongs
to the New Age Movement. Lewis wrote in 1970: "My friends, it is a New
Age. It is an age of warm delight in the Divine Presence."[52]

Nonetheless Lewis affirmed the Prophet Muhammad's supremacy because
he lived a perfect life in an "operative world":

> The Bible says that God created Adam in His image, but Adam is usually
> associated with "sin." There had to be a "perfect man" for redemption.... But
> the Buddhist does not live like the Buddha, nor the Christian like Christ, nor
> the Hindu like Ram or Krishna. We wish to live in an operative world—to raise
> families and go into business and study and do all those things which we consider
> human. It is on this point that Muhammad excels. He does not excel in
> being nearer to God, the Creator, but he does excel in being closer to man, the
> created.[53]

In this spirit of simplicity, Samuel Lewis summarized his teaching in these
words of the communal spirit: "Eat, pray, and dance together." Lewis
believed that three figures from the Islamic world offered particularly valuable

policies that might be applied today: the Caliph 'Umar (d. 644 CE), Sultan Salahaddin (d. 1193 CE), and Suleiman the Magnificent (d. 1566 CE).[54]

Lewis appointed Moinuddin Carl Jablonski (1942–2001) as the *khalif* (designated leader) of the SIRS (Sufi Ruhaniat Islamia Society), now Sufi Ruhaniat International (SRI). Pir Vilayat also initiated Jablonski as a *murshid,* but in SIRS. In 1977 SIRS, as part of an effort to make the murshid-murid relationship more central than in the formal organization, Jablonski decided to separate SIRS from the Sufi Order but to continue its sisterhood relationship to both the Sufi Order and the (European) Sufi Movement. Jablonski integrated a system of psychotherapy counselling from Frida Waterhouse called Soulwork to aid *murids* in both achieving psychological unity and refraining from overemphasizing transcendence. As his successor, Jablonski appointed another former student of Murshid Samuel Lewis, Shabda Khan, who is also a master vocalist and musician trained in classical Indian music.

Another prominent Ruhaniat leader, Saadi Neil Douglas-Klotz, has led the Dances of Universal Peace Movement. Under his auspices the catalog of dances now number at least 400. Klotz also leads a national movement of people studying, chanting, and dancing the words and prayers of Jesus in Aramaic.[55] Saadi uses distinctive etymologies of Arabic words as he learned them from his Pakistani Qur'an teacher Shemsuddin Ahmed. Introducing the workings of Semitic languages, he encourages people to meditate on them in the heart in order to open more mystical levels of meaning. In his most recent book he poetically presents the Names of God as "pathways of the heart" serving as techniques of meditation. The first meditation in the book is typical:

> With one hand lightly on your heart, breathe easily and gently. Feel the awareness of breath and heartbeat creating a clear, spacious place inside. Breathe with the sound *bismillah* (Bis-MiLLaaH). When we remember to connect our heart to the Heart of the Cosmos, we recall that, as the Sufis say, "God is your lover, nor your jailer."[56]

The Dances of Universal Peace have become mainstreamed and autonomous. Not only are they performed in the Sufi Order, but free dances open to the public are offered around the world. This innovative form of worship, syncretic in both its religious and its cultural framework, is one of the most obvious Sufi contributions to the New Age Movement and the Interspiritual Age.

Meher Baba (1894–1969)

Meher Baba declared that he was the Avatar, the manifestation of God in human form, not merely a teacher, but an awakener, sent to awaken love

through the power of divine love. He claimed to have lived before as
Zoroaster, Rama, Krishna, Buddha, Christ, and Muhammad. This list
echoes Inayat Khan's prayer "Saum" and Meher Baba's claim to be Muhammad locates him squarely in our discussion of teachers who are both steeped
in either Islam or Sufism and who are also harbingers of the New Age Movement and the Interspiritual Age. He transmitted Sufi teachings to disciples in
Europe, America, Australia, New Zealand, and around the globe. By 1958,
he had established two teaching centers in America, one in Australia, and
one in London. He represents a specific link between Sufism and the Interspiritual Age. In addition, he attempted to "re-orient" Inayat Khan's Sufi
Order.

Born in 1894 to a family of Parsis (Zoroastrians who emigrated from Iran
to India beginning in the tenth century CE) in Mumbai, he was introduced
to Sufism by his father Sheriar who had wandered as a dervish (Sufi mendi-
cant) for 18 years in both Iran and India. Of five Indian "perfect masters"
who initiated Meher Baba three had Muslim backgrounds. Meher Baba's
own teaching is infused with the Sufism of Persian and Indian cultures, especially from Hafiz (d. 1389 CE) and Rumi (d. 1273 CE).

Meher Baba's teachings pointed beyond the boundaries of scriptures, practices, and institutions:

> I am not come to establish any cult, society, or organization; nor even to
> establish a new religion. The religion that I shall give teaches the Knowledge of
> the One behind the many. The book that I shall make people read is the book
> of the heart that holds the key to the mystery of life. I shall bring about a happy
> blending of the head and the heart. I shall revitalize all religions and cults, and
> bring them together like beads on one string.[57]

Meher Baba declared the oneness of religious truth in love:

> There is no difference in the realization of Truth either by a Muslim, Hindu,
> Zoroastrian, or Christian. The difference is only in words and terms. Truth is
> not the monopoly of a particular race or religion.[58]
>
> I belong to no religion. Every religion belongs to me. My personal religion is
> being the Ancient Infinite One. And the religion I impart to all is love for God,
> which is the truth of all religions.[59]

Meher Baba culled from a variety of traditions, mostly those of his
previous Avataric manifestations as well the "perfect masters" Rumi, Hafiz,
Ramakrishna, Tukaram, Kabir, Milarepa, and St. Francis.[60]

In one of his two most important books, *God Speaks* Meher Baba takes a
famous poem by Rumi as his point of departure to describe and explain in
detail how souls return to God. This can be a challenging poem for some
Muslims since it seems to carry overtones of metempsychosis:

I died as a mineral and became a plant,
I died as a plant and rose to animal,
I died as animal and I was Man.
Why should I fear? When was I less by dying?
Yet once more I shall die as Man, to soar
With angels blest; but even from angelhood
I must pass on: all except God doth perish.
When I have sacrificed my angel soul,
I shall become what no mind e'er conceived.
Oh, let me not exist! For Non-existence proclaims
In organ tones. "To Him we shall return." [61]

This poem expresses God's immanent and empathetic experience as
He participates in all levels of being. (The Qur'an teaches that God sees
through the eyes of all creatures [Surat al-An'am (6):103].) God here is the
subject, the "I," who progresses through each of these stages. Meher Baba,
teaching that each soul is an individual "drop" of the divine ocean returning
to the divine ocean, sustains both this reading and his teaching that the soul
transmigrates.

Meher Baba explains the journey Rumi describes in three parts: "evolution," "reincarnation," and "involution." In "evolution" the soul traces a
path through the physical universe: gaseous forms; stone; metal; vegetable;
worm, insect, and reptile; fish; bird; and animal; before finally reaching human
form. In "reincarnation" the human soul goes through repeated rebirths and
through its thoughts, words, and actions acquires new "impressions"
(patterns, *samskara* [s]). As these impressions wind around it, they veil
the soul from God's presence. However, ultimately through rebirths characterized by morality, spiritual work and divine grace these impressions loosen
and unwind until they progressively wear away. After evolution and reincarnation the soul moves into its third phase: "involution." In this phase the soul
passes beyond the first body, the "gross body" of human incarnation.

Involution takes the soul on a journey through seven planes. The first six
planes are contained in two "bodies" or "spheres." In involution the soul
first progresses to the "subtle body" which contains energy impressions.
Next the soul moves into the "mental body" filled with impressions of
instinct, intellect, emotion, and desire, before the soul completes its return
to God. Located in the planes of the "subtle body" (the first four planes in
a series of seven) are "psychic" or "magical" experiences and powers. In
the "subtle body" one experiences—and is in danger of becoming distracted
by—a variety of paranormal phenomena: images, colors, bright lights, circles,
fragrances, music, and so on.

The fifth and sixth planes of the "mental body" symbolize the purification
of mind and heart: "...Those belonging to the mental sphere only use their
powers for the good of others."[62] The "mental body" planes also describe
the spiritual attainments of various holy people. The fifth plane represents

those known as *wali* (lit., "friend of God") the saints and yogis. The sixth plane includes the perfect masters: *murshid* (lit., "guide") and *pir* (elder). Those on the sixth plane see God face to face. The *qutb* (lit., "pivotal saint," or perfect master) stands beyond these on a "seventh plane," in a state Meher Baba describes as "God's realization of Himself as Infinite."

Using traditional Sufi terms, Meher Baba describes the seventh plane as that of *fana'* ("passing-away into God [becoming God]") and the immediate stage beyond it as *baqa'* ("abiding in God [being God]"). Beyond these two journeys, only five perfect masters in the position of *qutubiat* (central saints) embark on the third journey in which they are "living God's life (living both as God and man simultaneously)."[63] Meher Baba considered Inayat Khan a "sixth-plane" saint.

In *God Speaks* Meher Baba included a commentary on his text written by 'Abdul Ghani Munsiff, a Muslim disciple among the earliest of Meher Baba's *mandali* (inner circle of disciples). 'Abdul Ghani's commentary expresses the ideas of *God Speaks* mostly in Persian Sufi terms frequently quoting the Sufi poetry of Hafiz-i Shirazi (d. 1389 CE). Meher Baba repeatedly showed his supreme appreciation and reverence for Hafiz, whom he described as: "a Persian poet who was a Perfect Master."[64] Two hours before he died Meher Baba dictated three of Hafiz's couplets to be inscribed on his tomb.

In 1931, Meher Baba explained his mission in New Age terms:

> I intend to bring together all religions and cults like beads on one string and to revitalize them for individual and collective needs. This is my mission in the West. The peace and harmony that I talk of and that will settle on the face of this worried world are not far off. [65]

Meher Baba also chartered a Sufi organization, "Sufism Re-Oriented." Inayat Khan's successor Rabia Martin and her disciple Ivy Duce both followed Meher Baba. Duce, who felt unequipped to succeed Martin, asked Meher Baba for help. On July 20, 1952 Meher Baba announced that he would charter "Sufism Reoriented." As Meher Baba explained, through this action he intended to reinvigorate all spiritualities—all "isms"—Sufism in particular, and especially the work begun by Inayat Khan:

> So it is now time for me to re-orient these different isms which end in one God. I intend to make one unique charter regarding this re-oriented Sufism and send it to Ivy Duce from India in November with my signature, and entrust the American Sufism work to her.... [I]t will be applicable to the whole Sufi world—and will, by God's grace—be lasting in its effect and influence.[66]

One of Meher Baba's biographers summarizes the duties Meher Baba dictated in the charter:

Sufism as reoriented by Meher Baba is based on love and longing for God and the eventual union with God in actual experience. The Charter states that it is the duty of every member: (a) to become conversant with the principles of Sufism by reading and studying the literature of Sufi saints, poets, and authors such as Hafiz, Jalaluddin, Shams, Inayat Khan, Ibn 'Arabi, Shibli, Hujwiri, and others; (b) to necessarily read and study vigorously the Discourses by Meher Baba and the book by Meher Baba called "God Speaks" which depicts the ten states of God and other important truths, and which is his last and final book on this subject; (c) to necessarily repeat verbally daily one name of God for half an hour any time of the day or night; this is to be done consecutively if possible, but may be accomplished in smaller portions if necessary; (d) to meditate on the Master daily for fifteen minutes in any secluded spot.[67]

As a self-proclaimed Avatar of Zoroaster, Rama, Krishna, Buddha, Jesus Christ, and Muhammad, Meher Baba sometimes referred to himself as the *Qutb al-aqtab*—principal axial saint of all. But Meher Baba's concept of the Avatar was not only a self-reference. In a 1954 gathering with Western disciples he commented: "I know that I am the Avatar in every sense of the word, and that each one of you is an Avatar in one sense or the other." Delving into this universally shared "New Age" sense of Avatarhood, he explained:

Everything and everyone represents God in one way or another, in some state of consciousness or another, but the God-Man (Avatar, Buddha, Christ, Rasool) represents God in every way, in everything, and everywhere, in one and all states of consciousness, manifest or latent.[68]

One distinctive aspect of Meher Baba's work and life is that for 44 years he maintained absolute silence. "Things that are real are given and received in silence," he said. Feeling that the world had received and ignored so many words from so many teachers for so long, he remained literally silent.

I have come not to teach but to awaken. Understand therefore that I lay down no precepts.

Throughout eternity I have laid down principles and precepts but mankind has ignored them. Man's inability to live God's words makes the Avatar's teaching a mockery. Instead of practicing the compassion He taught, man has waged crusades in His name. Instead of living the humility, purity and truth of His words, man has given way to hatred greed and violence.

Because man has been deaf to the principles and precepts laid down by God in the past, in this present Avataric Form I observe Silence.[69]

You have asked for and been given enough words; it is now time to live them.[70]

Like many New Age teachers to follow, Meher Baba emphasized experience over belief. He taught and communicated, but without speech. In films and photos we can glean what he meant when he explained, "I am eternally talking.''[71] From July 10, 1925, until October 7, 1954, he pointed to an alphabet board and used hand gestures. From then on he used only gestures.

In a very New Age-sounding pronouncement, Meher Baba declared that he would speak a word of love into every heart that would transform the world:

> When I break my silence it will not be to fill your ears with spiritual lectures. I shall speak only One Word, and this Word will penetrate the hearts of all men and make even the sinner feel that he is meant to be a saint, while the saint will know that God is in the sinner as much as He is in himself.
>   When I speak that Word, I shall lay the foundation for that which is to take place during the next seven hundred years.[72]

Meher Baba declared that he was engaged in "universal work." He declared that his actions had an impact on all beings which would produce a "transformation of consciousness" and bring about a "New Humanity," focused on the oneness of life and even bringing about a cooperative relationship between science and religion. At the least Meher Baba's vision of renewal, optimism, and universal love—plus announcing his intention to inaugurate an awakening which would merge science and religion—parallels the vision of the New Age Movement and those who have embraced, or are anticipating, the unfolding of an Interspiritual Age.

Muhammad Raheem Bawa Muhaiyaddeen (1884–1986)[73]

Discovered in the 1940s emerging from the jungles of Sri Lanka by Tamil Hindus, Bawa Muhaiyaddeen taught disciples as a Hindu until he was recognized by Muslims as a *shaykh* and *wali* ("friend of God"). By 1955 he had laid the foundation for a mosque in Sri Lanka. Interestingly, this pattern was repeated when he came to Philadelphia in 1971. There he was first known as Guru Bawa until he gradually adopted an Islamic framework. Artist and disciple Michael Green describes him as "the sublime master Muhammad Raheem Bawa Muhaiyaddeen, who was also Guru Bawa, who was the Qutb [axial saint] that came to the West, may this secret be known."[74]

On August 11, 1976, Bawa inaugurated ablutions and *dhikr* which included parts of the *Salat* prayer until in 1981 he instituted the performance of *Salat*. He gave as the translation of the *Shahada:* "Nothing else is, only You are, God."

As photos and films disclose, Bawa was an extremely gentle and graceful man in his manner and speech. Although he looked youthful, legends surrounding him suggested he lived beyond a hundred years. In a practice rarely known among Muslims, he was a vegetarian. From living in the jungle, he had become deeply attuned to nature. His discourses reflected inner knowledge, more than intellectual knowledge. And although he technically belonged to the lineage of 'Abdul Qadir al-Gilani, the founder of the Qadiriyya Sufi brotherhood, Bawa's teachings were more inclusive and eclectic than sectarian. These facets of his teaching made him especially attractive to New-Age devotees and Interspiritually-oriented persons: pacifism, vegetarianism, healthy cooking and eating, nature-mysticism, ecumenism, and his inner or intuitive, rather than text-based knowledge.

Bawa's prominence in American Sufism has continued since Rumi translator Coleman Barks and Sufi author–illustrator Michael Green have become better known for their work and the role they acknowledge Bawa to have played in inspiring it. Since 1986, Bawa's tomb (*mazar*) in Coatesville outside of Philadelphia, Pennsylvania, has been a pilgrimage site.

Bawa consistently described Islam as unconditional peace and love.

Everything is Islam. Islam is the spotless purity of the heart, it is a vast ocean. If God's teaching is there, it is Islam. To act out the qualities of truth and embrace it with true love, that is Islam. The tired hearts, the hurt ones, to embrace them with love, and give them the milk of love, embrace them face to face, heart to heart, in unity, that is Islam.[75]

In *Islam and World Peace* (1987) Bawa describes a radically inclusive vision of Islam as a religion of nonviolence.

Truth is one and Islam is one. It shows no preference for any particular religion, sect race, or tribe.[76]

We must realize that the human society is one. We are all the children of Adam, and there is only one God and one prayer. The Bible, the Hindu Puranas, the Zend-Avesta, the Torah, and the Qur'an—all these scriptures contain the words of grace given by God to the prophets.[77]

Bawa conveyed the significance of the Prophet Muhammad as a reality within humankind. Gisela Webb describes Bawa's word play in Tamil:

...*muham* in Tamil means "face" or "countenance" and *aham* means "heart." Thus Bawa will say, "Muhammad is the beauty of the heart reflected in the face [*muham*]...that the Light of Muhammad, the Inner Muhammad, is the first reflection or "countenance" of [*aham*] God's very being[78]

In Bawa's view, Allah and the Prophet Muhammad exclusively intended nonviolence:

Praising Allah and then destroying others is not *jihad*. Some groups wage war against the children of Adam and call it holy war. But for man to raise his sword against man, for man to kill man is not holy war.... Allah has no thought of killing or going to war. Why would Allah have sent His prophets if He had such thoughts? It was not to destroy men that Muhammad came; he was sent down as the wisdom that could show man how to destroy his own evil.[79]

Bawa emphasizes absolute love and compassion:

It is compassion that conquers. It is unity that conquers. It is Allah's good qualities, behavior and actions that conquer others. It is this state which is called Islam. The sword doesn't conquer; love is sharper than the sword. Love is an exalted, gentle sword. [80]

Bawa's symbolic correspondences between the five prayers and the five elements (earth, fire, water, air, and ether) resonates with New Age holism. As Michael Green paraphrases and summarizes them: in the dawn prayer (*fajr*) "prayer loosens the earthly torpor...Fajr releases these grasping earth obsessions into the generosity of the dawn."[81] Noon prayer (*salat al-zuhr* tempers the fiery power reflected in the sun's zenith overhead and embodied within as the result of the day's build-up of "anger, arrogance, and impatience." The noon prayer transforms "these wild surging energies into a passionate search for God."[82] The afternoon prayer (*salat al-asr*), marked by the time when the sun casts shadows, carries us into the quality of water. In this watery flux the soul yearns for clarity. The sunset prayer (*salat al-maghrib*) finds the mind given to airiness and needing grounding. At the time of the night prayer (*salat al-isha'*), "solidity falls away, but the spacious quality of ether grows, hypnotizing us with twinkling illusion."[83]

Bawa's teachings about food and cooking also link Islamic and New Age values. He advocated vegetarianism as the real meaning of the practice of *zabih* (*halal*) slaughter of animals. He taught that the purpose of *zabih* was to make slaughter difficult so that people would eat less meat and that ultimately the symbolism of *zabih* means slaughtering the lower ego (*al-nafs al-ammara*).[84]

A final note on Bawa's influence on the New Age Movement is his role in motivating Barks to translate Rumi.

A NOTE ON RUMI AND THE NEW AGE MOVEMENT

Rumi, whom Coleman Barks helped raise to fame, has emerged as a bridge between Islam and the New Age Movement, and offers Sufi perspectives that appeal to New Age participants' need for spirituality outside religion. As 'Abd al-Rahman Jami (d. 1492 CE) once said, Rumi's *Mathnawi* is "the Qur'an in Persian." Mevlana Jalaluddin Rumi, a Sufi poet and master who lived in Konya, Turkey is widely read and quoted in the New Age Movement. In 1995, according to *Christian Science Monitor, Publisher's Weekly,* and Bill Moyers of PBS, Rumi emerged as "America's best-selling poet." Poets

Robert Bly and Barks had begun public readings and performances of Rumi's poetry in their paraphrased "translations." Barks became a best-selling celebrity and Rumi became an icon for the New Age Movement. Through recited and musical performances, Rumi's poetry also became part of the curriculum of the Men's Movement of the 1980s and 1990s and drew audiences at universities and auditoriums. At the time of this writing, Amazon.com ranked sales of Barks' anthology *The Essential Rumi* as 5,657 among over 600,000 titles. Recently author-illustrator Michael Green has collaborated with The Illumination Band, a group of bluegrass musicians from the Bawa Muhaiyaddeen Fellowship, to release a CD of Rumi's poems set to country-bluegrass music.[85] In his handbill for his lecture series on Sufi poets, Hazrat Inayat Khan wrote this about Rumi's *Masnavi:* "The Masnavi has all the beauty of the Psalms, the music of the hills, the color and scent of roses; but it has more than that, it expresses in song the yearning if the soul to be reunited with God."[86]

CONCLUSION: A "SUN RISES IN THE WEST"—AMERICAN SUFISM AND THE NEW AGE

Here I present conclusions about two questions: (1) What bridges Islam and the Interspiritual Age or New Age Movement? (2) How have the lineages of these four Sufi teachers helped contribute to and develop the New Age Movement and the Interspiritual Age?

(1) New Age Movement participants—both practitioners and consumers—typically affiliate more independently than they could in traditional Islamic cultures where family and community identification tend to regulate religious affiliation. In the course of their lifetimes, New Age participants have typically tried or followed a number of spiritual paths. This is true among many of the followers of the movements we have discussed. And while syncretism and innovation stand at odds with most Muslim rhetoric, they have appeared throughout Islamic history. Inayat Khan's lineage initiated Hindus. All the teachers we discussed studied in multiple traditions.

In spite of their eclecticism and syncretism, each of these movements accepts the *Shahada* or *kalima* as an ultimate statement of truth. What varies is how the *kalima* is interpreted. People in Inayat Khan lineages translate the *Shahada* as "There is no reality other than the One Reality." Bawa translated it as "Nothing else is, only You are, God." Both of these lineages acknowledge Muhammad as the Messenger of Allah. In a more complicated and problematic sense Meher Baba also accepted the *kalima,* (translated as "There is no one greater than God."), modified by the fact that he identified himself as Muhammad. It is no coincidence that teachers from India provide such continuity between Islam and the Interspiritual Age.

Many practitioners and consumers of New-Age Sufism approach only the inner (*batin*) dimensions of Islam. The one exception is the Bawa Muhayyiddeen Fellowship: in 1976, Bawa's followers began performing ablution and reciting *dhikr*, then in 1981 they began to perform *Salat* and continued to adopt the *Shari'a*. As we observed, even though Inayat Khan did not explicitly practice *Shari'a* he expressed it as a "law needed to harmonize with one's surroundings and with one's self within." Furthermore, he went on to say that Qur'an and Hadith warrant that the Shari'a is "meant to be subject to change, in order to suit the time."[87]

Islamic policies on environmentalism will always serve as a potential bridge between Islam and the Interspiritual Age. Ecology and Creation Spirituality will stand as other such bridges. The Qur'an's advocates studying nature's "signs" and manifestations for lessons about divine unity (*tawhid*), and other divine mysteries. Many Sufi teachers presented *tawhid* as a form of *wahdat al-wujud* ("unity of existence"). This correlates roughly with the popular New Age use of "holograms," "wave-particle theory," and the "Heisenberg Uncertainty Principle." But fundamentally, both Sufism, the New Age Movement, and Interspiritual thinkers, correlate science and spirituality as parallel expressions of harmonious unity in creation. Similarly the New Age and Interspiritualist interest in the sacredness of the earth matches that of the Qur'an which frequently presents nature as a book of signs and symbols (Qur'an 16:10–22; 27:64; 30:20–27). Ecology will be a bridge between Islam, the New Age Movement, and the Interspiritual Age.

Does Islam share a doctrine of tolerance with the New Age Movement and the Interspiritual Age? The New Age Movement's theological relativism contradicts most Muslim attitudes toward interreligiosity. Muslims have often embraced tolerance and ecumenism but usually in a context in which Islam is the supreme and final religion. Bawa alone among the teachers we discussed echoes this conservatism. The others taught a spiritual path (*tariqa*) outside of religion. In their time their movements were called by sociologists "New Religious Movements." In Wayne Teasdale's exemplification of Interspirituality there is at least a precedent for setting one's own religion as the single framework for inclusivity.

Many contemporary Sufis who practice meditation use a kind of *chakra* system, and practice theosophy (*ishraqiyya*). They may also provide a bridge between Islam and the New Age Movement. Sufism offers a teaching about the energy centers (*lata'if*) of the subtle body.[88] Technically, however, the system of centers differs from yogic and New Age *chakras*. Sufism shares with Transpersonal Psychology a recognition of extraordinary abilities. As in the New Age, Sufi saints are sought for spiritual healing. Most New Age Movement participants would be attracted to the Healing Concentration of the Sufi Order and Bawa's philosophy of farming, cooking, and eating.

(2) The four teachers discussed in this chapter are Islamic heralds of the New Age Movement and the Interspiritual Age. Since each stands on

an isthmus between his Islamic background and the Interspiritual Age, his life demonstrates how Muslims and non-Muslims might relate Islam and the Interspritual Age. Hazrat Inayat Khan, Samuel Lewis, and Meher Baba knew Islam intimately but did not follow the *Shari'a* based on the Five Pillars of Islam. Members of the Inayat Khan traditions meditate, practice *waza'if* (meditation on divine qualities), recite *dhikr,* and do Dances of Universal Peace. Meher Baba led *Salat* once as part of an Inter-Faith Prayer meeting in September 1954.[89] "Baba lovers" encounter Islam as part of Meher Baba's teaching and culture. Only for Sufism Reoriented's members did he prescribe the practice of reciting the Islamic Names of God. Still, these three teachers used Sufi literature extensively, especially Persian poets.

Bawa placed Qur'an and Hadith at the center of his discourses. Bawa alone established the conventional practice of *Shari'a* including and especially, *Salat.* Bawa's *dhikr* included traditional *salawat an-nabi* (recitations of blessings upon the Prophet Muhammad) and invocations to the head *pir* of Bawa's *qadiri* lineage, 'Abd al-Qadir Jilani.[90] Bawa alone considered worship of Hindu deities incorrect and expressed concern over the proliferation of false teachers in the United States in the 1970s and 1980s. Inayat Khan and teachers in his lineage have consciously incorporated Hindu, Zoroastrian, Buddhist, and Christian elements—more than one finds in most Islamic *tariqas.* The "Dances of Universal Peace," meetings, publications, and workshops all show an inclusive and "integral" approach to synthesizing ideas and practices across religious boundaries. Each of these teachers has in his own way invented an American Sufism that continues to contribute to and reflect the New Age Movement.

By introducing a new genre of worship, the "Dances of Universal Peace," Lewis was a herald of the New Age Movement. Inspired by Sufi *dhikr,* he created an American *dhikr* that also incorporated Hindu, Buddhist, Zoroastrian, Native American, and Goddess Worship songs. As Lewis wrote in 1970, "My friends, it is a New Age." As "spiritual teacher to the hippies," he was a founder of the New Age Movement.

Bawa's teachings offer a bridge between Islam and the Interspiritual Age, especially as outlined in his book on world peace and Barks' and Green's book on the *Salat* prayer. This is the only book on *Salat* I have ever seen featuring illustrations from Buddhist, Christian, and other traditions to describe, interpret, and give instruction in the Muslim prayer. Bawa's presentation of Islam as a religion of peace and nonviolence makes Islam more accessible and harmonious with the Interspritual Age. As a vegetarian who taught farming and cooking, Bawa was in harmony with the health-food movement. His yogic life-style, gentleness and charisma, were appreciated by people with New Age tastes in teachers.

In an era when many Muslims and Jews have struggled with their collective relationship in the world, it is instructive and encouraging that Pir Vilayat had a deep spiritual friendship and teaching relationship with the Hasidic Rabbi Zalman Schacter-Shalomi of the Havera ("friendship") movement. Both Pir Vilayat and Murshid Sam had deep relationships with the Rabbi and singer Schlomo Carlbach. It is also interesting that many members of the Sufi Order, the Ruhaniat, the Bawa Muhaiyaddeen Fellowship, and many other American Sufi Orders have come from Jewish backgrounds—so much so that some people describe them as "Jew-fis."[91] This in itself is a force for bringing about an Interspiritual Age. The following appreciation of Murshid Sam by Rabbi Zalman Schachter-Shalomi illustrates the potential for these movements to offer healing influences:

> Although the sages have said that since the destruction of the Temple, prophecy has been taken from the prophets and given to the children and fools, the door to prophecy has remained open to those who were prepared to be God-fools in a child-like fashion. Murshid S.A.M. entered that door by his "foolish" faith, his child-like simplicity and has drawn from Revelation life giving elixirs to sustain us through the chaos we must pass in order to enter the New Age. [92]

In short, the New Age Movement and Islam have intersected whenever Sufism has been introduced to the Euro-American baby-boomer, hippie, and yuppie generations. Most of these Sufis who hold New Age and Interspiritual values and ideals are well into their 30s, 40s, and beyond. Although many young people followed Pir Vilayat Inayat Khan, Murshid Sam, and Meher Baba in the 1960s as well as Bawa Muhayyiddeen, in recent decades newly entering community members have tended to be older.

If we have entered a New Age, an Interspiritual Age, or a second Axial Age, then its ideals of kindness, nonviolence, and "interspirituality" are clearly reflected in the lives and work of Inayat Khan, Lewis, Meher Baba and Bawa. These four teachers built a bridge between Islam and the Interspiritual Age and encouraged people of many backgrounds to venture across it.

NOTES

1. *Jameh al-Asrar; Rasa'il-e Nimatullahi* (vol. 1, p. 177) in *Traditions of the Prophet*, ed. Javad Nurbakhsh, vol. 1 (London and New York: Khaniqahi-Nimatullahi Publications, 1981), 45.

2. *Mesbah al-hedayah,* Nurbakhsh, *Traditions of the Prophet*, 80; Nurbakhsh, vol. 2, 28.

3. Divan ST XXXI, in *Selected Poems of Rumi,* ed. Reynold A. Nicholson (Mineola, New York: Dover Publications, 2000).

4. Wayne Teasdale, *The Mystic Heart* (Novato, California: New World Library, 1999, 2001), 5.

5.   Russill Paul, *The Yoga of Sound* (Novato, California: New World Library, 2003), 36; Karen Armstrong, "A New Axial Age," *What is Enlightenment* 31 (Dec. 2005–Feb. 2006): 34–36.

6.   Marilyn Ferguson, *The Aquarian Conspiracy: Personal and Social Transformation in Our Time* (Los Angeles, California: J.P. Tarcher, 1980, 1987); J. Gordon Melton, "Whither the New Age?" in *America's Alternative Religions,* ed. Timothy Miller (Albany, New York: SUNY, 1995), 347–352.

7.   Ferguson, *The Aquarian Conspiracy,* 8.

8.   Steve Bruce, *Religion in the Modern World: From Cathedral to Cults* (Oxford, U.K.: Oxford University Press, 1996), 204–212.

9.   Teasdale, *The Mystic Heart.*

10.   Armstrong, "A New Axial Age," 35–36.

11.   Karen Armstrong, *Buddha* (New York: Penguin, 2000) 10.

12.   Clifford Geertz, *The Religion of Java* (Chicago, Illinois: University of Chicago Press, 1965.)

13.   Teasdale, *The Mystic Heart.*

14.   Omid Safi, "The Sufi Path of Love in Iran and India," in *A Pearl in Wine: Essays on the Life, Music, and Sufism of Hazrat Inayat Khan,* ed. Pirzade Zia Inayat Khan (New Lebanon, New York: Omega Publications, 2001), 265.

15.   Pir Zia Inayat Khan. 2005 "Welcome Note." (Hejirat Day September 13, 2005) received and accessed at Anjumani Moderator (Anjumjani-owner@yahoogroups.com) on November 8, 2005.

16.   Hazrat Inayat Khan, *A Sufi Message of Spiritual Liberty* (London, U.K.: The Theosophical Publishing Society, 1914), 17.

17.   Ibid., 38.

18.   Hazrat Inayat Khan, *The Unity of Religious Ideals,* vol. 9, *The Sufi Message of Hazrat Inayat Khan* (Geneva: Sufi Movement, 1927, 1979), 194.

19.   Ibid., 196.

20.   Inayat Khan, *A Sufi Message of Spiritual Liberty.*

21.   Samuel L. Lewis, *Sufi Vision and Initiation: Meetings with Remarkable Beings,* (San Francisco, California: Sufi Islamia/Prophecy Publications, 1986), 219.

22.   Inayat Khan, *The Unity of Religious Ideals,* 199.

23.   Ibid., 200.

24.   Ibid., 199.

25.   Donald A. Sharif Graham. "Spreading the Wisdom of Sufism: The Career of Pir-o-Murshid Inayat Khan in the West," in *A Pearl in Wine: Essays on the Life, Music, and Sufism of Hazrat Inayat Khan,* ed. Pirzade Zia Inayat Khan (New Lebanon, N.Y.: Omega Publications, 2001), 144, n. 33.

26.   Gerhard Bowering, *The Mystical Vision of Existence in Classical Islam: The Qur'anic Hermeneutics of the Sufi Sahl At-Tustari (d. 283/896),* (Berlin and New York: Walter de Gruyter, 1980).

27.   Hazrat Inayat Khan, *The Heart of Sufism: Essential Writings of Hazrat Inayat Khan,* ed. H.J. Witteveen (Boston, Massachusetts: Shambhala, 1999), 80.

28. Andrew Rawlinson, *The Book of Enlightened Masters: Western Teachers in Eastern Traditions* (Chicago, Illinois: Open Court, 1997), 550.

29. Shams Kairys, "Invincible Spirit: Pir Vilayat Inayat Khan," *Elixir* 1 (Autumn 2005): 33.

30. Ibid., 33.

31. Pir Vilayat Inayat Khan, *Awakening: A Sufi Experience* (New York: Jeremy P. Tarcher Putnam, 1999), 67.

32. Rawlinson, *The Book of Enlightened Masters*, 543–553.

33. Ibid.

34. Kairys, *Elixir*, 37.

35. Ibid., 175.

36. Ibid., 90.

37. Ibid., 16–17.

38. The term Pirzade means the expected successor to the Pir.

39. Rawlinson, *The Book of Enlightened Masters*, 569.

40. "Suluk: A Journey Toward the One." Brochure. New Lebanon, New York: Suluk Academy of Sufi Studies.

41. www.sulukacademy.org (Accessed January 14, 2006).

42. Qur'an Sura al-Kahf (18:60–82). See my "Traveling with Khidr," *Elixir* II (Winter 2006). A comprehensive treatment of the significance of Khidr appears in my "Where Two Seas Meet: How the Story of al-Khidr and Moses is Interpreted by Sufi Qur'an Commentators as a Model for Spiritual Guidance," Dissertation, Duke University, 2000.

43. Wali Ali Meyer, "Preface," in *The Jerusalem Trilogy: Song of the Prophets*, ed. Samuel L. Lewis (Novato, California: Prophecy Pressworks, 1975), 11.

44. Lewis, *Sufi Vision*, 52.

45. Ibid., 119.

46. Ibid., 334.

47. Ibid., 45, 359.

48. Ali Meyer, *The Jerusalem Trilogy*, 12.

49. Ibid., 336.

50. Ibid., 338.

51. Ibid., 340.

52. Ibid., 333.

53. Ibid., 220.

54. Ibid., 19.

55. Neil Douglas-Klotz, *Prayers of the Cosmos: Meditations on the Aramaic Words of Jesus* (HarperSanFrancisco, 1990).

56. Neil Douglas-Klotz, *The Sufi Book of Life: 99 Pathways of the Heart* (Penguin Compass, 2005), 3.

57. Meher Baba, *God Speaks*, 2 ed. (New York: Dodd, Mead & Co., 1973), xxxvi.

58. Meher Baba, in *Silent Master, Meher Baba,* ed. Irwin Luck (Myrtle Beach, South Carolina: Irwin Luck, 1967), 15.

59. Ibid., 22–23.

60. Charles Haynes, *Meher Baba: The Awakener* (North Myrtle Beach, South Carolina: The Avatar Foundation, 1993), 22.

61. Rumi, *Mathnawi*, vol. III, 3901 in Nicholson, 43.

62. Meher Baba, *The Path of Love* (Myrtle Beach, South Carolina: Sheriar Press, 2000), 81.

63. Meher Baba, *The Everything and the Nothing,* (Myrtle Beach, South Carolina: Sheriar Foundation, 1995), 24–25.

64. Ibid., 8.

65. Quoted in Adi K. Irani *Messages of Meher Baba* (Ahmadnagar: Meher Baba Trust, n.d.), 83–84.

66. Meher Baba, in *The Beloved: The Life and Work of Meher Baba,* ed. Naosherwan Anzar (North Myrtle Beach, South Carolina: Sheriar Press, 1974,1983), 66.

67. Ibid.

68. Luck, *Silent Master, Meher Baba,* 16.

69. Haynes, *Meher Baba,* 65–66.

70. Ibid., 35.

71. Meher Baba quoted in Purdom, 5.

72. Charles Haynes, *Meher Baba: The Awakener* (North Myrtle Beach, South Carolina, 1993), 111.

73. The claims of Bawa's birth year are advanced by Sharon Marcus in her Introduction to Bawa's book *The Triple Flame: The Inner Secrets of Sufism* (Philadelphia Press, 2001) as reported in Gwendolyn Zoharah Simmons, "Are We Up To The Challenge? The Need for a Radical Reordering of the Islamic Discourse on Women," in *Progressive Muslims: on Justice, Gender, and Pluralism,* ed. Omid Safi (Oxford, U.K.: One World, 2003), 245, n. 14. I have also personally heard claims of Bawa's longevity from many of his students.

74. Coleman Barks and Michael Green, *The Illuminated Prayer: The Five-Times Prayer of the Sufis as Revealed by Jellaludin Rumi and Bawa Muhaiyaddeen* (New York: Ballentine Wellspring, 2000), 144.

75. Ibid., 14.

76. Muhammad Rahim Bawa Muhaiyaddeen, *Islam and World Peace: Explanations of a Sufi* (Philadelphia, Pennsylvania: Fellowship Press, 1987), 89–90.

77. Ibid., 38.

78. Gisela Webb, "Tradition and Innovation in Contemporary American Islamic Spirituality: The Bawa Muhaiyaddeen Fellowship," in *Muslim Communities in North America* (Albany, New York: State University of New York Press, 1994), 75–86.

79. Muhaiyaddeen, *Islam and World Peace,* 51.

80. Ibid., 34.

81. Barks and Green, *The Illuminated Prayer,* 48.

82. Ibid., 50.

83. Ibid., 52, 54, 56.

84. Webb, *Muslim Communities,* 96.

85.   The New Illumination Band: Devastation Song and Other Timely Ballads, Hymns and Harmonies Discovered in the Poetry of Rumi (Accessed March 13, 2006 at http://www.sing4life.com/listings/6.html).

86.   Inayat Khan, quoted in Hazrat Inayat Khan and Coleman Barks, *The Hand of Poetry* (New Lebanon, New York: Omega Publications, 1993), viii.

87.   Inayat Khan, *Unity of Religious Ideals,* 199.

88.   Henry Corbin, *The Man of Light in Iranian Sufism* (New Lebanon, New York: Omega Press, 1994), rpt.

89.   Charles Purdom and Malcolm Schloss, *Three Incredible Weeks with Meher Baba: September 11 to September 30, 1954* (North Myrtle Beach, South Carolina: Sheriar Press, 1979), 37–39.

90.   Muhammad Rahim Bawa Muhaiyaddeen, *Morning Dhikr at the Mosque of Shaikh M.R. Bawa Muhaiyaddeen* (Philadelphia, Pennsylvania: The Bawa Muhaiyaddeen Fellowship, 1996).

91.   This is not unprecedented. For example Maimonides' grandson Obadiah practiced Sufism. (Personal Communication from Prof. Jacob Adler of the University of Arkansas, July 2001).

92.   Rabbi Zalman Schachter-Shalomi quoted on jacket of Samuel L. Lewis, *Jerusalem Trilogy.*

SELECTED BIBLIOGRAPHY

Barks, Coleman. *The Essential Rumi.* San Francisco, California: HarperCollins, 1995.

Bawa Muahaiyaddeen Fellowship website. www.bmf.org. (accessed 4 October 2004).

Birge, John Kingsley. *The Bektashi Order of Dervishes.* London, U.K.: Luzac Oriental, 1937, 1994.

Bruce, Steve. *Religion in the Modern World: From Cathedrals to Cults.*Oxford, U.K.: Oxford University Press, 1996.

de Jong-Keesing. *Inayat Khan—A Biography.* London, U.K.: Luzac & Co. Ltd., 1974.

Ernst, Carl. *The Shambhala Guide to Sufism.* Boston, Massachusetts: Shambhala, 1997.

Fox, Matthew. *Creation Spirituality.* San Francisco, California: Harper SanFrancisco, 1990.

Frager, Robert. *Heart, Self and Soul.* Wheaton, Illinois: Theosophical Publishing House, 1999.

Graham, Donald A. Sharif. "Spreading the Wisdom of Sufism: The Career of Pir-o-Murshid Inayat Khan in the West." In *A Pearl in Wine: Essays on the Life, Music, and Sufism of Hazrat Inayat Khan,* edited by Pirzade Zia Inayat Khan, New Lebanon, New York: Omega Publications, 2001.

Halman, Talat Sait, and Metin And. *Mevlana Celaleddin Rumi and the Whirling Dervishes.* Istanbul: Dost Yayinlari, 1983, 1992.

Hixon, Lex. *The Heart of the Qur'an.* Wheaton, Illinois. Theosophical Publishing House, 1988.

Inayat Khan, Pir Vilayat. *Toward the One.* New York: Harper and Row, 1974.

Inayat Khan, Pirzade Zia, ed. *A Pearl in Wine: Essays on the Life, Music, and Sufism of Hazrat Inayat Khan*. New Lebanon, New York: Omega Publications, 2001.

Lewis, Franklin D. *Rumi: Past and Present, East and West*. Oxford, U.K.: OneWorld, 2001.

Lovelock, James. *Gaia: A New Look at Life on Earth*. Oxford, U.K.: Oxford University Press, 1979.

Melton, J. Gordon, Jerome Clark, and Aidan A. Kelly. *The New Age Encyclopedia*. Detroit, Michigan: Gale Research, 1990.

Meyer, Murshid Wali Ali. "A Sunrise in the West: Hazrat Inayat Khan's Legacy in California." In *A Pearl in Wine: Essays on the Life, Music, and Sufism of Hazrat Inayat Khan*, edited by Pirzade Zia Inayat Khan, New Lebanon, New York: Omega Publications, 2001.

Muhaiyaddeen, Muhammad Rahim Bawa. *Asma' al-Husna: The 99 Beautiful Names of Allah*. Philadelphia, Pennsylvania: Fellowship Press, 1979.

———. *Dhikr: The Remembrance of God*. Philadelphia, Pennsylvania: Fellowship Press, 1999.

Nicholson, Reynold. *Selected Poems of Rumi*. Mineola, NY: Dover Publications, 2001. Rpt of ibid. *Rumi Mystic and Poet (1207–1273)* London, U.K.: George Allen and Unwin, Ltd., 1950. Posthumously completed by A.J. Arberry.

Nurbakhsh, Javad. *Traditions of the Prophet*. 2 vols. London and New York: Khaniqahi-Nimatullahi Publications, 1981, 1983.

Schimmel, Annemarie. *Mystical Dimensions of Islam*. Chapel Hill, North Carolina: University of North Carolina Press, 1975.

Sufi Order International website www.sufiorder.org/activities/

Sufi Ruhaniat International website www.ruhaniat.org (accessed August 10, 2005).

Walbridge, John. *The Wisdom of the Mystic East: Suhrawardi and Platonic Orientalism*. Albany, New York: SUNY, 2001.

Wilbur, Ken. *A Theory of Everything: An Integral Vision for Business, Politics, Science, and Spirituality*. Boston, Massachusetts: Shambhala, 2000.

9

I and Thou in a Fluid World: Beyond "Islam versus the West"

Omid Safi

Another world is possible.

We as God's children are not bound to live in fear and poverty, humiliation and rage. Other paths are possible, and they must be sought. The path to there has to start here, with each and every one of us. There is a time for peace, a time for dignity, and a time for self-determination. And that time is now.

We are perpetually surrounded by clichés of "clash of civilizations," "Islam versus the West," and so on. We insist that it is part of our task to rise up to an acknowledgement of a fluid, hybrid world in which nationality and ethnicity, religion and race, sexuality and gender, class and political commitment each frame one facet of larger, broader, more cosmopolitan identities. Neither religion nor nationalism will be accepted as a monolith that somehow exhausts one's identity. In the words of Edward W. Said, in the aftermath of colonialism, all identities are hybrid, fluid, and overlapping: "Partly because of empire, all cultures are involved in one another; none is single and pure, all are hybrid, heterogenous, extraordinarily differentiated, and unmonolithic."[1]

The aim of this chapter is to conceive of an American Muslim identity in a way that allows for such a heterogenous and differentiated acknowledgment of the multiple layers of our identities. However, before doing so it is mandatory to visit, challenge, critique, and deconstruct the powerful and seductive paradigm of "Islam versus the West" (and the twin "clash of civilizations") before we can offer a more holistic alternative. To do so, we will first deal with Muslim Westernophobes and then with Western Islamophobes.

MOVING BEYOND MUSLIM WESTERNOPHOBIA

One of the tasks of Muslims committed to the highest mandates of ethical responsibility before God is to engage the voices and actions of Muslims who have declared a war on other Muslims as well as Westerners—governments and civilians alike. Many such expressions take place in the context of responses to Western colonialism and imperialism.[2] Whereas critiques of Western imperialism and colonialism are a time-honored and proud tradition of all anticolonial and postcolonial movements,[3] most of these movements have not historically redirected the violence of colonialism back against the civilians of Euro-American civilization, as well as engaging in guerilla tactics against fellow Muslims, as we see in the case of current Iraq. Yet these hideous practices are precisely the case for Al Qaeda today.

The piece of propaganda issued by the self-proclaimed "World Islamic Front," masquerading as an Islamic legal opinion (*fatwa*) and signed by Usama Bin Laden and Ayman al-Zawahiri, reads in part:

> ...In compliance with God's order, we issue the following fatwa to all Muslims: The ruling to kill the Americans and their allies—civilians and military—is an individual duty for every Muslim who can do it in any country in which it is possible to do it, in order to liberate the al-Aqsa Mosque and the Holy Mosque [Mecca] from their grip....[4]

This "fatwa," which appeared in the Arabic journal *al-Quds*, presented this duty as a "religious obligation" (*fard*) upon all Muslims.[5] Subsequent interviews with Bin Laden make it clear that he viewed the 9/11 attacks as targeted against the symbols of American military and economic structures. He justified the attacks as a form of "defensive jihad," and time and again came back to the notion that "the Jewish lobby has taken America and the West hostage."[6] Usama Bin Laden also dismissed out of hand the views of Muslim jurists who have challenged the jihad justification as "having no value." Other Al Qaeda members such as Sulaiman Abu Ghaith have also decried the "Crusader-Zionist" conspiracy, comprised of Bush, Blair, and Israel.[7]

The task of contemporary Muslims in confronting this perspective is quite complicated. We begin by a critical discussion of the spectrum of interpretations of jihad in Islamic history, and by making the case that no such attack against civilians can be justified under Islamic law. Yet ours is not a mere theoretical conversation, but one that seeks to transform societies as well. So we also seek to engage those in Muslim societies who gravitate toward such messages by calling them to the higher ground of pluralism and justice. Lastly, while questioning the usefulness of the "Crusader-Zionist" conspiracy as a totalizing explanation, we also have a responsibility to call Americans to envision a relationship with the Middle East which is not based on the unilateral support of Israel regardless of the latter's actions. We will have to insist that both Palestinians and Israelis observe international human rights regulations, and in cases where either is guilty of breaking these laws, to help in bringing them to justice and establishing alternatives on the ground. In the case of Israel, that means forming broad coalitions with

Jewish peace groups who wish to live side by side with their Arab neighbors in a peace rooted in justice.[8] It also means to admit at the most humane level the legitimate right of Israeli mothers and fathers to be able to send their children to schools or cafes without worrying about them being blown to pieces by Palestinian suicide-bombers. In the case of Palestinians, it means working with Palestinians to take a page from Gandhi, and express their legitimate resistance through nonviolent means, while bringing the world's conscience to focus on their plight.[9] It also means to admit at the most humane level that Palestinian children have the right to live in dignity and not to be mocked or shot at by the IDF (Israel Defence Force), and that Palestinian families have the right to live in their homes in peace and not have them bulldozed by the Israeli military. This is a long and daunting task, but we perceive of ourselves as bridge-makers whose task and calling it is to bring together the silent majority of humanity who wish to live in peace and harmony with one another. The Muslim extremists' hatred of the West is far too commonly known for me to devote more space to its discussion here. I will now move to its far less discussed mirror image, Western Islamophobia.[10]

MOVING BEYOND WESTERN ISLAMOPHOBIA

Contemporary Muslims in the West also have a task to critique Western Islamophobes in academia and policy circles, and to provide alternate models. With the ascent of the Neo-Conservative movement, it is hard to overemphasize the power this Islamophobic perspective currently has in America.[11] One of the gravest tasks of Western Muslims is to expose the ideological background of many "Islam versus West" proponents who are positioned in the highest places of power in the United States, and to offer viable alternatives. We will begin here by reviewing two of the most noted—and notorious—voices of Islamophobia in the West, Bernard Lewis and Samuel Huntington.

Bernard Lewis

Bernard Lewis is simultaneously one of the most celebrated and most vilified scholars of Islam and Middle Eastern Studies in the West. His scholarly life covers over 65 years, extending from 1938 to the present. He is frequently acknowledged, however disputed this claim might be, as "the foremost Western scholar of Islam." At the time of the writing of this chapter, two of the current four best selling books on Islam (*What Went Wrong* and *The Crisis of Islam*) were composed by Lewis.

Lewis is perhaps the best known example of scholars who have fine-tuned a textual and philological approach to the study of Muslim societies. He has also been criticized as the epitome of an "Orientalist" mode of scholarship.

It was precisely this accusation that informed so much of Said's paradigm-shifting study *Orientalism*.[12] In the years following the publication of *Orientalism*, Said and Lewis exchanged vitriolic personal attacks in the pages of *New York Review of Books*.[13] My concern here is not to undertake yet another personal attack on Bernard Lewis. Nor is it my intention to begin by calling attention to Lewis' involvement in right-wing politics and pro-Zionist groups. One cannot entirely avoid that topic in a thorough engagement with Lewis, because Lewis himself does not avoid it (especially in his TV appearances). However, I will begin by exploring his assessment of Islam, Muslims, and modernity.

Lewis' focus on Islam is bound up exclusively in the Middle East. In fact, in many of his works he uses the phrases "Muslims" and "Middle Easterners" interchangeably, as if all Muslims are Middle Easterners, and all Middle Easterners Muslims. This confusion even shows up in the titles of Lewis' works.[14] For a scholar of his rank, he seems unaware or unconcerned with the fact that over half of all Muslims in the world live east of Lahore, Pakistan. In reality, Muslims are more South Asian than Arab, more Southeast Asian than Middle Eastern. The Muslim populations of Indonesia, Bangladesh, India, and Pakistan easily dwarf the entire population of the Middle East. However, Lewis' focus on the Middle East is entirely consistent with the Arab-centric view of Orientalist scholars whose approach to Islam is primarily mediated through the study of Arabic (and to a far lesser extent, Persian) texts. In fact, so much of Lewis' concerns with Islam and Muslims begin and end with the broader Eastern Mediterranean in general, and Palestine/Israel more particularly.

Lewis' voluminous and prominent publications extend back to the year 1950. As John Trumpbour reminds us, Lewis had used the idea of a clash among civilizations as far back as 1964.[15] However, the most recent phase of his public polemic against Muslims dates back to four decades later, to a 1990 article in *The Atlantic Monthly*, titled "The Roots of Muslim Rage."[16] The subtitle of this piece was even more specific: "Why so many Muslims deeply resent the West, and why their bitterness will not easily be mollified." The essay starts in the same way that many of Lewis' works do, with an acknowledgement that "Islam is one of the world's great religions." Whenever this phrase appears in Lewis' book, it is followed by a brief paragraph praising the achievements of premodern Muslims in scientific areas and in creating a culture of tolerance. Lewis oftentimes compares this medieval achievement with what he identifies as the more inferior medieval situation of Christendom. Almost without fail, the praising of premodern Muslims serves as a foil against which Lewis posits the alleged backwardness and failure of modern Muslims. The rest of the "Muslim rage" essay is a long and totalizing diatribe against modern Muslims. The first significant idea that Lewis introduces without any supporting evidence is the notion that Muslims harbor hatred for the West not for any particular action of the West—specifically not for colonialism, or for U.S. support of corrupt and dictatorial regimes in the Muslim world. Rather, Lewis posits that Muslims hate the West simply because it is the West, and represents Western ideals:

> At times this hatred goes beyond hostility to specific interests or actions or policies or even countries and becomes *a rejection of Western civilization as such, not only what it does but what it is,* and the principles and values that it practices and professes. These are indeed seen as innately evil, and those who promote or accept them as the "enemies of God."[17] [emphasis added]

This notion of "they hate us because we are Western civilization" has proven surprisingly resilient. It is echoed, as we shall see, by Samuel Huntington in his "Clash of Civilizations" theory. In the days following September 11, 2001, even the usually astute Colin Powell stated that the attacks on New York City and Washington were "attacks on civilization,"[18] as if the members of Al Qaeda simply represented a vacuum of civilization, as opposed to a violent movement with a vastly different set of values. To attribute the reason for hatred to another group is of course not a task to be undertaken haphazardly, and can only be undertaken through engaging—even if ultimately dismissing—the rationale provided by one's opponents. Lewis does neither in this case, simply deciphering the motivations of the unspeaking and unnamed (and thus unable to resist and challenge) *Other.*

There is a good bit of scholarly debate regarding the very issue of whether or not it is proper to speak of a single Western civilization, rather than a plurality of strands of history and schools of thought. Even if we grant the existence of a singular Western civilization, one has to be willing to specify exactly what Western civilization is thought to stand for. If we assume that it stands, among other things, for freedom, democracy, individual rights, and so on, then it is a legitimate question to ask why anyone (that is, Muslims) would hate freedom or democracy? The argument of "they hate us for what we are, not what we do" is ultimately a convenient exercise in allowing the "us" to construct an enemy, attribute a motivation to "them," and ultimately to demonize them. However, it does not allow the audience to move any closer to understanding the real objectives that any adversary might have with our specific policies. Even when we are likely to disagree with those gripes and critiques, it behooves us to understand more clearly the perceptions and motivations of an oppositional group.

A more fundamental critique is the positing and positioning of Muslims as an "other," an oppositional group. But I will come back to this notion in a concluding remark on pluralism in the North American scene. Lewis then presents the "struggle between these rival systems"—which he identifies as Islam and Christendom—and traces this rivalry back to the very foundation of Islam: "It began with the advent of Islam, in the seventh century, and has continued virtually to the present day." Islam is Islam, and Christendom is Christendom, and never the twain shall meet, so Lewis would have one believe. One would be well advised to ask whether it is proper to speak of a distinct, crystallized identity for Europe (a term that Lewis takes as identical with Christendom) in the seventh century, as opposed to particular entities such as the Byzantine empire, and so on. Also, Lewis' depiction of the relationship between the Islamic and Christian civilizations consists of "long series of attacks and counterattacks, jihads and crusades, conquests and reconquests." This model of focusing on clashes is again appropriated by Huntington and others. What is missing from this picture is the entire range of intellectual collaborations, intermarriage, trade, diplomatic exchanges, indeed peaceful coexistence between the two civilizations. In Lewis' assessment, places like Cordoba where Muslims, Jews, and Christians lived side by side in peace, and engaged the deepest aspects of each others' traditions simply do not register.

In subsequent sections of this essay, Lewis summarily brings up various reasons for potential anti-Americanism among Muslims today: U.S. support for Israel, American support for "hated regimes," and colonialism. He quickly moves to dismiss the relevance of all these factors as ultimate explanations, through phrases such as "This accusation has some plausibility.... But it does not suffice." The very wording of these reasons as "accusations" betrays Lewis' own positioning. In place of an examination of these ideas, Lewis moves into what he identifies as "something deeper that turns every disagreement into a problem and makes every problem insoluble." This "deeper" problem is none other than "Muslim rage." The very language of "rage" as a psychological profile of over a quarter of the world's population is a sad reminder of earlier nineteenth-century discussions of "the savage mind," "the Negro mind," and so on. While the limitations, indeed absurdity, of those terms are now fully recognized, Lewis still feels entitled to use terms like "Muslim rage." In doing so, he places himself in the nineteenth-century racist Euro-colonial discourse.

It is later in this essay that Lewis introduces the problematic phrase "a clash of civilizations," which Huntington would later borrow. Lewis starts out in a fairly conventional manner diagnosing the ills of Muslim society through identifying what is "lacking" from Islam. In identifying the importance of secularism, Lewis states: "Muslims experienced no such need and evolved no such doctrine." Said, among others, has pointed out the problematic of explaining Muslim events through what is *not* there.[19] Lewis' approach is as helpful in identifying the course of action that is Islamic history as describing an orange by stating that it is not an elephant. Lewis, while not a psychologist —and quite averse to anthropology—does not hesitate to offer a psychological model which seems to detect something quite perverse in the most ordinary of Muslims. Even when Muslims display kindness and generosity, these emotions are seen by Lewis as potentially masking a deeper, more underlying hatred and violence. Of course no proof can be offered for this, apart from Lewis' own authority. Yet again unnamed, unspeaking, and unexaminable subjects are evoked to observe the following: "There is something in the religious culture of Islam, which inspired, in even the humblest peasant or peddler, a dignity and a courtesy toward others never exceeded and rarely equaled in other civilizations." In typical Lewis fashion, this compliment must be followed with a brutal insult:

> And yet, in moments of upheaval and distortion, when the deeper passions are stirred, this dignity and courtesy toward others can give way to an explosive mixture of rage and hatred which impels even the government of an ancient and civilized country—even the spokesman of a great spiritual and ethical religion—to espouse kidnapping and assassination, and try to find, in the life of their Prophet, approval and indeed precedent for such actions.[20]

The last item that needs to be noted in Lewis' essay is his assessment of the responsibility of the West in ameliorating the "clash of civilizations." According to Lewis, there must be a "hard struggle" within Islam between fundamentalism and a more tolerant version of Islam (which Lewis is not quite sure what to call). And what is to be the role of the West in this struggle? Significantly, nothing. "We of the West can do little or nothing. Even the attempt might do harm, for these are issues that Muslims must decide among themselves." To sum up Lewis' worldview, the U.S. support for Israel and other oppressive regimes in the Middle East are overblown excuses, colonialism is not really an explanation of the political resentment of Muslims against the West, and finally, there is nothing that the West can do to help. The fault and the responsibility rest solely with Muslims.

Muslims can do no more than partially agree with Lewis, even as they part ways with him in a profound fashion. Clearly, we as Muslims have a responsibility to ensure justice and pluralism within our own communities. To that extent, we as Muslims have a responsibility to be "witnesses for truth, even if it means to speak against" our own selves and our community—as the Qur'an reminds us.[21] However, Muslims also insist that the responsibility to urge humanity toward an age of pluralism rests not just on the shoulders of Muslims, but on all of humanity. As the most politically and militarily hegemonic civilization that the world has ever known, the West is not exempt from this responsibility. Contrary to Lewis, there are things that those of us in the West—particularly in the United States—can and need to do in order to bring about a day where justice and freedom are guaranteed for all.

Lewis has pursued the same theses more recently, but with greater ferocity. All that seems to have changed is that he is now afforded an even more visible public platform. His *What Went Wrong: Western Impact and Middle Eastern Response* concludes with a section in which he describes the Muslim encounter with modernity using clichés such as "badly wrong," "poor," "weak," "ignorant," "disappointing," "humiliating," "corrupt," "impoverished," "weary," "capricious," "shabby," "dictatorships," repression," and "indoctrination." All of the above descriptions are simply from one page (p. 151) of *What Went Wrong*. This barrage of totalizing insults comes unnamed and unchecked and is directed at any and all Middle Easterners/ Muslims. In the subsequent pages, Lewis is even more direct than he was in "Roots of Muslim Rage." Whereas the Muslim resistance to Western imperialism had been an "accusation" before, in *What Went Wrong* it is now a "scapegoat." Furthermore, Anglo-French rule and American influence are posited as a benign "consequence, not a cause" of "the inner weakness of Middle Eastern states and societies."[22]

The brutal oppression of Palestinians in the past century, the forcible exile of hundreds of thousands of Palestinians from their homeland, the ongoing illegal occupation of the West Bank and Gaza, all of these are handled by Lewis as part of his narrative on "anti-Semitism."[23] The Palestinian peoples, if they exist at all for Lewis, are only the subjects of hatred for Jews, not even capable of experiencing loss and lament. It is hard indeed to read Lewis' diatribe against modern Arabs and Muslims as being entirely separate from his profound Zionism. His description of the state of Israel, with one of the most potent armies in the world according to the IDF itself[24], armed with over 220 nuclear warheads (in violation of U.N. resolutions[25]), as "surrounded, outnumbered, and outgunned by neighbors"[26] seems either out of touch with reality or deliberately misleading. Lewis' dismissal of modern Arabs (and indeed Muslims) is intrinsically tied to his insistence that Arabs accept not the right to existence of the State of Israel (which Arab governments have affirmed on a number of occasions), but rather the very brutal system of occupation of Palestinians in the West Bank and Gaza. As Said remarked in 1978, Lewis' project is to explain why the "Muslims (or Arabs) still will not settle down and accept Israeli hegemony over the Near East."[27]

The very last paragraph of *What Went Wrong* starts with this sentence: "If the peoples of the Middle East continue on their present path, the suicide bomber may become a metaphor for the whole region…."[28] In reading Lewis' verdict, one cannot help but wonder if at the beginning of the twenty-first century, it would be acceptable for a noted public figure such as Lewis to describe any other group of humanity apart from Middle Easterners *as a whole* as being represented by the suicide bomber. One can only imagine the outrage that would be felt and heard from many corners if instead of talking about Middle Easterners (read: Muslims), a public scholar of Lewis' rank had described all Chinese, all Africans, all women, all Jews, or all Hindus in such a derogatory fashion. Nonetheless, this characterization is perfectly consistent with Lewis' trajectory from his earlier scholarship. Absolving the West of all guilt and the responsibility to help, Lewis concludes by putting the fault and the responsibility for fixing "what has gone wrong" entirely on the Muslims: "For the time being, the choice is their own."[29]

Samuel Huntington

Whereas Lewis casts a long and dark shadow over the fields of Middle Eastern and Islamic studies, Huntington is even more implicated in policy circles. As the past president of the American Political Science Association, and a University Professor at Harvard, Huntington is a figure whose political theories deserve a serious engagement. It would be hard to overestimate the level of influence that he and his ideas have had on public policy circles and successive administrations. The perspective of Huntington carries a great deal of weight with many Neo-conservatives in George W. Bush's administration, such as Paul Wolfowitz, Condoleezza Rice, and so on.

Huntington published his widely read and highly influential essay titled "The Clash of Civilizations?" in the 1993 edition of *Foreign Affairs*. It is important to review and critique this much-discussed thesis. According to Huntington, the primary source of conflict in the emerging world order was to be not ideological or economic, but rather cultural. He further identified the various civilizations that were to be the agents of this process:

> Civilization identity will be increasingly important in the future, and the world will be shaped in large measure by the interactions among seven or eight major civilizations. These include Western, Confucian, Japanese, Islamic, Hindu, Slavic-Orthodox, Latin American, and possibly African civilization.[30]

There are at least two points worth noting from this list: first, some civilizations are identified based on religious identity (Islamic, Confucian, Hindu, Slavic-Orthodox), whereas others are based on geographical location (Japanese, Western, Latin America, African). It is not clear from Huntington's list why some—but not all—civilizations are identified based on religion, a feature that he identifies as the most important differentiator of civilizations. Many critics have pointed to the profound racism of this schema, which seems deeply uncertain as to whether or not Africans deserve to be named as having their own civilization: "and possibly, African."[31] This revelation of Huntington's underlying racism was quickly covered up in the 1996 book version, where Sub-Saharan Africa was listed as African civilization, without any qualifiers. Between 1993 and 1996, he seems to have recognized the inappropriateness of describing all Chinese as "Confucian," and renamed that civilization as "Sinic." Likewise, for him, Buddhists had emerged as their own civilization between 1993 and 1996.

In discussing the interaction among these civilizations, Huntington relies on a favorite metaphor, to which he returns time and again: "fault lines."[32] The language of "fault lines" comes from geology, where the tectonic plates on the Earth's crust shift ever so slowly, inching along till they bump into each other, causing earthquakes. He applies the same concept to civilizational units: "The fault lines between civilizations will be the battle lines of the future."[33] The choice of the metaphor is particularly intriguing, as it reveals Huntington's conception of civilizations as rock-solid, distinct entities that go bump in the night—causing a clash of civilizations. What is so intriguing about this depiction is that it bears almost no resemblance to the way that people who study cultures and civilizations—sociologists and anthropologists—often talk about these entities. Anthropologists in particular are mindful of the fluidity of civilizations, and are particularly aware of the adaptability of each culture. Huntington's work bears almost no indication of having engaged that whole body of scholarship.

By the publication of the book bearing the title *Clash of Civilizations*,[34] Huntington attempted to tease out some of the assertions in the earlier article. For example, he offered a flowchart in which he traced the development of what is termed "Eastern Hemisphere civilizations." What is termed "Classical (Mediterranean)" civilization is said to give rise to both the Islamic and the Western civilizations (both of which also receive input from the "Canaanite" civilization), as well as the Orthodox (Russian) civilization.[35] What is missing from this crude evolutionary schema is any sense of interaction *among* civilizations. There is no sense of how Islamic civilization may have interacted with, contributed to, and learned from Western civilization.[36] The chapter which is supposed to deal with "intercivilizational issues" engages only weapons transfer and an obsession with immigration, without any possibility of intellectual, aesthetic, or other mutually beneficial cultural exchanges.[37] For Huntington, the primary mode of interaction among civilizations is one of conflict and clash. He states:

> The civilizational "us" and the extracivilizational "them" is a constant in human history. These differences in intra- and extracivilizational behavior stem from:
>
> 1. feeling of superiority (and occasionally inferiority) toward people who are perceived as being very different
> 2. fear of and lack of trust in such people;
> 3. difficulty of communication with them as a result of differences in language and what is considered civil behavior;
> 4. lack of familiarity with the assumptions, motivations, social relationships, and social practices of other people.[38]

But is this historically what has happened throughout human history? What is one to do with the transmission of Greek philosophy to the Western world through Muslim commentators? What about places like Andalusia, where Muslim, Jewish, and Christian religious communities lived side by side in peace, while their scholars engaged one another in pluralistic academies?[39] One could point to countless other examples. While there have of course been many situations of superiority/inferiority complex exasperated by conflict, it also is the case that many civilizations have sought to study one another and have strived for a pluralistic coexistence. These "non-clash" situations and possibilities do not register for Huntington.

Huntington, following Lewis, has a problematic relationship with Islam. The main problem from Huntington's perspective is not Al Qaeda, the Taliban, or the Wahhabis, not that ever present bogey-man of "Islamic fundamentalism," "Muslim terrorism," and so on. The problem for Huntington, simply, is *Islam* itself, the entire religious tradition, the full spectrum of interpretations, practices, and so on. He states:

> The underlying problem for the West is not Islamic fundamentalism. It is Islam, a different civilization whose people are convinced of the superiority of their culture and are obsessed with the inferiority of their power.[40]

In Huntington's formulations we also have the classic markers of difference, "a different civilization," with the typical superiority/inferiority association. Taking his cues from Lewis' assertion that the Muslims hate "us" (that is, the West) not for what the West does but simply for what it is, Huntington goes on to assert:

> The problem for Islam is not the CIA or the U.S. Department of Defense. It is the West, a different civilization whose people are convinced of the universality of their culture and believe that their superior, if declining, power imposes on them the obligation to extend that culture throughout the world.[41]

In the 1993 article Huntington had made the infamous assertion that "Islam has bloody borders."[42] While that statement was criticized heavily, it did not prevent Huntington from expanding upon it in the book version:

> In all these places [Palestine, Lebanon, Ethiopia, bulge of Africa, Sudan, Nigeria, Chad, Kenya, Tanzania], the relations between Muslims and peoples of other civilizations—Catholic, Protestant, Orthodox, Hindu, Chinese, Buddhist, Jewish—have been generally antagonistic; most of these relations have been violent at some point in the past; many have been violent in the 1990s. Wherever one looks along the perimeter of Islam, Muslims have problems living peacefully with their neighbors.[43]

This assertion is a serious one and obviously is tied to a reading of Islam and Muslims as being essentially incapable of living in peace with those different from them. The most substantial and thorough factual critique of this assertion by Huntington is that offered by the Harvard historian Roy Mottahedeh. Mottahedeh, a leading Middle East historian, rightly points out that Huntington selectively picks the historical episodes that fit his model, while neglecting parallel examples that would undermine his argument.[44]

Huntington's thesis is predicated on a number of assumptions about authentic American identity being white, Anglo-Saxon, and Protestant. While his misgivings about Islam betray part of this racial/racist anxiety, it is his more recent writings that have made this point painfully clear. Case in point is his 2004 article called "The Hispanic Challenge."[45] The summary for this article reads:

> The persistent inflow of Hispanic immigrants threatens to divide the United States into two peoples, two cultures, and two languages. Unlike past immigrant groups, Mexicans and other Latinos have not assimilated into mainstream U.S. culture, forming instead their own political and linguistic enclaves—from Los Angeles to Miami—and rejecting the Anglo-Protestant values that built the American dream. The United States ignores this challenge at its peril.

Even more troubling is the conclusion of the essay, in which Huntington even seeks to deny Mexican-Americans the right to dream in their mother tongue if they wish to be participants in the American dream: "There is no Americano dream. There is only the American dream created by an Anglo-Protestant society. Mexican Americans will share in that dream and in that society only if they dream in English." Nowhere in Huntington's worldview, not about Muslims and not about Hispanics, is there an awareness of culture in the way that anthropologists, sociologists, and scholars of religion discuss: the notion of overlapping, fluid spheres of identity. Possibilities of bilingualism and multiculturalism are indeed anathema to the Huntingtons of the world.

One can criticize Islamophobes such as Lewis and Huntington, and indeed both deserve serious engagements. Yet the measuring stick of the ethical demands of Islam is the amount of change Muslims can produce in lived communities, urging all of us toward ever-higher ideals of justice and pluralism. In doing so, one has to acknowledge the fundamental challenges that the American Muslim community faces.

CHALLENGES TO NORTH AMERICAN ISLAM

Participation and Representation in the Media and Cultural Productions

American Muslims form the fastest growing block of citizens in the United States. In 1970, there were a scant 100,000 Muslims in America. By 2006, accurate estimates put the number at more than six million. This 60-fold growth in slightly over 30 years represents a phenomenal achievement. It is due to both the immigration of Muslims from South Asia and the Arab world to the United States and the mass conversion of many Americans (largely African Americans) to Islam. Yet when one compares American Muslims with other religious groups with similarly large populations, there is a noticeable gap. The most frequent comparison, one filled with admiration and envy, is with the American Jewish population. Comparisons by Muslims with American Jewry are filled with admiration for their political clout, envy for their civic institutions, outrage at the support of U.S. government for Israel, and hope for achieving exactly the same level of prominence. Being weary of charges of anti-Semitism (and not always innocent of them), these comparisons with the Jewish community are usually voiced inside the Muslim community.

By now, many scholars of religion such as Diana Eck have noted that numbering at six million, there are as many American Muslims as American Jews, more Muslims than Episcopalians, and more Muslims than Presbyterians.[46] There is no shortage of Muslims on TV, but most portrayals are in the context of either terrorism or political leaders of other countries. Both of these reinforce the erroneous impression of Muslims as quintessentially "other," fundamentally different from "us" Americans.[47] One is hard-pressed to think of a single Muslim intellectual, artist, or musician who is nationally known at the level of ABC, CNN, NBC, or CBS. (Fox "News" is beyond hope.) The only American Muslims that most Americans would be able to name come from the realm of sports: Muhammad Ali, Hakeem Olajuwon, Kareem Abdul-Jabbar, and so on. There are no high-profile Muslim journalists (apart from the half-Iranian Christiane Amanpour who does not self-identify as a Muslim) on these TV shows. In short, American Muslims are in the society but have almost no representation in terms of popular culture aside from negative stereotypes.

When there are Muslims who show up on TV, they show up as "obviously Muslim," with a singularly religious identity that does not reflect the multiple and fractured identities of most Muslims today. The women almost invariably wear a conservative type of *hijab,* and the males are typically conservative, immigrant, bearded, and speak with an accent. Going back to the analogy with Judaism, it would be similar to having only Ultra-Orthodox Jews on TV, rather than a full spectrum that would cover everything from Orthodox to Conservative and Reformed. That great marker of humanity, humor, is uniformly lacking from Muslim subjects on TV. Muslims on TV experience grief or outrage, but almost never joy or laughter. Also absent from media depictions are the delicious wit and affectionate sarcasm for which so many Muslim cultures are known. When we laugh not at someone but with them, we have experienced their full humanity. The humanity of American Muslims will be acknowledged only when we come up with our own successful and widely distributed version of Adam Sandler's "Chanukah Song"! That project and others similar to it will have to take place alongside the daily struggle to achieve social justice, gender equality, and so on. Yet it would be foolish to underestimate the interconnectedness of issues of culture and politics, as Said and others have reminded us.

Political Participation

It is one of the great ironies of American political life that some 72 percent of American Muslims voted for George W. Bush in the 2000 elections,[48] only to see the Bush regime impose the most severe erosion of civil liberties in the last 40 years and initiate a hostile and potentially unending "war on terrorism" almost exclusively on Muslim populations all over the world. The assault on civil liberties, which affected Muslims in America more directly than other Americans, began with the so-called PATRIOT Act, passed hastily and without any opposition after the 9/11 attack.[49] Even more terrifying attempts to erode civil liberties are underway in the so-called "PATRIOT 2" Bill.[50]

Muslims have underdeveloped infrastructures of participation in American politics. It is fair to say that no other group with over six million members in American society is so politically fragmented and ill-organized.[51] While one is beginning to see the formative stages of development of Muslim Public Affairs Committee groups, there are still a number of substantial challenges ahead. The first is overcoming the divide between immigrant and African American communities. It remains to be seen how much unity can be forged between the immigrant Muslim population in America and the African American Muslim population. There are profound class divisions between the two, which often dictate communal, social, and political participation.[52] The second challenge is that of investing in American political structures: this is a particular problem for immigrant Muslims. Many came to this country for the same reasons that other immigrants have: the pursuit of a better life, the promise of freedom, and so on. Yet at least the first generation of immigrants have often looked back toward their origin as their real "home" and have not fully invested monetarily and emotionally in American political and civic structures. Many immigrant Muslims have led lives of political neutrality and passivity, seeing their primary mission as that of providing for their families. There are, however, signs that this political lethargy is beginning to change in the charged post-9/11 environment, particularly among the second-generation immigrant Muslims.[53] The foremost leader of African American Muslims, Warith Deen Muhammad, is a conservative Republican who is largely uninterested in engaging the critiques of American foreign and domestic policy that many Muslims are invested in. Western Muslims realize that one has no way of transforming a society along the lines of justice without participating in it and remaining engaged with it. Passivity is no longer an option, if it ever was, for American Muslims.

Education

As previously mentioned, there are currently no credible institutions of higher learning for training of Islamic scholars in the United States, although organizations such as Zaytuna and the International Institute of Islamic Thought are moving in that direction. There are ongoing conversations about a Crescent University to be established outside of New York City. Many of the leading scholars of Islam in America, such as Seyyed Hossein Nasr and John A. Williams are involved in this ambitious project. It seems clear that this is a necessary step in the further evolution of an American Islamic identity.

American Muslims, like other Americans, are drawn into the controversies over the teaching of religion in public education systems. A vivid recent example was the University of North Carolina controversy in which a translation of the Qur'an (by American scholar Michael Sells) was chosen for a summer reading program.[54] These struggles are not confined to university curricula, and in some ways, the most widespread impact will come from revising junior high and high school offerings. The founder of the Council for Islamic Education, Shabbir Mansuri, recalls how he became involved in these struggles. His daughter's eighth grade social studies textbook included sections on every major world civilization. Whereas the chapter on every culture began with a picture of a historical figure, the chapter on Islam was introduced by a picture of a camel![55] This dehumanizing depiction of Muslims is so widespread that it will take a massive engagement with the system to transform it.

Christian Zionism: the Bastard Offspring of Christian Evangelical Movements and Pro-Zionist Organizations

One of the largest obstacles to the integration of Muslims into American civic and political life is the power and pervasive influence of what has been called Christian Zionism. The usage of this term requires some background explanation. It is far too customary for American Muslims to point to the power of Jewish lobby groups such as AIPAC as part of conspiracy theories. It is equally common for supporters of AIPAC (American Israel Public Affairs Committee) to describe those who undertake a critical discussion of pro-Zionist political structures in America as anti-Semitic. One has to enter this minefield with caution and clarity.

On one hand, it is important to recognize AIPAC as one of the four or five largest and most powerful lobby groups in Washington, according to the sources as varied as *Fortune* and BBC.[56] This power and prestige from a group that has roughly the same population in America as American Muslims has led to situations of resentment and envy. On the other hand, it is simplistic to imagine that the entire American foreign policy support for Israel is due to the influence of groups like AIPAC. An equally important reason has to be sought in the political emergence of the Evangelical Christian Movement. Depending on the survey that one consults, one-fourth to one-third of all Americans describe themselves as Evangelical or "born again" Christians. It is in the context of this Evangelical Christianity that an unwavering support for Israel has developed in American Protestantism. In terms of number, funds, and political influence, this voting block vastly dwarfs the impact of groups like AIPAC. It is perhaps one indication of the secular bias of much of the American media that this group by and large goes unexamined (or at least under-examined) in the national media.[57]

In 2006, another episode indicated the extent to which discussions of the extent of the influence of the Israel lobby are contested in the public sphere. A Harvard professor at the Kennedy School of Government, Stephen Walt, working in tandem with a University of Chicago professor, John Mearsheimer, published a lengthy study titled "The Israel Lobby and US Foreign Policy." This 82-page study represents one of the lengthiest documentations of the extent to which American foreign policy in the Middle East is shaped by Israeli interests.[58] The fury over the debate—although not so much the particular evidence and the conclusion—is another representation of the taboo nature of this topic. In an ironic twist, the pressure put on Harvard to remove its seal from the paper (an unprecedented move) supports the argument for the power of the Zionist lobby in the United States. A more balanced perspective can be obtained from across the Atlantic, where an English journalist, Geoffrey Wheatcroft wrote:

> The degree to which this has affected American policy, up to and including the war in Iraq, has been discussed calmly by sane British commentators – though also, to be sure, played up maliciously by bigots.
>
> In America, by contrast, there has been an unmistakable tendency to shy away from this subject.[59]

The power and relevance of Christian Zionist groups is underscored by the fact that they were largely responsible for bringing the George W. Bush regime to power. It is no accident that the South and the Midwest, regions that largely voted for Bush in the 2000 elections, are the parts of the country with the largest percentage of self-identifying "born-again" Christians. Furthermore, many prominent members of the administration, including President George W. Bush himself, identify themselves as Evangelical Christians. One such member is former attorney general John Ashcroft, who summed up his views on Islam and Christianity as follows: "Islam is a religion in which God requires you to send your son to die for him. Christianity is a faith in which God sends his son to die for you."[60] While many members of the secular media scoffed at President Bush's evocation of Jesus Christ (at a strategic Republican debate in Des Moines, Iowa) as his "favorite philosopher," they failed to understand the implication of that signal for the Evangelical voting block.[61]

It is this circle of Evangelical Christianity that is responsible for perhaps the most vigorously pro-Zionist and simultaneously anti-Islamic statements in the American public scene. The two need not be linked, but in today's America they are increasingly emerging from the same corner. Evangelical leaders such as Jerry Falwell and Pat Robertson repeatedly recall that "The Bible Belt in America is Israel's only safety belt right now." Linked to this support for a vision of an exclusive Jewish state in the "Holy Lands" (as they prefer to call it) is a distinct hatred of Islam, Arabs, and Muslims. Falwell's ministry has even put together a webpage to spread some vicious and hateful accusations against the Prophet Muhammad and Islam.[62] Some of the tension with Muslims is traceable to medieval theological polemics between Islam and Christianity. More pertinent is the distinct messianic, premillennial theology of Evangelicals who believe that the establishment of the state of Israel is a necessary prequel for the return of the Messiah. The massive popularity of Christian fiction genres such as the "Left Behind" series is directly due to this messianic eschatology. This has made for a very strange relationship between Evangelical Christians and largely secular Zionist Jews in their one-sided support for Israel.[63] It is for this reason that I referred to Christian Zionism as a "bastard" child. This is no permanent "marriage," but a convenient assignation. Theologically speaking many of the same Evangelical Christians may be guilty of horrendous levels of anti-Semitism. If asked openly, they would recognize Judaism either as an incomplete or a misled religious tradition, since according to their reading of the Bible, "none shall come to the Father except through Christ." Furthermore, according to this Evangelical eschatology, when the Messiah returns, two-third of the Jews will perish. The rest will convert. While many American Jews and Israelis are aware of the bigotry of these Evangelicals, for the time being it has proven convenient to prolong this cooperation to bring "security" for the state of Israel (that is, military and foreign aid support, United States vetoing of U. N. resolutions). A joint meeting of Christian and Jewish Zionists in the summer of 2003 declared President Bush's "road map" for Palestinians and Israelis to be a breach of God's 4000-year-old covenant with Israel.[64]

It is hard to overemphasize the degree to which this Evangelical component is responsible for creating and maintaining a hostile attack on Islam in America. Franklin Graham is the son of Billy Graham, the famed Crusader (pun intended) who has counseled almost every single American president for five decades. In the weeks after the 9/11 attack, Graham (Jr.) disagreed with Bush (Jr.) over the President's description of Islam as a religion of peace that had been hijacked. Graham instead stated that Islam is an "evil and wicked religion" and maintained that any attempts to describe Islam as containing peaceful messages were fundamentally mistaken. It was only much later that President Bush distanced himself from these comments, and even then he did so without referring to Graham by name.[65] Still, Graham delivered the Good Friday sermon in April of 2003 at the Pentagon, which confirmed the worst Muslim anxieties about the juxtaposition of Evangelical prejudice and arrogant militarism in the Bush administration.[66] Graham speaks for many Evangelicals in this country who do not share President Bush's benevolent, if somewhat simplistic, attitude toward Islam.[67] Nor was Graham's comment the only such statement. The former president of the Southern Baptist Convention, Jerry Vines, who is from Jacksonville, Florida (this author's birthplace and hometown), described the Prophet Muhammad as a "demon-possessed pedophile." Vines, who was also the board chairman of Jerry Falwell's Liberty University, went on to repeat typical Evangelical assertions that Muslims worship a different God than Jews and Christians, thus revealing a fundamental misunderstanding of Islamic thought according to both Muslims and most Christian theologians from various denominations.[68] Christianity has had to come to terms with the insidious anti-Semitism that it nurtured for centuries. Now, it will have to reckon with its "new anti-Semitism," Islamophobia.

NATIONALISM OR PATRIOTISM?

Hyper-nationalism and flag waving are entrenched modes of response to both tragedy and war in America.[69] Many American Muslims have participated in this mode, becoming more flag-waving than all the rest in order to protect themselves from charges of serving as a fifth column in this country. Much of the visual imagery put forth by American Muslim organizations—and distributed by mainstream media sources—has consisted of "obviously Muslim" figures (meaning veiled women and bearded immigrant males) carrying the American flag. At least one intended meaning of such symbols is to assure us that Muslims are "just as American" as everyone else in this country.[70]

There are groups of contemporary progressive Muslims who have responded to the above by going over to the other end of the spectrum, one which rejects all nationalist based forms of identity. They see Muslims instead as a part of a global spiritual community (the *Umma*), or simply as human beings whose humanity both precedes and transcends their national identity. These are important means of showing solidarity with all those outside the world hegemon, the United States.

There exists yet another option for American Muslims, especially ones who wish to engage both their Muslimness and in some sense their American affiliation. This distinction is one introduced by other liberal social critics, and seeks to identify a distinction between being patriotic and nationalistic.[71] The majority of American Muslims reject nationalism as a mode of identity politics, since rooted in the very idea of nationalism is affiliation with those members of humanity who happen to be born inside a modern nation-state above and beyond other human beings outside of those borders. For many

Muslims, this form of identity ultimately serves to create an "us" versus "them" means of identity, one that is ultimately divisive rather than unifying. Patriotism, on the other hand, is a more redeemable term. The term "patriotic" is also contested. Some use the term as virtually synonymous with nationalism. For others, it means an unquestioning, unwavering support for the foreign policy of United States, especially in time of war. For them, being patriotic means to "support the soldiers" when they are overseas fighting wars. There is, however, another usage of the term that would seek to resort to a type of being American where one is simultaneously invested in being patriotic but feels called to hold America responsible for the highest standard of justice it is capable of. This type of a patriotism is reminiscent of the attitude of civil rights leaders such as Dr. Martin Luther King, who fully recalled the high ideals of the unfulfilled American dream while remaining mindful of the realities of injustice against Native Americans, women, African Americans, and others throughout American history. It is this variety of patriotism that many American Muslims who wish to engage their American-ness as a significant aspect of their multilayered identity call upon.

CONCLUSION: WHAT DOES THE EMERGENCE OF ISLAM MEAN FOR AMERICA?

It is safe to say that the engagement of Islam with America is now entering its critical stage. In the next two generations, both Islam and American society at large will have to change to accommodate each other. At the heart of this emerging relationship is a central set of questions: Will America be an ostensibly (Judeo-)Christian country, whereby other religious communities are merely tolerated? Muslims have pointed out that the term "tolerance" has its origin in medieval toxicology and pharmacology, dealing with how much foreign substance and poison a body can tolerate before it dies. For Muslims, as indeed for other pluralistic human beings, there has to be a higher calling than merely *tolerating* those different from us until it kills us! Our challenge is to push America toward what Eck and others tell us it has already become, the "most pluralistic nation on Earth." This America will be more than merely "Abrahamic," since even that wonderful umbrella which brings together Jews, Christians and Muslims still leaves out our Hindu, Buddhist, Taoist, Jain, Sikh, Zoroastrian, Wiccan, Atheist, and Agnostic friends.

Will this America be one that truly believes in the equal protection of all human beings before the law, or rather will it target disempowered racial, religious, and ethnic minorities? Will civil rights be seen as necessary sacrifices in an ongoing "war on terrorism," or will they be seen as the very foundation of what is worth saving about America itself? Will immigrant Muslims realize that in every civilization where Islam has flourished it has done so through the interaction of timeless spiritual teachings and timely cultural contexts? Will the highest and most humanistic elements of American culture be blended into the collage of Islamic values? Can American Muslims be a part of the movement to confront the racism, sexism, classism, consumerism, and militarism of American society while upholding the yet unfinished American dream as a noble experiment?

These are open-ended questions, and the answers, as Bob Dylan tells us, "are blowing in the wind."

NOTES

1. Edward Said, *Culture and Imperialism* (New York: Vintage Books, 1993), xxv.

2. Seyyed Vali Reza Nasr, "European Colonialism and the Emergence of Modern Muslim States," in *The Oxford History of Islam,* ed. John L. Esposito (Oxford, U.K.: Oxford University Press, 2000), 549–600; Bruce Lawrence, *Shattering the Myth: Islam Beyond Violence* (Princeton, New Jersey: Princeton University Press, 1998).

3. The classic statement of this perspective is Frantz Fanon, *The Wretched of the Earth,* trans. Constance Farrington (New York: Grove Weidenfeld Press, 1968).

4. "Jihad Against Jews and Crusaders," available through http://copia.library. cornell.edu/colldev/mideast/wif.htm.

5. Letter cited in http://www.library.cornell.edu/colldev/mideast/fatw2.htm.

6. From the interview "Muslims have the right to attack America," published in *The Observer,* November 11, 2001. See http://www.observer.co.uk/afghanistan/ story/0,1501,591509,00.html.

7. http://news.bbc.co.uk/2/low/middle_east/1598146.stm. It is worth noting that Bush and Blair are personalized, while Israel remains a state entity. It is as if Al Qaeda members can conceive of a non-Crusader American and British leadership, but Israel is beyond redemption.

8. One such example is that of the group Tikkun, led by Rabbi Michael Lerner: www.tikkun.org.

9. For an example of nonviolent, civil disobedience by a Palestinian Christian, see Mubarak Awad in http://www..org/Media%20Project%202/mpaa1002.html.

10. See the witty cover on Tariq Ali's *The Clash of Fundamentalism,* which shows George W. Bush and Usama Bin Laden morphing into one another.

11. A sympathetic study is Irving Kristol, *Neoconservatism: The Autobiography of an Idea* (New York: Free Press, 1995). One critical evaluation is Michael Linds' "The Weird Men Behind George W. Bush's War," http://www.newamerica.net/ index.cfm?pg=article&pubID=1189. Also worth seeing is Gary Leupp's essay exposing the anti-democratic and Neo-Straussian foundations of the Neo-con movement, which is available at http://www.counterpunch.com/leupp05242003.html. Seymour Hersh's exposé in *The New Yorker* is a solid source of journalistic investigation in demonstrating the business interest of Neo-con Richard Perle. See: http:// newyorker.com/fact/content/?030317fa_fact.

12. Edward W. Said, *Orientalism* (New York: Pantheon, 1978).

13.   Edward Said, "Orientalism: An Exchange." [Letter] *New York Review of Books* 29 (13) (August 12, 1982): 44–46. On Bernard Lewis, "The Question of Orientalism," *New York Review of Books* 29 (11) (June 24, 1982): 49–56. Lewis' reply is on 47–48.

14.   The hardback version of *What Went Wrong,* which came out in 2001, bore the subtitle: "Western Impact and Middle Eastern Response." By the time the paperback version came out in 2003, "Middle Eastern" had mysteriously morphed into Islam/Muslim, resulting in: "The Clash between Islam and Modernity in the Middle East." Modernity among Muslims is assumed by Lewis to be entirely due to "Western impact."

15.   Bernard Lewis, *The Middle East and The West* (Bloomington: Indiana University Press, 1964), 135; cited in John Trumpbour, "The Clash of Civilizations: Samuel P. Huntington, Bernard Lewis, and the Remaking of Post-Cold War World Order," in *The New Crusades: Constructing the New Enemy,* eds., Emran Qureshi and Michael A. Sells, 93.

16.   Bernard Lewis, "The Roots of Muslim Rage: Why so many Muslims deeply resent the West, and why their bitterness will not easily be mollified," *Atlantic Monthly,* September 1990. Available online at: http://www.theatlantic.com/issues/90sep/rage.htm.

17.   Lewis, "The Roots of Muslim Rage."

18.   http://www.pbs.org/newshour/bb/military/july-dec01/powell_9-13.html.

19.   By attempting to define through a discussion of the absent item (posited to be present in Western civilization, Lewis follows in the footsteps of anti-Semitic Orientalists like Ernest Renan, who described the "Semitic race" as "recognized almost entirely by negative characteristics. It has neither mythology, nor epic, nor science, not philosophy, nor fiction, nor plastic arts, nor civil life; in everything there is a complete absence of complexity, subtlety or feeling, except for unity." For Renan, both Muslims and Jews belonged to the "Semitic race." Lewis subsumes the Jewish civilization under Western, but the framework remains much the same.

20.   Lewis, "The Roots of Muslim Rage."

21.   Qur'an 4:135.

22.   Lewis, *What Went Wrong: Western Impact and Middle Eastern Response* (New York: Oxford University Press, 2002), 153.

23.   Ibid., 153–4.

24.   See *Jerusalem Post,* April 30, 2001, interview with Maj.-Gen. Yitzhak Ben-Yisrael, head of military research and development, Israeli Defense Force.

25.   One such resolution (A/RES/46/30) of the General Assembly on December 6, 1991, states: "Bearing in mind the consensus reached by the General Assembly at its thirty-fifth session that the establishment of a nuclear-weapon-free zone in the region of the Middle East would greatly enhance international peace and security, Desirous of building on that consensus so that substantial progress can be made towards establishing a nuclear-weapon-free zone in the region of the Middle East, Welcoming all initiatives leading to general and complete disarmament, including in the region of the Middle East, and in particular on the establishment therein of a zone free of weapons of mass destruction, including nuclear weapons,…"

See http://www.un.org/documents/ga/res/46/a46r030.htm Resolution 687 of the UN Security Council (April 3, 1991), in addition to ending the first Gulf war involving Iraq also calls for a nuclear-weapons free Middle East: http://ods-dds-ny.un.org/doc/RESOLUTION/GEN/NR0/596/23/IMG/NR059623.pdf? OpenElement.

26.   Lewis, *What Went Wrong*, 155.

27.   Said, *Orientalism*, 316.

28.   Lewis, *What Went Wrong*, 159.

29.   Ibid.

30.   Samuel Huntington, "The Clash of Civilizations?" *Foreign Affairs* 72, 3 (1993): 22–25.

31.   I am here (and elsewhere) indebted to the wonderful insights of a dear friend and leading anthropologist, Carolyn Fluehr-Lobban, who pointed out Huntington's racism in a lecture at Colgate University in Spring 2003.

32.   See for example, Samuel Huntington, *The Clash of Civilizations: Remaking of World Order* (New York: Simon & Shuster, 1996), 207–208, 245–265, 266–298, 312.

33.   Huntington, "The Clash of Civilizations?" 22.

34.   It is tempting to note that in the article the Clash was posited as a question mark, whereas by 1996 Huntington was confident enough to remove the question mark and affirm the self-fulfilling prophecy.

35.   Huntington, *The Clash of Civilizations*, 49.

36.   One could easily point to many encounters in the realms of science, medicine, philosophy, trade, and so on.

37.   Huntington, *The Clash of Civilizations*, 184–206.

38.   Huntington, *The Clash of Civilizations*, 129.

39.   For an excellent study of Muslim Andalusia as a model of pluralism, see Maria Rosa Menocal, *The Ornament of the World: How Muslims, Jews, and Christians Created a Culture of Tolerance in Medieval Spain* (Boston, Massachusetts: Little, Brown, 2002).

40.   Huntington, *The Clash of Civilizations*, 217.

41.   Huntington, *The Clash of Civilizations*, 217–218.

42.   Huntington, "The Clash of Civilizations?" 35.

43.   Huntington, *The Clash of Civilizations*, 256.

44.   Mottahedeh offered a point by point refutation of Huntington in his "The Clash of Civilizations: An Islamicist's 'Critique," *Harvard Middle Eastern and Islamic Review* 2, 2 (1996): 1–26. This essay has been reprinted in the Emran Qureshi and Michael Sells volume, *The New Crusades*.

45.   http://www.foreignpolicy.com/story/cms.php?story_id=2495.

46.   Diana Eck, *A New Religious America: How a "Christian Country" Has Become the World's Most Religiously Diverse Nation* (San Francisco, California: Harper Collins, 2002), 2–3.

47.   The classic study here is Edward Said, *Covering Islam: How the Media and the Experts Determine How We See the Rest of the World* (1997; repr., New York: Vintage Books, 1981).

48.   http://www.beliefnet.com/story/54/story_5402_1.html.

49.   Very useful here is Bill Moyer's interview with the head of the Center for Public Integrity, at http://www.pbs.org/now/transcript/transcript_lewis2.html For ACLU's evaluation of the PATRIOT Bill, see http://www.aclu.org/SafeandFree/SafeandFree.cfm?ID=12126&c=207.

50.   Center for Public Integrity has obtained a leaked copy of this memo. Among other powers, this bill would grant the Attorney General the power to strip U.S. citizens of their citizenship. See: http://www.publicintegrity.org/dtaweb/downloads/Story_01_020703_Doc_1.pdf.

51.   http://www.beliefnet.com/story/50/story_5010_1.html.

52.   For a frank discussion of these tensions, see Sherman A. Jackson, *Islam and the Blackamerican: Looking Toward the Third Resurrection* (New York: Oxford University Press, 2005).

53.   Rachel Zoll, AP religion writer, "U.S. Muslims Lobbying for Civil Rights," June 8, 2003. The article can be accessed at: http://www.newsday.com/news/nationworld/nation/wire/sns-ap-american-muslims,0,2912861.story?coll=sns-ap-nation-headlines.

54.   For this controversy, see http://www.haverford.edu/relg/sells/UNC_ApproachingTheQur'an.htm.

55.   As conveyed in the video *Islam in America*, produced by the Christian Science Monitor.

56.   http://news.bbc.co.uk/2/hi/middle_east/1969542.stm (BBC) and http://www.fortune.com/fortune/power25 (Fortune), which ranks AIPAC as the fourth most powerful lobby group in the United States.

57.   One notable exception was a 60 Minutes piece (June 8, 2003). Access at http://www.cbsnews.com/stories/2002/10/03/60minutes/main524268.shtml.

58.   The paper, minus the JFK Seal which was removed, can be downloaded at: http://ksgnotes1.harvard.edu/Research/wpaper.nsf/rwp/RWP06-011/$File/rwp_06_011_walt.pdf.

59.   "Most Favored Nation," http://www.boston.com/news/globe/ideas/articles/2006/04/02/most_favored_nation/?page=1.

60.   The statement is from an interview with the syndicated columnist Carl Thomas, at http://www.crosswalk.com/news/1108858.html.

61.   http://www.cnn.com/1999/ALLPOLITICS/stories/12/15/religion.register/.

62.   http://www.falwell.com/historical_data.html.

63.   For a historical overview of this complicated relationship, see *On Behalf of Israel: American Fundamentalist Attitudes Towards Jews, Judaism, and Zionism, 1865–1945* (New York: Carlson Publishing Inc., 1991).

64.   "Zionist meeting brands 'road map' as heresy": http://www.washtimes.com/national/20030518-114058-5626r.htm.

65.   "Bush Takes on Christian Right Over Anti-Islam Words," http://middleeastinfo.org/article1607.html.

66.   http://www5.cnn.com/2003/ALLPOLITICS/04/18/graham.pentagon/.

67.   See for example Bush's comments about Islam inside the Washington Islamic Center (http://usinfo.state.gov/usa/islam/s091701b.htm), and the comments as part of the speech to the joint session of the congress after 9/11(http://usinfo. state.gov/usa/islam/s092001.htm).

68.   Susan Sachs, "Baptist Pastor Attacks Islam, inciting cries of Intolerance," *The New York Times,* June 15 (2002).

69.   Chris Hedges, *War Is a Force That Gives Us Meaning* (New York: Public Affairs, 2002).

70.   This discourse has been advocated by authors ranging from Asma Gull Hasan to Feisal Abdul Rauf.

71.   For an insightful commentary, see Bill Moyers http://www.pbs.org/now/commentary/moyers19.html.

INDEX

⎯⎯⎯⎯⎯⎯⎯⎯⎯⎯⎯ • ⎯⎯⎯⎯⎯⎯⎯⎯⎯⎯⎯

ABOUT THE EDITORS AND CONTRIBUTORS

———————————•———————————

VINCENT J. CORNELL is Asa Griggs Candler Professor of Middle East and Islamic Studies at Emory University. From 2000 to 2006, he was Professor of History and Director of the King Fahd Center for Middle East and Islamic Studies at the University of Arkansas. From 1991 to 2000, he taught at Duke University. Dr. Cornell has published two major books, *The Way of Abu Madyan* (Cambridge, U.K.: The Islamic Texts Society, 1996) and *Realm of the Saint: Power and Authority in Moroccan Sufism* (Austin, Texas: University of Texas Press, 1998), and over 30 articles. His interests cover the entire spectrum of Islamic thought from Sufism to theology and Islamic law. He has lived and worked in Morocco for nearly six years and has spent considerable time both teaching and doing research in Egypt, Tunisia, Malaysia, and Indonesia. He is currently working on projects on Islamic ethics and moral theology in conjunction with the Shalom Hartmann Institute and the Elijah Interfaith Institute in Jerusalem. For the past five years (2002–2006), he has been a key participant in the Building Bridges Seminars hosted by the Archbishop of Canterbury.

OMID SAFI is Associate Professor of Islamic Studies at the University of North Carolina at Chapel Hill. He specializes in Islamic mysticism, contemporary Islamic thought, and medieval Islamic history. He is Co-Chair of the Study of Islam Section at the American Academy of Religion, the largest international organization devoted to the academic study of religion. He is the editor of the volume *Progressive Muslims: On Justice, Gender, and Pluralism* (2003). His work *The Politics of Knowledge in Premodern Islam*, dealing with medieval Islamic history and politics, was published by UNC Press in 2006. He is now finishing a volume for HarperCollins on the historical expansion of Islam. He is also finishing two works dealing with Islamic mysticism: his translation of Ayn al-Qudat Hamadani's *Tamhidat* is forthcoming from Classics of Western Spirituality series at Paulist Press and his translation and analysis of Rumi's biography is forthcoming from Fons

Vitae. He has been featured a number of times on NPR, Associated Press, and other national and international media.

UMAR F. ABD-ALLAH heads the Nawawi Foundation in Chicago, an educational nonprofit organization dedicated to thought leadership in the American Muslim community. He received his PhD from the University of Chicago in 1978 in Arabic and Islamic Studies and taught academically in Canada, the United States, and other countries from 1977 until 2000. He has recently completed a biography of one of the earliest and most significant American Muslim converts, *A Muslim in Victorian America: The Life of Alexander Russell Webb* (2006). He is concluding *Roots of Islam in America: A Survey of Muslim Presence in the New World from Earliest Evidence Until 1965* and also writes on general Islamic cultural history and his specialization, Islamic law.

MOHAMMAD AZADPUR is Assistant Professor of Philosophy at San Francisco State University. His most recent publication is "The Sublime Visions of Philosophy: Fundamental Ontology and the Imaginal World (*'Alam al-mithal*)," *Islamic Philosophy and Occidental Phenomenology on the Perennial Issue of Microcosm and Macrocosm* (March 2006).

HUGH TALAT HALMAN is Research Assistant Professor in the King Fahd Center for Middle East and Islamic Studies at the University of Arkansas, Fayetteville. From 2004 to 2005, he served as a Fulbright Senior Scholar based at the Universitas Islam Negeri Syarif Hidayatullah, Jakarta, Indonesia. He has published articles on Sufi saints, Islamic advocates of nonviolence, and Indonesian Islam. His forthcoming book on the story of al-Khidr will explain its significance for select Sufi Qur'an commentators.

JAMILLAH A. KARIM is Assistant Professor of Religion at Spelman College. She obtained her PhD in Islamic Studies from Duke University. She specializes in Islam in America, women and Islam, race and Islam, and Muslim immigration. She is currently completing a book project tentatively titled *Imagining the American Ummah: Muslim Women Negotiate Race, Class, and Gender.* Her most recent publications include "Between Immigrant Islam and Black Liberation: Young Muslims Inherit Global Muslim and African American Legacies," *Muslim World* 95, no. 4 (October 2005): 497–513.

SCOTT SIRAJUL HAQQ KUGLE is an independent scholar of religious studies and Islamic culture. He received a PhD from Duke University for a comparative study of reformist Sufism in North Africa and South Asia. He has taught at Swarthmore College and was a research fellow at the Institute for the Study of Islam in the Modern World in the

Netherlands. He has published *The Book of Illumination* (2005) and *Rebel Between Spirit and Law: Ahmad Zarruq, Sainthood, and Authority in Islam* (2006).

AMINAH BEVERLY McCLOUD is Professor of Islamic Studies in the Department of Religious Studies at DePaul University and Director of the Islamic World Studies Program. She is the author of *African American Islam, Questions of Faith, Transnational Muslims in American Society*, and *American Muslim Women*. She is currently working on *The Nation of Islam: A Closer Look* and is the author of over 20 articles on topics ranging from Islamic law to Muslim women. Also, she is a Fulbright Scholar, consultant on Muslim affairs for the courts, and current editor of the *Journal of Islamic Law and Culture*. She is the founder of the Islam in America Conference at DePaul University, which houses the "Islam in America Archives." Since January 2005, she has run the only undergraduate baccalaureate Islamic World Studies program. She is a board member of CAIR (Council on American Islamic Relations) Chicago, "the Healing Project" at Boston University Hospital, Radio Islam, the Institute for Social and Policy Understanding, the Feminist Sexual Ethics Project (Brandeis University), and she works as an educator for the Middle East Policy Council on understanding Islam and Arabic cultures. She has received grants for her work from the Ford Foundation, the Illinois Humanities Council, the Graham Architectural Foundation, and the Lilly Foundation. Dr. McCloud has also worked on a number of television projects on Muslims and is currently working on task forces for the East West Institute and Chicago Council on Foreign Relations relating to Islam and Muslims.

ZIBA MIR-HOSSEINI is a consultant, researcher, and writer on Middle Eastern issues, specializing in gender, family relations, and Islamic law and development, based in the London Middle East Institute. Her books include *Marriage on Trial: A Study of Islamic Family Law in Iran and Morocco* (1993; repr., 2000), *Islam and Gender: The Religious Debate in Contemporary Iran* (Princeton, New Jersey: Princeton University Press, 1999), and (with Richard Tapper) *Islam and Democracy in Iran: Eshkevari and the Quest for Reform* (2006). She has also directed (with Kim Longinotto) two award-winning feature-length documentary films on contemporary issues in Iran: *Divorce Iranian Style* (1998) and *Runaway* (2001).

EBRAHIM MOOSA is Associate Professor of Islamic Studies at Duke University and Associate Director of the Duke Islamic Studies Center (DISC). He is the author of *Ghazali and the Poetics of Imagination* and has numerous publications on Islamic law, ethics, theology, and historical studies. He is also the recipient of the 2005 Carnegie Scholar's Award.